ALFRED A. KNOPF
1915 · 100 YEARS · 2015

MICHELLE OBAMA

MICHELLE OBAMA

A LIFE

Peter Slevin

ALFRED A. KNOPF   NEW YORK
2015

THIS IS A BORZOI BOOK
PUBLISHED BY ALFRED A. KNOPF

www.aaknopf.com

Knopf, Borzoi Books, and the colophon are registered
trademarks of Penguin Random House LLC.

Library of Congress Cataloging-in-Publication Data
Slevin, Peter.
Michelle Obama : a life / by Peter Slevin.—First edition.
pages   cm
ISBN 978-0-307-95882-2 (hardcover)   ISBN 978-0-307-95883-9 (eBook)
1. Obama, Michelle, 1964–   2. Presidents' spouses—
United States—Biography.   3. African American women lawyers—
Biography.   4. African American lawyers—Biography.   I. Title.
E909.O24S54   2015   973.932092—dc23
[B]   2014041100

Front-of-jacket photograph by Ben Baker/Redux
Jacket design by Carol Devine Carson

Manufactured in the United States of America
First Edition

For Kate

Contents

MICHELLE
OBAMA

Introduction

In June 2010, when Michelle Obama cast her eyes across the class of graduating high school seniors from one of Washington's most troubled black neighborhoods, she saw not only their lives, but her own. The setting was Constitution Hall, where the Daughters of the American Revolution had prevented opera singer Marian Anderson from performing in 1939 because she was black. So much had changed in seven decades, and yet much had not. Michelle spoke to the graduates about the troubles facing African American children in Anacostia, and she spoke about racism. She pointed out that the neighborhood within sight of the U.S. Capitol once was segregated and that black people had been prohibited from owning property in parts of the community. "And even after those barriers were torn down," she said, "others emerged. Poverty. Violence. Inequality."

Michelle drew a straight line from her struggles with hardship and self-doubt in working-class Chicago to the fractured world the Anacostia students inhabited thirty years later. She told them about being written off, about feeling rejected, about the resilience it takes for a black kid in a public school to become one of the first in her family to go to college. "Kids teasing me when I studied hard. Teachers telling me not to reach too high because my test scores weren't good enough. Folks making it clear with what they said or didn't say that success wasn't meant for a little girl like me from the South Side of Chicago." As she spoke of her parents—their sacrifices and the way they pushed her "to reach for a life they never knew"—her voice broke and tears came to her eyes. As the students applauded in support, Michelle went on, "And if Barack were here, he'd say the same thing was true for him. He'd tell you it was hard at times growing up without a father. He'd tell you that his family didn't have a lot of money. He'd tell you he made plenty of mistakes and wasn't always the best student."

She knew that many of the Anacostia students faced disruptions and distractions that sometimes made it hard to show up, much less succeed. It might be family turmoil or money troubles or needy relatives or children of their own. Or maybe the lack of a mentor, a quiet place to study, a lucky break. "Maybe you feel like no one has your back, like you've been let down by people so many times that you've stopped believing in yourself. Maybe you feel like your destiny was written the day you were born and you ought to just rein in your hopes and scale back your dreams. But if any of you are thinking that way, I'm here to tell you: *Stop it.*"

There were no cheap lines in Michelle's speech that day, seventeen months after she arrived in the White House as the unlikeliest first lady in modern history. In a voice entirely her own, she reached deep into a lifetime of thinking about race, politics, and power to deliver a message about inequity and perseverance, challenge and uplift. These were the themes and experiences that animated her and set her apart. No one who looked like Michelle Obama had ever occupied the White House. No one who acted quite like her, either. She ran obstacle courses, she danced the Dougie, she hula-hooped on the White House lawn. She opened the executive mansion to fresh faces and voices and took her show on the road. She did sitcoms and talk shows and participated in cyber showcases and social media almost as soon as they were invented. Cameras and microphones tracked her every move. Maddening though the attention could be, she tried to make it useful. Amid a characteristic media fuss about a new hairstyle, she said of first ladies, "We take our bangs and we stand in front of important things that the world needs to see. And eventually, people stop looking at the bangs and they start looking at what we're standing in front of."

Michelle's projects and messages reflected a hard-won determination to help the working class and the disadvantaged, to unstack the deck. She was more urban and more mindful of inequality than any first lady since Eleanor Roosevelt. She was also more steadily, if subtly, political. Not political in ways measured by elections or ephemeral Beltway chatter, although she made clear her convictions from many a campaign stage. Rather, political as defined by spoken beliefs about how the world should work and purposeful projects calculated to bend the curve. Her efforts unfolded in realms that had barely existed for African Americans a generation earlier, a fact that informed and complicated her work. "We live in a nation where I am not supposed to be here," she once said.

Michelle's prospects as first lady delighted her supporters and helped get Barack elected, but her story and its underpinnings remained unfamiliar to many white Americans in a country where black Americans often felt relegated to a parallel universe. "As we've all said in the black community, we don't see all of who we are in the media. We see snippets of our community and distortions of our community," Michelle said. "So the world has this perspective that somehow Barack and Michelle Obama are different, that we're unique. And we're not. You just haven't seen us before." She belonged to a generation that came of age after the civil rights movement. It was fashionable in some circles for people to declare that they no longer saw race, but translation would be required. As her friend Verna Williams put it, "So many people have no idea about what black people are like. They feel they know us when they really don't." Lambasted early as "Mrs. Grievance" and "Barack's Bitter Half," Michelle knew the burden of making herself understood. One of her favorite descriptions of her Washington life came from a California college student who described the role of first lady as "the balance between politics and sanity."

During her years in the spotlight, Michelle became a point of reference and contention. She built and nurtured her popularity and emerged as one of the most recognizable women in the world. "You do not want to underestimate her, ever," said Trooper Sanders, a White House aide. Indeed, Michelle seemed to stride through life, full of confidence and direction. Comfortable in her own skin, friends always said. Authentic. But when asked what she would say to her younger self, as an interviewer flashed her high school yearbook photo onto a giant screen, Michelle paused to consider. "I think that girl was always afraid. I was thinking 'Maybe I'm not smart enough. Maybe I'm not bright enough. Maybe there are kids that are working harder than me.' I was always worrying about disappointing someone or failing."

At Constitution Hall, addressing 158 Anacostia seniors dressed in cobalt blue gowns, Michelle shared her history and her self-doubt. She offered advice and encouragement but skipped the saccharine. "You can't just sit around," she instructed. "Don't expect anybody to come and hand you anything. It doesn't work that way." She asked them to think about the obstacles faced by Frederick Douglass, their neighborhood's most illustrious former resident, born into slavery and self-educated in an era when it was illegal to teach slaves to read or write. His mother died when he was a boy and he never knew his father. But he made it, "persevering through thick and thin," and spent decades fighting for equality. She also asked them to consider the current occupants of the White House. "We see ourselves in each and every one of you. We are living proof for you, that with the right support, it doesn't matter what circumstances you were born into or how much money you have or what color your skin is. If you are committed to doing what it takes, anything is possible. It's up to you."

ONE

Chicago's Promise

In the DuSable High School swim team photograph, Fraser C. Robinson III stands in dark swimming trunks in the back row, third from the left. He is bare-chested, lean and fit. His arms are strong and his gaze is sure. The year was 1953 and the seventeen-year-old senior was close to having all the formal education he would get. In five years, he would be an army private on his way to Germany. In five more, he would be married and a father, a Democratic precinct worker soon to be on the payroll of the city of Chicago. The work he would do for much of his life, tending high-pressure boilers at a water-filtration plant, was tedious labor done in eight-hour shifts and it paid just enough for him to get by. At home, where he invested his considerable smarts and energy in his family, the swimming days of his youth would give way, far too soon, to years of physical decline. Multiple sclerosis left his brain increasingly unable to control his body. He walked with a limp, then a cane, then crutches; finally he used an electric scooter. Before work, his children watched him struggle to fasten the buttons on his blue work shirts. After work, he would sometimes call them to help carry shopping bags up the stairs to their apartment. Known on the job as Robbie, to his family as Diddley, he worked long after he could have taken disability. "The gutsiest guy I have ever known," said water plant colleague Dan Maxime.

In 2008, sixteen years after Fraser Robinson died, Michelle told voters that her father remained her north star. "I am constantly trying to make sure that I am making him proud," she said. "What would my father think of the choices that I've made, how I've lived my life, what careers I chose, what man I married? That's the voice in my head that keeps me whole and keeps me grounded and keeps me the girl from the South Side of Chicago, no matter how many cameras are in the room, how many autographs people want, how big we get." That voice in her head emerged from Fraser's own South Side upbringing and the narrow but steady path he followed. The oldest of five surviving siblings born to a deeply religious mother and an ambitious father who arrived from South Carolina in the Great Migration, he secured a foothold in the working class. He was the least professionally accomplished of the children, but he occupied a central position in the family—"the glue," a cousin said—and he propelled his own two children yet further. Fraser was the one to whom the others turned with their problems, the one who kept track of the family lore, the one who worked hardest to knit together a large clan with its share of triumphs, failures, and frustrations. In the final lines of her speech to the 2008 Democratic National Convention, Michelle called on voters to elect her husband Barack as president "in honor of my father's memory and my daughters' future." She would also say that year, on the cusp of occupying a White House perch that she would devote to opening doors for others, "I remember his compassion. I remember the words, his advice, the way he lived life, and I am trying each and every day to apply that to how I raise my kids. I want his legacy to live through them. Hopefully it will affect the kind of first lady I will become because it's his compassion and his view of the world that really inspires who I am, who I want my girls to be, and what I hope for the country."

Fraser's story, and hers, begins in the Chicago of the 1930s, when any child of the first wave of the great black migration learned what was expected of him. Fraser would come to know possibility and the rewards of discipline and perseverance, lessons he would bequeath to Michelle and her older brother, Craig. He would encounter, too, the profound obstacles that faced African Americans in Chicago in the middle of the twentieth century, despite living hundreds of miles up the well-traveled Illinois Central tracks from the South of slavery and Jim Crow.

RICHARD WRIGHT, author of the memoir *Black Boy*, pulled into Chicago on a bitterly cold day in 1927, seeking a job more than anything. Not yet twenty, he was hungry and weighed less than 125 pounds, the minimum weight for a postal worker. He was uncertain about what lay ahead, but he was sure there was nothing for him in Memphis, where he had earned $8 a week, with little chance of advancement, as an errand boy in an optical company. "I could calculate my chances for life in the South as a Negro fairly clearly now," he wrote, remembering the decision to head north. Wright's white co-workers in Memphis belittled his choice, and as he rumbled into town aboard a northbound train, the Chicago that he spied through the window hardly seemed encouraging. That first glimpse "depressed and dismayed me, mocked all my fantasies," he wrote. Once he stepped off the train, however, he witnessed scenes that brightened his mood. Before he left the station, he saw that a black man could buy a newspaper "without having to wait until a white man was served." He saw black people and white people striding along purposefully, strikingly unmindful of one another. "No racial fear," he thought. Yet for a young black man born near Natchez, Mississippi, even the encouraging scenes triggered anxiety: "I knew that this machine-city was governed by strange laws and I wondered if I would ever learn them."

The blessings of Chicago, as Wright and later waves of migrants would find, were mixed. The sense of freedom was undeniable. Indeed, for many, it was overwhelming. Many of the rules were different, and in a better way. Streetcars had no seating code. Work paid better. Decent public schools beckoned, even if overcrowding forced many black schools to operate on double shifts. Chicago offered a rich menu of music, culture, and religion, not to mention gambling, liquor, and pursuits of a less savory kind. On the one hand, so many people crowded into African American districts marked by invisible boundaries that it sometimes seemed there was no room to move. On the other, the concentrated South Side community generated energy and drive and, for some, a common purpose. Sociologists St. Clair Drake and Horace R. Cayton described "a city within a city," and likened the intersection of 47th Street and South Parkway to a busy town square. In their study, *Black Metropolis*, published in 1945, they sketched a "continuous eddy of faces." Within view on a typical morning were black doctors, dentists, police officers, shopkeepers, and clerks, along with newsstands selling black-owned newspapers that included the *Defender*, the *Bee*, the *News-Ledger*, and the *Metropolitan News*. In one direction was a library named for Dr. George Cleveland Hall, chief of staff at Provident Hospital. In another was the Regal Theater, scene of performances by Cab Calloway and Louis Armstrong, Lena Horne and Duke Ellington, Lionel Hampton and Nat King Cole. Starting in 1939, the Regal was managed by a black man, a significant achievement for the time. As New York's Harlem Renaissance ebbed away, in its place stood Chicago. One writer would christen the South Side "the capital of black America."

Four years after Wright arrived, Fraser C. Robinson Jr. alighted on the South Side. He had traveled north and west from a small town in coastal South Carolina called Georgetown—in honor of King George II, not George Washington. It was known locally for rice farming, timber mills, and the plantation economy. Robinson was born in 1912 to a one-armed father as imperious as he was successful, a lumber company worker and businessman who owned his own home on an integrated block. Just one generation earlier, and for generations before that, the family had lived in slavery, when countless Robinsons and their kin were owned by white people. After the Civil War came and went and Abraham Lincoln signed the Emancipation Proclamation, they stayed put. They continued to speak Gullah, a distinctive English-based creole language descended from languages brought from West Africa.

African American voters held a majority in Georgetown as late as 1900, when the town's white leaders decided enough was enough. The tipping point came in September, when hundreds of black residents massed outside the county jail to protect a black barber named John Brownfield from a lynching. A white sheriff's deputy had tried to arrest Brownfield for failing to pay a poll tax. There was a scuffle. The deputy caught a bullet from his own gun and died a few hours later. Brownfield went to jail on suspicion of murder. As word spread that white men were organizing a lynching party, as many as a thousand black residents gathered outside the jail and chanted "Save John!" The demonstrations grew, and Georgetown's white mayor persuaded the state's governor to send soldiers to restore order.

In court, Brownfield was convicted and sentenced to death for capital murder, while he and eight others were found guilty of crimes connected to the protests. White community leaders formed a White Supremacy Club and used literacy tests and poll taxes to cull black citizens from voter rolls. By 1902, only 110 of the city's 523 voters were black. The same was true in other southern states. In Louisiana, about 130,000 black people were registered to vote in 1896; in 1904, the total was 1,342. In Alabama, 2 percent of eligible black men were registered "and they risked serious reprisals if they attempted to exercise their right to vote." With the white minority firmly in control, the portents looked uniformly bad. "The whites in power," wrote Rachel Swarns in *American Tapestry*, a study of Michelle Obama's ancestry, "made it clear that there was no future for ambitious black men in Georgetown."

Finishing Howard High School at the end of the 1920s, Fraser Robinson Jr. considered himself "a young man destined for better things." Others saw him the same way. A skilled debater and strong student, he envisioned college and perhaps a career in the emerging field of electronics. But he felt certain that such a future did not await him in Georgetown, where he found himself working in a timber mill as the Depression took hold. "He wanted a different kind of life. He had high hopes," recalled his daughter, Francesca. When a friend left for Chicago, Fraser followed.

FROM THE START, things went poorly for the man who would one day be Michelle's exacting paternal grandfather. Jobs in Chicago were scarce and Fraser always seemed to be a temporary hire. He set up pins in a bowling alley. He washed dishes. He worked in a laundry and undertook the workaday chores of a handyman. It soon became clear that college was out of the question, as was a career in electronics. To get steady work as an electrician required membership in a union that barred African Americans. He eventually found a regular income with the Depression-era Works Progress Administration, but the money did not stretch far. As he made his way, he gave up the African Methodist Episcopal church of his youth in favor of a South Side Pentecostal church called Full Gospel Mission. There, he began courting a focused and prayerful teenager in the choir, LaVaughn Johnson. She was the daughter of James Johnson, a sometime Baptist preacher who had done duty as a Pullman porter and owner of a shoe repair shop. After a quiet stretch in Evanston, Illinois, in the 1920s, the Johnsons moved around as he sought stable work. Financial pressure brought trouble, and the marriage between James and his wife, Phoebe, came undone. James moved out, leaving Phoebe on the South Side with their seven children, the oldest twenty-seven, the youngest five. LaVaughn stayed in school, but soon began spending her off hours working alongside her mother in the homes of white families. She did laundry and took care of children in Hyde Park, where her granddaughter Michelle would live seventy years later in relative splendor.

Fraser and LaVaughn married in October 1934. He was twenty-two years old, three years removed from South Carolina. She was nineteen, barely eight months out of high school. In August 1935, they had a son and named him Fraser C. Robinson III. The city, in the teeth of the Great Depression, was overflowing with unskilled black laborers who had streamed into town in search of something like a future. The pace of migration was startling. In 1910, one in fifty Chicago residents was black; in 1940, it was one in twelve. During those thirty years, the city's African American population grew 530 percent, to 277,731 residents. The population would continue to climb during the boom years of World War II and beyond as passenger trains delivered thousands of new residents each month to the imposing Illinois Central terminal, within sight of the downtown skyscrapers. Chicago was called the city of big shoulders, not the city of open arms, and the vast majority of African Americans found themselves squeezed into a slice of the South Side called the Black Belt. Some called it North Mississippi. To others, it was Darkie Town.

Segregation in housing was the rule. For years, white community leaders used restrictive covenants and race-minded civic organizations—known without irony as "improvement associations"—to keep blacks out. Mob violence and intimidation played a part. The Federal Housing Administration, founded in 1934, refused to insure mortgages in neighborhoods that were home to more than a small number of black people. The policy, known as redlining, meant that banks would not loan money to most African Americans, which kept property largely out of reach. In 1940, when Michelle's father was five years old, three-fourths of Chicago's black population lived in neighborhoods that were more than 90 percent black. Fully 350 of the city's 935 census tracts had not a single black resident. Housing in the Black Belt tended to be inhospitable and, as more African Americans arrived from the South, increasingly cramped. To accommodate the newcomers and line their own pockets, landlords carved buildings into smaller and smaller units, often without plumbing, even as they charged rents far higher than white people paid elsewhere in the city.

Overcrowding and poor sanitation contributed to rates of illness and death that were higher among black Chicagoans than among white ones. Tuberculosis in 1940 was five times more prevalent among black residents. Three black infants died before their first birthday for every two white infants who did. By 1945, more than half of the Black Belt was considered "blighted" by city planners and real estate assessors. Equality was at best a mirage, at worst a hoax. Which is not to say that Chicago did not hold out hope for a better future. But the equation was a complicated one. The deck was stacked, and it would remain that way well into Michelle's lifetime. As Barack Obama would say of his in-laws and their lives in the 1960s, "They faced what other African American families faced at the time—both hidden and overt forms of racism that limited their effort to get ahead."

IN THE MID-1930S, when Michelle's father was born, money was tight in the Robinson household. LaVaughn again took up housecleaning. She gave birth to Nomenee in July 1937 and later to a third son, John, who died as a baby. Under the strains that grew as the decade passed, the relationship between husband and wife that had started strongly ended abruptly. By the end of the 1930s, the elder Fraser was through with the marriage. Soon after, he was through with Chicago, at least for the time being. He enlisted in the army in March 1941, giving his height as five feet, eight inches, and his weight as 153 pounds. A form noted his marital status as "separated, without dependants [*sic*]."

LaVaughn's day-to-day challenges grew harder. Living on East 57th Street near State Street, she turned to public assistance before finding her way into a federal job, working in the publications office at the U.S. Department of Agriculture. Her sons visited her there. With Fraser leading the way, the boys climbed aboard a northbound streetcar and stepped off downtown. They rode upstairs in an elevator cage and visited their mother in the room where she operated a mimeograph machine. To help with the boys during the early years, LaVaughn looked to friends and relatives. She relied especially on two older women from Georgetown, who sometimes spoke Gullah as the children listened. She also remained close to her church, taking young Fraser and Nomenee with her to Full Gospel Mission on Sundays. The storefront church had rigid rules and lively music. "If a church doesn't jump, so to speak, I don't feel that there's any holy spirit there," said Nomenee, who called it a wonderful experience. He remembered the boost he got from a pastor who called him "my little preacher" and told him he had a gift for words. As for his mother, in his telling she was "religiously sheltered" while growing up and, as an adult, always proper and "very, very prayerful." Finding a way to blend faith with a measure of professional ambition, LaVaughn would go on to manage a Moody Bible Institute store in Chicago, the first African American woman to do so. In 1958, her twenty-two-year-old son Fraser gave her a Bible for Mother's Day. Fifty-five years later, with Michelle holding that Bible in the Blue Room, Barack Obama would take the oath of office for his second term in the White House.

Although money was always scarce, LaVaughn strongly encouraged Fraser and Nomenee in musical and artistic pursuits. "Everything educational, they got it," her sister Mary Lang said. They learned to swim and ice-skate and to always do their schoolwork. Money mattered, but

Nomenee recalled a time when his mother's caution about his safety trumped her concern about the family's finances. For Christmas one year, he received a set of molds in the shapes of Mickey Mouse, Donald Duck, Pluto, and other Disney characters. "I just loved that little toy because you had some plaster and you'd take that off and let it sit and harden. You'd shellac them and paint them. So, one day, I just decided to keep making them. I had forty sitting on the table or something. I came up with this idea that I'm going to sell them." He put them in an old shoebox and asked his mother to buy him a receipt book. "I never told her what I was doing. I said I'm going to try to go into business. She was just laughing."

While his mother was at work, Nomenee began walking through the neighborhood, knocking on apartment doors. "I said, 'Miss, would you like to buy one of these? Thirty-five cents, three for a dollar.' You know, she'll say, 'Honey, come here, look at this! Look at this little boy!' So, one week, I collected thirteen-something dollars, a lot of money. I put it on the table in front of Mom." Shocked, she asked where the money had come from. Nomenee said he had gone into business selling Disney figures and reminded her that she was the one who had bought the receipt book. LaVaughn was not amused. "Don't you dare go out there again knocking on people's doors," she told her son. "Somebody's going to snatch you." That ended the sales enterprise.

World War II took Fraser Jr. to Europe and, by his children's accounts, made him stronger. He worked with radios and climbed in rank in a segregated unit, years before President Harry Truman ordered the military's integration in 1948. "I think he finally had the opportunity to use his skills and gifts in the army. He had a sense of autonomy in some respects," said Francesca, his only daughter, born in Chicago long after the war. Fraser would return to the South Side, but for years he kept a certain distance from the family. "He'll come by once a year or so and take us to the circus. That was our encounter with him," said Nomenee, who recalled visits to a railroad fair in downtown Chicago and occasional trips to the movies. His father lived just a few blocks away, but it might as well have been across the state. His mother knew the location; the children did not.

After Fraser's army stint and several years back on the South Side, he returned to the family, which in time would grow to include three more children. They were Andrew, Carlton, and Francesca, named for a friendly Italian woman who delivered milk and eggs to Fraser and other black American soldiers bivouacked near her farm. It had been more than a decade since his departure, but he rejoined the household as a prideful man, confident and often stern, a disciplinarian possessed of firm ideas about right and wrong. It was no accident that he became a master sergeant during his army years. He could be hard on the boys, recalled Nomenee, who said he challenged his father's authority more than his brother did. Once, in Nomenee's early teens, his father started to whip him for a misdeed, now forgotten. Young Fraser stepped in. "He happened to hear me screaming. He came in and said, 'That's enough, Dad. That's enough.' He held his hands and Dad couldn't move, couldn't pull away. We never had any whippings after that." When he was raising his own children years later, Fraser III would not spank them. He left that chore to his wife.

When Fraser III and Nomenee grew older, they were expected to work in addition to fulfilling their school responsibilities. "We had to contribute. It's not like we were making that much money, but it's just that that was Dad's system," said Nomenee, who recalled that one boy might be responsible for the phone bill, another for the light bill or groceries. One of Fraser's first jobs was as a dairy helper, hefting glass bottles of Wanzer Dairy milk—motto: *"Wanzer on milk is like sterling on silver"*—to customers' doorsteps and returning with the empties. He worked on the horse-drawn cart of a vegetable deliveryman, also for a hat-maker and a cleaning company. Being a swimmer on his high school team, the Sea Horses, Fraser sometimes found work as a lifeguard. When he could, Fraser passed along his old jobs to Nomenee, two years younger. "We had to be hustlers, in the positive sense of hustling," Nomenee said. "We had to figure out ways."

LAVAUGHN WAS DETERMINED to open a door to a wider world for her children. In the mid-1940s, when he was about eleven years old, Fraser caught a bus on Saturday mornings to the Art Institute of Chicago, a grand beaux-arts edifice on Michigan Avenue. There, he discovered painting and sculpture. With classmates at what was then called the Junior School, he worked in an array of disciplines. One of his teachers was Nelli Bar Wieghardt, a German-Jewish sculptor and refugee from wartime Europe. "Her style was very open, looking to discover what strengths the student had and encouraging them," said Richard Hunt, another black student of hers, born the same year as Fraser. "More embracing than strict," Hunt said, and less wedded to academic conventions than to approaches more abstract and flowing. Hunt remembered lunch discussions about race relations in the United States. Wieghardt was startled by what she found after "escaping and coming to the land of the free and then discovering what it was in terms of black-white relations." For Hunt, who traveled to the Junior School on Saturdays from the bustling working-class streets of Englewood, one discipline led to another as he studied drawing and painting, watercolors and oils, still life and figures. Looking back after becoming a professional sculptor, he remembered an eclectic and engaging array of Art Institute instructors. Classrooms and studios were tucked into basement spaces, but, just upstairs, students had the run of a flourishing museum. "The teachers might suggest, 'Why don't you go up and look at Rodin?'"

Fraser's passion for art was understated, but enduring. It set him apart at DuSable High School, where his interests ran from painting and sculpture to swimming and boxing. A full-page photograph in the 1953 *Red and Black*, the school yearbook, shows him dressed in a sport coat, sculpting a bust. "You'd hardly know he was around," said classmate Reuben Crawford. "He was going about the business of being the business, as we used to say. He was very quiet and into his art." If he could have afforded it, Michelle said later, her father would have made art his profession. "He was quite an artist," Nomenee agreed, acknowledging a certain envy that started at an early age. He saw Fraser, who led parades and took trips as a young drum major, as smoothly talented and sociable, a steady soul who made friends easily. He had fashion sense and style. "He was very self-confident," his brother said. "He was secure with himself."

. . .

FRASER CELEBRATED his seventeenth birthday in 1952, shortly before starting his final year at DuSable. The previous year, Nelson Algren had published his essay *Chicago: City on the Make*, mocking the bilious self-promotion of city leaders and their notion of Chicago as a place where color did not matter. He argued that race relations were grounded in a "protean awareness of white superiority everywhere, in everything." Algren, a white novelist later known for his novel about heroin addiction, *The Man with the Golden Arm*, told of rents pegged higher for black residents, and restaurants and bars that were unofficially, but certainly, off-limits. "Make your own little list," he wrote. "Of the streets you mustn't live on, the hotels where you can't register, the offices you can't work in and the unions you can never join."

Among DuSable students, many of them children of the Great Migration, blackness was widely discussed and understood. It was not only a fact of life, it was the X factor in their futures. Encounters with racism, studied in school and experienced outside, would shape their thinking and their decisions, not least about what lessons to teach the next generation. The high school itself was named for Jean-Baptiste Point du Sable, a black fur trader regarded as the first permanent settler of Chicago. Born in 1745 in what is now Haiti, his story was important to the high school's identity from the time it was christened in 1936. "We were taught the history of Jean-Baptiste Point du Sable," said Charlie Brown, a 1954 DuSable graduate who reported that African American history lessons stretched throughout the school year. Students regularly discussed "all the hardships the black people went through."

One of the most freewheeling and influential teachers during Fraser Robinson's years at DuSable was the main art teacher, Margaret Burroughs, who laced her lessons with African American history and current events. A young girl when she moved to Chicago from Louisiana with her family in the early 1920s, she joined the NAACP Youth Council as a teenager and studied at the Art Institute on her way to helping create a South Side art center and the DuSable Museum of African American History. Beseeching her students to take pride in their history, she instructed them to press onward when "faced with abhorrence of everything that is black." Burroughs's attitudes and activism were evident, not just to her students, but to higher-ups at the Chicago Board of Education who summoned her downtown in 1952 to explain herself. At first, she thought she might be getting a promotion. Instead, they questioned her views of communists and their sympathizers, including Earl Browder and one of her heroes, Paul Robeson. Burroughs said she was never given a reason, but she suspected it was her advocacy of black history, which, she said, "was considered subversive at the time."

The central message at DuSable was perseverance in the face of inequality, the idea that it was important to know the past but not be bound by it. Painted above the stage in DuSable High's ornate auditorium were the words "Peace if possible, but justice at any rate." The phrase came from Wendell Phillips, a white abolitionist in the nineteenth century and president of the American Anti-Slavery Society. "An agitator by profession," a prominent historian called him. Nearly sixty years after graduation, Charlie Brown could recite the DuSable epigram from memory. To him, the eight words registered as a demand for fairness, for it was undeniable that African Americans faced long odds. "When you lived in Chicago back then," he said, "you understood how white society described a black person, or a Negro. One drop of blood, you were a Negro." Brown was the star of the DuSable basketball team, a six-foot-two forward on the 1953 and 1954 squads that won the city title and became the first all-black teams to compete downstate in the Illinois state tournament. When DuSable played a white team, the coach warned his players to be at least 20 points ahead entering the fourth quarter, especially if it was an away game. "We didn't look for any favorable calls from the refs," Brown said. "In those days, racism was not hidden at all."

LONG BEFORE the civil rights movement became national news, African American adults on the South Side of Chicago often conveyed a message that acknowledged the obstacles without surrendering to them. Young people learned that they needed to work hard to prove themselves; they needed to be twice as good as whites to get just as far. They had less room for error than their white peers. Unfair? Yes, but that was the deal. No cavalry would ride to their rescue. "If one word came out of my father's mouth more than any other word, it was discipline, self-control," said Bernard Shaw, who grew up on the South Side and became an on-air reporter for CNN. "My mother used to say, 'It's not what you do, it's how you do it.' My father used to say, 'It's not what you say, it's how you say it.'" Yet these were not the standard admonitions that parents of any ethnicity might deliver about character and good manners. Rather, the Shaws were instructing their son on how to succeed in a society dominated by white people. "Racism pervaded city life," he said. "It certainly trickled down to the high school level." To succeed, as Fraser's classmate Reuben Crawford had said, you had to be about the business of being the business.

Children of the Great Migration learned that their job was to reach a higher rung than the one their parents occupied. "You *had* to do better. So much was expected of you," said Crawford, whose father supported his family by working two jobs, one of them as a window washer for the Chicago Board of Education. "You knew to respect your elders and do what you had to do. No nonsense, that was the key." Crawford played the clarinet, made the honor roll, and held an after-school job, working as a busboy at Gus' Good Food on North Dearborn. He learned a trade, dye-setting. The values ran deep. Going to church every Sunday was not required, but the moral imperative was strong: "Just do what you're supposed to do when you're interacting with people. Treat all people alike. Don't misuse them. That's God's will."

The message was very much the same at Fraser and LaVaughn Robinson's dinner table, said to Capers Funnye, a nephew, who recalled "an absolute conviction for what's right. You don't embarrass your family. You don't embarrass yourself." He ascribed a "tenacity" to the elder Fraser, recalling his message to the younger generation, especially to black boys: "You don't have time to be a slacker. If that's what you want to be, you're wasting your life. You're in competition. And as a person who's a Negro, you have to work twice as hard. You have to always be willing to step forward to prove your worth. You have to adjust to the situation. Move forward." In a world of equal opportunity, Fraser might have become a college professor, believed Funnye, who attended Howard University, converted to Judaism, and became a South Side rabbi. Indeed, some people who knew Fraser in South Carolina in the early years called him "professor." He "encouraged striving, he encouraged pushing," Funnye said. If someone in the family were wasting talents and opportunities, he would demand, "What are you doing? We don't have time for this." Although the system might be rigged, the message was to carry on, steadfast and undaunted.

FRASER III TURNED TWENTY in 1955, the summer of Emmett Till. On August 28, two white men in a Mississippi Delta town kidnapped the visiting fourteen-year-old from his great-uncle's house, lynched him, and dropped his body, weighted with a hundred-pound cotton gin fan, into the Tallahatchie River. His alleged crime was whistling at a white woman who tended a shop in rural Money, Mississippi. After Till's mutilated body reached Chicago on an Illinois Central train, his mother, Mamie Till Bradley, decreed that the casket should remain open so that "all the world" would bear witness. For anyone living in the city—and certainly on the South Side, where mourners paid their respects at the A. A. Rayner & Sons Funeral Home—there was no avoiding the shocking news. The papers were filled with it. A photographer from *Jet* magazine took photographs, one with Bradley looking on. "Few photographs . . . can lay claim to equally universal impact upon black observers," wrote historian Adam Green, who traced the ripples. Langston Hughes and Gwendolyn Brooks wrote poems about the case. James Baldwin made it the foundation of his play *Blues for Mister Charlie*. Eldridge Cleaver and Anne Moody said the killing influenced their political paths. Muhammad Ali told an interviewer, "I couldn't get Emmett Till out of my mind."

In Chicago, thousands upon thousands of people filed past the casket during five days of shock and mourning that ended with a large funeral service at the Roberts Temple Church of God in Christ. Before the month was out, a rally at the city's Metropolitan Church had attracted another ten thousand. Three months later, Rosa Parks refused to give up her seat on a city bus in Montgomery, Alabama. One thought running through her head as she sat there, she said many years later, was Till's death.

BY THE TIME of Till's murder, Fraser Robinson Jr. was earning his living in a post office job offered to war veterans, a valuable pathway to the middle class in an era when prejudice often limited private-sector opportunity. It was not electrical engineering, his long ago dream, but it was steady and it allowed him to salt away some savings. He was a frugal man who believed that when you put money in the bank, you never take it out. Settling back in together as a family, he and LaVaughn took a step rare for African Americans at the time and bought an apartment. It was located in the Parkway Gardens Homes, rising on fifteen acres at the old White City Amusement Park grounds in Woodlawn, just east of the rail yards. Parkway Gardens, described as "the largest mutually-owned apartment project to be owned and operated by Negroes in America," got its start in 1945. It was an initiative of the Dining Car Workers Union, whose leaders aimed to ease living conditions for the black laborers who crowded into scarce and substandard dwellings during the World War II manufacturing boom. In the immediate post-war years, 20 percent of the nation's steel was made in Chicago, and jobs were more plentiful than housing. Beyond delivering 694 apartments in 35 buildings, the shared ownership model of Parkway Gardens was designed to make decent housing more affordable and keep slumlords at bay. After an initial payment—$2,500 for families who had signed up by 1949—co-op owners paid a monthly amount at something less than market rates. The project, built with several million dollars in Federal Housing Administration support, made it easier to own property at a time when African Americans rarely had access to credit on the same terms as white people. The complex opened in the early 1950s and was completed in 1955. In 2011, Parkway Gardens was added to the National Register of Historic Places.

The ceremony to lay the Parkway Gardens cornerstone in September 1950 attracted political notables from across the city including, as keynote speaker, civil rights leader Mary McLeod Bethune who considered the ownership model "the opening of a new frontier to progress." Michelle Obama would live in Parkway Gardens, across the hall from her grandparents, for the first eighteen months of her life. In future years, she would visit often from her childhood home in nearby South Shore.

FRASER AND LAVAUGHN ROBINSON'S MOVE into an apartment of their own in the 1950s signified advancement, a solid step on a road that would carry each of their five children through high school, in some cases through college and graduate school, and into the middle class. They reached Parkway Gardens in a decade that would advance the slow-growing consensus that racial discrimination was wrong, symbolized most publicly by the Supreme Court's 1954 ruling in *Brown v. Board of Education*. Yet court victories masked as much as they promised. It was two steps forward, a step or two back. At times, success itself was thwarted. Carl Hansberry was a banker, real estate investor, and unsuccessful Republican candidate for Congress. In 1937, he secretly bought a house in a white part of Woodlawn, not far from the University of Chicago. He wanted not only to provide for his family, but to challenge housing restrictions, called restrictive covenants, a form of legalized segregation designed to prohibit black residents from living in certain places. "Literally howling mobs surrounded our house," his daughter Lorraine wrote, calling the block "hellishly hostile." Although a neighbor sued and Illinois courts ordered the Hansberry family to leave, the U.S. Supreme Court ruled otherwise in November 1940, invoking a procedural issue, not the constitutional question. By then, the Hansberrys had given up on the new house at 6140 Rhodes Avenue and returned to a home in the heart of the Black Belt, where they hosted many figures in the black cultural elite, including W. E. B. Du Bois, Paul Robeson, Duke Ellington, Langston Hughes, and Joe Louis.

Eighteen years after the ruling, a group of actors gathered in New York to rehearse a play written by Lorraine Hansberry, who said the drama was largely autobiographical. "Mama," she wrote to her mother, "it is a play that tells the truth about people, Negroes and life, and I think it will help a lot of people to understand how we are just as complicated as they are . . . people who are the very essence of human dignity." The play was *A Raisin in the Sun,* and it became the first drama by a black author to reach Broadway. Hansberry set the story in a black neighborhood on the South Side, the very one where she grew up and the Robinsons now lived. The central character is Lena Younger, a black domestic worker who receives an insurance windfall of $10,000, a princely sum. To help her family escape their shabby apartment, she uses some of the money to buy a house in a white neighborhood. Appalled, the white community sends an emissary to buy her out. Lena struggles with what to do and announces that her family will reject the payoff. They will not surrender to self-doubt, or to the connivings of their foes. "We ain't never been that poor," she explains. "We ain't never been that . . . dead inside." Even as she moves up and out, however, she is aware that not everyone in their old neighborhood, or even their own family, will make it. For many black families like them, the dilemma of obligation—to oneself, to family, to others—would become a feature of life, a perpetually renewing riddle. After seeing a revival of *A Raisin in the Sun* in 2014, Michelle would declare the play "one of America's greatest stories," and call it one of her favorites.

FRASER III SPENT his final stretch of high school living at Parkway Gardens and making his way to DuSable for class. After graduation in 1953, he enrolled at the University of Illinois at Navy Pier, a temporary campus built to accommodate the post–World War II college boom. He ran out of money, dropped out, and soon was helping to support his brother Nomenee, who would graduate from the Illinois Institute of Technology with a degree in architecture. Fraser joined the army in May 1958 at age twenty-two, prompting younger brother Andrew, not yet eight years old, to cry in worry that Fraser was going off to war. But these were the quiet years between the end of the Korean War and the start of hostilities in Vietnam. His first stop was Fort Leonard Wood, 130 miles southwest of St. Louis. Eight days later, he was on his way to

Fort Riley, Kansas. Six months after that, he headed to southern Germany.

At Fort Riley, soldiers converged from all over the country for eight weeks of basic training and eight weeks of advanced combat preparation. Once they reached their barracks near Munich, they joined the 24th Infantry Division, soon to be commanded by Major General Edwin Walker. A complicated figure, Walker had directed the federal troops that defended the integration of Little Rock's Central High School in 1957, but he was bounced from the army in 1961 for distributing right-wing political messages to soldiers under his command in Germany. In 1962, he was arrested for demonstrating against James Meredith's enrollment at the University of Mississippi. Walker demanded a spirit of discipline and dedication built on the presumption that a cold war in the era of superpower competition could quickly become hot. Drill time and physical training seemed endless, the rules unbending. "You fell out for formation every day. Every Saturday morning you had barracks inspection and God help you if everything wasn't perfect," recalled Joe Hegedus, who served in a mortar battery in Fraser's regiment. Before he left active duty, Fraser would win an expert marksmanship qualification with a rifle and a sharpshooter's qualification with a machine gun. He was awarded a good conduct medal and left active duty on May 23, 1960, as a private first class. He would complete his service with four years on the roster of the Illinois National Guard.

FRASER TURNED TWENTY-FIVE the summer after he returned home to the South Side. He looked for work and spent time with a young woman named Marian Shields. Chicago was teeming, and in flux. As African Americans continued to migrate northward, the city was home to 500,000 more black residents in 1960 than it was in 1940. It was now nearly thirty years since his father's generation had arrived from the old Confederacy and for all of Fraser Jr.'s frustrations, the family seemed to be gaining traction. In the next decade, it would be the turn of Fraser III and Marian to see what they could make for their children of Chicago's gruff promise.

TWO

South Side

Fraser Robinson and Marian Shields met through mutual friends when he was nineteen and she was seventeen, a senior at Englewood High. They broke up before he went into the army and got back together when he returned. They were vibrant, energetic, and athletic. Their interests were eclectic, their feet were on the ground, and they laughed a lot. Less than six months after Fraser returned from Germany, they were married in Woodlawn on October 27, 1960. The presiding African Methodist Episcopal minister was the Reverend Carl A. Fuqua, who doubled as executive secretary of the Chicago NAACP. On January 17, 1964, Marian gave birth to Michelle, who joined their oldest son, Craig, not quite two. The Robinsons' ambitions ran more to family happiness and their children's advancement than to professional success, particularly after Fraser was hit with multiple sclerosis. In the family's shorthand, Marian was the disciplinarian, while Fraser was the motivator and "philosopher in chief." Emerging from complicated families in a city that recognized them first and foremost as black, they saw it as their mission to provide strength, wisdom, and a measure of insulation to Michelle and Craig. Attitudes were changing, if slowly, and opportunities were growing. But the lessons echoed the ones their own parents had taught: Play the hand you were dealt and do it without complaint. "If it can be done, you can do it," Marian once said, describing the family motto. "It's a matter of choice."

Neither Fraser nor Marian finished college, a disappointment that fueled the push they gave to their children. Fraser served on reserve status with the Illinois National Guard and, like his father, worked at the post office. Three days before Michelle's birth, he started the city water plant job that he would keep until his death. Marian spent an unsatisfying two years studying to be a teacher, a profession favored by her parents but unattractive to her. She worked at Spiegel, the retail company, and then stayed home with the children until Michelle was in high school. "I come from a very articulate, well-read, highly productive, strong moral background. We weren't rich but we had the same aspirations as middle- and upper-middle-class African American families . . . ," Michelle explained in 2005. "People tend to either demonize or mythologize black communities that aren't wealthy. But my experience is that my community was very strong, the parents had strong values—the same as other people have throughout this country."

MARIAN SHIELDS ROBINSON WAS BORN in Chicago on July 30, 1937. Her parents arrived in the city as grade-school children, each already knowing much about sadness and loss. Rebecca Jumper and Purnell Shields came from the South, one from North Carolina, one from Alabama. Born early enough in the new century that people were alive who had lived in slavery, they joined the growing tide that became the Great Migration, attracted to what writer Isabel Wilkerson, borrowing from Richard Wright, called "the warmth of other suns." They traveled to the big city with adults who were determined to escape the race-based constraints of the South and grasp the economic opportunities that Chicago appeared to offer. Marian's parents arrived roughly a decade before Fraser C. Robinson Jr. and lived through the 1920s there. Married by age twenty, they would raise seven children on the South Side. But their path was hardly smooth, professionally or personally. By the end of their lives, they would be living apart.

Rebecca Jumper, Michelle's maternal grandmother, was born in 1909 in North Carolina, the seventh child in the family and the first to be born away from the Virginia farm where her father, James Jumper, had been an illiterate sharecropper. The family had followed relatives across the state line to Leaksville, where businesses sprouted to mill the cotton, process the tobacco, and hew the trees grown nearby. James worked as a laborer and his wife, Eliza Tinsley Jumper, the daughter of former slaves, took in laundry, scrubbing other people's clothes on a washboard. As adults, they both learned to read and Eliza could write "a little." Before Rebecca was ten years old, however, her parents died, perhaps in an influenza outbreak that killed thousands of people in North Carolina, the majority of them black. The family split apart. Rebecca joined her mother's younger sister, Carrie Tinsley Coleman, and her husband, John, who had moved north in 1907. After starting in Baltimore, they were on their way to Chicago to try their luck. They settled on the bustling South Side as a cobbled-together family of three. As an adult, Rebecca found work as a seamstress. "The women in my family were dressmakers," said Marian, who would also learn to sew. John went to work in a meatpacking plant, not five years after Upton Sinclair wrote his dark history of the industry, *The Jungle*. He then found work as a plasterer.

Purnell Shields, too, knew loss at a young age. He was born in Birmingham, Alabama, in 1910, the newest member of a family that had climbed several rungs since slavery. The city was deeply segregated and would remain so for decades, yet his grandfather had succeeded as a businessman and acquired property. His father, Robert Lee Shields, worked as a Pullman porter—desirable work that delivered a solid income, a measure of prestige, and a window onto a wider world. Purnell was not yet ten when his father died suddenly, leaving his mother, Annie Shields, to pay the bills while caring for her two children. Her work life until then had consisted of working at home as a seamstress, and she struggled with the new responsibilities. She soon remarried. Her new husband was a tailor. With Purnell and his sister, the family moved from Alabama to Chicago in the early 1920s.

Purnell, working in a syrup factory by the time he was nineteen, would spend much of his adult life as a carpenter and handyman whose passions ran to music, especially jazz. When he was a young man, Chicago was a music mecca. "When I finally came to Chicago on May 9,

1930," said Floyd Campbell, a renowned drummer of the era, "there was plenty of work for musicians. I used to say that there were at least 110 full-time musicians working on salaries of up to $75 a week within a one-block radius of 47th Street and South Parkway. There were two bands at the Regal Theater and three large orchestras working at the Savoy Ballroom.... Chicago was a musician's town." The greats, the sidemen, and the dreamers flowed through town in the years to come. Louis Armstrong and Earl Hines. Bessie Smith and King Oliver. Duke Ellington and Cab Calloway. Count Basie and Benny Goodman. Ella Fitzgerald and Gene Krupa. They all played at the Lincoln Gardens Cafe or the enormous Savoy Ballroom, capacity four thousand, or in the galaxy of other South Side clubs.

It was clear to everyone who spent time with Purnell Shields that jazz animated him. "He played it 24 hours a day on the highest volume he could put it on," recalled Michelle, who credited him with presenting her with her first album, *Talking Book,* released by Stevie Wonder in 1972. She reported that he had speakers in every room, including the bathroom, and quoted her mother as saying of her upbringing, "You learn to sleep through jazz." Craig said the grandfather they called Southside was "by calling a chef, drummer and jazz aficionado, an impresario and all around magnet who made everyone in the family gravitate to his side." He experienced frustration, as well, particularly about the racism he encountered throughout his life. He was denied better jobs and pay because, as an African American, he could not join a labor union. "I had a father who could be very angry about race," Marian once said. "My father was a very angry man."

IN NO DECADE since the Civil War and Reconstruction had race been more consistently central to the national conversation than it was in the 1960s, when Fraser and Marian were beginning to raise their children. The Kerner Commission, delivering its 1968 report on racial unrest in America's cities, made its elemental conclusion plain on the very first page: "Our nation is moving toward two societies, one black, one white—separate and unequal." The commission, established by

President Lyndon B. Johnson during the angry summer of 1967 and chaired by Illinois governor Otto Kerner Jr., was hardly stacked with iconoclasts or seers. Rather, months of testimony and analysis yielded the inescapable conclusion that America's cities were bitterly broken and black people were getting the short end of the stick. "Segregation and poverty have created in the racial ghetto a destructive environment totally unknown to most white Americans," wrote the eleven members of what was officially named the National Advisory Commission on Civil Disorders. "What white Americans have never fully understood— but what the Negro can never forget—is that white society is deeply implicated in the ghetto. White institutions created it, white institutions maintain it, and white society condones it." In establishing the commission, President Johnson declared that the nation should attack, as a matter of "conscience," the urban conditions that bred despair and violence: "All of us know what those conditions are: Ignorance, discrimination, slums, poverty, disease, not enough jobs."

What the commission found in cities across the country was commonplace in Chicago, where progress toward equal opportunity had been grudging in the aftermath of the 1948 Supreme Court decision in *Shelley v. Kraemer*, which ended racially restrictive housing covenants, and the 1954 ruling in *Brown v. Board of Education*. Protests had been launched and civic battles fought, notably over segregated schools, but avenues to advancement through education, work, and politics remained stubbornly narrow. When the Reverend Martin Luther King Jr. decided to carry his nonviolent southern protest movement to the urban north in 1966, he chose Chicago. To draw attention to slum housing and discrimination, he made a show of moving his family into a dilapidated West Side apartment with a broken boiler and stairwells that stank of urine.

That same year, a team of university researchers concluded that poverty and lack of opportunity in Chicago's African American neighborhoods owed much to discriminatory policies in housing and employment. Redlining and usurious contract-buying practices were common. Although the income of an average black family in 1966 was just two-thirds of the income of an average white family, average rents were identical. Noting that rents and home prices in African American neighborhoods were artificially high. Academics called it a "color tax" and demonstrated the ways that housing discrimination rippled through other aspects of the lives of black citizens: "This difference has its source in the prejudice that deprives the Negro of the free choice of his residence. Regardless of his living standards or of his preferences, the Negro is confined to certain areas of the city. Residential segregation by extension tends toward segregation of residentially oriented facilities such as schools, parks, libraries, beaches and public transportation lines." Schools became increasingly overcrowded with black children, but the Chicago public school leadership refused to redraw boundaries to allow black students to fill unused classroom space in largely white schools.

As for employment, the gap was stark. Black people were generally unwelcome in jobs in the Loop, the city's downtown business center. A 1966 report on major Chicago businesses by the U.S. Equal Employment Opportunity Commission found that white workers were ten times more likely than black workers to have professional or managerial jobs and five times more likely to have sales jobs. Black employees were three times more likely than whites to be laborers or service workers. In raw numbers, the survey found that African Americans held 4.5 percent of the 33,769 white-collar jobs in the insurance industry and 12 percent of the 78,385 retail jobs. In the health care field, black people were found to have 7.9 percent of the 23,783 white-collar jobs.

All ten of Chicago's poorest communities were in the so-called "Negro Belt" on the city's South and West Sides. Seven of the ten communities were found to be at least 90 percent nonwhite. Meanwhile, only one in sixty-five African Americans lived in neighborhoods that were at least 90 percent white. The most downtrodden neighborhood in the city was Altgeld, on the city's far southern edge, where Barack Obama would work as a community organizer in the 1980s.

WOODLAWN, WHERE MICHELLE LIVED for the first eighteen months of her life across the hall from Fraser and LaVaughn Robinson in

Parkway Gardens, was also going downhill. The community's population was expanding and becoming increasingly African American, with Woodlawn moving from 40 percent nonwhite in 1950 to 98 percent nonwhite in 1966. It was also becoming poorer by every measure, its housing stock deteriorating, juvenile delinquency rising, and jobs moving away. "Statistically, Woodlawn had become just another slum," wrote one author. In 1965, when Craig was three years old and Michelle was one and a half, the Robinsons moved about three miles away to a house on a quiet street in South Shore, a middle-class neighborhood in transition from all white to all black. At the time, some called the move going "way out south." They packed up their things, from Fraser's artwork to the children's toys, and settled into the upstairs apartment of a red-brick bungalow purchased that year by Marian's aunt, Robbie Shields Terry, a strong-willed schoolteacher active in the Woodlawn AME church choir, and her husband, William Terry, a Pullman porter. With no children of their own, they liked the idea of having the young Robinson family close by. The apartment was small, but the house had a yard in front and back with plenty of room to turn cartwheels.

At about the time Marian and Fraser were moving to 7436 South Euclid Avenue, Gloria and Leonard Jewell bought a home two blocks south. "Because it was an integrated neighborhood," Gloria Jewell told a *Chicago Tribune* reporter in 1967. "We wanted to bring up our two children, ages 5 and 4, in a world that would be far more pleasant than it had been to us." She said, "People here are dedicated and have high standards." Gloria worked as a Head Start coordinator after earning a teaching certificate. Leonard was a commercial artist who had studied and taught at the Art Institute of Chicago but was routinely denied jobs because he was African American. One of the first black families in the 7600 block of South Euclid, the Jewells stayed and built a life even as a steady stream of white people moved out. "I had the best childhood ever. It was awesome," said Leonard Jewell Jr., known as Biff to his friends, including Craig Robinson. "I had so much fun. There were tons of kids, we played tons of games. It was all outside, simple stuff. Riding your bike, playing softball, playing football. There was always something going on. Climbing my garage, swinging from the trees into my backyard. It was a blast."

Two blocks away it would not be long before Craig and Michelle could ride their bikes on the sidewalk and around the block to the back alley. Across East 75th Street was a large city park with a grass field and playground equipment. Its name, Rosenblum Park, signified an earlier wave of South Shore residents, now moving out. When they were old enough, Craig and Michelle could walk safely to class at Bryn Mawr Elementary, where Marian, one of the very few stay-at-home mothers in the neighborhood, volunteered her time. "There were good schools, that's why people moved, and it was the reason *we* moved," Marian said. "It was fine with me that it was changing. Some people felt the schools were too geared to whites. People were very conscious and wanted black artists in the schools. My point was just to go to school and learn what you have to learn." To the children, it seemed pretty great. Craig called it "the Shangri-La of upbringings."

IN 1966, when Martin Luther King arrived in North Lawndale, a grittier precinct on Chicago's West Side, he found a latticework of racial politics so intricate that it made him long for the television-ready segregationists in Selma and Birmingham. Not that the hatred in Chicago was any milder, he would soon conclude, for the structural inequality that hindered and harmed black people had deep roots. King began leading interracial vigils and protest marches in support of open housing. He met with gang members, civic activists, and city officials. Pickets stood outside real estate offices and banks, instructing passersby about discrimination that kept more people from doing what the Robinsons did. In the city's central business district demonstrators carried signs that read "We are here because the Savings and Loan Associations refuse to loan money to Negroes who wish to buy beyond the ghetto."

On July 10, six months into what became known as the Chicago Freedom Movement, King headlined a rally on a ninety-eight-degree day at Soldier Field, where tens of thousands of people listened to performances by B.B. King, Mahalia Jackson, Peter, Paul, and Mary, and sixteen-year-old Stevie Wonder. Several thousand then marched three miles to City Hall, where King emulated Martin Luther and taped a parchment with fourteen demands to an outside door. Five days later, a neighborhood argument over opening fire hydrants for black children in the brutal summer heat had ricocheted into riots that left two dead, hundreds under arrest, six police officers wounded by gunfire, $2 million in property damage, and four thousand National Guardsmen patrolling the streets.

The troubles continued. Three weeks later, King led a march of 550 white and black Freedom Movement supporters through Marquette Park, a white southwest Chicago neighborhood. Despite the deployment of two hundred police officers in riot helmets to protect the demonstrators, the protest turned ugly. The marchers, including Andrew Young and Jesse Jackson, were met with rocks, bricks, and cherry bombs; forty-two people were hospitalized. White youths slashed tires and set fire to marchers' cars, which were identified by their "End Slums" stickers. King addressed 1,700 supporters a few days later by saying the protests and the picket lines would continue: "I *still* have faith in the future. My brothers and sisters, I *still* can sing 'We Shall Overcome.'" The next afternoon, when King returned to Marquette Park, an angry crowd of more than four thousand white people was waiting. One sign read "King Would Look Good with a Knife in His Back." A King supporter who had helped plan the march route heard a singsong chant to the tune of the Oscar Mayer Weiner jingle:

> *I wish I were an Alabama trooper.*
> *This is what I would truly love to be.*
> *Because if I were an Alabama trooper,*
> *Then I could kill the niggers legally.*

A rock hurled by someone in the crowd hit King behind his right ear and knocked him to the ground. Someone else threw a knife; it missed him and stuck in the shoulder of a white heckler. The three-mile march continued, as did the attack, with windows shattering, bones breaking, and men setting protesters' cars afire. Six Chicago policemen, seen by the crowd as collaborators, were cornered and beaten until reinforcements fired gunshots into the air and rescued them. "I have never in my life seen such hate," King told reporters later. "I've been in many demonstrations all across the South, but I can say that I have never seen—even in Mississippi and Alabama—mobs as hostile and hate-filled as I've seen in Chicago. I think the people from Mississippi ought to come to Chicago to learn how to hate."

The protests, the bad publicity, and the potential for more conflict pushed Mayor Richard J. Daley and the business community to promise modest action. But when King left town, the status quo remained undisturbed. "We should have known better," King's Southern Christian Leadership Conference ally Ralph Abernathy said later, "than to believe that we could come to Chicago and right its wrongs with the same tactics we had used in Montgomery, Birmingham and Selma." What the Chicago project did, however, was demonstrate to a national audience that racism in the mid-1960s was not confined to the byways of the old Confederacy. The violence and vitriol in the heartland, wrote author Taylor Branch, "cracked a beguiling, cultivated conceit that bigotry was the province of backward Southerners, treatable by enlightened but firm instruction." In the aftermath of the bloody Chicago campaign, the editors of the *Saturday Evening Post* wrote, "We are all, let us face it, Mississippians."

THE TUMULT EXPOSED a mean side of Chicago, a city dominated by Daley, a quintessential political boss who was elected to six terms between April 1955 and December 1976. More than any mayor in twentieth-century America, Daley perfected the power of patronage to bend the city to his vision and his will. He earned the loyalty of many, co-opted others, and bulldozed the rest. This was particularly true in the growing black community, which experienced Daley's tactical largesse as a limited blessing. "Daley had a special weak spot. He never accepted African American Chicagoans on an equal basis," said Leon Despres, an independent white South Side alderman who often found himself on the lonely end of 49–1 city council votes. "He used their committeemen and officeholders to get votes. He allotted them their mathematical share of patronage. He reserved the highest offices for whites. He resisted a genuine opening of the police and fire departments. He arranged the construction of the Dan Ryan Expressway to serve, he hoped, as a barrier to expansion of black residence. He resisted genuine fair housing legislation as long as he could."

By the early 1960s, there were six African American aldermen on the city council. They were known derisively as the Silent Six for their supple responses to Daley's demands. The mayor granted his loyalists considerable license to dispense jobs to constituents, so long as election day turnout was high and aldermen voted the right way when called upon. At its height, the Chicago machine controlled as many as forty thousand patronage jobs, by one estimate, ranging from gardeners, garbagemen, and drivers to city inspectors and department heads. For some, patronage meant respectable work at a decent salary, a path to the middle class. For others, it was a gateway to greased palms; cash flowed from numbers rackets, business schemes, and kickback operations that were limited only by the boundaries of human imagination. For still others, it was a ladder to public office. Very few people stepped into one of the fifty city council seats during the Daley years without a nod from the man who ruled City Hall.

Everything was a transaction and everyone understood the rules. "It was impossible to do business in Chicago at that time without dealing with Mayor Daley," said John Johnson, the African American chairman of the downtown media company that published *Jet* and *Ebony*. "You couldn't cut a deal with underlings; you had to see him personally. Which meant that you were personally obligated to him." Harold Washington, who became the city's first black mayor in 1983, got his start with the machine. So did Eugene Sawyer, who took office when Washington died. William Barnett, a precinct captain who later became one of the Silent Six, said matter-of-factly, "We gave out jobs. A man had to carry his precinct to keep his." A former Black Panther named Bobby Rush would say in 1975 that Barnett's perspective had been "blunted by the taste of polish from Mayor Daley's boots," but defenders argued that the bargain made by the Silent Six was not entirely venal, particularly when work possibilities for African Americans were so limited. "You went along with things in order to make sure that we were able to help people," Sawyer told the *Chicago Tribune* after he himself became mayor. "They were people who wanted somehow to break that shackle, but they had so many people that would get hurt, so many people who would lose jobs and positions." Far down the food chain, precinct workers owed the jobs that sustained their families to the labor they did for the machine. "There are no virgins in Chicago politics," Sawyer said. "We all started in the Daley machine."

Sawyer's political mentor was Robert Miller, one of the Silent Six. A funeral director by profession, Miller ran the 6th Ward on the South Side, dispensing favors, getting out the Democratic vote, and toeing the party line. Miller not only understood patronage as the way politics was played, but defended the tradeoffs as the price of progress for his black constituents. Just as Sawyer owed his job on the city payroll to Miller, who put him to work at the city water plant in June 1959, so did Nomenee Robinson, Michelle's uncle, who talked his way through the 6th Ward patronage system into a water plant job one year later. As Robinson recalled the moment, he was attending the Illinois Institute of Technology, helped to a scholarship by Robert Chorley, director of the Woodlawn Boys Club. When Chorley asked what he intended to do for the summer, Robinson replied, "Mr. Chorley, I need a good job." The year before, Robinson had worked as a city janitor and he was looking to move up. Chorley wrote a letter of introduction and sent him to Miller, who dispatched him to City Hall. There, he met Matthew Danaher, Daley's patronage chief, who had started as the mayor's driver and risen to become the 11th Ward alderman before his indictment on federal bribery charges. Danaher, in turn, sent Robinson to see the public works commissioner, James Wilson, who thumbed through a thick employment ledger.

"Okay, we have this laborer job," Wilson said. "How's that fit you?" Robinson took a chance and said that, well, he had held a better job before. Wilson turned back to the ledger and saw a different slot. "Chlorine attendant," he said. "It's like an engineer's job at the old water tower. Are you up to that?" Robinson asked how much it paid. When Wilson said it paid $543.50 a month, Robinson was floored. It was a sum equal to the median family income for a Chicago family of four. He accepted on the spot. Miller, of course, asked something of

Robinson in return, assigning him to be an assistant precinct captain. As Robinson recalled, "He put it very nicely: 'If this conflicts with your studies, you let me know.'" Miller tied the request in a bow, but both parties understood that declining was not an option.

Fraser Robinson followed his younger brother into a low-level job with the machine, serving as a Democratic precinct captain and reporting to the city water department. He was twenty-eight years old when he started work as a water plant "station laborer," or janitor, for a salary of $479 a month. One of his colleagues in later years was Dan Maxime, a white man from the North Side who had started working for the Democratic machine in 1957. When Maxime got his first patronage job, serving as a Cook County zoning inspector, he said it was "the beginning of the good old days of politics. With the graft, even for the cop on the street. When you got stopped, he asked for your license and you had either a five- or a ten-dollar bill you handed him with your license. We were all part of the system. Every election was war and the Republicans were the enemy. You did everything you needed to win that war. That included stealing votes." But Fraser Robinson was not one to falsify registrations or steal votes, Maxime said. "He wasn't the type. He was strait-laced. Just the salt of the earth."

For Fraser, the role of precinct captain suited his outgoing personality. It was also "a ladder, a stepping stone to a job," said his brother Andrew. The water plant job, while tedious, afforded him a steady living with reasonable hours. In five years, he had been promoted to foreman at $659.50 a month, and seven months later, in May 1969, he began tending boilers for $858 a month. He would keep that job until his death. Marian recalled that Fraser "felt local politics was the most important" and saw his precinct work as a way to do good works. "He loved trying to help people. The city was set up so that precinct captains were the go-between with the city," she said. "If they needed an answer, he was the liaison. He was always going to the precinct. He would head there in the evening. He loved to talk." She called him "a visiting kind of person."

. . .

THE HOUSE AT 7436 South Euclid Avenue where the Robinsons lived was neither the nicest nor the poorest on a quiet street stretching three blocks north to a commercial strip on East 71st Street that would later be called Emmett Till Way. It had two entrances on the south side, with one door leading to a staircase that rose to their second-floor apartment. With help from Marian's father, Purnell, the Robinsons turned two rooms and a kitchen into a home for a family of four. The parents took the bedroom while Purnell installed paneling that divided a narrow living room into a shared bedroom and play space—later, a homework space—for Michelle and Craig. The kitchen, down a hallway from the children's room, did double duty as the dining room, and the family shared a single bathroom. "If I had to describe it to a real estate agent, it would be 1BR, 1BA," Craig said. "If you said it was 1,100 square feet, I'd call you a liar."

"Everything that I think about and do," Michelle said later, "is shaped around the life that I lived in that little apartment in the bungalow that my father worked so hard to provide for us." The family made a point of sitting down to dinner together every evening, apart from the nights when Fraser pulled the late shift at the water plant, a twenty-minute drive up Lake Shore Drive to downtown Chicago. Aunt Robbie gave piano lessons to the children, who played outdoors together in good weather. When Craig rode the bicycle he got for Christmas, Michelle followed on her new tricycle. "It was almost as if we were twins, rather than siblings close in age," Craig recalled. There are stories of practical jokes played in the dark and scenes that made the children fall out laughing. Also, all sorts of contests, from hunts through dictionaries and encyclopedias to a jumping game staged by Fraser, who sometimes put a quarter atop a door jamb for young Craig to leap and reach. Michelle had an Easy Bake Oven and a passel of Barbie dolls, including the impossibly contoured blonde Malibu Barbie—the first doll she owned—and a black Barbie imitation. "I liked everything Barbie. I was a big Barbie doll kid and every Christmas, I got a new Barbie. One year, I got the Barbie townhouse and the camper." Only later, after she started to read the work of Maya Angelou, particularly her poem "Phenomenal Woman," did she reflect on the cultural messages contained in the curves of the tiny-waisted plastic figurines. Barbie seemed to be "the standard for perfection," she said later. "That was what the world told me to aspire to."

AT THE ROBINSON HOUSE, Fraser made time when he returned from work to play sports with the kids—baseball, basketball, soccer, football. He gave Craig a pair of boxing gloves and taught him how to use them. Craig remembers boxing with Michelle, who told the International Olympic Committee in Copenhagen that her father "taught me how to throw a ball and a mean right hook better than any boy in my neighborhood." She described herself as "kind of a tomboy" and recalled sports as "a gift I shared with my dad." The children were limited to one hour of television a day. *The Brady Bunch* was a particular favorite of Michelle's, and she developed an encyclopedic knowledge of the show. For the parents, nights out of the house on their own were a rarity. The family typically devoted Saturday nights to games: Chinese checkers, Monopoly, a bluffing game called Hands Down, and, later, epic Scrabble battles. From an early age, Michelle hated to lose.

When the weather was warm, in a house without air conditioning, the children staged camping trips on the back porch, later converted to a bedroom for Craig. During football season, they backed the Bears, with Fraser parking himself in front of the television on Sunday afternoons. They rooted for the White Sox, the nearby South Side baseball team. But they invested more passion in the Cubs, the team that played in the North Side's iconic Wrigley Field. The star was the effervescent Ernie Banks, ace fielder, slugger, and two-time National League most valuable player who had once earned $7 a day in the Negro Leagues. Fans called him Mr. Cub. He and two black teammates, Billy Williams and Ferguson Jenkins, reached the Baseball Hall of Fame despite years on desultory squads that never saw the first inning of a World Series. Craig once said he considered baseball his main sport as a young boy. He liked to imagine himself as the next Ernie Banks.

When Michelle launched her healthy eating campaign during her husband's first term in the White House, she recalled how active she had been as a girl in South Shore. The streets were safe and Bryn Mawr Elementary still had recess. Before school, she played freeze tag and other games in the schoolyard until the bell rang, "and after school we'd head home to our neighborhood and play outside for hours. There were always plenty of kids around, and we'd play softball or a game called Piggy with a batter, a pitcher, a catcher, and a 16-inch softball rather than the standard 12-inch ones." When a fielder caught a batted ball on the fly or on one bounce, the fielder got to bat. "Later, we played chase, which was basically just boys chasing girls and then girls chasing boys. And all the girls in the neighborhood knew how to jump Double Dutch. We would also ride on our bikes and ride around for hours."

MARIAN DEVOTED considerable time to the education of her children, starting when they were young. Craig recalled his mother's diligence in teaching him to read at age four, before he started school. She was ready with flash cards and, as soon as he showed an interest, spent hours with him, describing the letters and sounds and how they connected. He was far ahead of his classmates when he arrived at Bryn Mawr. When she tried the same strategy with her daughter, the little girl refused. "I guess she figured she could figure out how to read on her own, but she was too young to say that," Marian recalled. On her way to becoming grandmother in residence at the White House, Marian would report that Michelle's younger daughter, Sasha, then age seven, reminded her of Michelle at the same age. "Just like Sasha. She always had her own opinions about things and she didn't hesitate to say so, because we allowed it." LaVaughn Robinson, Michelle's paternal grandmother, told a co-worker that Michelle was "hard-headed" and needed a spanking from time to time, but that she and Craig were good kids. A friend, meanwhile, recalled hearing Michelle tell a story about a Bryn Mawr teacher who complained to Marian about the girl's attitude. "Her mom told the teacher, 'Yeah, she's got a temper, but we decided to keep her anyway.'"

The Robinsons' standards for achievement were very high, but they emphasized effort and attitude over grades. They instructed the children that hard work would be rewarded. And it was. Michelle skipped second grade, and Craig, who remembered being bored in second grade, skipped third. It was known as "doing a double." When they finished eighth grade at Bryn Mawr two years apart, Craig was the valedictorian of his class and Michelle was the salutatorian of hers. In making clear the importance of education—not just attending school, but excelling—Marian and Fraser used their own experience as an example, explaining to Michelle and Craig how much they regretted not finishing college. "We told the kids how dumb it was," Marian said.

The lessons at home expanded on what the children learned in school and filled gaps in a Chicago Public Schools curriculum that could not keep up with the politically charged times. The Civil Rights Act and the Voting Rights Act had both become law, yet the children would see on Sunday drives through the city and summer trips to the South that segregation and bigotry endured. Martin Luther King was assassinated in April 1968, when Michelle was four years old, sparking riots in black neighborhoods on the West Side and across the country. When Bryn Mawr lesson plans began to include black history and Craig began asking questions, Marian bought a set of encyclopedias "written from the black perspective," as Craig put it. "Now I could understand not only what the tragedy of Dr. King's killing meant, but also what he represented in terms of the dream of equality that belonged to all races," Craig recalled. "I also learned why 'turn the other cheek' wasn't always easy to do and a little more about other civil rights leaders in [the] 1960s like Malcolm X." It was no coincidence that Malcolm was Craig's middle name. In 1962, he said, his mother "read an article about his work and, as she was looking for a middle name for a boy if she should have one, decided Malcolm had a nice ring to it." Or, as he put it another time, "Now, you've got to remember, my dad grew up in the Black Panther era—my middle name is Malcolm!"

In the tumult of the 1960s, Malcolm X personified an array of images of black people in America, some of them contradictory. He was the petty criminal born as Malcolm Little and known as Big Red who spent time behind bars. He was the ascetic who preached against drugs, deceit, and moral decay. Lanky and stylish, operating from behind silver and black glasses that lent him a studious air, he befuddled white questioners with calm rejoinders about the fundamental rights that any decent society owed its citizens. Yet he also raised his fist in a black power salute. He advocated separatism and militancy, and asked what progress nonviolent protest had ever delivered to African Americans. He dismissed the 1963 March on Washington, which culminated in King's "I Have a Dream" speech, as the "farce on Washington."

Through all of Malcolm's intellectual and spiritual wanderings, even many African Americans who were skeptical or disdainful of his fulminations drew strength from his personal narrative and his celebration of blackness. Jackie Robinson, the first black baseball player in the major leagues, offered up his opinion in *The Defender* in March 1964. The piece appeared in the weeks after Cassius Clay defeated Sonny Liston for the heavyweight boxing title and converted to Islam, becoming Muhammad Ali. Robinson said the new champ, who called himself "the greatest," was loud and sometimes crude, but his message of black self-worth was right. "I am not advocating that Negroes think they are greater than anyone else," Robinson said. "But I want them to know that they are just as great as other human beings." He said critics missed the point in worrying that Ali and Malcolm X would entice Negroes to become Black Muslims. The black people who marched for civil rights "want more democracy, not less," Robinson said. "They want to be integrated into the mainstream of American life, not invited to live in some small cubicle of this land in splendid isolation. If Negroes ever turn to the Black Muslim movement, in any numbers, it will not be because of Cassius or even Malcolm X. It will be because white America has refused to recognize the responsible leadership of the Negro people and to grant us the same rights that any other citizen enjoys in this land."

"Before Malcolm X," wrote cultural critic Ta-Nehisi Coates, "the very handle we now embrace—*black*—was an insult. We were *coloreds* or *Negroes*, and to call someone *black* was to invite a fistfight. But Malcolm remade the menace inherent in that name into something mystical—*Black Power; Black Is Beautiful; It's a black thing, you wouldn't understand*. . . . For all of Malcolm's invective, his most seductive notion was that of collective self-creation: the idea that black people could, through force of will, remake themselves." In *Dreams from My Father*, his memoir about his search for identity, young Barack Obama wrote of Malcolm X that his "repeated acts of self-creation spoke to me. The blunt poetry of his words, his unadorned insistence on respect, promised a new and uncompromising order, martial in its discipline, forged through sheer force of will. All the other stuff, the talk of blue-eyed devils and apocalypse, was incidental to that program." As president, Obama said he found Malcolm's theology, analysis, and policy advice to be "full of holes." And yet, he told writer David Remnick, Malcolm gave voice to the growing conviction in the African American community that black people must believe in themselves and assert their worth. "If you think about it, of a time in the early 1960s, when a black Ph.D. might be a Pullman porter and have to spend much of his day obsequious and kowtowing to people, that affirmation that 'I am a man, I am worth something,' I think that was important. And I think Malcolm X probably captured that better than anybody."

WHEN MICHELLE AND CRAIG WERE in elementary school, Marian made herself a familiar presence among the teachers and students. Fraser also spent time in their classrooms, and other relatives pitched in. Aunt Robbie ran an operetta workshop for children in the school district, once casting Craig as Hansel in *Hansel and Gretel* when he was in second grade. He had a singing part, as did Michelle, who wore a tutu and played the good fairy. Singing a solo was "humiliating," she said, but the performance was a win. "I liked it because of the costume."

Robbie was a formidable presence. Always had been. Years before, she had lived with Marian's large family at 6449 South Eberhart Avenue, helping with the children in ways that, as Marian recalled, "my mother would not or could not." She became youth choir director at the politically progressive Woodlawn AME church and, in 1943, registered for a church and choral music workshop at Northwestern University. Late on a summer night, when she arrived at Willard Hall to claim her room, a clerk informed her that Negroes were not permitted to spend the night on campus. Although it was nearly midnight, the clerk sent her to a rooming house for "coloreds" elsewhere in Evanston. Robbie reported the news to Woodlawn's pastor, the Reverend Archibald J. Carey Jr., who mustered a *Chicago Defender* reporter and an officer of the Chicago Civil Liberties Committee to investigate. "We know that Negroes prefer to live with members of their own race," a school official told the delegation. Five months later, backed by the Woodlawn church, Robbie sued Northwestern in state court, alleging discrimination. The lawsuit charged that the university had treated her as "inferior to other normal young American women and unfit to live and associate with them."

Robbie, who became the Woodlawn choir director, retained her high standards, a trait that ran in the family. "She was friendly, but that music had to be perfect," remembered Betty Reid, who sang at Woodlawn and rehearsed from time to time at the South Euclid house. "Let me tell you, in the middle of your performance, if you were off-key, she would stop. 'We are going to start at *this* place. If you aren't interested in singing, you should just sit this out.' We would feel so embarrassed, but she wanted to make sure you never made that error again. She was a hard taskmaster, but the choirs and the performers were right on target." Reid became a friend, sometimes giving Robbie a ride home from church. Later, Reid would leave Woodlawn and minister to her own congregation. She presided over Fraser's memorial service in 1991.

Michelle said both sides of the family had a "strong connection to faith and religion," although she and Craig were infrequent worshippers as children. They sometimes attended Woodlawn, which was preferred by the Shields family, and sometimes the Baptist church favored by the Robinsons. She remembered enduring the endless Chicago winters with the help of romps in a church basement much larger than the cellar at 7436 South Euclid. As an adult, she said she wanted her own daughters to have "a basic foundation, understanding and respect for [a] higher being . . . because it's what I grew up with." In religious matters as with many other things, Fraser and Marian left it to the children to choose their own way. Their approach, according to Craig, was to expose them to church and encourage them "to explore and find our own basis for faith by thinking for ourselves." After his father's funeral years later, Craig noted that Betty Reid's remarks were not "about how Fraser had gone on to a better place, which would have been counter to his belief that life is what it is, here on earth."

THROUGH THE YEARS, Craig and Michelle frequently described their childhood as an idyll rooted in family solidarity that flowed from their parents' evident affection for each other and their determination to get the parenting equation right. "That love for one another," Craig wrote, "was simply a fact of our lives, the foundation of the strong family unit they chose to build, and the reason they always seemed to be happy to me—even when circumstances might have dictated otherwise." Fraser and Marian made clear their rigorous expectations for achievement and citizenship, while deploying a sense of humor that, among other things, kept the children from getting too big for their britches. Craig recalled their parents as "relentless." Michelle, who remembered "a mother who pushed me," cleaned the bathroom every Saturday, scrubbing the sink and toilet and mopping the floor. She and her brother took turns doing the dishes. The parents "didn't overdo the praise," yet something in the mix kept the children from being overly concerned with the negative opinions of others. "It was very disciplined and there was a lot of accountability," Craig said. "But there was a whole lot of respect, a whole lot of love, and the biggest thing I think my parents gave us was self-esteem." They also modeled a sense of responsibility, to oneself and others, that would be echoed in countless choices Michelle made as an adult.

The freedom granted to Michelle and Craig to make their own decisions was not unlimited. It existed within a framework that emphasized hard work, honesty, and self-discipline. There were obligations and occasional punishment. But the goal was freethinking. "Don't be a follower," Marian told her children. "You follow people for one reason and they'll lead you for another." She advised them to use their heads, yet not to be afraid to make mistakes—in each case always learning from what goes wrong. "If it sounds like they are using good judgment," she said, "then you don't settle on the rules, because you want them early on to start making decisions on their own. I think that gives kids a lot of confidence."

The highs and lows of Marian's own childhood taught her some enduring lessons, ones that she would pass along. She attended segregated schools. In her extended family, she saw struggle and sacrifice alike. "That's where we got our understanding that it was going to be hard, but you just had to do whatever it takes," she said. "We all went to church. I was a Brownie. I was a Girl Scout. We all took piano lessons. We had drama classes. They took you to the museum, the Art Institute. They did all these things, but I don't know how." She saw to it that Craig and Michelle went to the symphony, the opera, and the city's fine museums. Recalling times in her childhood when she "resented it when I couldn't say what I felt," she also aimed to raise her children to stand up, speak up, and always ask why. "More important, even, than learning to read and write was to teach them to think. We told them, 'Make sure you respect your teachers, but don't hesitate to question them. Don't even allow us to just say anything to you.'"

It was understood in the Robinson household that no matter what obstacles Michelle or Craig faced because of their race or their working-class roots, life's possibilities were unbounded. Fulfillment of those possibilities was up to them. No excuses. Not that the strategy emerged fully formed when the kids were born. Marian said she raised her children "by ear, day by day." She explained, "You know, we always tried to look at things like we might not be right. I learned a lot from my kids simply because I didn't pretend to act like I knew everything, and my husband was good at that, too. Kids can be smart if you let them; they can think on their own."

From the Robinsons' vantage point on the South Side in the 1960s and 1970s, prejudice and opportunity existed side by side. Amid the undeniable perils, Marian and Fraser recognized that their children would inhabit a world of greater possibility than the one that had greeted their own coming of age a generation earlier. They calculated that a black child stepping into the tumult of modern urban America would find a certain independence of mind to be not just an asset, but a necessity.

THREE

Destiny Not Yet Written

Fraser and Marian Robinson mastered the art of the Sunday drive, a form of entertainment that matched their budget and not incidentally furthered their educational goals for their children. In the early 1970s, gas was affordable and the city beckoned in all of its complexity. When they had time, the family would pile into the Buick Electra 225—Fraser called it the "deuce and a quarter"—and meander through Chicago neighborhoods as the children asked questions and Fraser told stories. With Fraser at the wheel and the children in the back seat, Marian would sit with her back against the passenger door to watch her family as the conversation unfolded. Michelle's exploration of the wider world began on those drives and would continue on neighborhood bicycle rides, treks across town to high school, summer trips across state lines, and, one day, airplane flights to the East Coast to attend university. Fraser was a devoted reader of books and newspapers, as was Marian, and he was the keeper of the family lore. As he drove, he connected the scenes spooling beyond the windows with stories and wisdom he kept stashed in his head, drawing on his own experiences and his long, solitary hours tending the equipment that kept the city's tap water flowing. Craig Robinson, who loved hearing stories about the family, remembered the Sunday drives as important moments in the children's consideration of life beyond the relative comfort and neighborliness of South Shore.

In 1974, when Craig was twelve and Michelle was ten, one expedition led the Robinsons to a neighborhood lined with mansions. Craig asked why so many of the homes had an extra little house in the back. "My parents explained that those were carriage houses where black folks who took care of the family stayed," he recalled. "Thus began a conversation about racism and classism, integration and segregation, along with the history of slavery and Jim Crow." In South Shore by this time, there were few white residents and the children encountered few white people on their daily rounds. If they experienced animosity in those early years, it was likely from African American kids who heard their good grammar, saw their classroom diligence, and accused them of "trying to sound white." On that particular Sunday drive, the children wanted to know why some kids, black and white, were judgmental and mean. Marian remarked that meanness often stemmed from insecurity. Fraser said it was important to understand the nature of ignorance instead of dismissing it without reflection. The antidote to meanness was self-knowledge. No one can make you feel bad, they said, if your values are solid and you feel good about yourself. "When you grow up as a black kid in a white world, so many times people are telling you—sometimes not maliciously, sometimes maliciously—you're not good enough," Craig said later. "I remember [my father] saying you don't want to do things because you're worried about people thinking they're right; you want to do the right things. You grow up not worrying about what people think about you."

The national debate about racism was intense in the early 1970s, thanks, on the positive side, to the civil rights movement and, on the negative, to Republican president Richard Nixon's adoption of a race-baiting "Southern strategy." Opportunities for African Americans were unquestionably growing. Legalized discrimination was ebbing, aided by federal law, and the "firsts" were piling up, even if the few exceptions continued to prove the rule. Yet obstacles aplenty remained. In Chicago, the world of young African Americans was different in degree, but not in kind, from the city their parents had known in their youth. The lessons they heard—grounded in education, personal responsibility, and self-esteem—emerged from the experience of the generations that preceded them, including the ones that had flowed north during the Great Migration. For Michelle and Craig, that meant wisdom imparted by Fraser and Marian, but also by their four grandparents and a sprawling extended family on the South Side. Fraser was one of five children, Marian one of seven. It required considerable concentration simply to name all the cousins.

Purnell Shields, Michelle's maternal grandfather, was the jazz lover called Southside. He was lively, a good cook, and a master of barbecue whose home became "the headquarters for every special occasion," Michelle said. Beyond birthdays, holidays, and his annual Fourth of July extravaganza, she recalled visiting frequently, "packed into his little house, eating those ribs for dinner, talking and laughing, listening to jazz, playing cards late into the night. And then, when we could barely keep our eyes open, Southside would jump up and ask, 'Anybody want cheeseburgers and milkshakes?' He didn't want us to leave." One of Purnell's most memorable messages, said his daughter Grace Hale, came the day she arrived home in tears and told her father that other children did not like her. "They might not like you, but you need to make sure they respect you. Always work to get respect outside, but get your love at home," he replied, adding, "Don't ever come to me again with something so unimportant." Michelle's maternal grandmother, Rebecca Shields, was a model of a different sort. She raised her children, then returned to school in her fifties to become a licensed practical nurse, learning to speak French along the way. "Very smart, but very quiet," Hale recalled. "Sometimes you didn't even know she was in the room."

Michelle owed her middle name to her paternal grandmother, LaVaughn Robinson, who was formidable in her own way, becoming the first African American woman to manage a Moody Bible Institute store. When customers were scarce, she chose sections of scripture and prayed with her fellow workers. "She had very strong values," said store clerk Jacquelyn Thomas, who reported to her. "She would tell us how we should dress, how we should carry ourselves as Christian young women." Thomas considered her "a beautiful lady," and yet felt troubled by the way LaVaughn treated her. "I used to think she was picking on me. The other girl, she didn't make her do the things she made me do. I would go home and pray on it." But the teaching and prodding made sense after LaVaughn announced that she was moving, reluctantly, to South Carolina following Fraser's retirement. It turned out that she wanted Thomas to succeed her and had been preparing her for the role.

Yet no one carved a stronger profile in the family than LaVaughn's husband, Fraser C. Robinson Jr., who delivered acerbic lessons in nonsense avoidance to his grandchildren whenever they visited. If he had been born white, Michelle once said, he would have been a bank president. Despite his teenage aspirations in South Carolina in the 1920s, he retired fifty years later from the Chicago workforce as a post office employee, his dreams unfulfilled. Michelle saw "a discontent about him." Even Craig, who tended to look on the bright side, described him as "scowling" and "very stern." He said the crusty grandfather they called Dandy was "not always enjoyable to be around." Fraser was, however, punctilious in all things. "As precise as a drill sergeant when it came to the use of the English language," Craig said. He liked to use unfamiliar words. If the children did not recognize them, he would send them to the dictionary. "On one visit," Craig recalled, "I went to greet him and as soon as I said hello, Grandpa barked, 'Well, that was perfunctory!' . . . Sure enough, before I could respond, he asked, 'Do you know what *perfunctory* means?' 'No, I don't know.' 'Then go look it up!' . . . But then he smiled, which was not only shocking, since it was so rare, but also made me wonder if it made him happy to use a word we didn't know." Years later, when Craig coached basketball at Oregon State University, his players found a dictionary permanently positioned in the locker room.

Fraser Jr. was fiercely disciplined and famously tight with a nickel, recalled his nephew, Capers Funnye, born in 1952. To borrow money from him was to invite a lecture about responsibility. "His whole demeanor was that men have to be responsible." Fraser's own record, of course, was mixed. He had left LaVaughn and his two young boys on their own for many years, although when he returned to the family, he stayed for good. "He was wrestling with something that you and I would never be able to understand," reported his second son, Nomenee, who said he made it through college and graduate school without his father's help, drawing on scholarships, summer jobs, and other sources of money, including loans from his brother Fraser. His father did not show up for Fraser's graduation from DuSable High, Nomenee's graduation from Hyde Park High, where he was a top student, or his college commencement. Younger brother Andrew said his father "didn't exactly spew love or anything. Everything was his way or no way or the highway." This was true no matter how grand the success. "When I was at my ballgames and winning awards at the Museum of Science and Industry for my drawings, he wouldn't come or say anything. When I was quarterback in the city championship, he didn't come. We had to do it on our own."

Nomenee went to India with the Peace Corps, where a 1962 photograph in *The New York Times* showed him meeting Jacqueline Kennedy. He later worked for the federal Office of Economic Opportunity and, in 1971, graduated from Harvard Business School. To his surprise, his father broke with precedent and traveled to Cambridge for the commencement ceremony. After his father's death in 1996, Nomenee discovered among his father's papers a folder marked EENEMON—his name spelled backward. In the folder was a thick stack of newspaper stories that mentioned his son, whose achievements had drawn local attention. The family found something else that stunned them: the frugal soul who refused to pay for his sons' college education had died a prosperous man, leaving a six-figure sum to LaVaughn.

FRASER JR. ALSO DRUMMED into the grandchildren a larger message fundamental to their upbringing, one that Fraser III and Marian and countless other African American parents perfected in the 1960s. The message was rooted in a paradox that required elders to hold two seemingly contradictory ideas in mind simultaneously. One was the fact that the playing field was tilted away from their children because of their race and class. The other was the conviction that a combination of love, support, perseverance, and upright living could win out.

Michelle sketched the juxtaposition in a speech to a largely black audience in South Carolina during the first presidential campaign. On the one hand, she spoke of the "veil of impossibility that keeps us down and keeps our children down—keeps us waiting and hoping for a turn that may never come. It's the bitter legacy of racism and discrimination and oppression in this country." On the other, she said her grandfather Fraser "filled my brother and me with big dreams about the lives we could lead. He taught me that my destiny had not been written before I was born—that my destiny was in my hands."

Whatever their frustrations and demons, Michelle's grandfathers did not appear to be fixated on the injustices of the past. Nor were her parents. Whether because the history was too painful or too much of a distraction or a little of both, the elders did not want their children to feel beaten down by knowledge of the barriers that had halted their own progress. Even Purnell, whom Marian perceived as angry about racism, "did not let it carry over," she said. "We couldn't be racially divisive. That wasn't allowed. We could not be prejudiced." This was typical for the times. Sterling Stuckey, who graduated from DuSable High School in 1950, had an uncle with an Ivy League degree, from Cornell. Yet the best work his uncle could find in those days was managing a business that sold ice. "An ice house!" Stuckey marveled. "But never did he say something discouraging to the young people in the family. He said, 'Things will be different for you.'"

"Parents were trying not to burden their children, but to give them hope and keep them moving forward," said Rachel Swarns, who traced Michelle's family back to slavery, finding white ancestors and slaves on both sides of the family tree, along with generations of travail. The unspoken message from Fraser and LaVaughn was pragmatic. "We want you to get what you can. We want you to look forward. We don't want you to look back," daughter Francesca Gray, who graduated from Simmons College, remembered limiting excavations of the past, the adults created a buffer, a security zone that made it possible for many African American children to grow up in a nurturing, optimistic world even as prejudice persisted up the street or around the corner or a bus ride away. Michelle noticed and later paid homage, praising "the mothers and the fathers who taught their children to stand with dignity during a time when it was hard to get our kids to dream big."

THE LESSON WAS FAMILIAR to Deval Patrick, who grew up in an impoverished family on the South Side. "We didn't think of it as segregation," he said, "just the neighborhood." He saw elders who had every reason to surrender to cynicism, yet they told him he could shape his future. Seven years older than Michelle, he endured penury worse than anything faced by the Robinsons, particularly after his father, a baritone saxophonist, split for New York to play with the Sun Ra Arkestra. The day his father stormed away from the family in a rage, four-year-old Deval ran after him. "Go home! Go home!" his father shouted. A block from their apartment, he turned and slapped Deval, knocking him to the ground. "From that position, I watched him walk away," said Patrick, whose childhood was punctuated by his mother's stint on welfare, gang threats on his way to DuSable, and summer days wishing his family could afford orange juice. His bright and able grandfather, Reynolds Wintersmith, worked for more than fifty years as a South Shore Bank janitor, sweeping floors and cleaning toilets four blocks from the Robinsons' house on South Euclid Avenue.

"I was surrounded by adults who had every reason to curb my dreams," Patrick said. "My grandparents had grown up with Jim Crow. My mother knew all too well the humiliation of poverty and betrayal." Yet he and his older sister reached adulthood with "just no sense at all that there were limits on us," confident that they could chart their own course. "The true gift of my childhood," he called it. With an unexpected boost from a white South Side teacher who relayed news of a scholarship possibility, Patrick escaped to boarding school at Milton Academy, then earned two degrees from Harvard before being elected the first African American governor of Massachusetts. "They did not want me trapped by bitterness, but liberated to believe that the wider world could be a special place," Patrick said. It was only much later that he realized how far his family had gone to protect him. His grandmother's decision to pack food for the family's monthly visits to Kentucky was not about saving time or money on the road. Rather, it was an attempt to avoid the indignity of stopping at roadside restaurants that refused to serve black customers.

CRAIG ROBINSON DID NOT REALIZE how little money the family had, or how small their apartment was, until he reached Princeton in 1979. At that point, he concluded that the Robinsons were "poor." His father had received regular raises at the water plant, and the family kept its expenses down through general frugality and the chance to share the house on South Euclid. When they took a vacation, it was by car. When they went out, it was usually to dinner at a relative's house. When they went to a drive-in movie, Marian popped the popcorn at home. Desserts were reserved for Sunday dinner and Fraser cut Craig's hair, saving the expense of a barber. "Lunch on school days was often a sandwich made from leftovers. Going to the circus once a year was a big deal. Getting pizza on Friday was a treat," Michelle said, noting that pizza was often reserved as a reward for good grades. The purpose of a rare visit to State Street or Michigan Avenue was usually not to shop, but to peer into the windows of bustling stores decorated for Christmas. "If the TV broke and we didn't have any money to have it fixed, we could go out and buy another one on a charge card," Marian explained, "as long as we paid the bills on time."

One day when Craig was in elementary school and feeling inquisitive about the family finances, he caught up with his father at the kitchen table and asked, "Are we rich?" He told Fraser that it looked as though they were rich, since Marian did not work outside the home and Fraser had a steady city job. When Fraser received his next paycheck, instead of putting it in the bank, he cashed it and brought home a wad of cash, probably about $1,000. When he spread out the bills on the foot of the bed, it was more money in one place than Craig had ever seen. "Wow, we are rich!" he exclaimed. Then Fraser pulled out the family's bills, for electricity, gas, telephone, rent, and the monthly car payment. He had a stack of envelopes and he placed the matching amount of money in each. He set aside money for groceries and each of the ordinary costs of a typical month. When he was finished, a lone $20 bill remained. Craig said gamely that $20 still seemed like a lot. "You get to keep $20 every time you get paid?" Fraser reminded Craig of the trips to the drive-in and the occasional takeout meal. There was nothing left.

IN CONTRAST TO his own father, Fraser C. Robinson III channeled great energy into the children he called "Cat" and "Miche" and took very public pride in their doings and accomplishments. He would even make time for them in the mornings after an overnight shift, which ran from 10 p.m. to 6 a.m., sometimes fixing their breakfast before he headed to bed. He attended Craig's games and Michelle's dance recitals. He spent hours with Craig on neighborhood courts, and shot baskets with him at Dukes Happy Holiday Resort, a rustic getaway in central Michigan where the Robinsons sometimes rented a cabin, and helped him find a principled coach who would teach him well. He took Craig with him to the barbershop, so that his son could hear the talk of the day—advising him, however, not to repeat the bawdy jokes to his mother. He dispensed aphorisms. One favorite was "A smart man learns from his own mistakes; a wise man learns from the mistakes of others." There was something about Fraser that made his children want to live up to his high standards. "If you disappointed my dad, everybody was, like, crying," reported Craig, who said he did not drink his first beer until a college recruiting trip. "I never had any friends who could talk me into doing something that my parents would be disappointed in. Never. Because it was the ultimate insult to me as a son to disappoint my mom and dad."

Friends and relatives universally described Fraser as gregarious and generous, honorable and trusted. "Unofficial counselor to family, friends and strangers all around Chicago," as Craig once put it. "Fraser was the type of person, whatever he did, he put his all into it. Whatever he did, he did it all the way," said Grace Hale, Marian's sister. "The way he thought about his job. The way he went out there every day, determined to make it. The way he insisted that his children would get an education. He always assumed he would make a way for them to get their education. He wanted the best for them and he gave it to them—and he never got to see it." When Marian's uncle William Terry's health failed, Fraser would check on him before leaving for work and again when he arrived home. He would shave Terry's whiskers, cut his hair, bathe him, and take him to the toilet. To others in the family, he listened well and was not shy about offering advice. "That's where I went to talk about my issues in life, wife, children. We would get a bottle of Old Fitz and ginger ale and some beer nuts and sit down and really talk. He taught me a lot," said Nomenee, who described being dismissed at times by other relatives as a vagabond or, worse, a schemer. "Not that I always made the best decisions, but whatever decisions I made and I wanted to recover from, he wanted the best for me. I always felt that way. He could put things in perspective."

A major source of Fraser's perspective was his debilitating multiple sclerosis. The illness held him back on many fronts, not least in pursuing his passion for painting and sculpture. "Before he got really sick and had to work and raise us, he probably, if he had his choice, would have been an artist," Michelle said. Multiple sclerosis is unpredictable in whom it afflicts and how seriously. It also is notoriously difficult to diagnose, but by 1965, the year he turned thirty and the family moved to South Shore, it seemed likely that he had the disease. Long before the children knew why he was ill, they saw that he was becoming weaker, walking with a limp and struggling against tremors to button his work uniform. "I never knew my father as a man who could run," Michelle once told an audience. He walked first with a cane, then with one crutch, the kind with a cuff that wraps around the arm. Then with two and then with a walker. By the time the children were in college, he used a wheelchair and a motorized scooter.

"Even as a kid, I knew there were plenty of days when he was in pain. And I knew there were plenty of mornings when it was a struggle for him to simply get out of bed," Michelle told delegates to the 2012 Democratic National Convention. "But every morning I watched my father wake up with a smile, grab his walker, prop himself against the sink, and slowly shave and button his uniform. And when he returned home after a long day's work, my brother and I would stand at the top of the stairs of our apartment, patiently waiting to greet him, watching as he reached down to lift one leg and then the other to slowly climb his way into our arms." He took pride in not going to the doctor, Michelle said, and he almost never missed a day of work. By all accounts, he did not complain about yet another bad break in a life afflicted with more than his fair share. Michelle, who often talked about the example her father set, did not volunteer details about how her father's illness had influenced her, but there were signs in her preference for organization and discipline. "When you have a parent with a disability," she said, "control and structure become critical habits, just to get through the day."

Dan Maxime started work at the water plant in 1970 and remembered Fraser walking with a limp even then. As the years went by, he watched his health decline. "Here's a guy who could have gone on medical disability," Maxime said. "Every day, he worked. He was the gutsiest guy I have ever known in my life. He was honest, conscientious, hardworking. Here he had this disability and he never complained about it. A mild-mannered guy. I only heard him cuss once." It happened one payday, when a co-worker stopped by the plant to pick up his paycheck, then called in sick two hours later when he was due to start his shift. Maxime recalled attending one of Craig's basketball games, impressed that Craig had addressed him as Mr. Maxime. "We had a lot of laughs. We talked a lot of sports. . . . Every time there was some kind of accomplishment by Craig or Michelle, he would always tell me. 'Guess what? Craig made his first dunk today.'"

Nor was he timid about sharing his pride and good feelings with the children themselves. Fraser "thought he had the greatest kids that God ever gave anyone," Marian told an interviewer. None of it was lost on Craig or Michelle. "To have a family, which we did, who constantly reminded you how smart you were, how good you were, how pleasant it was to be around you, how successful you could be, it's hard to combat. Our parents gave us a little head start by making us feel confident," Craig said. "It sounds so corny, but that's how we grew up."

BEFORE MICHELLE was old enough to ride by herself on the trains that rumbled along 71st Street, her bicycle provided an escape. A favorite destination, and the apogee of one of her first solo rides, was Rainbow Beach, a large patch of public sand on the shores of Lake Michigan, an easy pedal from home. Michelle sometimes gathered friends, riding their own bikes, to join her. At a city-run summer camp there, ten-year-old Michelle missed out on the best camper award because of her salty tongue. "I was going through my cursing stage," she said. "I didn't realize until my camp counselor at the end came up and said, 'You know, you would have been best camper in your age group, but you curse so much.'" The news floored her. "And I thought I was being cool."

The fact that Rainbow Beach could occupy a spot on Michelle's itinerary in the mid-1970s was a sign of changing times. Barely a dozen years earlier, the stretch of sand and water from 75th Street to 79th Street was contested territory, as more African Americans moved beyond the borders of the traditional Black Belt. White lifeguards and beachgoers made it clear that black people were not welcome, prompting protests. In July 1961, an interracial group of demonstrators, including members of the NAACP Youth Council, staged a "freedom wade-in." Opponents threw rocks, injuring demonstrators. Although the conflict was history to the South Shore kids of Michelle's generation, Craig had an encounter in the 1970s that reinforced a sense that the city was making only halting progress. One warm day, he was riding his new bicycle, bought at Goldblatt's department store, along the lake at Rainbow Beach. A black Chicago police officer ordered him off the bike and accused him of stealing it. Craig protested, to no avail, and the officer drove the boy and the bicycle home. Standing in the front yard, Marian lectured the officer for a good half hour about jumping to conclusions about black children as Craig watched from an upstairs window. She insisted that the officer return the next day and apologize. He did.

Leonard Jewell Jr., Craig's friend from the 7600 block of South Euclid, considered bike rides an important part of his South Shore childhood. He recalled the feeling of freedom when he pedaled east toward the lake, away from his block. Yet he, too, had one ride that troubled him for years. It happened when he rode with elementary school friends to South Shore Country Club, home to a nine-hole golf course and private beach. The country club, originally open only to white Protestants, refused to allow Jews or African Americans to join. A white gatekeeper

stopped the bike-riding group. "He said, 'You guys can't come in here.'"
Jewell felt sure they were turned away because of their skin color, and he
said the hurt was "horrible." But just as Rainbow Beach had yielded to
changing times, so would the club. As whites moved away, membership
dwindled and the place was put up for sale. One group of bidders was
headed by Muhammad Ali, who lived nearby. In the end, the Chicago
Park District purchased the property. In 1992, Michelle and Barack held
their wedding reception there.

AS MICHELLE PROPELLED herself through school, she developed a
ferocious work ethic. "Michelle works harder than anyone I know,"
Craig once said. "I'd come home from basketball practice and she'd
be working. I'd sit down on the couch and watch TV. She'd keep working. When I turned off the TV, she'd still be working." Although they
were two grades apart at Bryn Mawr, they both attended an acceler-
ated learning program at Kennedy-King College, where Michelle took
classes in biology and French. Jewell, who joined them there, recalled
an engaging day each week away from the neighborhood. While he,
too, skipped a grade, he recalled that Michelle and Craig worked harder
than he did, a trait that he traced to the ethos that infused the Robinson household. Fraser and Marian, he said, were "strong, strong,
strong, like steel." They honored values that seemed beyond his reach.
"Mrs. Robinson, I loved her a lot. I would not want to piss her off, ever.
Mr. Robinson, I was really scared of. I was so much of a chameleon
back then, I remember my grandmother telling me, 'You have to have
more of a backbone, you have to have character.' And I'm like, 'What is
character?'"

Jewell tumbled through a series of identity crises before becoming
a successful Chicago veterinarian. "I set my own schedule when I was
in eighth grade. And when I got into high school, I was making my
own activities, I was calling the shots. I remember sitting at the kitchen
table with Mr. Robinson and he could just look right through me. He
was kind of stoic and quiet and tough. I felt like such a phony." Jewell
could not help but notice the contrast in the way the two families lived.

"We had so much. My house was like fucking elegance, and they were crammed in this little, tiny, itsy-bitsy space. It was a box. One little cubicle was Michelle's place and one little cubicle was Craig's. They had a small living area and this itsy-bitsy kitchen and one little tiny bathroom. They were the most disciplined people I have ever known."

Michelle hated to be bad at anything. She "really does hate to lose, and that's why she's been so successful," Craig once said. One of her first pursuits was piano, guided by Aunt Robbie. Craig played, too, on the upright that was parked along a wall in the upstairs apartment, but not nearly as well or as diligently. "She would practice the piano for so long, you'd have to tell her to stop," her mother said. By the time Michelle was a teenager, she played Broadway show tunes, jazz, and pop songs. To soothe Craig's nerves before a basketball game, she would play the *Peanuts* cartoon theme song. At the games themselves, Michelle and Marian were regulars. They loved easy wins, but could not bear suspense. If the game was close and the clock was ticking down, they would turn away or leave the gym.

The children did not have the only competitive streaks in the family. In 1996, shortly before she turned sixty, Marian competed in the sprints at the Illinois Senior Olympics, running 50 meters in 9.39 seconds and 100 meters in 20.19 seconds. She finished third in her age group in both events. The following year, she turned sixty and ran faster—8.75 in the 50 and 18.34 in the 100—and won both races in the 60-to-64 category. She finished second in both events in 1998. After a fall and an injury, she stopped competing. "If I can't do it fast, I'm not doing it," Marian said at age seventy. "You don't run just to be running. You run to win."

Michelle herself, although competitive and skilled at sports in a sports-minded house, generally avoided joining teams, although she put in some time with the track squad. "Tall women *can* do other things. I wasn't going to be typecast that way," she said. She would grow to five feet, eleven inches, yet basketball was Craig's sport and she was already known as Craig Robinson's little sister in many other things. She started with ballet as a girl and continued to dance at Whitney M. Young High School, where a 1981 yearbook photograph shows her in a leotard onstage, springing off her left foot, her right leg raised high, toe extended, arms stretched out for balance, her body fully under control. As an adult, Michelle hung on her wall a photograph of Judith Jamison doing her iconic solo dance performance, "Cry," which choreographer Alvin Ailey dedicated in 1971 to "all black women everywhere—especially our mothers." Jamison wrote that her character in the dance "represented those women before her who came from the hardships of slavery, through the pain of losing loved ones, through overcoming extraordinary depressions and tribulations. Coming out of a world of pain and trouble, she has found her way—and triumphed."

MICHELLE'S HIGH SCHOOL WAS NAMED for a black man born into segregation in Kentucky. Whitney Young took control of the National Urban League in 1961 and maneuvered the organization into a position of influence. Yet at a time of growing racial ferment, Young drew criticism among some African Americans for courting the support of Lyndon Johnson and white business leaders. Pushing for what would become known as affirmative action, he saw himself as a bridge and considered constructive compromise a virtue. "I think to myself, should I get off this train and stand on 125th Street cussing out Whitey to show I am tough? Or should I go downtown and talk to an executive of General Motors about 2,000 jobs for unemployed Negroes." Michelle learned his story and praised him. At a White House film screening of *The Powerbroker: Whitney Young's Fight for Civil Rights,* a documentary about his life, she told schoolchildren that Young "drew on his decency. He drew upon his intelligence and his amazing sense of humor to face down all kinds of discrimination and challenges and all kinds of threats."

The high school named for him was something of an experiment when it opened in 1975, a magnet school designed to mix talented students of different races and ethnicities. It would "force you outside your bubble," said Ava Greenwell, a black graduate from the South Side. The Chicago Urban League called the school "probably the finest ever built in Chicago. It has facilities, equipment and a curriculum plan which give it unique power to attract students." The league had been pushing the concept for years, while recognizing the quandary the new public school created: Each year, several hundred students would win a coveted spot, but thousands of Chicago teenagers would be left behind in second-rate schools. "We are delighted with the recent progress of the magnet school idea," league director James W. Compton said. "But we do not want this idea to be advanced at the cost of neglecting the interests of areas and people who need help first."

By 1974, as the city's African American population grew, 51.7 percent of high school students were black, along with 57.8 percent of elementary school students. Only 28.3 percent of elementary school students were white. At Whitney Young, enrollment goals by race and ethnicity were explicit. By design the school would draw students from all over the city. Plans called for a student body that was 40 percent black, 40 percent white, and 10 percent Spanish-speaking, with 5 percent "other," and 5 percent in the patronage-friendly category of "principal's option." Overall, when geography was factored in, the principal's option accounted for 10 percent of all students. Academically, at least 80 percent of entering students would be "average or above" on citywide test scores. Principal Bernarr E. Dawson, in describing the waiting list, said the information accompanying the applicant's name would include residence, race, sex, "achievement grouping," and comments from the applicant, teachers, and counselors. He said he would choose "in such a way that students' characteristics are best matched with the educational program of Whitney Young."

Opened two years before Michelle arrived, the school brought together teenagers from the South, West, and North Sides. The fortunate ones who made their way to a rundown area just west of downtown Chicago soon discovered that Whitney Young was an island—some thought an oasis—populated by students who would not otherwise have met. They studied, attended classes, and hung out together on campus. But when they scattered to their homes in far-flung neighborhoods, they often would not see each other again until the morning bell. Jeffrey Wilson was in the group of students that entered in 1975. He played center and defensive tackle on the football team and sang in the choir. It felt odd to be away from his West Side neighborhood, where he had friends from the earliest years of elementary school. Instead of walking to a nearby school, he rode an L train and walked the last two blocks.

"Whitney Young was built in the middle of a slum. It was barren," Wilson recalled. "There were different mills and factories, brick buildings, around. And most of them were empty. There was a skid row just two blocks away on Madison, where transient and homeless people walked through the neighborhood all the time. We'd be at football practice and they'd be standing on the sideline. Sometimes they'd talk to us in the middle of practice." Wilson said the school's purpose and spirit were clear. "It was a grand experiment in integration at a time when Chicago was considered the most segregated city in the country. I think we just dealt with it matter-of-factly. I had white friends. I had black friends. I had white male friends, white female friends." At the same time, as an African American student, he learned that there were neighborhoods where a black teenager should not go. "It wasn't all that unusual for a black kid to go off to a certain neighborhood and get his brains beaten in. That affected all of us," said Wilson, who appreciated the ways that life inside the school was different from life outside. "At the end of the day, back in those days, your white friends went where they went and your black friends went where they went. The only time they would mingle would be at school or an event connected to school, or if you were dating someone in another neighborhood." Wilson laughed about the classroom material delivered by Chicago daily life. "Particularly for the social studies teachers, it was like Christmas. They got to bring the message directly to where we lived. It wasn't abstract."

Wilson remembers feeling tugged between different worlds, not just between white and black, but within different black communities. His upbringing was thoroughly working class in a family so large—he had seven siblings—that they could never go anywhere in the same car. His father came from Mississippi and worked as a mixer at Entenmann's bakery. His mother came from Alabama and spent twenty-eight years working on a conveyor belt at Sara Lee. Starting at 4 a.m. more than an hour's drive away, she fit dough into pans before they rolled into the oven. His parents delivered a clear and timeless message: Life is hard.

You can make it. Keep pushing. Education, education, education. Yet when Wilson enrolled at Whitney Young, some kids in the neighborhood mocked him. They said he must be so special, so smart, so stuck up. One of Wilson's defenses was to talk black, even at Whitney Young. In the hall one day, he said to a friend, "I'm fixin' to go to the gym," but in his telling, the words were guttural and slurred, something like "Ahmfinninuhgotagym." A French teacher overheard and said, "Young man, why did you say that?" Wilson repeated the phrase. The teacher motioned him into her classroom, closed the door, and commanded, "Don't ever say that again." She made him say the sentence correctly several times and sent him back into the hall. "Not two minutes later, someone else asked me where I was going and I said it the same way, 'Ahmfinninuhgotagym.'" The teacher was still watching. "I saw her fixing me with this icy stare and I never did it again." He loved being at Whitney Young. "We enjoyed being in school that much, we would stay and watch the basketball team, the volleyball team, the swim team just practice."

MICHELLE WAS THIRTEEN when she started riding public transportation from the South Side to Whitney Young, then in its third year of operation. She caught a bus not far from her house and traveled a route that led to Lake Shore Drive, then about eight miles north along Lake Michigan into a thicket of skyscrapers downtown. From there, she caught another bus or a train and walked the final stretch. The trip took at least an hour in each direction. In the depths of Chicago's winters, she would travel both ways in the dark. Sometimes, to get a seat on the crowded northbound bus, she would catch a different bus south and board the downtown bus a few stops earlier. The maneuver could take thirty minutes, but it guaranteed her a chance to sit and study. Her frequent traveling companion and closest friend was Santita Jackson, daughter of the Reverend Jesse Jackson, the civil rights leader and future presidential candidate. The girls visited one another's homes as teenagers and remained close as young adults. Jackson would sing at Michelle's wedding.

For the Robinsons, the distance was daunting, but the decision to apply to the new magnet school was straightforward. South Shore High School had been plagued by construction defects, vandalism, and a lack of supplies since its opening. Envisioned as a "model in function and design" when proposed in the mid-1960s, it had opened two years late, millions of dollars over budget and still unfinished. Craig bypassed the school to attend the all-male Mount Carmel High School, where he played varsity basketball and described himself as "the outsider, the racial minority and the brainy athlete I had always been." In attending Whitney Young, Michelle knew she was taking a valuable step beyond the limitations of her neighborhood high school, yet just like James W. Compton, the Chicago Urban League director, and Lena Younger in *A Raisin in the Sun*, she also knew that hundreds of her peers would not have the same option. It was the kind of thing she noticed from a young age. When she and Craig shared a bedroom, they often compared notes before they fell asleep. He said, "My sister always talked about who was getting picked on at school or who was having a tough time at home."

Once at Whitney Young, Michelle built on the work she had done in the gifted program at Kennedy-King and the record that had made her salutatorian of her eighth-grade class. She sang in a choir that traveled around the city. She helped organize social activities and ran for office, becoming treasurer of her senior class after a close race that required her to give a speech that jangled her nerves. She served on the publicity committee for school fundraisers, took Advanced Placement classes, and made the National Honor Society, whose president was Santita Jackson. College was the goal, she said. "I signed up for every activity that I could fill up my applications with, and I focused my life around the singular goal of getting into the next school of my dreams . . . It seemed like every paper was life or death, every point on an exam was worth fighting for." She earned extra money by teaching piano, babysitting, and training the occasional dog. Her senior year, she worked in a bookbinder's shop and witnessed at close range the lives of adult co-workers who were low on options and relegated to doing the same repetitive job for the rest of their working days.

A trait not lost in the transition to high school was Michelle's confidence in challenging authority. A typing teacher at Whitney Young told the students that their grades would be calculated according to their typing speed. By the end of the course, Michelle typed enough words per minute to earn an A, according to the teacher's chart, but the teacher said she simply did not give As. "She badgered and badgered that teacher," Marian said. "I finally called her and told her, 'Michelle is not going to let this go.'" Another time, a substitute teacher did not know her name. "Michelle said, 'What is my name?'" her mother related. "She sat on his desk until he knew her name. I told her, 'Michelle, don't sit on a teacher's desk.'" Michelle's diligence paid off. In addition to her job in the bindery, she spent three summers as a typist at the Chicago headquarters of the American Medical Association.

Michelle's ambitions grew at Whitney Young as her gaze expanded. As a young girl, she wanted most to be a mother, "because that's who I saw. I saw my mom caring for me. Those were the games that I played. I didn't play doctor, I didn't play lawyer." New professional imaginings developed toward the end of her high school years. For a time, she thought she would become a pediatrician, but she felt she was not strong enough in math and science and, anyway, did not much like those subjects. Test taking was a weakness, although in her mother's eyes, smarts were not the problem. "I'm sure it was psychological, because she was hardworking and she had a brother who could pass a test just by carrying a book under his arm," Marian said. "When you are around someone like that, even if you are okay, you want to be as good or better."

The disparity in work ethic and test results was also something Craig thought about. "She saw I never studied. I could always take tests and do well," he said. "She always studied. She was always up late, until 11 or 12 o'clock, doing homework." She burned the candle at the other end, too. Frustrated that the house felt crowded and noisy, she sometimes rose at 4:30 or 5 a.m. to do homework when she could hear herself think. Marian recalled those late nights, telling Michael Powell of *The New York Times*, "She'd study late but she had a discipline about her. I would ask, 'Aren't you through yet?' And she'd just keep going. She's always been pretty good in school, and if she works for the grade, you'd better give it to her. She was very independent, very strong-willed."

MICHELLE GRADUATED thirty-second in her class, solid if not stellar. As she headed to college, she received a small scholarship from a South Side foundation created by Ora C. Higgins, who had helped integrate Spiegel, the Chicago retailer. The company was ahead of its time in 1945, when M. J. Spiegel hired Higgins, a Chicago Urban League field-worker, as a "personnel counselor" and tasked her with hiring hundreds of African Americans for the company's catalog business and its twenty-six Chicago department stores. She recruited and hired workers in dozens of capacities, from secretaries and typists to stencil cutters, commercial artists, accountants, and packers. Word got around fast, particularly at a time when decent jobs for African Americans were scarce. "They said, 'Go to Spiegel. There's a black lady there who can get you hired,'" recalled Reuben Crawford, Fraser Robinson's high school classmate, who worked on a Spiegel loading dock. Another beneficiary was Marian, who worked as a Spiegel secretary as a young woman. Seeing Higgins's success, other department stores hired her, making her a noted Chicago figure. She earned two degrees from Northwestern University, and in the 1960s, traveled to Washington, where she spoke at the Labor Department and had her picture taken with President Johnson.

Higgins was Michelle's great-great-aunt. She was a regular at Shields family gatherings, as was her daughter, Murrell Duster, a college administrator who was married to Benjamin C. Duster III, a civil rights lawyer and grandson of Ida B. Wells. "They talked about everything," Murrell Duster said of family gatherings. "My mother always talked about human rights. We were very aware as children of what was going on in Chicago and other places." When Higgins turned 100 in 2010, Michelle sent a letter of congratulations from the White House, saying what an inspiration she had been.

AS MICHELLE WAS FINISHING high school, Craig was taking his final exams at the end of his sophomore year at Princeton. He had starred at

Mount Carmel and played well at a summer basketball camp in Wisconsin that was scouted by a Princeton assistant coach. When the Ivy League program flew him east for a recruiting trip, the school's head coach, Pete Carril, picked him up at the Newark, New Jersey, airport wearing a trademark gray sweatshirt and messily smoking a cheap White Owl cigar. Craig, who remembered equating Princeton and Yale with "Princestone" and "Shale" in *The Flintstones* cartoons, appreciated the attention. He was all the more impressed when Carril flew out to Chicago and made his way to South Euclid Avenue, where he climbed the steep stairs and met the Robinsons. One day, the mail brought a fat acceptance letter. Craig said, "People reacted as if I were Neil Armstrong just come back from the moon."

Marian recalls being clear with Craig that Princeton was the right choice: "It's like I say, 'You're tall and black. Nobody's going to notice the smartness.' So you had to go." Yet there was the matter of money. Craig felt torn. Other colleges were offering him full scholarships, while Princeton's financial aid package would require Fraser and Marian to come up with perhaps $3,000 toward the yearly cost. "It might as well have been $2 million to me," Craig said years later. As his mother stood at the sink doing the dinner dishes one night, Craig sat at the kitchen table and told his father that he craved the chance to go to an Ivy League school, but he was thinking of accepting an offer from the University of Washington. Good school, good coach, good basketball program—and it was a free ride. His father did not react with histrionics or tell his son what to do. Rather, after a deep sigh, he nodded and stroked his chin and said in a measured voice, "Well son, you know I'd be awfully disappointed if I thought you were making a decision this important on the basis of what we could afford." Craig said nothing after the conversation with his father. He simply agreed to think about it overnight, but he felt elated, "like the weight of the world was being lifted off my shoulders." His father's offer, as his health worsened and Michelle remained at home, testified to a "generosity greater than I have ever witnessed in any other human being." Craig, who later learned that his parents financed much of their share of his Princeton education with credit cards, would recall that conversation as one of the most important of his life.

Michelle's view, when it came time to apply to college, was that if Craig could get into Princeton, she could, too. By her reckoning, she was just as smart and certainly worked harder. Her counselors at Whitney Young, however, did not see it that way. They said her grades and scores were too low and her sights were too high. Their assessment knocked her off stride, leaving her feeling uncertain. "It made me mad, too," she said more than thirty years later. The moment would stay with her, becoming an essential component of her campaign stump speech and her message to young audiences. She folded her story into the narrative of Barack Obama's run for president. His election, she said, would send a message to "thousands of kids like me who were told, 'No.' 'Don't.' 'Wait.' 'You're not ready.' 'You're not good enough.' See, I am not supposed to be here. As a black girl from the South Side of Chicago, I wasn't supposed to go to Princeton because they said my test scores were too low." Michelle applied to Princeton and Harvard, as well as the University of Illinois and the University of Wisconsin. Her Princeton essay was "long, long," recalled Marian, who said Michelle "talked her way in." Like her brother, she was accepted and soon was on her way. She was stepping up and out, making the biggest leap of her young life.

FOUR

Orange and Blackness

Princeton in September 1981 was a world away from the South Side. It was a world away from most of the world, in fact. From the leaded glass and gargoyles to the sleek and sculpted columns of I. M. Pei, the campus telegraphed privilege, a trait the university leadership did not hesitate to advertise. Every freshman knew that Nassau Hall was home to the Continental Congress in 1783 and that Princetonians had populated America's top tier since the beginnings of the republic. *Dei sub numinae viget* read the Latin saying etched on Princeton's orange and black shield. Translated, the phrase meant "under God she flourishes," but wags rendered it as "God went to Princeton." Princeton's leaders touted the institution as a pinnacle of undergraduate education and had the applicant pool to prove it. Of 11,602 aspirants to the class of 1985, only 17.4 percent were admitted, a very low acceptance rate at the time. Among them were more high school valedictorians, class officers, team captains, and newspaper editors than anyone could count.

President William Bowen addressed them on September 13, 1981, the last time they would gather as a class before commencement week nearly four years later. Standing among towering stone pillars and stained glass in the grandly opulent Princeton chapel, he urged them toward a path of self-discovery and purpose. He invited them to aim high and advocated learning for its own sake, "not merely as a means to some more prosaic end." It would be a shame, he said, to choose narrow goals too easily achieved, ones that in retrospect "turn out to be trivial." He challenged them to pursue "lives lived generously, in service to others," and asserted that "the most worthwhile goals are often elusive and almost always just beyond reach."

For a text, Bowen read aloud a translation of Constantine P. Cavafy's poem "Ithaka," an ode to the joys of a great, lifelong journey. Ithaka was the home of Odysseus and the talismanic destination of his adventures after the fall of Troy. Bowen made an explicit reference to the racial divide that plagued Princeton and the country at large. "I sometimes feel," he told the freshmen, "that in developing friendships, especially those that require us to reach across such complex boundaries as race and religion, we are too self-protecting. . . . You can spare yourselves discomfort by keeping your distance, by remaining safely aloof, by maintaining what are largely superficial friendships. But if you do, you will deprive yourselves, and others, of one of the greatest opportunities for learning and for personal growth."

MICHELLE ROBINSON REACHED campus three weeks early to attend an orientation for minority students and other freshmen who might want extra time to adjust. Five months shy of her eighteenth birthday, she was daunted at first, a trepidation shared by many of her classmates. "When I first got in," she remembered, "I thought there's no way I can compete with these kids. I mean, I got in, but I'm not supposed to be here." During the first days on campus, she felt overwhelmed. Her sense of being at a loss was symbolized by the bedsheets she brought from home, too small for the standard university-issue mattress. She stretched the bottom sheet as far as she could from the head of the bed, then draped her covers over the part that the sheet did not reach. She slept with her feet resting on the bare mattress. Then there were the clothes, the furniture, and the cars. "I remember being shocked by college students who drove BMWs," she said. "I didn't even know parents who drove BMWs."

Michelle sometimes felt her head was barely above water. Her first semester, she took a class in Greek mythology and found herself "struggling just to keep up." On the midterm, she got a C. "The very first C I'd ever gotten and I was devastated." She pressed ahead, talking repeatedly with the professor and pouring heart and soul into her final paper. She soon discovered a secret of elite American universities: The tricky part is getting in the door; flunking out is hard to do. She gravitated to the sociology department and the Third World Center, created in 1971 as an oasis for the growing community of students of color. The center featured discussions about race, black culture, and the African diaspora, and served as a social hub. For Michelle, who found a work-study job there and was elected to the governing board, it became a refuge. Following the pattern set at Whitney Young, she chose not to join a sports team, nor did she try to prove her mettle in campus politics. She made close friends and stayed grounded during her first foray into an elite realm where African Americans and, especially, African American women, were a distinct minority.

It helped, when Michelle arrived, that she had a significant anchor in Craig, who was entering his junior year as a sociology major and basketball star who spun records at Third World Center parties. His early jitters foretold her own. When he stepped off a bus on Nassau Street on a muggy August afternoon in 1979, he felt as though he was entering "a world that existed practically in its own time and space continuum." It seemed that every second classmate had come up with a medical breakthrough or published a novel. By the time he received his midterm grades, he was standing at a pay phone, trying to keep from crying. He had agreed to an adviser's recommendation that he enroll in the engineering program, but his record showed one C, two Ds, and an F. A worrier by nature, especially anxious about disappointing his parents, Craig told his father that he was not sure he would make it. "Maybe I'm over my head," he said. "Maybe I shouldn't be here. Maybe coming here I reached too far."

Fraser interrupted and told him to pull himself together. You won't be finishing first in your class, he said, but you won't be finishing last, either. With a Princeton degree in your pocket, Fraser said, "You think people will care what your grade was in freshman calculus?" Craig recalled his father saying that the Ivy League school had chosen him not because he was "just like everybody," but "because of what made me distinctive and because of the contribution that I could make to the school." Reassured, Craig stuck it out, although he did switch out of engineering. He later said that he loved history and African American studies, but gained the most from philosophy and religion classes— and the on-court tutelage of coach Pete Carril, who would be named to the basketball hall of fame.

AS A FRESHMAN, Michelle was "enormously concerned as all young people are, especially black women, with identity problems," said sociology professor Marvin Bressler, who befriended Michelle and Craig and supervised the beginnings of her senior thesis. "There existed in universities at that time various competing strains of what an ideal minority should be. She had to make up her mind to what extent she regarded herself as black, as a woman, as simply a person." The matter of making up her mind was not an exercise performed in a vacuum. For all of its remarkable academic offerings, Princeton was by tradition and reputation the most southern of the elite northern universities. Michelle would write that the school was "infamous for being racially the most conservative of the Ivy League colleges." The color barrier remained virtually unbroken for two hundred years after the university's founding in 1746. The dawn of the civil rights movement prompted the admissions office to declare in 1963, "Princeton is actively seeking qualified Negro applicants," yet it was years before any entering class included more than 20 African American students. The class of 1985 included just 94 black students, or 8.2 percent of the entering cohort of 1,141 students. The class was also unbalanced along gender lines, with 721 men and 420 women, a dozen years after Princeton admitted women for the first time. Tuition, room, and board cost roughly $10,000 her first year.

Not for the last time, Michelle felt herself walking in two worlds, one black and the other white. She was living what W. E. B. Du Bois in 1897 called "two-ness." For Du Bois, who not incidentally had been a black man at Harvard, it was the idea that an African American was in a perpetual struggle to reconcile his blackness with his Americanness, "to be both a Negro and an American without being cursed and spit upon . . . , without having the doors of Opportunity closed roughly in his face." Being a Negro at the end of the nineteenth century, Du Bois suggested, was to face a looming question from white people: "How does it feel to be a problem?" He observed that a black man often felt at sea, striving to develop an independent identity yet enduring "double-consciousness, this sense of always looking at oneself through the eyes of others, of measuring one's soul by the tape of a world that looks on in amused contempt and pity."

Hilary Beard, a friend of Michelle's who arrived on campus one year earlier, had been stunned by what she found. "I grew up around a lot of white people. What was new to me was to be around white people who had had so little exposure to people of color. Nothing prepares you to have somebody you don't know, and shares a room with you, ask you something like if your skin color rubs off. I didn't just get asked that once. I got asked that all the time. I was suddenly confronted with negative assumptions about me and people who looked like me that I had never encountered before. It was shocking. I was unprepared. It was a lot, to be dropped in the middle of this environment and be confronted with that as part of your transition."

Minority students, more than most of their white peers, faced profound choices tied to race and ethnicity. For Michelle, questions about race, class, and values would inform her academic pursuits and her senior thesis, which explored issues of identity and purpose among black Princeton graduates. She wrote in the introduction, "My experiences at Princeton have made me far more aware of my 'Blackness' than ever before. I have found that at Princeton, no matter how liberal and open-minded some of my White professors and classmates try to be toward me, I sometimes feel like a visitor on campus; as if I really didn't belong. Regardless of the circumstances under which I interact with Whites at Princeton, it often seems as if, to them, I will always be Black first and a student second."

THE FIRST SIGN THAT Michelle would encounter racism at Princeton happened before classes even started. One of her freshman year roommates was a white teenager named Catherine Donnelly. She had been raised in New Orleans by her schoolteacher mother, Alice Brown, who labored, much as the Robinsons had, to position her daughter for a first-rate education. Catherine was settling into her fourth-floor room in Pyne Hall on her first day when Craig Robinson dropped by. He was searching for Michelle, who was not there. Catherine headed up campus and told her mother the news: One of her roommates was black.

Brown was horrified. She first called her own mother, who recommended pulling Catherine out of school and driving right back to New Orleans. That seemed extreme, so Brown charged into the student housing office and demanded a room change. "I told them we weren't used to living with black people, Catherine is from the south," Brown said. Hoping to strengthen her hand, she returned to her room at the tony Nassau Inn, where she and a friend called everyone they knew with Princeton ties and beseeched them to intervene. Nothing worked. The housing office said no beds were available.

Second semester, when a room came open, Donnelly moved out. At that point, she was simply glad to escape a cramped room. She had come to admire and enjoy Michelle, although they traveled in entirely different circles. She called her "one of the funniest people I've ever known." Donnelly had forgotten about Michelle Robinson a quarter century later when she noticed a lovely black woman with long fingers and a familiar face, the one whose husband was running for president. She did an Internet search to test her hunch and was chagrined to learn that she was right. Looking back to her freshman year, she regretted not standing up to her mother. By then, she had another reason to shake her head at her family's prejudice. Donnelly, a high school homecoming queen and basketball captain, had come out as a lesbian while at Princeton. When she did, she felt judged, and she learned a few things about being an outsider.

TO BE BLACK at Princeton was to be anything but unthinking. Racial politics compelled African American students to make decisions about how to live their blackness—where to sit in the dining hall, where to live on campus, where to socialize, what friends to make and what causes to claim. The pressures came not just from white teachers and classmates, but from African Americans. Walking in a black world was not without its own dilemmas. Indeed, it was possible to sketch not just two worlds confronting a black student at Princeton, but three or more, each tugging in a different direction. "There were those black students who wanted to be part of the storied Princeton they had heard about," said Ruth Simmons, one of a relative handful of black faculty members during Michelle's time at Princeton. "There were those who 'hung' black and those who did that to an extreme degree and did tend to resent people who were too impressed with the white society of Princeton." Simmons, who would later become president of Smith College and Brown University, felt the pressure herself. "You had to prove yourself to everybody."

Robin Givhan knew this well. She graduated from Princeton in 1986, one year after Michelle, and went on to win a Pulitzer Prize for criticism at *The Washington Post*. A black woman from Detroit, she visited the Third World Center from time to time—"it was a little like checking in with family"—but decided not to become a regular. "I didn't want this Third World place to be the focus of my social life, because if I had wanted that, I would have gone to Howard." She never forgot a speech at the center early in her Princeton career by a student from, she thinks, the Organization for Black Unity (OBU), a group that Michelle joined. "I had no idea who this guy was. He basically was giving this spiel about what it meant to be black at Princeton and what it entailed and what you should think. I felt what he was saying was, 'You are not black.' I remember coming back to my dorm and being just so upset about it, a little tearful."

By contrast, Sharon Holland felt a pull toward the Third World Center, which counted more than two hundred members. "I wanted to create a different social life for myself," said Holland, a doctor's daughter raised in Washington, D.C. Like Michelle, she took a job there, answering telephones, taking messages, typing memos, running errands. "An amazing time to be at the center. Lots of outreach, lots of attempts at multi-ethnic community building." She recalled her Princeton years as a mix of highs and lows as she struggled to chart a path that was not constrained by white privilege or what she called black "codes of responsibility," unwritten rules about how a black person should act toward other black people. Those were "some of the best of times," said Holland, who would become an American studies professor at the University of North Carolina, "but they were also really difficult times."

Some afternoons, as Michelle drifted into the Third World Center after class, she entertained Jonathan Brasuell, the young son of the center's director. His favorite tune was the theme song from *Peanuts*, the same song she had played to calm her brother's nerves before basketball games back in Chicago. Hilary Beard remembers Michelle playing the piano as Jonathan, not yet ten, sat beside her on the bench. "She took time to talk with him," Beard said, "not at him." Michelle worked with center director Czerny Brasuell to start an after-school program for the children of Princeton staff, principally young children of color whose parents wanted "a program that would be more sensitive to the needs of their children." Simmons was one of them. She enrolled her daughter and became a Third World Center regular. Recruiting black professors to Princeton was difficult "because of the isolation that African American families felt," Simmons said. "We spent so much time there as a family and faculty and staff because it was the one place we could go where we could feel part of that community. Just as we felt very comfortable there, others felt very uncomfortable with the activities of the Third World Center because it was, in a way, an activity that resegregated the campus."

As a place for discussions about social justice at home and abroad, the center welcomed speakers with political views to the left of much of the Princeton student body and more international in scope. Craig Robinson called it a "sanctuary." "You learned about politics, you learned about culture, you learned about people from different backgrounds. . . . I remember using those debates as practice for my in-class debates, and how I felt so fortunate to have that kind of support that made me feel good about going into class and competing." On weekends, the TWC, as it was often called, was central to Michelle's social life. "She was generally where the party was," said Ken Bruce, two years ahead of Michelle at Princeton, adding that "black parties mostly revolved around the music and dancing, and less around drinking or anything like that." Michelle ate meals at Stevenson Hall, and she lived on campus for four years, as did almost all of her classmates. She was active in the Organization for Black Unity and helped bring speakers to campus, recalled classmate and OBU officer Lauren Robinson, later Lauren Ugorji, who became Princeton's vice president for communications. She said Michelle also played a role in the Black Thoughts Table, an informal forum where African Americans and other interested students could talk about social and political questions. "As a black student at Princeton at that time," Ugorji said, "whether you wanted to deal with race issues or not, you had to."

While at Princeton, Michelle walked the runway in an occasional fashion show. At a February 1985 benefit that helped raise $15,000 for Ethiopian famine relief, she modeled a sleeveless red velvet gown and a voluminous white floor-length dress. She was pictured in a photograph on the front page of the school newspaper, *The Daily Princetonian*. To raise money for a local after-school program, she wore a yellow peasant skirt intended to suggest the Caribbean countryside. The student designer, Karen Jackson Ruffin, said she asked Michelle to model the skirt "because she is so tall and carries herself so well. Michelle is very mellow and she said, 'Sure.'"

Sometimes, Michelle and Beard would team up to do Third World Center errands. "If I drove, I would speed," Beard said. "Michelle would drive the speed limit. We were twenty years old, we were supposed to speed and do dumb, reckless things. Michelle would always do the right thing." The same qualities struck Beard that would strike Michelle's friends through the years. She was independent without being arrogant or aloof; she was "always rooted in her values." When people sought her advice, and many did, she listened carefully and did not simply react, "unlike the rest of us who were twenty and thought we knew so much. When you're twenty and you go to Princeton, you think you're smart and life is about you." As Beard recalled it, "Her thoughts were never the popular opinion or the Princeton opinion or the black opinion."

Beard also said Michelle was a "fighter" who had "feistiness in her spirit." That came out in amusing ways, as when Michelle was annoyed with her French teacher. "Michelle's always been very vocal about anything. If it's not right, she's going to say so," Marian Robinson said. "When she was at Princeton, her brother called me and said, 'Mom, Michelle's here telling people they're not teaching French right.' She thought the style was not conversational enough. I told him, 'Just pretend you don't know her.'" Her convictions emerged in sharper ways, as well. After Crystal Nix became the first black editor of *The Daily Princetonian*, Michelle disapproved of a story about an African American politician. She told Nix in a calm voice, "You need to make sure that a story like that doesn't run again." In her senior year, Michelle felt punched in the stomach when a professor assessed her work by telling her, "You're not the hottest thing I've seen coming out of the gate," despite the fact that she had aced his class. Her response was revealing: "I decided that I was going to do everything in my power to make that man regret those words. . . . I knew that it was my responsibility to show my professor how wrong he was about me." She became his research assistant and poured herself into the effort. He noticed and offered to write an extra letter of recommendation. She concluded that she had "shown not just my professor, but myself, what I was capable of achieving."

Brasuell took Michelle on her first trip to New York and made her feel welcome in her Princeton apartment, which Michelle described as "a place of peace and calm." But her most memorable experience was folding Craig and Michelle into a rental car for a surprise Mother's Day expedition to the Carolinas, an overnight drive from central New Jersey. The Robinsons dropped Czerny and young Jonathan in North Carolina and continued to Georgetown, South Carolina, to see their grandparents, Fraser and LaVaughn. After the visit, they picked up their traveling partners on the way back north. Time was short. "It was sort of like, 'Are we crazy?' But it was worth it," said Brasuell, who invited Michelle to be a bridesmaid at her wedding. "There was an evenness about her, a self-assurance about her, a consistent center of gravity about the way she moved in the world." Marvin Bressler, the professor who supervised the junior year independent work that led to Michelle's sociology thesis, remembered her for a combination of discipline—"she has a certain puritanical streak"—and sense of humor, which he called "impish." He described her as thoughtful, prone to reflection, and committed to what he considered social responsibility. "One of the things that is always said about her is that she was grounded," said Bressler, who traced the trait to her parents, who sometimes visited. The Robinsons, he said, seemed to step from the pages of *The Saturday Evening Post* like characters in a Norman Rockwell painting. "That family more nearly embodied that conception than any I've ever seen," Bressler said. He recalled Craig, the Ivy League's best basketball player, a two-time player of the year, holding court in the lobby of Jadwin Gymnasium after games, "his mother standing next to him, tugging at his sleeve and saying, 'How's your senior thesis, Craig?' He knew it was funny. Their father, he was disabled, was barely able to conceal his pride. He knew as a male you weren't supposed to go around being sentimental about your children, but he was. That kind of thing sustained her."

ON A STRETCH of Prospect Street known as the province of the university's private eating clubs, the Third World Center was the odd building out. For generations, sophomores took part in "bicker," the clubs' fraternity-like interview and assessment process that determined who would receive invitations, or bids, and which bids the most coveted students would accept. Next door to the center was the all-male Tiger Inn, famous on campus for its boisterous parties. Across the street, behind a low red-brick wall and a swinging gate, was Cottage Club, whose alumni included Secretary of State John Foster Dulles, basketball star and U.S. senator Bill Bradley, and writer F. Scott Fitzgerald, author of *The Great Gatsby*. As an undergraduate, Fitzgerald began writing a Princeton-based novel in the upstairs library at Cottage and later published it as *This Side of Paradise*. Princeton's president, John Grier Hibben, said after reading the book, "I cannot bear to think that our young men are merely living four years in a country club and spending their lives wholly in a spirit of calculation and snobbishness."

Seventy years later, many of the clubs of Michelle's era had dropped their selective status, and most admitted women, several relenting under the pressure of a civil liberties lawsuit. For all of the progress, the clubs along Prospect Street remained overwhelmingly white, while the service workers tended to be African Americans or immigrants. Black students in Michelle's generation learned to walk with care down Prospect on party nights. "Even walking across Prospect Street when a lot of people had had a lot to drink was a very challenging experience. People would say things, they would shout things, they wouldn't give you space on the sidewalk. It was almost like they felt a sense of ownership and they felt we were supplementary guests," said Ken Bruce, a Princeton junior when Michelle arrived. "I don't think they looked at us as equivalent stakeholders at the time, and I think it was hard for us to look at ourselves as equivalent stakeholders." Bruce, an African American engineering student who played football, ran track, and went on to become a New York investment manager, sometimes found himself the only black face in class. "Across the board," he said, "students and professors saw us as black first."

ONE COMPLICATING FACTOR—some would say *the* complicating factor—for African American students in the Ivy League in the 1980s was affirmative action. A policy that delivered opportunity could also be an unwelcome cloud, especially in relations with white students and faculty. The effort, begun in the mid-1960s, was straightforward enough: Identify talented black students who previously would have gone unnoticed and invite them into the club, even if their record appeared weaker than those of white students. One result was to create a reflexive doubt in the minds of skeptics about the worthiness and smarts of black students. The policy was also deeply unpopular among the public at large. At Princeton, where the admission of a black student often meant the rejection of a white student, perhaps the son or daughter of an alumnus, the tension was unmistakable. The dangling question, which trailed African American students like a shadow, was whether they belonged. "There were the beginnings of a lot of resentment about affirmative action. People asked you over dinner what your SAT scores were," Sharon Holland recalled of the early 1980s. Lauren Ugorji remembered the slights clearly: "The question that bothered me most was, 'Why are you here?'"

The public purposes of affirmative action, a policy described more precisely in Britain as "positive discrimination," were clear enough. When it came to college, the objective was to give an increasing number of black children opportunities that were comparable to ones enjoyed for generations by white children. In the wake of the civil rights movement and assessments by the likes of the Kerner Commission, credible research suggested that black students were paying the costs of racial subjugation endured by them, their parents, and their parents' parents, all the way back to slavery times. Compared with a white child, a black child born in the United States in the 1960s was likely to have less money, fewer models of achievement, and a poorer education. All of which, it was assumed, translated to lower scores on standardized tests and rejection letters from selective universities. When combined with the likelihood that African American families had less financial wherewithal to pay the high costs of competitive schools, it became clear to some progressive thinkers that equality of opportunity would not come naturally, at least not any time soon. In 1965, President Lyndon Johnson argued the case in a speech at Howard University. The Civil Rights Act of 1964, he said, was an important step, but an insufficient one. "You do not take a person who, for years, has been hobbled by chains and liberate him, bring him up to the starting line in a race and then say, 'You are free to compete with all the others'—and still justly believe you have been completely fair." One year later, Harvard Law School began admitting black law students with standardized test scores markedly lower than those of their white classmates, and other schools followed suit.

In 1978, three years before Michelle reached Princeton, the battle over the fairness of affirmative action policies reached the Supreme Court in the case of *Regents of the University of California v. Bakke.* The instigator was Alan Bakke, a white medical school applicant who said he was rejected by the University of California–Davis in favor of minority students with inferior credentials. He sued, citing Title VI of the Civil Rights Act, which stated that no program receiving federal money can discriminate "on grounds of race, color, or national origin." The high court was divided. Four justices agreed with Bakke, while four justices said racial preferences were justified to overcome the residual effects of past discrimination. Justice Lewis Powell cast the deciding vote, concluding that Bakke should not have to pay for wrongs committed by others. But Powell also cited the educational benefits of various kinds of diversity and ruled that universities could consider race when deciding who should be admitted, just as they might consider grades, test scores, orchestral achievements, or speed in the 100-yard dash. The decision left it to admissions officers to determine how to weigh an applicant's many traits. Standardized tests, increasingly shown to be culturally biased against disadvantaged minority students, would be just one factor. This benefited high-achieving black and Hispanic students while persuading critics that white students were now the losers in a rigged game.

"WE CREATED A COMMUNITY within a community," Michelle once said, discussing the challenges of being a minority student at Princeton. She also used space on her senior yearbook page to talk about what sustained her: "There is nothing in this world more valuable than friendships. Without them you have nothing." She grew particularly close to two women. One was Angela Kennedy, the third of three African American siblings to attend Princeton, each of whom would develop a richly meaningful career. The other was Suzanne Alele, born in Nigeria and raised partly in Jamaica before finishing high school in suburban Maryland. The three women were inseparable. They lived in dormitory rooms, using the workaday desks, dressers, and single beds provided by the university. No sofa, no television. "We couldn't afford any furniture, so we just had pillows on the floor, and a stereo," reported Kennedy, who said they listened to a lot of Stevie Wonder and "giggled and laughed hysterically." During spring break one year, they went on a ski trip with a Jewish student group. "We were three black women on a trip with all of these white Jewish kids. We stuck out like sore thumbs, but we had a great time."

Angela Sadie Edith Kennedy grew up in the nation's capital, where her father was a postal clerk and her mother commuted to work as a teacher at the upscale and very white Chevy Chase Elementary School, known in the neighborhood as Rosemary. Henry Harold Kennedy Sr., born in 1917 in Covington, Louisiana, "never forgave American society for its racist treatment of him and those whom he most loved," recalled Angela's brother, Randall Kennedy, a Harvard Law School professor whose research and teaching focused on race and society. He described his father as "an intelligent, thoughtful, loving man who, tragically, had good reason to doubt his government's allegiance to blacks and, thus, to himself." He attended segregated schools, saw doors closed to him because of his race, and watched as African Americans were "terrorized and humiliated by whites without any hint of disapproval from public authorities." His children saw their strong-willed father being humiliated and never forgot it. As Randall Kennedy told the story, his father was pulled over several times by white police officers as he drove the family to South Carolina, "simply because he was a black man driving a nice car. I am not making an inference here. This is what the police openly said." As the children watched, the officers would instruct Kennedy to behave himself, since he was not "up north" any longer. Their lectures would end with the words "Okay, boy?" There would be a pause as the policeman waited for Kennedy's response. "My dad reacted in a way calculated to provide the maximum safety to himself and his family: 'Yassuh,' he would say with an extra dollop of deference."

And yet, just as Michelle would recall of her elders, the Kennedy parents made clear that there would be no hand-wringing or excuses. Nor, by the way, would there be any talk of taking to the streets and getting arrested at civil rights protests. "We were expected to get a great education and be excellent at whatever we did. Racism? So what? Overcome it by being better," said Henry H. Kennedy Jr., Angela's oldest brother, who came of age during the civil rights years. All three Kennedy children chose legal careers after graduating from Princeton. Henry attended Harvard Law School and became, at thirty-one, the youngest judge appointed to D.C. Superior Court, later becoming a U.S. district judge. Randall went to Oxford on a Rhodes Scholarship and then to Yale Law School before clerking for Supreme Court justice Thurgood Marshall. Angela wrote a senior thesis titled "Attitudes Toward Femininity and Masculinity of Princeton University Women" and graduated from Howard Law School. She dedicated her professional life to defending indigent clients at the D.C. Public Defender Service, remaining close to Michelle during the White House years. Asked how the three children managed to prosper, Randall Kennedy described an approach that echoed life on South Euclid. He said of his parents, "They created a family that told the kids that they were deeply loved, no matter what. They also told the family, the kids, to be ambitious and to go out into the world and do what you want to do. They were not people who stood over us every minute. . . . They did have a rule that said to the kids, especially once we turned 11 or 12: 'You have to be interested in something. You have to have a particular passion. Frankly, we don't care what that passion is, but you have to have a passion.'"

SUZANNE ALERO ALELE HAD LIVED in the United States for only two years when she reached Princeton in late summer 1981. Born four days after Michelle and half a world away, she spent her early childhood in Lagos, the Nigerian capital, where her parents were doctors with medical degrees from prominent universities in the United Kingdom. Her mother was an obstetrician-gynecologist, her father a specialist in nuclear medicine who graduated from the University of London. They spoke Itsekiri and English at home. Alele spent the first half of high school in Jamaica and the second half in Bethesda, Maryland, where she attended a large suburban high school. She high-jumped and ran the hurdles, took advanced classes in biology and physics, and made the county honor roll. She was also an accomplished pianist, winning a certificate of merit at a London music school and performing in a folk music group during her time in Jamaica.

What fascinated Alele academically, she said in her Princeton application, were biology and biochemistry. "What are the important items in the food that I eat? Why am I 5'10" tall and why do I look like my mother?" She learned several computer languages and, as a teenager, envisioned a career in applied mathematics. Teachers commented on her "originality" and clear understanding of difficult subjects. "Integrity and a real sense of responsibility and purpose," wrote Sharon Hell-ing, her Advanced Placement biology teacher. "Compassionate beyond her years," wrote guidance counselor Dorothy J. Ford.

At Princeton, Alele took science classes, ran track, and became manager of the lightweight football team. She staffed the help desk at the computer center and joined the International Center. Her academic record was mixed—she found herself on disciplinary probation—but she graduated with a degree in biology after writing her senior thesis on the molecular basis of abnormal red blood cells in sickle-cell anemia, a hereditary disease that primarily afflicts people of African descent. Friends admired her for her ability to resist the pressure to conform. "Suzanne was the spirit that we all should have, the voice inside you that tells you to listen to your own heart," Czerny Brasuell said. Michelle, more cautious and conventional by nature, said her friend "always made decisions that would make her happy and create a level of fulfillment. She was less concerned with pleasing other people, and thank God."

While Alele counted herself a member of the Third World Center, she decided to bicker at selective eating clubs. She was invited to join Cap and Gown, a club with a decidedly upper-crust feel across the alley from Cottage Club. There, she knew Terri Sewell, who had been mentored by Michelle through a Third World Center program designed to support new black students on campus. Sewell arrived at Princeton from Alabama. She had graduated as valedictorian of her class at Selma High School, where her father taught math and her mother, the first black woman on the Selma City Council, worked as a librarian. She attended Brown Chapel AME Church, the starting point of Martin Luther King Jr.'s fateful Selma-to-Montgomery march. "She never accepted the status quo," Sewell's mother once said, "from grade school on up." At Princeton, she became a varsity cheerleader and junior class president and wrote an award-winning senior thesis, "Black Women in Politics: Our Time Has Come." After graduation, she moved on to Oxford and Harvard Law School. In 2010, she became the first black woman elected to Congress from Alabama.

· · ·

MICHELLE SPENT the summers after her freshman and sophomore years in Chicago, living on Euclid Avenue and commuting to the downtown office of the executive director of the American Medical Association. She spent much time as a typist, later lamenting that meaningful internships and summer jobs with community groups "seemed to be a luxury that a working-class kid couldn't afford." Such positions paid little, if anything, and students on financial aid could not justify giving up a paycheck for the adventure or the experience. "I felt guilty to even ask parents who were already working hard to let me take a summer or a semester off to do something like that," Michelle said during the White House years in praising a law designed to triple the size of AmeriCorps, a national service program underwritten by the federal government. "So, oftentimes I never asked. I studied. I worked. I worked and I studied. . . . I had to work all the time because I had to have enough money for books for the year and I had to help out with tuition."

In 1984, the summer before her senior year, Michelle and Angela signed up as counselors at a camp in the Catskills for underprivileged girls from New York City. They reported to Camp Anita Bliss Coler—Camp ABC, for short—sixty-five miles north of Manhattan, where 216 girls between the ages of nine and twelve arrived for one of four two-week summer sessions, sleeping in wooden cabins without doors, electricity, or running water, taking long hikes, and listening to nature, often for the first time. Activities at the rustic facility, one of four *New York Times* Fresh Air Fund camps, ranged from swimming and dance to sewing and pottery. Many of the games organized by counselors were noncompetitive, designed to build trust and self-esteem. Each day, the girls sang grace before lunch. "Being in the woods builds up their confidence," camp director Beverly Entarfer said in 1985. "Especially the girls [who] have been told that they can't do this and they can't do that. Well, they go walking through the forest at night without a flashlight, build a fire or go without hot water for a while, and they find out they can do a lot."

Urban church groups and community service organizations chose the campers. In 1984, the summer Michelle was there, some campers came from the Rheedlen Foundation, whose educational director was

Geoffrey Canada, the future head of the Harlem Children's Zone. Canada believed that many impoverished children could get ahead if they had support and caught a break. These were fundamentally good kids, he said, who lacked the experiences and opportunities considered elemental in a middle-class upbringing elsewhere. "Average kids with a chance," he called them. His thinking would mirror Michelle's own. As first lady, she called Canada "one of my heroes."

At first, Canada was skeptical that the Fresh Air Fund adventures would make a difference. He pointed out that many children in his program, economically disadvantaged and living in broken or violent households, were two years behind their peers in reading and math. Their summers were, at best, unstructured and all of the kids had "a problem with adult authority." In the end, however, he concluded that the summer projects worked. The children got out of town, they tasted something new, they learned about themselves. "I liked the hayride, and getting away from my enemies in the city," an eleven-year-old girl said of Camp ABC in the summer of 1984. Another camper in the same era said, "The first time I came here, I liked the nights here, the way you could sit by the lake, talk to people with the moon shining." Counselors who converged on the camp from the United States and Europe also tended to grow. Helen Macmillan, a young Scottish woman who worked at Camp ABC the year Michelle was there, said, "You learn a lot about yourself here—what you can't tolerate, what your boundaries are, and what makes you mad."

WHEN MICHELLE RETURNED to Princeton for her senior year, the politics-plagued Los Angeles Olympics were over and Ronald Reagan was coasting toward a lopsided reelection victory during a stretch that would see five of six presidential elections won by Republicans. Her largest task before graduation was her senior thesis, which would combine her sociology studies with her interest in African American affairs. She spent many hours designing and refining a study of the racial attitudes and habits of black Princeton alumni, trying to assess the likelihood that successful African Americans would work to help less fortunate black people. Her sixty-four-page paper revealed much about the questions that interested her as she tried to square her upbringing on the South Side of Chicago with the elite world she now inhabited.

In a survey sent to four hundred black alumni, she asked their reaction to nine statements about "lower class Black Americans and the life they lead." Among the choices were "I feel guilty that I may be betraying them in some way" and "I feel ashamed of them; they reflect badly on the rest of us." Other options included "I feel lucky that I was given opportunities that they were not given" and "I feel they must help themselves." The final choice: "There is no way they can be helped; their situation is hopeless." For each statement, she asked the respondents to mark boxes ranging from "very true" to "false." The six-page survey also asked the graduates about their upbringing, their heroes, their connection to God, their relationships of various kinds with white people and black people, and how they perceived those relationships before, during, and after their time at Princeton.

The thesis was built on twin truths that applied beyond Princeton as African American class differences grew. The first was that some black people were making their way to ever higher rungs on the ladder. The second was that vast numbers of black people were being left behind. Michelle and her friends had opportunities their parents could hardly have imagined, a fact they recognized every time they sat down to Christmas dinner with their extended families. The broad racial solidarity of the civil rights movement was giving way to economic stratification. It was an "illusion" of the Civil Rights Act, wrote University of Chicago sociologist William Julius Wilson in 1978, "that when the needs of the black middle class were met, so were the needs of the entire black community." As it happened, it was Wilson's drives through the nicest parts of South Shore, Michelle's increasingly middle-class Chicago neighborhood, that crystallized his recognition of the growing divide. But where did the obligations lie? Michelle had been taught from childhood that every rising African American must reach back with a helping hand. It was a familiar understanding—"From those to whom much is given, much is expected"—and she considered it part of her cultural DNA. Now she was asking whether success far above the norm had changed the equation.

Michelle's literature review sketched a continuum of opinion about black identity and the wide array of essentially political choices available to African Americans in U.S. society. At one end of the spectrum, she borrowed a 1967 definition of black power from Charles V. Hamilton and former Freedom Rider and Student Nonviolent Coordinating Committee leader Stokely Carmichael. "Before a group can enter the open society," they wrote in *Black Power: The Politics of Liberation in America*, "it must close ranks. By this, we mean that group solidarity is necessary before a group can operate effectively from a bargaining position of strength in a pluralistic society." From Andrew Billingsley's *Black Families in White America*, she described the idea that African Americans must take responsibility for black communities and "define themselves by new 'Black' standards different from the old White standards." And from the other end of the spectrum, distant from Hamilton and Carmichael, she cited the conciliatory position of her thesis adviser, Walter L. Wallace, who taught a class called "Race and Ethnicity in American Society." In his *Black Elected Officials*, he argued that blacks and whites must work together toward "representative integration." Michelle wrote that such integration, according to Wallace and his co-author, James E. Conyers, meant the inclusion of black politicians and public servants in "various aspects of politics." She explained, "They discuss problems which face these Black officials who must persuade the White community that they are above issues of race and that they are representing all people and not just Black people." Michelle's description strikingly foreshadowed a challenge that she and her husband would face twenty-two years later as they aimed for the White House.

To say that during her Princeton years she could not envision an African American president is like saying that the sun rises and sets every day. Even the acceptance of black people as equals seemed unlikely. The "White cultural and social structure will only allow me to remain on the periphery of society, never becoming a full participant," she wrote in her thesis. Indeed, Michelle believed that there existed a separate "Black culture" and "White culture." Among the reasons she perceived black culture to be different were "its music, its language, the struggles, and a 'consciousness' shared by its people." Those elements "may be attributed to the injustices and oppressions suffered by this race of people which are not comparable to the experience of any other race of people through this country's history." She expected her research to show that the more thoroughly a Princeton student or graduate became immersed in white culture, the less connected that person would feel to the plight of lower-class black people—the "black underclass," as Wilson described it, "in a hopeless state of economic stagnation, falling further and further behind the rest of society." But, to Michelle's surprise, the eighty-nine surveys returned by black alumni did not confirm her hypothesis. Black graduates could, and did, care about the fate of African Americans who had been less successful.

To Michelle, the most interesting finding suggested that African American students identified more with other black people while they were at Princeton than they had before or after. Indeed, after graduation the sense of identification "decreased dramatically." She called it her major conclusion. The survey did not address the reasons, but Michelle offered two. Calculating the ages of the respondents, she reasoned that most had been on campus in the 1970s and might have sought solidarity in keeping with the teachings of the black power movement. Her other theory was rooted in the isolation that she and others felt. Noting that the university had just five tenured African American professors, a small African American studies program, and only the Third World Center "designed specifically for the intellectual and social interests of Blacks," she suggested that black students turned to each other for support "because it is likely that other Blacks are more sensitive to respondents' problems."

As for her own views of Princeton and life beyond, she wrote that her sense of alienation made her more determined to muster her skills "to benefit the Black community." And yet in a season when recruiters for blue-chip banks and companies descended on Princeton, she felt her professional aspirations shifting and the temptation of a large paycheck growing. "It is conceivable," she wrote, "that my four years of exposure to a predominately White, Ivy League university has instilled within me certain conservative values. For example, as I enter my final year at Princeton, I find myself striving for many of the same goals as my White classmates—acceptance to a prestigious graduate or professional school or a high paying position in a successful corporation." Howard Taylor, a sociology professor who helped advise Michelle while she was working on her thesis, said she "was not an assimilationist, but she wasn't a wild-eyed militant, either. She was able to straddle that issue with great insight."

The questions Michelle was asking represented familiar territory for black students at the time, said fellow graduate Ken Bruce. "How her experience at Princeton would affect her place in society, that's pretty much what all of us were thinking. You get this great education and what do we do with that, both in the majority environment and in our minority environment?" Few questions seemed to have easy answers, and one conundrum led to another, even about where to live. "Do you become the wealthiest person in a black neighborhood," Bruce asked, "or the only black person in a white neighborhood?"

MICHELLE EARNED sociology department honors. Her thesis also won an honorable mention and a $50 prize from the African American studies program. The questions she raised would stay with her. "One of the points I was making, which is a reality for black folks in majority white environments, is it is a very isolating experience, period. The question is how do people deal with that isolation. Does it make you cling more to your own community or does it make you try to assimilate more? Different people handle that in different ways," Michelle said in 2007. Tacking to the value of diversity, she continued, "It is incumbent on us, whether we are in city government or sitting around the corporate boardroom or in policy or education, to have critical masses of diverse voices at the table. I challenged my colleagues in the nonprofit world to look around and say, 'What does the leadership look like? Does it look like you? What are you doing to branch out and to make sure there aren't just one or two black folks, women, or Hispanics around the table?' In all sectors, we still struggle with that. At many of the top universities, we still struggle with that. That's one of the core points that comes out of my thesis and I don't think that's changed significantly since I wrote it. We've made marginal change. The question for

Princeton is what does the ratio of underrepresented minority students look like today? What about faculty? What about top administrators? Those are the questions we have to continue to ask as a country."

ALTHOUGH MICHELLE WORRIED that her time at Princeton would diminish her desire to serve, there never seemed much chance that she would forget her South Side roots. For one thing, her parents had drilled the message of community deep into her consciousness. "We teased them about how some people went away to college and never came back to their community," Marian said of Michelle and Craig. For another, Michelle nurtured a connection to family not five blocks from the lush Princeton campus. From time to time, she crossed Nassau Street and the town-gown divide to visit a woman who lived in a small apartment at 10 Lytle Street, just downhill from the gates of the university. Born in 1914, barely two generations removed from slavery, the woman was raised in rural South Carolina and made her way to Princeton to find work. When Michelle knew her, she was cooking and cleaning for a prosperous white family. Although her name was Ernestine Jones, Michelle knew her as Aunt Sis, for she was a younger sister of her paternal grandfather, Fraser C. Robinson Jr. How sweet it was, considering the southern world that Jones had known and the Princeton she had first encountered, that two of her brother's grandchildren would graduate from one of the finest schools in the land.

Four years at Princeton left Michelle freshly conflicted about her own ambitions. "My goals after Princeton are not as clear as before," she wrote in her thesis. The picture-book university, with its neo-Gothic quadrangles of carved stone and its clutches of self-assured white people, was an elite realm that delivered an elite education. It was a combination that cut both ways, reminding her all too often that she was a black student from the Chicago working class, while also telling her that Michelle LaVaughn Robinson could play in the big leagues. After another summer back home, she moved on to Harvard Law School, where the opportunities and the conundrums presented themselves anew.

FIVE

Progress in Everything and Nothing

arvard Law School, when Michelle arrived in 1985, was a lofty perch, every bit as privileged as Princeton, but certainly more competitive once classes began. Some critics derided the school as a factory, in part because it was the largest law school in the country, in part because it turned out so many corporate lawyers. At graduation, diligence would be rewarded with admission to the upper echelons of American society. It was no accident that nearly half of the Supreme Court justices appointed after 1955 bore a Harvard pedigree or that Michelle pressed ahead with her application after being waitlisted, despite being accepted everywhere else she applied. The place had an undeniable mystique, polished and perpetuated by the 1973 film *The Paper Chase,* whose iconic Professor Kingsfield explains theatrically to his cowed students, "You come in here with a skull full of mush and you leave thinking like a lawyer." Chicago writer Scott Turow turned anxiety into memoir in *One L,* published in 1977. He said Harvard beckoned "those of us compulsively pursuing some vague idea of distinction." A former federal prosecutor who wrote a string of crime thrillers, he drew a stark portrait of the first-year pressures. "It is Monday morning, and when I walk into the central building, I can feel my stomach clench," he wrote. "For the next five days I will assume that I am somewhat less intelligent than anyone around me. At most moments I'll suspect that the privilege I enjoy was conferred as some kind of peculiar hoax. I will be certain that no matter what I do, I will not do it well enough." Years later, Turow said being at Harvard meant "feeling like you were playing an unwinnable game of king of the hill."

For many black students, the hill seemed yet steeper. Robert Wilkins would go on to become president of Harvard's Black Law Students Association and a judge on the high-profile U.S. Court of Appeals for the D.C. Circuit. But as he finished his undergraduate chemical engineering degree at a small school in Terre Haute, Indiana, Harvard seemed a mirage. "I almost didn't apply," he said. "And if I applied, I probably couldn't afford it. And if I could afford it, I probably wouldn't like it. *The Paper Chase* was all I knew." Wilkins described himself as a "small-town kid who didn't really know that much about the world." But he did apply, and he got in. In spring 1986, the Black Law Students Association (BLSA) invited him to its annual gathering of students past, present, and future. He remembers being broke and unable to afford the trip until a visiting fraternity brother said he could drive him as far as Philadelphia, where he could catch a train to Cambridge. Wilkins felt welcomed that weekend. The students he met, including Michelle—"You can't really forget her because she's a tall, striking woman"—impressed him not only as smart and substantive, but caring.

The discovery of community and common cause was unexpected, considering the school's cutthroat reputation. Yet the attitude, a kind of constructive embrace, would shape many of the black students who enrolled at Harvard in the mid-1980s, particularly those who became active in campus efforts to diversify the faculty and curriculum. "The black community at Harvard was really sustaining to me," said Verna Williams, a close friend of Michelle's who grew up in Washington, D.C., and preceded Wilkins as BLSA president. Williams moved uncertainly into one of the world's great crossroads of the elite, doubting that she would measure up, yet she discovered people with similar experiences "who were really, really smart and really cool—the most amazing people I had ever met." Harvard struck her as a better fit than Yale, particularly because of her interests in race and social justice. True, she found the whiteness and maleness of the Harvard faculty "stunning." But she felt encouraged by the recent recruitment of black professors, and the black students, numbering 170 among the 1,796 students on campus in 1985, struck her as "more active and more dynamic" than their counterparts in New Haven. "We had a critical mass of black folks," she said. "Why would you go to Yale?"

It was certainly a contrast from twenty years earlier, when barely one percent of U.S. law students were black, and one-third of those attended predominantly African American schools. Being at Harvard with smart, committed black people, Williams said, was "a lifesaver for me. It contributed to the formation of my identity as a black professional, as a black woman. Feeling like I have this opportunity, I have this incredible opportunity, and it's not just about me. It wasn't just about me when I got here, and it can't be just about me when I get out of here." Williams remembered bull sessions in the cluttered basement offices of the Black Law Students Association, where friends including Michelle discussed conundrums of obligation and purpose. " 'What are you going to do for black folks when we get out of here?' We did think a lot about that, about what it means to be a lawyer, what it means to be a black lawyer." Such questions became central to Michelle's thinking at Harvard and beyond, connecting the lessons of the South Side with her experiences at Princeton and the looming decisions about where to aim her career.

The 575 1L students of the Harvard Law School class of 1988 split into sections to move through their introductory year of torts, contracts, and constitutional law. The required classes tended to be less than scintillating, with plenty of rote learning in the mix. It was law school, after all, and it was all-consuming. Michelle had been known for her discipline at Princeton, so self-controlled that she imposed a personal ban on all-nighters. At Harvard, too, she stayed focused and, according to friend Jocelyn Frye, avoided being "caught up in all that goes with being at an elite law school. She was a regular person. We had fun." To help pay the bills, she held a campus job and added to her Princeton debt by taking out loans. One year, she worked as a research assistant for Randall Kennedy, the law professor brother of Angela, her college roommate. With her friends, she sat in front of a big television set in the BLSA office on Thursday nights to watch *L.A. Law* and *The Cosby Show,* the most popular show on television, featuring the Huxtables, an upper-middle-class black family headed by Cliff, a gregarious obstetrician, and Clair, a smart and plainspoken lawyer. Their oldest daughter, Sondra, went to Princeton and planned to be a lawyer, but veered in another direction, deciding to open a wilderness store, instead. When she announced that she had changed her mind, her mother erupted. "Change it back!" she demanded. "After all that money we spent sending you to Princeton? Sondra, you owe us $79,648.22 and I want my money now!" The line got a big laugh, but Clair was also making a deeper point about contributing to society, according to Phylicia Rashad, the actress who played her. "Parents know their children," Rashad said, "and Clair wasn't telling her daughter to become a lawyer just to be a lawyer—but don't cop out."

As the Harvard students bumped along with varying degrees of competence and sanity, Williams noticed that her classmate seemed unusually serious and self-possessed, but not in a preening, call-on-me way. "She was not the person in class who was constantly raising her hand, showing she's smarter than everyone," Williams said. "But you know she's got it going on. She's got the quiet air of confidence—and it's confidence, not arrogance." Jocelyn Frye saw her in similar terms, describing Michelle as "down-to-earth, reasonable, practical, solution-oriented." She explained, "The thing about law school is that you get caught up in the theory so much. She has always been a person who's thinking about the bottom line—here's what makes sense, here are the practical results we can and should be trying to achieve."

Toward the end of every Harvard student's first year came the moot court competition, the first exercise where the students could stand up in a courtroom setting and act the part of the lawyers they would soon become. When it came time to choose partners, Williams made a beeline for Michelle. Her calculation was simple: "She's really cool and really smart, I'd better ask her before someone else does." It was a criminal case. The details escaped her memory, but Williams recalled that as they set to work, there was an easy way and a harder way to proceed. They chose the harder way: an evidentiary hearing to prevent the prosecution from entering a weapon into evidence. Williams was struck again by Michelle's cool forcefulness. "Damn, she is good," she thought to herself, watching as Michelle pushed the envelope and drew objections from opposing counsel. "She is saying something that she knows is objectionable, and she's just going to do it. The kind of question, 'How long have you been beating your wife?' Look at her, she knows she's not supposed to be doing that. She's so confident."

They lost the motion to suppress the evidence, but their friendship blossomed. Williams was the more overtly vocal and political, while Michelle generally preferred roles out of the spotlight—helping indigent clients of the school's legal aid bureau, adding heft to BLSA's annual conference, and doing some editing for a student-run law journal that aspired to be a vehicle and a voice for African American legal minds. "Michelle always, everything she wrote, the things that she was involved in, the things that she thought about, were in effect reflections on race and gender," said Charles Ogletree, a high-profile Harvard professor who mentored her. "And how she had to keep the doors open for women and men going forward."

IN THE SPRING of 1986, Michelle's first year in Cambridge, she volunteered as an editor for the *Harvard BlackLetter Journal,* which had been created a few years earlier on the largely white campus to address questions of race and rights from a black perspective. This was the journal's third issue and the editors presented a discussion of "The Civil Rights Chronicles," an allegorical essay by African American law professor Derrick Bell published in the November 1985 issue of the *Harvard Law Review.* The article ran as The Foreward, the review's annual disquisition on the previous Supreme Court term. In selecting Bell to write the piece, student editors Elena Kagan, Carol Steiker, and William B. Forbush III signalled the prominence of discussions about race and the law. "All the talk and the debates were shifting to race," said Kagan, a 1986 graduate who would become dean of the law school and a Supreme Court justice.

The *BlackLetter Journal* had gotten its start in the late 1970s as a blend of essays, poetry, news, and interviews. "A voice for black expression," later editors would say. In 1984, students relaunched the journal as a race-conscious alternative to the lofty law review, which had never had a black president until Barack was elected to the position in 1990. The goal was to produce "scholarly presentations of legal issues of interest to blacks. . . . without some of the stylistic constraints of other law reviews." The editors were hungry to squeeze into the conversation, but the journal was underfunded, understaffed, and decidedly outside the mainstream. Entirely different, in other words, from the hypercompetitive law review, which was as much a part of Harvard's self-image as the elegant law library, with its 1.4 million volumes and the inscription over the main entrance that read *Non sub homine sed sub deo et lege,* or "Not under man, but under God and law."

For African Americans, the law review had long proved difficult to navigate, even from the inside. Kenneth Mack, a Harvard student in the late 1980s and later a faculty member, called his time on the law review "the most race-conscious experience of my life." He said prejudices crossed political and ideological lines. "Many of the white editors were, consciously or unconsciously, distrustful of the intellectual capacities of African-American editors or authors. Simply being taken seriously as an intellectual was often an uphill battle." Bradford Berenson, politically conservative and white, said, "I've worked at the Supreme Court. I've worked at the White House. I've been in Washington now for almost 20 years. And the bitterest politics I've ever seen, in terms of it getting personal and nasty, was on the *Harvard Law Review.*"

In the Spring 1986 issue of the *BlackLetter Journal,* nine of the twelve articles directly responded to Bell's "Chronicles." Two others dealt with affirmative action, including one by Harvard professor Elizabeth Bartholet entitled "The Radical Nature of the Reagan Administration's Assault on Affirmative Action." The staff dedicated the issue to Bell's fictional protagonist and muse, Geneva Crenshaw, a confident black lawyer in the 1960s whose "pride in her color and her race," Bell wrote, "flourished at a time when middle class 'Negroes' (as we then insisted on being called) were ambivalent about both." Crenshaw saw herself continuing the work of nineteenth-century black abolitionists Sojourner Truth and Harriet Tubman, crediting them with an inner vision that allowed them to "defy and transcend the limits that the world tried to impose on their lives." In Bell's telling, Crenshaw, recently hired as a law professor at Howard University, is driving to a voter registration meeting during the Mississippi Freedom Summer of 1964 when a white driver runs her off the road. She survives in a catatonic state, emerging twenty years later to survey American race relations and conclude, "We have made progress in everything, yet nothing has changed." She says, "It is incredible that our people's faith could have brought them so much they sought in the law and left them with so little they need in life."

Despite a string of victories for African Americans in courthouses and statehouses across the land, Crenshaw is perplexed that the United States has made so little progress on racial fairness. "What is impossible is making the public understand that blacks continue to endure subordinate status, despite the legal advances of the last two decades," Crenshaw laments. "Blacks demand nothing more than their rightful share of opportunities long available to whites. But whites believe that blacks are demanding privileges they have not earned to remedy injustices they have not suffered."

Charismatic and soft-spoken, Bell was an engaging provocateur and high-profile protests against Harvard's disappointing minority-hiring practices put him at the center of the school's racial politics. Prone to wage his fights through sit-ins and threats to resign, he challenged the persistence of racial bias, questioning not just Ivy League demographics, but the very role of laws and lawyers in building a more equitable society. He believed that racism was pervasive in the American establishment and could not be sliced out with a scalpel or a lawsuit. As a principal proponent of critical race theory, he argued that racism was more than simply a random array of bigots who said and did bigoted things. Rather, he posited racism as an attitude and an affliction embedded in laws, legal institutions, and relationships—"a legal system which disempowers people of color." He considered it the product of a history of black subjugation so distant in the minds of most white people that attempts to shift the balance were dismissed as a form of racism in reverse. Bans on overt discrimination allowed some talented

African Americans—"the spotlighted few," he labeled them; W. E. B. Du Bois called them "the talented tenth"—to rise and prosper. Yet, even as they rose, the vast majority of black people remained hostage to stubbornly enduring patterns of inequality.

Bell cited the work of William Julius Wilson, the prominent Chicago sociologist who wrote in *The Declining Significance of Race* that "the patterns of racial oppression in the past created the huge black underclass, as the accumulation of disadvantages were passed on from generation to generation." In Bell's view resistance was essential. He believed significant progress, if it ever came, would emerge from the ground up, assisted by a recognition by white people that black advancement served their own interests. "History gets made through confrontation. Nothing gets done without pushing," Bell said during one of his many standoffs with the Harvard administration. Harvard professor Robert Clark cracked in 1987, "This is a university, not a lunch counter in the Deep South." Bell's retort: "I feel that Harvard is long overdue for change, just like the South was."

When it came to the Harvard curriculum, Bell's thinking led him to develop a set of positions about faculty diversity that went well beyond the assertion that women and African Americans deserved to join the faculty as a matter of equitable hiring practice. In an argument that Michelle would advance in a 1988 essay for incoming students, Bell said that women and faculty of color enhance university teaching because of who they are, how they teach, and what experiences they carry into classrooms and corridors. "Even liberal white scholars have to imagine oppression, and have to imagine they are not oppressors," Bell said upon the publication of *We Are Not Saved*, his book based on the "Chronicles." "Black people have stories and experiences that provide the basis not only for their lives but for their scholarship."

As a former NAACP attorney who did not attend a prestigious law school or clerk for a federal judge, Bell did not forget that he owed his own job to students who pressed Harvard to hire a tenured black professor during the civil rights ferment of the late 1960s. "You'll be the first, but not the last," Harvard president Derek Bok told him when offering him a spot on the faculty. That proved true, but barely. In 1967,

Harvard Law School had fifty-three tenured faculty, all of them white men. Twenty years later, when Michelle was there, the school had sixty-one tenured faculty, including five white women, but still only two black men and not a single woman of color. In other words, 96 percent of the faculty at one of the country's most elite and ostensibly progressive law schools was white.

THE CAMPUS AIR may have been rarefied, but developments at Harvard reflected the dawning national realization that so much and yet so little had changed in matters of race and opportunity. More than thirty years after *Brown v. Board of Education*, African Americans were winning elections and stepping into academic and corporate positions in greater numbers. But the decade in race relations was largely defined by the presidency of Ronald Reagan, who launched his 1980 campaign with an endorsement of states' rights in Neshoba County, Mississippi, where three civil rights workers were murdered in 1964. He peppered his public speeches with exaggerated or apocryphal stories about Cadillac-driving welfare queens and "young bucks" who bought T-bone steaks with food stamps. Reagan opposed affirmative action programs, a product of the Civil Rights Act of 1964, as a fount of unfair advantage. He curtailed the enforcement work of the Justice Department's civil rights division and tried to defund the Legal Services Corporation. To run the Equal Employment Opportunity Commission, he appointed Clarence Thomas, a future Supreme Court justice and unabashed foe of affirmative action.

The political debate between Reagan and his antagonists carried over to the law school. In 1987, as the country celebrated the two-hundredth anniversary of the Constitution, Harvard and the National Conference of Black Lawyers hosted a scholarly conference, "The Constitution and Race: A Critical Perspective." The gathering provided "time for re-evaluation in the midst of the pomp and circumstance." Bell was the keynote speaker, and black Harvard professors Charles Ogletree and David Wilkins led workshops. For all of the glorification of "original intent" by conservatives—this was the year of Reagan's highly contentious nomination of Robert Bork to the Supreme Court, an event that drew campus protests—many Harvard students and faculty thought "original sin" was more like it. After all, the men who built the framework of American democracy wrote a contradiction into the nation's founding documents when they promised liberty but permitted slavery. They did not endorse voting rights for women, black people, or men without property. Indeed, many of the founders owned slaves.

On campus, students and instructors not only discussed the causes and costs of three centuries of racial inequality, but asked what could change and how. Was it appropriate to promote diversity as a tool of learning? Was affirmative action a legitimate approach? "We were trying to search for the meaning of all that. We were writing about that and talking about it," Robert Wilkins said. In the fiery debate over affirmative action, critics not infrequently questioned the abilities of African American students, who were outnumbered nine to one. "The absence of minorities feeds the perception that blacks are not qualified to be here . . . as students, as professors, and as future lawyers," Verna Williams said at the time. "The idea that we're here as a twist of fate is totally false, when in fact to be here we've had to sustain a great deal of stress, along with the abuse that we experience on a daily basis as African Americans." Williams's comments appeared in a profile written for a special report of the Black Law Students Association's *Memo,* a newsletter designed to share the wisdom of the class of 1988 with newer students. That year seemed "as good a time as there has ever been to recognize, celebrate and preserve the achievements of black students at Harvard Law School," according to an editor's note. Black students in the class led more Harvard organizations than ever before. Among them were the *Women's Law Journal,* the *Harvard Journal on Legislation,* and the *Civil Rights and Civil Liberties Law Review,* as well as the Legal Aid Bureau, Students for Public Interest Law, and even the Harvard Law School Republicans. The longest essay in the fifty-page newsletter was written by Michelle, who devoted more than three thousand words to an appeal for greater faculty diversity.

In the essay, "Minority and Women Law Professors: A Comparison of Teaching Styles," she spoke up for a more human understanding of law and the work of lawyers and argued that women and people of color connected with students in fresh and valuable ways. She suggested, referring to *The Paper Chase*, that space should be cleared for instructors who did not conform to the Professor Kingsfield model of imperious superiority. However cinematic, the image of law school cultivated in *The Paper Chase* and Scott Turow's *One L* constrained student expectations and influenced faculty teaching styles—and not in a good way, she argued. "In the name of tradition, these images serve to mold perceptions of what one should look for in a 'genuine' law school experience. . . . Unfortunately, this sense of security and comfort that students find with traditional notions of the law school experiences engenders an inherent distrust of anything that does not resemble or conform to those notions." Michelle predicted that old-school teaching models, if left unchallenged, would be replicated in the hiring process. Instructors who tested boundaries would find themselves on the outs with a majority of students and undervalued in hiring and promotion. "The faculty's decisions to distrust and ignore non-traditional qualities in choosing and tenuring law professors merely reinforces racist and sexist stereotypes," she said.

Michelle chose three instructors—two black men and one white woman—to study and interview. She concluded that all three had received a chilly reception from white male colleagues and faced hostility from some students. A number of students, "solely on the basis of race and sex . . . feel justified in rudely challenging their authority and doubting [their] credibility," she wrote. But when given the chance, minority and women faculty were able "to introduce innovative methods of teaching and to invoke their perspectives on different issues. Now, unlike before, students are being made to see how issues of class, race and sex are relevant to questions of law. Not only do students find that these issues are relevant, they are finding them interesting."

Different as they were from the traditional faculty, the professors she chose were also quite different from one another. Charles Ogletree grew up in Merced, California, his father a truck driver, his mother a housekeeper, one from Alabama, the other from Arkansas. A counselor recognized his talent, and he thrived at Stanford University "despite academic and cultural disadvantages stemming from inadequate basic educational training," Michelle wrote. Ogletree, known to friends as Tree, had doubts about the merits of law school, but he enrolled at Harvard after concluding that legal training would make him a more effective advocate. He served as president of the National Black Law Students Association and the organization's Harvard chapter.

On a different path, David Wilkins was the son of a black graduate of Harvard Law School. He attended the University of Chicago Laboratory Schools, won honors as a Harvard undergraduate, and made the *Harvard Law Review* before clerking for Justice Thurgood Marshall. The third professor, Martha Minow, was raised in a world of some privilege as the daughter of former Federal Communications Commission chairman Newton Minow. She earned a master's degree in education at Harvard, graduated at the top of her Yale Law School class, clerked for Marshall, and developed specialties in human rights and the status of women and racial and religious minorities. When Michelle wrote the essay, Minow was the only one of the three with tenure. Ogletree and Wilkins would later be awarded tenure and Minow would be named law school dean.

"IN PROFESSOR OGLETREE's criminal law class," Michelle wrote, students "could close their eyes and imagine what it would be like to see him in action in a courtroom. Like a successful trial, this professor approaches each class with a game plan and he merely uses the Socratic Method to extract from students the information necessary to make that plan work. He manages to do this, however, without interrogating students with confusing questions designed to catch them off-guard. Inflections in his voice are always calm, soothing and patient, but yet he is able to get to the point very quickly and with the precision of an artist." Ogletree used role-playing, assigning students to play prosecutor and defense attorney. He served as moderator, "interjecting or intervening when necessary." Discussing an issue that would remain relevant for decades, he told Michelle that context counted. "When we talk about whether or not a stop and frisk is permissible, it makes a difference to see how a stop and frisk can be abused against certain groups and, therefore, students will not be as willing to say that such a procedure is acceptable." Years later, Ogletree said he pushed Harvard students "to understand that they're here for a reason, and it's not just to work at law firms and be successful in and of itself."

David Wilkins, in Michelle's account, adopted a more traditional approach, in part because he felt a need to demonstrate his own authority. He told her, "You don't think that I'm going to walk into a class of Harvard Law students being young, looking even younger, black and a first-time teacher and say, 'Hey guys, call me Dave!'" Michelle said Wilkins encouraged class participation without using intimidation or motivation-by-fear. "I make it a point not to cut off or treat any comment as stupid," he said. "Also, I run my class in a way that makes discussion important and I absolutely forbid any hissing or booing." He told Michelle that he wanted to create an atmosphere where minorities and women felt comfortable speaking out. He also made sure that students were exposed to uncommon or unfamiliar reasoning. "Part of the reason why I'm here, as opposed to a white professor," Wilkins said, "is to bring issues of race, class and other issues into the classroom and make them part of the debate. I want to show students how a lot of what goes on in cases is fueled by issues of race and class."

Michelle likened being a student in Minow's family law class to being a member of the studio audience during a taping of *The Phil Donahue Show*. Like Donahue, the prototype of the empathetic daytime talk show host, Minow paced the classroom, "probing deeply," using smiles and humor as she worked to make everyone feel welcome. She told Michelle that sharp analysis remained essential, but that "safety and a sense of reinforcement is more likely to produce motivation and learning than fear." A by-product of her openness was the stream of students who sought her advice. "Students come to me because I look like someone who listens and cares," Minow told her. "And partly because they know that I won't turn them away. It's important for students to feel they have a place to go."

In her essay, Michelle called for new approaches to the recruitment and assessment of law school faculty. She emphasized hands-on teaching and the human side of education, rather than intellectual heft for its own sake. Let others count angels on the head of a pin; she cared about outcomes. Her interests and, indeed, her orientation to the world were close to the ground. An emerging professional skeptic, she wanted to know how the law connected to real lives, not least to African American ones. Thus, she highlighted Ogletree's "primary objective" as bringing "reality into the classroom." She cited Wilkins's efforts to demonstrate the roots of conflict and noted that Minow did whatever she could "to shake students out of the complacency of being in a class-room and to force them to think long and hard." Describing Michelle's own approach, Wilkins said later that she thought hard and spoke up. She listened to others, he said, and yet was "strong on what her opinions were. She was always the person who was asking the question, 'What does this have to do with providing real access and real justice for real people? Is this fair? Is this right?' She was always very clear on those questions."

THE DISCUSSION MOVED from theory to practice when Michelle volunteered at Harvard's Legal Aid Bureau, a student-run clinic for low-income clients. She worked in a small house on the edge of campus and rode a shuttle to a down-at-the-heels Boston neighborhood. The volunteers met with clients and the attorneys for the opposing party, whether a landlord, a spouse, the gas company, or perhaps a state or federal agency. They drafted pleadings and occasionally argued the issues in court. In return for hands-on experience, students were expected to devote at least twenty hours a week to their cases. For some, the bureau defined their identity. Notable bureau alumni included Supreme Court justice William J. Brennan Jr. and Massachusetts governor Deval Patrick. Yet only a small subset of each Harvard class volunteered, about sixty students a year.

At the clinic's seventy-fifth anniversary celebration in 1988, public interest lawyer Alan Morrison suggested that all graduates should spend a year with a legal services organization after collecting their diplomas. "You can't begin to approach the problems of the poor unless you have experienced them directly," he said. "Working for poor people shows you the difference between the lives of the people who have to fight the system and those who simply enjoy it." Ronald Torbert, an African American student who led the bureau during Michelle's third year, wished more African American students were among the volunteers. "A large number of our clients are blacks and minorities. Lots of folks just don't have the background experience to understand," Torbert said.

Michelle worked with clients on at least six cases between September 1986 and June 1988, when she graduated. Three are listed in bureau records as family cases, a category that encompassed domestic disputes, divorce, and custody fights. Two were housing cases, which a bureau administrator said were probably evictions. One was a matter whose details are not reflected in the files. A 1988 bureau summary referred to a case in which her client's opponent had no attorney. It said Michelle "experienced the tactical difficulty of negotiating against a *pro se* party in the tense emotional environment of visitation and custody issues." In each of her cases, Michelle was the lawyer of record and would have been responsible for developing her strategy, consulting if necessary with one of the bureau supervisors. Ogletree, who ran a trial advocacy workshop, described Michelle as "tenacious." He said Michelle's work flowed from a sense of purpose grounded in her South Side upbringing and "a commitment to her father, who did not go to college, that she would pursue her talents to help her community."

Supervisor Ilene Seidman recalled a visit by Michelle to a satellite court in a white, upper-crust Boston suburb. "People looked at her as though she was an exotic bird. You didn't see women on the bench or in the courtroom in the same way you do now, and certainly not out of the city. Definitely very few women of color." Michelle had labored over a careful memorandum for the judge, Seidman said, while the opposing counsel, a white courthouse regular, had come unprepared. "So she's sitting very upright and serious with her beautiful memo and the other lawyer is flailing around. The judge started really admonishing the other lawyer, 'She did this beautiful memo; you didn't do anything.'" Things went well. On the forty-five-minute ride back to Cambridge in

Seidman's minivan, they replayed the events with delight. "She had just been in a situation that might have made some people justifiably angry, because she had been treated like an alien," Seidman said. But the two women shook their heads and laughed. Michelle was "keenly aware of everything going on around her and had a very mature way of assessing what she would respond to and how."

THE LEGAL AID BUREAU STINT was the only time in Michelle's career when she practiced street-level law, although it was far from the last time she would pay attention to working-class Americans in need. It was a persistent dilemma, what to do with the education and opportunity presented by Princeton and Harvard. She conceded that she had been neither selfless nor particularly purposeful when she set out for Cambridge. "Law school was one of those 'Okay, what do I do next? Don't want to work,'" she said in 1996. "It was less a thoughtful experience than 'Hey, this is a good way to develop a good income. Being a lawyer is prestigious and socially acceptable.'" She worked at corporate law firms in Chicago after each of her first two years at Harvard and entertained lucrative offers to start her career the same way. By the same token, the conversation about responsibility and purpose coursed through her law school years. "There was a real sense among the black students at Harvard of the old adage 'From those to whom much is given, much is expected,'" said Robert Wilkins, the former Black Law Students Association president. Even as they themselves were struggling with where to land, Michelle and several friends saw a vehicle in the group's spring alumni conference, a once-substantive forum that by the mid-1980s had become little more than a social event. They decided to add a measure of meaning about the law, lawyering, and black responsibility. Areva Bell Martin, who co-chaired the 1987 gathering, said one theme "permeated" it: "You guys, this is not just about you going to a cushy firm on Wall Street and doing the fat cat part . . . You will be doing your community and your family a disservice if you leave here and buy your penthouse apartment and never do anything else. There's more to your life than your own personal gain."

The temptations of corporate law firms could be hard to resist, as Michelle was learning. Big-city firms flew Harvard students into town, put them up in fine hotels, and wined and dined them "like you wouldn't believe. We were treated like celebrities," said Martin, who remembered taking more than a half-dozen trips early in her Harvard career. Many students succumbed to the allure, not least some who graduated with substantial student loan debt, including Martin, whose upbringing in a St. Louis housing project was harder than most. She described the BLSA conference as an attempt to present an alternative narrative, for use immediately or later: "Yes, you're privileged. Yes, these firms are courting you. Yes, you'll be offered these huge salaries. But there's more to it and don't get caught up in it."

The BLSA conference, as Martin and the other organizers saw it, needed to convey a sense of purpose, even as it developed into a more effective recruiting and networking event for law firms and students. The organizers set out to lure not just alumni and African Americans in private practice, but also black lawyers who had chosen public interest law, elective office, and other forms of public service. The keynote speaker in 1987 was L. Douglas Wilder, lieutenant governor of Virginia. In 1988, Michelle's third year, it was Bruce M. Wright, a retired New York Supreme Court justice. Known for spotlighting racial disparities in the criminal justice system, Wright titled his 1996 memoir *Black Justice in a White World*. In 1935, Wright had been admitted to Princeton, but when he showed up on campus, administrators saw the color of his skin and refused to allow him to enroll. He sat on his trunk on the sidewalk for several hours as his father drove from New York to pick him up. Asked later why he did not protest, he replied, "I was timid then. And there was a campus police officer standing there." Wright did receive a response in 1939 when he finally asked Princeton why he had been turned away. Radcliffe Heermance, director of admissions, replied that Princeton had a nondiscrimination policy, but that southern students in particular would not approve. "My personal experience," Heermance wrote in a letter that Wright was carrying when the university publicly embraced him in 2001, "would enforce my advice to any colored student that he would be happier in an environment of others of his race."

Jocelyn Frye was one of the spring conference organizers that year, joining Michelle and fellow student Karen Hardwick. Raised in Washington, D.C., the daughter of federal workers, Frye would become Michelle's policy director in the White House. She attended the National Cathedral School and the University of Michigan before alighting at Harvard in 1985. She was glad to find a critical mass of motivated and accomplished black students who shared a number of experiences and goals. "There's no other black student at Harvard who's going to think 'What the heck are you doing at Harvard?'" Frye said. "It was nice to be around people like that and not to feel you were being fitted in boxes that people created for you."

Her feelings of good fortune about being at Harvard aside, Frye came to believe that the law school administration should do more on issues of diversity. "There weren't enough of us. There weren't enough faculty of color. I think Harvard is like any other institution that is a predominantly white institution: They are not good about doing a meaningful assessment of their strengths and weaknesses. They think they're better than they are." She went on, "We had—and we should have—higher expectations for schools that are considered the best or among the best in the country. If you want to brag about Harvard being the preeminent law school, you ought to be able to brag about Harvard being the preeminent law school with faculty and students of color." In May 1988 many of the most active members of BLSA would take a very public step to adjust the balance.

BLSA LEADERS HAD BEEN MEETING in small groups to discuss protest options since April 1988, when law school dean James Vorenberg announced that he was stepping down. The new dean would be Professor Robert Clark, who had been dismissive of Derrick Bell's protests. The students, concluding that the moment before Vorenberg's departure was an opportunity to petition for faculty diversity, decided on an overnight sit-in in Vorenberg's office, where they would present a dozen demands. Seeking maximum publicity, they drafted a mock complaint resembling a lawsuit and assembled a list of likely media outlets. The target was May 10, two days before a full faculty meeting. One objective was to be invited to the meeting to argue their case.

When Robert Wilkins presented the plan to BLSA members, the response was far from the unanimous support he had expected. It was exam season and some students said they could not afford to take time away from their books. Others worried that an arrest would hurt their professional chances. Wilkins reminded his audience that a generation of protesters in the South had risked beatings and jail for their convictions and, anyway, nothing so severe was going to happen in the hushed halls of Harvard Law. Whether or not they joined the sit-in, he and others argued, BLSA members should not weaken the impact of the demonstration by voting against it. The leadership counted enough votes to go forward.

Geneva Crenshaw would have been proud. The vote was a victory, however modest, for Derrick Bell's cherished activism and the narrowing of the distance between theory and practice. Verna Williams described a determination to make BLSA "something more, not a social club," and she gave Bell some of the credit. "He said nothing's going to happen unless you speak up. He was always reminding us of that." If three years at Harvard had confirmed anything to the most politically active students, it was the elemental lesson from Frederick Douglass that power concedes nothing without a demand.

THE TWENTY-FOUR-HOUR SIT-IN began on schedule on Tuesday, May 10. Roughly fifty students participated, the majority of them African American. The BLSA leadership called it a "study vigil." Television news footage showed students seated quietly in Vorenberg's suite preparing for exams. Wilkins presented the demands to the dean, among them that the law school hire a black female professor that year and add at least twenty women or members of minority groups in tenured or tenure-track jobs over the next four years. The list called on the administration to do more to prepare black and minority students to teach law and to "diversify the curriculum to reflect the experience of people of color and women," a page from Bell's playbook and Michelle's

BLSA essay. For good measure, the students also demanded that Bell be named the next dean and Ogletree be offered tenure. A student press release said the protest had become necessary when Vorenberg and the faculty appointments committee showed "a refusal to take any concrete steps or make any tangible commitment." The statement went on to say that minority hiring was important to address "the breadth of legal issues that face America's lawyers. Many of these issues are now omitted by the predominately White male faculty."

In response, Vorenberg made no promises on hiring, but pledged to support a broadening of the curriculum and efforts to give students a stronger voice. Wilkins was permitted to speak to the faculty at its meeting, the day after the sit-in ended. He recalled a decidedly mixed reaction from the assembled professors. Some applauded, some folded arms, some showed stern faces. At least one faculty member did not look up from his newspaper.

GRADUATION DAY DAWNED GRAY, but the rain-soaked outdoor ceremony in Harvard Yard carried the familiar pomp of commencement exercises everywhere, this one all the sweeter because it was Harvard. The recipients of honorary degrees at the university's 337th commencement included soprano Jessye Norman, economist John Kenneth Galbraith, and Nobel Peace Prize winner Óscar Arias from Costa Rica, who admonished the graduates to acknowledge their rare and privileged position and embrace the accompanying responsibilities. "The majority of young people in this world are neither here nor in other university graduations," he said. "That majority, if they are lucky, got up early today to plow fields or to start up machines in factories. Young people like yourselves are dying in futile wars or barely subsisting with no hope. The privilege of knowledge bears a social responsibility." Harvard president Derek Bok, too, spoke of civic duty that day. He lamented the low salaries paid to teachers and public servants and contrasted those roles with the career choices of the graduates of Harvard Law. He pointed out that just 2 percent of the graduates of one of the most prestigious law schools in the country entered government jobs right after graduation. An even smaller number, he said, chose public interest or legal aid work. The vast majority joined corporate law firms.

After the ceremony, David Wilkins saw from a distance the Robinson family sheltering under an arch. Michelle was there, elegant and tall, her brother Craig still taller, and Marian Robinson standing with them. Fraser, who would die less than three years later, sat alongside in a wheelchair. Wilkins introduced himself to the Chicago visitors. "Harvard Law School is a hard place," he told them. "It's a hard place for anybody, but it's a particularly hard place for black students and more for black women students. Michelle not only did well in this place, but she did something quite unique: She tried to change it. I don't know what your daughter's going to do, but I promise you, whatever she decides to do, she's going to be somebody special."

Michelle was leaving Harvard more confident and skilled, if not necessarily more certain about her direction, than when she arrived nearly three years before. For all of the impassioned discussion about purpose, she chose corporate law, returning to the name-brand Chicago firm where she had worked the previous summer, stepping onto the cushy corporate track that she had mused about at Princeton. The new job would cover some bills and provide some legal experience. And then she would see. In the Harvard yearbook, her parents bought space for a message, reminding her with proud bemusement that she might have fancy degrees from Harvard and Princeton, but she was still a South Side girl, still a Robinson: "We knew you would do this fifteen years ago when we could never make you shut up."

SIX

Finding the Right Thing

W hen Michelle packed her boxes in Cambridge and moved back to Chicago after seven years in the Ivy League, she traded one privileged institution for another, embarking on the corporate path that she had begun to foresee in her college years. She started work in the summer of 1988 as a first-year associate at Sidley & Austin, one of the city's most prominent firms—very white, very male, very pleased with its blue-chip client list. By education and affiliation, she was now a certified member of the elite, and from her first day on the job, she was earning more money than her parents combined. And yet she was no closer to resolving her essential dilemma, the one that had informed so many conversations at Princeton and Harvard: What is possible for a black person, especially a black woman, in America? What is desirable? What is right when judged by whom?

It was more than Michelle's fine education that made her new career possible, although the pair of diplomas inked in Latin offered impressive evidence of her potential. The fact was, Chicago was changing. The city she found when she returned to the bungalow on South Euclid was not the Chicago of Richard Wright or her grandfathers or her parents. It was not the city where a talented young black woman's options ranged about as far as the nearest classroom or secretarial pool. Nor was it the Chicago of Richard J. Daley, who had wielded power atop a largely white power structure from 1955 until his death in 1976. A generation after

Martin Luther King's northern campaign fizzled, black economic and political clout was growing. African Americans accounted for nearly 40 percent of the city's population, sprawling across dozens of square miles. There were more than one million black people within the city limits, compared with 240,000 in 1930, when Michelle's grandparents were coming of age. With the population and the changing times came greater opportunity and perhaps the biggest shift of all: The mayor of Chicago during much of Michelle's time away had been Harold Washington, a black man.

Chicago's election, in 1983, of its first African American mayor came later than most. Five years after New Orleans and Oakland. Ten years after Detroit, Atlanta, and Los Angeles. Sixteen years after Cleveland and Gary. Frustration with the white establishment had been growing, fueled by the unequal treatment of black neighborhoods and residents. Anger had spiked in 1968, as it had in many cities, with the assassination of Martin Luther King Jr., and again in 1969 when Chicago police raided an apartment and killed Fred Hampton and Mark Clark, leaders of the Black Panthers. In 1972, police mistreated two black dentists, Herbert Odom and Daniel Claiborne, fueling the conviction that the rock-no-boats strategy of the Silent Six black aldermen had run its course. "I have been asked why it took me so long to take a stand," Representative Ralph Metcalfe, an Olympic gold medalist who had been one of the six, said that year as he broke with Daley and the Democratic machine. "My answer is this: It's never too late to become black. And I suggest some of you try becoming black also."

After Daley's death in December 1976, Harold Washington lost the race to succeed him. In 1983, however, he rode into office with the backing of an energized coalition. The election, for all the progress it represented, also revealed the city's enduring racial fissures. Washington received just 11 percent of the white vote in the primary. Many white Democrats chose race over party and voted Republican in the general election. But the bitterness of the campaign and the lateness of the date made the achievement all the sweeter for Washington's supporters, particularly residents of the heavily black communities on the South Side and West Side. It was like the moment in *The Wizard of Oz* when the

Wicked Witch of the West melts away. Washington had paid his own dues to Daley and the Democratic machine, rising within it, yet his election promised progress and patronage alike.

"His picture was everywhere," wrote a young community organizer who arrived in Chicago in July 1985, two years into Washington's tenure. "On the walls of shoe repair shops and beauty parlors; still glued to lampposts from the last campaign; even in the windows of the Korean dry cleaners and Arab grocery stores, displayed prominently, like some protective totem." A black barber in Hyde Park asked the organizer if he had been in Chicago during the election. No, the newcomer said, he had not. The barber explained, "Had to be here before Harold to understand what he means to the city. Before Harold, seemed like we'd always be second-class citizens." Another man spoke up and said it was "plantation politics." The barber agreed. "That's just what it was, too. A plantation. Black people in the worst jobs. The worst housing. Police brutality rampant. But when the so-called black committeemen came around election time, we'd all line up and vote the straight Democratic ticket. Sell our soul for a Christmas turkey. White folks spitting in our faces and we'd reward 'em with the vote."

The new organizer who went to the barber shop and recalled the conversation was Barack Obama, who spent three years doing grassroots political work on the South Side. He headed off to Harvard Law School in 1988, just as Michelle was settling into her job at the law firm. They would not meet until the following year.

A FEW MONTHS AFTER Washington won a second term, Alan Greene sat down to dinner in Cambridge with twenty-three-year-old Michelle Robinson. It was the fall of 1987 and she was in her final year at Harvard, starting to choose among job offers from prominent Chicago law firms. One of those firms was Chadwell Kaiser, whose specialty was complex business litigation, particularly the profitable work of defending corporations against anti-trust complaints. She had spent the summer after her first year of law school at Chadwell, where the partners had been impressed. It was unusual for the firm to hire a first-year law student, but Michelle was "so obviously a quality candidate," Greene said. The lawyers were struck by her aptitude for the law, her self-confidence, and her accomplishments at Princeton and Harvard. Greene described her as "hard-charging" and "sophisticated," not somebody "you would just stick in a library to do research." And there was something else. Michelle was a talented black woman entering a hypercompetitive field that for decades had been very white and mostly male. The firm needed her. Not because it was the moral thing to do—an argument that was appealing but insufficient—but because its business model demanded it.

"Our firm, like everybody else in the mid-eighties, was realizing that the world of law firms was too insular," Greene said. The firm's interest in Michelle, he said, "started with the idea that here is somebody who seems to get along fine." If all went well and she proved to be as talented as she appeared, she could become a magnet for black clients and minority lawyers, as well as for other clients who valued a diverse team. The firm had once been entirely Protestant, male, and white, only later hiring Catholics, Jews, and women. "So, she would be the next breakthrough in the firm. That's a lot of pressure and it didn't seem to faze her, which was one of the things in her favor."

Despite Greene's entreaties, Michelle chose to start her career at Sidley & Austin, a larger, more dynamic, and marginally more diverse firm—the clients of one black Sidley attorney included Muhammad Ali and boxing promoter Don King. It was not a hasty decision; hasty was not her style. She aimed to build her credentials and start to repay student loans that totaled tens of thousands of dollars. She had a good idea of the air she would breathe, having been a summer associate at Sidley the previous year. The firm was founded in 1866, five years before the Chicago Fire tore through the heart of the city. It was a classic white shoe operation that had expanded and changed through mergers and collaborations. One of the firm's best-known partners in the modern era was Newton Minow, a Democrat, who, as director of the Federal Communications Commission, famously decried television as a "vast wasteland." Yet the firm's politics were broadly Republican, and there was no disguising the fact that the firm's business was distinctly corporate. There would be no trips to distant courthouses to work with indigent clients, no sit-ins for change. When she rode the elevator to her office on the forty-seventh floor of a downtown skyscraper, she was halfway to the clouds. And yet, as the novelty wore off, she would recognize ruefully that she could stand in her gleaming window and still not quite see the South Side neighborhood of her youth.

MICHELLE'S ASSIGNMENTS as a young associate at Sidley ranged from the AT&T account to a series of marketing matters for Coors beer and Barney, the purple dinosaur on public television. One colleague said the work could be thankless and, frankly, dull—for example, reading storyboards to determine whether a beer advertisement conformed to television industry rules and standards. "I knew Michelle was frustrated," said John Levi, a senior partner who remained a friend. "Things in that group were unsettled at that time." Colleagues recall her efforts as thorough and her voice as independent. "She was very at ease with herself. Confident in her attitude. I don't think she suffered fools easily," said Mary Hutchings Reed, one of the firm's few senior women attorneys, who supervised Michelle in Sidley's intellectual property group. Other young lawyers had stronger records when they were hired, but Michelle's personality and high standards stood out, another senior colleague recalled. "A lot of people come with great résumés, but without a lot of common sense and without the kind of personal strength that she had," said Nate Eimer, who joined the firm in 1973. "She was very poised, she was extremely articulate, she was very smart, she obviously was not intimidated by anything or anybody," Eimer said. "She was the perfect associate, the perfect lawyer for Sidley. She would have done extraordinarily well had she stayed there."

Early on, in a conversation with Levi, Michelle volunteered to play a role in the firm's recruiting efforts. She had not been at Sidley for a year, but Levi invited her to sift applications from Harvard students, and help recruit the best of them. He reasoned that she knew the school, possessed a winning personality, and would speak positively about the firm. The fact that she was African American was a bonus. In the next step of Sidley's hiring and orientation process, her race played a role. "There was always a bit of an effort to introduce black people who were coming through to black people who were here, just to let them know they wouldn't be the sole black person here," said Steven Carlson, a white Princeton graduate who had been Michelle's first contact at Sidley. That year, the firm invited a black first-year law student from Harvard to join Sidley's class of summer associates in 1989, just as Chadwell Kaiser had done with Michelle. He was a star and the firm wanted him to have a good summer. Would Michelle, the higher-ups wanted to know, be his adviser?

ON HIS FIRST DAY, Barack was late. Michelle took note. Despite what she described as "all this buzz about this hotshot," she expected to be unimpressed. For one thing, after examining the photograph he had sent for the Sidley directory, she concluded that he was not much of a looker. It was the ears, she later said. For another, she knew how little it sometimes took for well-meaning white people to be wowed by a black person. Everyone was making a big fuss, she thought to herself, because Barack was "probably just a black man who can talk straight."

"But he walked into the office and we hit it off right away because he is very charming and he was handsome—I thought he was handsome. And I think we were attracted to each other because we didn't take the whole scene as seriously as a lot of people do. He liked my dry sense of humor and my sarcasm. I thought he was a really good, interesting guy, and I was fascinated with his background because it was so different than mine." How different? "Well, Barack grew up in a multiracial environment," she explained in 1996. "His mother is white, his father is Kenyan, he lived in Hawaii." He had spent several years as a child in Indonesia with his anthropologist mother and he had seen some of the world. His worldliness gave him a dimension that she did not encounter on the South Side or among the well-heeled lawyers at Sidley, where "you tend to find people that sort of fit one mold."

Not that she intended to date him. That would be going too far. Besides, as she told her mother while feeling luckless at love, she had sworn off romance that summer, declaring, "I'm going to focus on me." Michelle had dated an array of young men all the way back to high school, when she went to the Whitney Young prom with David Upchurch. She had posed for a photo that night in a silken evening gown with a V neck and a thigh-high slit, a pattern she chose and modified, insisting on the slit. Her mother did the sewing. At Harvard, one beau was law student Stanley Stocker-Edwards, the adopted son of singer Patti LaBelle. Nothing lasted. She said later, "My family swore I would never find a man that would put up with me."

WHEN BARACK ARRIVED at Sidley, it was the second time he had lit out for Chicago. His background was, indeed, exotic, and he had made many ports of call in his search for purpose and identity. His parents met in the autumn of 1960 at the University of Hawaii, where his mother, Stanley Ann Dunham, born in Kansas, had just enrolled as a seventeen-year-old freshman. Barack Hussein Obama Sr. was six years older, married, with one child in Kenya and another on the way. Within a few weeks of the start of classes, Ann was pregnant. She left school after the first semester and the couple quietly married in a county courthouse in Wailuku. At the time, laws prohibiting interracial marriage were on the books in twenty-one states. Barack Hussein Obama II was born in Honolulu on August 4, 1961, at Kapiolani Maternity and Gynecological Hospital. In Arabic, Barack means "blessed by God," while Hussein means "good" or "handsome." Within months, his parents had split up and young Barack would see his father only once more, when he was ten years old. For four years in his childhood, he lived with his mother and her Indonesian husband, Lolo Soetero, in Jakarta. His younger sister was born there. Dissatisfied with the Indonesian elementary schools, his mother often awakened him at 4 a.m. and tutored him, sometimes for as long as three hours. When Barack complained, her refrain was always the same: "This is no picnic for me either, buster."

By the time Barack was ten, Ann had decided he should be schooled in the United States. While she stayed in Indonesia to continue her research, he moved to Honolulu, where he lived in a small apartment with his middle-class midwestern grandparents, Stanley and Madelyn Dunham. They, too, had married young, eloping before her eighteenth birthday, on the night of her high school prom. During World War II, Stanley served in the Third Armored Division while Madelyn, known to the family as Toot, worked in a B-29 bomber factory. After Ann was born, their peripatetic existence took them to California, Oklahoma, Texas, Washington State, and, eventually, Hawaii, where Stanley found work in a furniture store and Madelyn worked as a bank secretary. Stanley was a bluff man, a dreamer and a drinker considerably less industrious than his wife. Basically a good man but "too old and too troubled to provide me with much direction," Barack said. They "stayed married through thick and thin," said Charles Payne, Madelyn's younger brother, who retired in 1995 as assistant director of the University of Chicago library. "They were both strong-willed persons and Stanley believed that he was the master of the household in all things. Madelyn made the money that paid the rent. In fact, Madelyn was the one, year after year, who got up and went to work and earned some money. Stanley could never do that consistently." In Payne's view, it was the women in Barack's life—his mother and his grandmother—who set the terms and the tone: "They were both very strong and tended toward the domineering." Musing about their impact on the future president, he said, "Well, he ended up pretty strong himself." Barack, in fact, once told Michelle, "You know, I got my toughness from Toot."

When Barack—then known as Barry—returned to Honolulu from Jakarta, his family enrolled him in the elite, private Punahou Academy. In *Dreams from My Father: A Story of Race and Inheritance*, the memoir he published at age thirty-three, Barack described a directionless adolescence. "Indifferent" was how he recalled himself. He played basketball, studied only as much as necessary, and smoked so much pot that he and his friends called themselves the Choom Gang. "I rebelled," he once said, "angry in the way that many young men in general, and young black men in particular, are angry, thinking that responsibility and hard work were old-fashioned conventions that didn't apply to me." By senior year, he had doubts about going to college. His mother asked him one day whether he was being a little casual about his future. He mused that he might stay in Hawaii, take a few classes, maybe get a part-time job. "She cut me off before I could finish," he said. "I could get into any school in the country, she said, if I just put in the effort. 'Remember what that's like? Effort? Damn it, Bar, you can't just sit around like some good-time Charlie, waiting for luck to see you through.'"

Barack roused himself. He made his way to Occidental College in Southern California. "A few miles from Pasadena," he wrote, "tree-lined and Spanish-tiled. The students were friendly, the teachers encouraging." In Hawaii, he had spent time with Frank Marshall Davis, a dashiki-wearing black nationalist poet and former Chicago newspaperman. Before Barack set out for the mainland, Davis warned him that the price of admission to college was "leaving your race at the door, leaving your people behind," a bluntly phrased version of the dilemma that absorbed Michelle at Princeton and Harvard. Davis said the experience would give the young man "an advanced degree in compromise." Indeed, when he arrived at Occidental—a first-rate school, but no one's idea of the Ivy League—Barack found that most of the concerns of black students "seemed indistinguishable from those of the white kids around us. Surviving classes. Finding a well-paying gig after graduation. Trying to get laid. I had stumbled upon one of the well-kept secrets about black people: that most of us weren't interested in revolt; that most of us were tired of thinking about race all the time; that if we preferred to keep to ourselves, it was mainly because that was the easiest way to stop thinking about it."

His own internal conversation about race and identity, however, was deep and unremitting, a product of his biracial heritage and an upbringing unconventional in white and black terms alike. Hawaii, Indonesia, the absent Kenyan father. Even the Dunhams. "We always just thought of Barack as just being Barack. Not black or white. Another family member who was just like us, only not quite," Charles Payne said. Barack said his grandmother more than once "uttered racial or ethnic stereotypes that made me cringe" and "once confessed her fear of black men who passed her by on the street." He came to envy, perhaps idealize, traits he saw in black students from working-class urban neighborhoods, young people who came from Watts or Compton or, as it happened, Chicago. In *Dreams from My Father,* which relied on composites of characters from his life, he assigned the role of alter ego to a black woman from the South Side.

He called her Regina, Latin for "queen," and identified her as an Occidental student, "a big, dark woman who wore stockings and dresses that looked homemade." She was studious—she spent a lot of time in the library—and she helped organize black student events. She had an evenness about her, an honesty and authenticity that "made me feel like I didn't have to lie." Her father was absent, her mother was struggling to pay the bills in a Chicago apartment cold in winter and so hot in summer that people sometimes slept outdoors to keep cool. Regina, he wrote, spent many "evenings in the kitchen with uncles and cousins and grandparents, the stew of voices bubbling up in laughter. Her voice evoked a vision of black life in all its possibility, a vision that filled me with longing—a longing for place, and a fixed and definite history."

When Barack told Regina that he envied her memories, she started to laugh. Confused, he asked why. "Oh Barack," she said, "isn't life something? And here I was all this time wishing I'd grown up in Hawaii." Barack published *Dreams* six years after meeting Michelle. They were married by then and he had been steeped in her South Side life, even living with her for a time in the house on Euclid. In his second book, *The Audacity of Hope,* he would use similar language to describe the real-life Michelle and her family.

ONE THING THAT STRUCK Michelle that first summer in Chicago was the way Barack seemed to move so easily among many different worlds. She also saw a sense of purpose not tied to wealth or corporate success. The Sidley brass took a keen interest, hoping to lure him back to the firm for good. He went to one cloth-napkin lunch after another. A member of Sidley's executive committee took him to a board meeting, while Newt Minow urged him to enhance his credentials by becoming a federal law clerk. The estimable attorneys saw what the Harvard professors saw. "Barack Obama, One L!" wrote constitutional scholar

Laurence Tribe on his desk calendar on March 29, 1989, commemorating an encounter with the first-year student. "I was impressed by his maturity and his sense of purpose, his fluency. Barack wasn't just a wonk of some kind. He cared about how people ticked."

The man was undeniably smart and smooth and it did not take long before Michelle found him intriguing "in every way you can imagine. He was funny. He was self-deprecating. He didn't take himself too seriously. He could laugh at himself. I mean, we clicked right away." But she hesitated to date him. She thought it might be inappropriate, given the responsibility conferred by Sidley in assigning her to be his mentor. And quite possibly tacky, should two of the firm's relatively few black professionals find themselves in a romantic relationship. "When I first met him, I fell in deep *like*," Michelle explained. "Right off the bat, I said, 'This guy can be my friend. We're going to be friends.' And it was later on, when he pressed for a little more than friendship, that's what I pushed away from. Because I thought, you know, we're working together." She even tried to set him up with her friends. Over the course of several weeks, with no small amount of verbal jousting, Barack wore her down, challenging her professed reasons one by one. Along the way, she learned something more about him: "He is very persistent."

"So," she recalled, "I said, okay, we'll go on this one date, but we won't call it a date. I'll spend the day with you." The day arrived sunny and warm. Michelle was living in South Shore. Barack had an apartment in nearby Hyde Park, not far from the University of Chicago. They started at the Art Institute, where Michelle's father had studied forty years earlier. They ate lunch in the museum's leafy stone courtyard to the sounds of a jazz combo and then took a long walk to see the new Spike Lee movie, *Do the Right Thing*. Afterward, they had a drink on the ninety-sixth floor of the John Hancock building, as the city and the lake stretched into the distance. "I was sold," she said.

Barack saw many things to like in Michelle, including her beauty: "I thought she looked real good." He admired her "strong sense of herself and who she is and where she comes from." But he also spotted a trait that was not part of her public persona. "In her eyes," he said later, when Michelle was in her early thirties, "you can see a trace of vulnerability, or at least I do, that most people don't know, because when she's walking through the world, she is this tall, beautiful, confident woman and extremely capable. But there is a part of her that is vulnerable and young and sometimes frightened and I think seeing both of those things is what attracted me to her." Michelle's vulnerability flowed from a sense that life was "terrifyingly random," Barack wrote in *The Audacity of Hope*. He said he spotted "the slightest hint of uncertainty, as if, deep inside, she knew how fragile things really were, and that if she ever let go, even for a moment, all her plans might quickly unravel."

One afternoon after a Sidley picnic, they went for ice cream in Hyde Park. As they sat on a curb outside Baskin-Robbins, they shot the breeze. Barack told Michelle how he had once scooped ice cream at a Baskin-Robbins in Hawaii. He said he would like to meet her family. He asked if he could kiss her.

"WE SPENT THE REST of the summer together," trading stories and getting to know one another, Barack wrote in *The Audacity of Hope*. To impress him, she borrowed her mother's seafood gumbo recipe, persuading him that she was a more versatile cook than she actually was. She was saving money by living with her parents in the Euclid house, which Fraser and Marian had bought from Aunt Robbie for $10 in April 1980. Later, when he was president and Michelle told acquaintances the story of their courtship and what attracted her to him, Barack chirped merrily, "Black man with a job! Black man with a job!"

Barack said it was not until he met Michelle's family that he "began to understand her." In the Robinson household in those early days, he saw what he described as joy. He said visiting the bungalow on Euclid was like "dropping in on the set of *Leave It to Beaver*." Beyond Fraser, Marian, and Craig, who graduated from business school and became a Chicago investment banker, "there were uncles and aunts and cousins everywhere, stopping by to sit around the kitchen table and eat until they burst and tell wild stories and listen to Grandpa's old jazz collection and laugh deep into the night." It was language that echoed his descriptions in *Dreams* of Regina's extended family and its effect on him. The contrast could hardly have been greater between his untethered life and the world of the Robinson and Shields clans, so numerous and so firmly anchored in Chicago. He felt embraced and it surprised him. "For someone like me, who had barely known his father, who had spent much of his life traveling from place to place, his bloodlines scattered to the four winds, the home that Fraser and Marian Robinson had built for themselves and their children stirred a longing for stability and a sense of place that I had not realized was there."

MICHELLE WAS STRUCK by Barack's community organizing work and the way he still talked about making a difference. He seemed to care little about the legal profession's traditional ladders of success, and even less about money. He reported to Sidley in serviceable clothes— "cruddy" was Michelle's word. His only pair of shoes was a half size too small and he drove a car so rusty that she could sit in the passenger seat and see the road through a hole in the door. "He loved that car. It would shake ferociously when it would start up. I thought, 'This brother is not interested in ever making a dime.'" He had graduated from Columbia University in 1983 after becoming more serious about his studies and transferring from Occidental. He worked in New York City for Business International, a publishing operation that produced newsletters and research reports, and he considered working in Harold Washington's administration. But when he wrote to the mayor's office, he received no reply. If he had cared more about money, he would not have answered a newspaper ad and spent three years before law school in Chicago, working for the Developing Communities Project, where the starting pay was $12,000 a year, plus $1,000 to buy a rattletrap.

The project descended from the work of Saul Alinsky, a Chicago organizer best known for his cagey opposition to Daley and his authorship of a book that was part manual, part manifesto, called *Rules for Radicals*. Still in New York, Barack aced the interview, took the job, and set off for Chicago. His mission was to mobilize the largely apolitical residents of Altgeld Gardens and Roseland to demand a fairer shake from the government—more attention, better services, a stronger chance of pulling their neighborhoods together. Fellow organizer Mike Kruglik said Barack possessed "a basic belief in the humanity of the folks on the South Side and their right to a decent life" and was "emotionally committed to African Americans getting ahead." Political critics who disapproved of Alinsky's philosophy, real or imagined, later accused Barack of being an acolyte. In fact, athough his supervisor, Gregory Galluzzo, liked to describe himself as Alinsky's St. Paul, Barack borrowed some bits and discarded others, crafting his own strategies as he went.

Looking back, Barack said the work gave him "the best education I ever had." In those deathly poor neighborhoods where he worked with African American ministers, he found persistent racial inequality that defied the progress that had erased the worst of segregation. He interviewed black Chicagoans, heirs to the Great Migration, whose family history mirrored Michelle's, with grandparents barred from labor unions and parents kept out of good schools and jobs because of their skin color. Some had succeeded, while many others had stalled out, perhaps permanently. It was the paradox of the talented tenth all over again. He was troubled by "this dual sense, of individual advancement and collective decline." The need was clear enough, but what to do? Feeling his way, Barack saw limits to what he could accomplish as a local organizer and set out for Harvard, thinking maybe he could do more as a lawyer or a politician.

Back in Chicago that summer after his first year of law school, he invited Michelle to join him as he met South Side residents he had known as an organizer. It was there, in a church basement, watching Barack talk with African Americans living from paycheck to paycheck, that she fell in love. His theme that day was the world as it is and the world as it should be. "He said that all too often we accept the distance between the two and we settle for the world as it is, even when it doesn't reflect our values and aspirations," Michelle said in a campaign speech. "But he reminded us that we also know what the world should look like. He said we know what fairness and justice and opportunity look like, and he urged us to believe in ourselves, to find the strength within ourselves to strive for the world as it should be." Barack's talk that day, in a year that would see peaceful revolutions across Central Europe and an unarmed man defying a column of tanks in China's Tiananmen Square, stayed with Michelle long after they were married. It would take two years and two jarring emotional blows before she quit Sidley, but what she saw in Barack strengthened her view that there was more to life than billable hours.

In Barack, Michelle felt she had found a man whose values meshed with her own, someone with whom she could share a purposeful life. "There are a lot of women who have the boxes—did he go to the right school, what is his income? It was none of that," Michelle told British high school girls in 2011.

It was how he felt about his mother. The love that he felt for his mother. His relationship to women. His work ethic. We worked together in a firm. He did his work, and he was good, and he was smart, and I liked that. And he was low-key. He wasn't impressed with himself, and he was funny. And we joked a lot. And he loved his little sister. And he was a community organizer—I really respected that. Here we are in a big law firm, right? And everybody was pushing to make money. He was one of the smartest students at Harvard Law School, one of the smartest associates in our firm. He had the chance to clerk for the Supreme Court and I thought, "Well, you're definitely going to do that, right?" Only a few people even have the chance to do that. He was, like, "Not really. I think I can do more work working with folks in churches." I was like, whoa, that's different. And he meant it. It wasn't a line. He wasn't trying to impress me. It was those kinds of values that made me think, "you don't meet people like that often." And when you couple that with talent, and he's cute. You know, I always thought he would be useful."

"WE GAVE IT a month, tops," Craig Robinson said after Michelle introduced Barack to the family. Not because there was anything wrong with him. He was quick, engaging, handsome, and six-foot-two, which mattered to Michelle, who stood nearly six feet tall. "But we knew he was going to do something wrong, and then it was going to be too bad for him. She held everybody to the same standard as my father, which was very high." Craig usually found no reason to dislike Michelle's boyfriends, but "you sort of felt sorry for them because you knew it was just a matter of time before they were getting fired." He called her "one tough girl" and made clear that she could be demanding. "She's very accomplished, so she needs someone as accomplished as her, and she also needs someone who can stand up to her. So, we in the family, we were just hoping she could hang onto this guy, because it was readily apparent he could stand up to her."

Marian, no pushover, was favorably impressed with Barack. "She found that he never talked about himself. He was always focused on who was around him," Michelle said. "He was somebody that shared the values of our family. He believed in honesty, treated people with respect and kindness, no matter who they were." Marian had white cousins and aunts who had married into the family, and one of her brothers married a white woman. But she was wary of Barack's biracial heritage. "A little bit," she said. "That didn't concern me as much as had he been completely white. And I guess that I worry about races mixing because of the difficulty, not so much for prejudice or anything. It's just very hard."

Barack's odds remained unclear. Fraser always said that you could tell a lot about a man by the way he played basketball. So one day Michelle asked Craig to include Barack in a pickup basketball game and report back. "When she asked me, I thought, 'Oh, no, she's going to make me be the bad guy,'" Craig said. But Barack was neither selfish with the ball nor shy about taking an open shot. He got extra points for not being overly deferential to his girlfriend's big brother during that first session, where they played for hours on a public court near Lake Michigan. "Confident without being cocky, selfless without being wimpy, and willing to sublimate his ego for the team. I gave her a good report."

After the summer in Chicago, Barack returned to Harvard for his second year of law school while Michelle continued her work at Sidley. He pursued a job in a different Chicago firm, but his plans to spend a leisurely summer in the Windy City were interrupted by his ground-breaking February 1990 election to the presidency of the *Harvard Law Review.* Never in its 104-year history had a black person led the esteemed journal, and his election drew media attention. He told *The New York Times* that he expected to spend two or three years at a law firm, then return to community work or enter Chicago politics. "The fact that I've been elected shows a lot of progress. It's encouraging," Barack, then twenty-eight, told the reporter. "But it's important that stories like mine aren't used to say that everything is okay for blacks. You have to remember that for every one of me, there are hundreds or thousands of black students with at least equal talent who don't get a chance."

FOUR MONTHS LATER, Suzanne Alele died.

Michelle's effervescent Princeton friend, the one she admired for making decisions based on fulfillment, not expectations, lost a fight with cancer on June 23, 1990. She was only twenty-six, barely five years out of college. Her devastated friends had pulled together during her illness, supporting her in Washington, D.C., where she had become a computer specialist at the Federal Reserve after earning an MBA. Angela Kennedy, who helped organize a memorial fund, said of Michelle, "If Suzanne or I picked up the phone and needed or wanted anything, she was here in a heartbeat. Suzanne's death was the first time I really got to see the depth of her love for her friends, how loyal she is." Alele's passing had a profound effect on Michelle, putting into focus frustrations she was feeling at Sidley and reminding her, against the backdrop of Barack's more purposeful inclinations, that the choice was hers to make. If she herself died young, she wondered, was being a corporate lawyer "how I would want to be remembered in life. Was I waking up every morning feeling excited about work and the work I was doing? The answer to the question was no."

She soon suffered an even deeper blow. Her father, after many years of living with multiple sclerosis, had been growing weaker. He started having breathing problems, but delayed telling anyone. One late winter night, Marian awakened to find him struggling for air. He passed out.

She called an ambulance. Doctors at the University of Chicago found a host of problems, including a large growth in his airway and bleeding ulcers. Surgeons operated, but unable to get enough oxygen to his brain, he slipped into a coma. The family gathered and Barack flew in from Boston to be with Michelle. On March 6, 1991, at age fifty-five, still employed at the water plant, Fraser died. He was buried a few days later at Lincoln Cemetery on the South Side. In their grief, Michelle and Craig argued over the wording of a remembrance. "Would you just stop it?" Marian demanded. "Do you know why you're arguing? You're arguing because you miss your father." The three of them burst into tears.

At the gravesite, Michelle rested her head on Barack's shoulder. "As the casket was lowered," Barack wrote later, "I promised Fraser Robinson that I would take care of his girl. I realized that in some unspoken, still tentative way, she and I were already becoming a family."

MICHELLE KNEW THAT she needed to find more meaning in her professional life. Exactly how, she had no clear idea, but she knew she had to leave Sidley. Among other factors, she was increasingly uncomfortable with the money she was making. She asked herself, figuratively, "Can I go to the family reunion in my Benz and be comfortable, while my cousins are struggling to keep a roof over their heads?" More than the matter of dollars and cents, she saw that making a difference in the city where her cousins, neighbors, and friends lived was important to her. "Just like that, I'd lost two of the people I loved most in the world," she told North Carolina A&T students in 2012. "So there I was, not much older than all of you, and I felt like my whole world was caving in. And I began to do a little bit of soul searching. I began to ask myself some hard questions. Questions like, 'If I die tomorrow, what did I really do with my life? What kind of a mark would I leave? How would I be remembered?' And none of my answers satisfied me."

SEVEN

Assets and Deficits

The file that landed on Valerie Jarrett's desk in Chicago City Hall was relayed by a colleague who had just interviewed a startlingly impressive young woman dissatisfied with her job at Sidley & Austin. The colleague was Susan Sher, a senior attorney for Mayor Richard M. Daley, elected two years earlier to his father's old job. Sher quickly realized that she could not tempt Michelle Robinson with a position in the legal department. "I don't want to be a lawyer," Michelle told her. "I want to do public service, but I think lawyers look at things from too narrow a perspective." Not wanting to let her get away, Sher alerted Jarrett, who was on the lookout for talented recruits, especially African Americans. Jarrett was so impressed after meeting Michelle that she offered her a job in the mayor's office on the spot. On the receiving end, Michelle was gratified and intrigued, but wary. She had an unusual request: Would Jarrett be willing to meet with her boyfriend, Barack Obama, and talk things over?

"He wanted to kick my tires," Jarrett recalled. The three of them—Jarrett the oldest at thirty-four, Barack turning thirty, and Michelle twenty-seven—met for dinner at a restaurant in the West Loop. Jarrett, who would become a friend, mentor, and one of the most powerful players in the Obama White House, recalled that Barack did much of the talking. He spoke little about himself. "I remember him, in a very nonthreatening way, tickling out what I was all about. He did it not in an intimidating way, but in a way that made me want to talk." He wanted to know where she was born. Iran, she told him. "He wanted to know how I'd gone from being born in Iran to Mayor Daley's office." That was a longer story.

Born in November 1956, Valerie Bowman had grown up in a highly educated family with ambitions to match. "Valerie, put yourself in the path of lightning," her grandmother used to tell her. For an African American family in the middle of the twentieth century, the educational lineage was exceedingly rare. "Everybody in my mother's generation went to college," said Jarrett's mother, Barbara Taylor Bowman, who was born in Chicago in 1928. "And the generation before that went to college. My grandfather, his brothers, all of their kids and, of course, us. We all went to college." One great-grandmother attended seminary at Oberlin before the Civil War. One grandfather was the first black graduate of the Massachusetts Institute of Technology and a deputy to Booker T. Washington at the Tuskegee Institute. Her father was the first black chairman of the Chicago Housing Authority, and she herself graduated from Sarah Lawrence College in 1950. Two weeks later, she married James Bowman, a dentist's son born in 1923 in Washington, D.C. He and his siblings all attended college, with Jim earning two degrees from Howard University. Yet, for all of their drive and success, the Bowmans experienced prejudice firsthand. Barbara recalled that, as one of about thirty black students at an integrated South Side elementary school, no white child would hold her hand as they walked into the building after recess.

In the Bowman family, the messages about racial identity were as clear as the ones about the importance of education. "My grandmother always kept telling us that they cannot make you uncomfortable; only you can make yourself uncomfortable," Barbara recalled. She said her grandmother could have passed as white, "but she took pride in being black and I also took pride in being black. . . . My great-grandmother, she took her stick and she would say, 'You know, you are a Negro. You should always be proud of that.'"

Valerie spent much of the first six years of her life outside the United States because her father was fed up with racial inequality in Chicago, where he had embarked on a medical career. With two internships behind him, he became the first African American resident at St. Luke's Hospital. Showing up for work in 1947, he was told that black employees were expected to use the back entrance. He defied the dictum and walked through the front door. The next day, he arrived to find other black employees waiting out front to walk through the door with him. He spent three years as chairman of pathology at Provident Hospital and three more as an army pathologist in Colorado, but when Provident executives invited him to return in 1955, they offered him less than half the salary white doctors were making. That was the breaking point. He said, "My wife and I decided that we were not going back to anything that smacked of segregation."

"We said, 'Let's look for someplace to go, and we may or may not ever come back,'" Jim Bowman recalled. He accepted a job as pathologist at Nemazee Hospital in Shiraz, an ancient crossroads in southern Iran, not far from the Persian Gulf. When they finally did head back to Chicago, following a stint in London, it was largely for Valerie's sake. "Because she didn't know who she was, and we wanted her to know who she was. In those days, we were called Negroes, but when we would say to our daughter, 'You are Negro,' she would say, 'Well, what does that mean?' We tried to explain it to her, but she said, 'Everywhere I look, I see lots of people with dark skin, but they are not called Negroes. Why aren't they called Negroes?'"

As educators who prospered in Chicago after their return, the Bowmans passed their wisdom along to their students, as well as to their daughter. Barbara Bowman helped create the Erikson Institute, a graduate program in early childhood education. Born seven years before Michelle's father, she told students that her generation took a certain satisfaction in confronting racism. "Because it was so hard, we thought about ourselves as being made stronger by the struggle." Jim Bowman told his black medical students at the University of Chicago that feeling sorry for themselves would get them nowhere. "In order to compete, you have to be better than the rest," he said. "You can't be just as good. You have to be better. And once you realize that and stop feeling sorry for yourself, then and only then will you succeed."

Like Michelle, Valerie became a lawyer at a blue-chip firm before reporting to City Hall, but she arrived by a different path. She attended the private University of Chicago Laboratory Schools and graduated from prep school in Massachusetts before attending Stanford and the University of Michigan. Well into adulthood, by her own account, she was "painfully shy." In the Chicago legal community in the 1980s, she felt much the same lack of fulfillment that Michelle would experience a few years later. She worked in plush surroundings on the seventy-ninth floor of the Sears Tower, then the world's tallest building. "I had a great office overlooking the sailboats on Lake Michigan, but I was miserable. A friend advised me to think about city government. I was hesitant. I was on my path and, miserable as I might be, it was my path. But Harold Washington had become the first black mayor of Chicago, and I made the move."

GIVEN HER OWN INITIAL DOUBTS, Jarrett was not surprised by the questions posed by Michelle and Barack over dinner. Michelle had long been suspicious of politics and the practitioners of its more unsavory arts. She knew from growing up as the daughter of a Democratic precinct captain the many ways that City Hall could seem remote, at best, from the lives of average citizens. Abner J. Mikva, an independent Democrat first elected to Congress in 1968, put it more bluntly. Until Washington's 1983 election, he said, "there was no reason to be happy with Chicago politics if you were black." Washington's tenure was messy and short. He died at his desk in November 1987 and was followed briefly in office by Eugene Sawyer, appointed by the city council. Now occupying the fifth-floor office was the unproven scion of Richard J. Daley, who had ruled City Hall for twenty-one years without paying more attention than absolutely necessary to his African American constituents.

Barack was a student of Chicago politics, and Jarrett recalled that he had "a certain trepidation" about Michelle working in the highly politicized office of the mayor, where she would not have a network to nourish and protect her. "She was a political novice," Jarrett said. "Was Mayor Daley going to be committed to the kinds of ideas Michelle cared about? Was he going to do only what he wanted to do or was he open to ideas? I think I convinced her that, together, we could do some unique things for the city." As they moved on to other subjects, Jarrett sensed that during the rest of the evening the younger couple was silently assessing whether they should trust her judgment. The experience told Jarrett that "before they were married, they were best friends. They had each other's back."

There was, of course, the matter of money. Although Michelle had concluded that finances would not be the deciding factor in her professional choices, the quest for fulfillment was going to cost her. Leaving Sidley for City Hall meant cutting her salary roughly in half, to $60,000 a year, when she still had significant student loan debt. "It just seemed incredible at the time that she'd leave," Angela Kennedy, her Princeton friend, said. The elder Robinsons had always counseled Michelle and Craig that if they took a job for the money alone, "ultimately you're not going to make enough money to put up with the mess." But even her father, aware before his death of her restlessness, had been concerned about a move. He asked Michelle, "Don't you want to pay your student loans?"

From the time she was young, Michelle had watched her pennies even as she made calculated indulgences. One was a Coach handbag she bought with her babysitting money. Marian gasped when Michelle informed her of the cost, telling her daughter that she would never spend such a crazy amount on a purse. Right, Michelle answered, but you'll go through ten handbags in the time I have this one. In fact, without the debt from her years at Princeton and Harvard, Michelle said she might have gone straight from Sidley to a nonprofit or a grassroots organization, a move she would make less than two years after reporting to City Hall. "City government, in addition to being interesting, was less of a setback to me, and I could manage that," she said. "My stint in city government was amazing. I was very young, but got a lot of responsibility."

AS MICHELLE WAS SETTLING into a job in the Daley administration, Barack was choosing an unconventional path of his own, one substantially less lucrative than the ones open to him as president of the *Harvard Law Review.* He spurned coveted judicial clerkships and six-figure law firm positions even though he could have had his pick. Instead, he cobbled together an eclectic array of jobs and pursuits, to the frustration of his mother and grandmother, who had both known financial hardship. His mother, Ann, in fact, had once been on food stamps. They believed Barack should fill his own pockets before he tried to save the world. Madelyn Dunham, his grandmother, "despaired" about his early choices, said her brother, Charles Payne. "We all thought Barack was going to make a lot of money. Because he was so good, so well spoken and, even with his dark skin, so white. Barack could fit in anywhere and he did. And with a Harvard law degree." He recalled his sister lamenting that she did not know what Barack was doing with his life. "Sometimes she was supporting six or seven people and her great hope was that Barack would make an awful lot of money and there wouldn't be these money problems."

Mikva, then a judge on the U.S. Court of Appeals for the D.C. Circuit, tried and failed to recruit Barack for a clerkship following his law review election. Barack informed Mikva that he intended to return to Chicago and go into politics. His political ambitions at that moment remained unchanneled, but they were not entirely unknown. He was twenty-six years old and on his way to Harvard when he had a drink in Chicago with Bruce Orenstein, an organizer for the United Neighborhood Organization. The two men had worked on a proposal, supported by Harold Washington, to fund South Side neighborhood improvements with fees from local landfills. After they ordered beers, Barack asked Orenstein what he wanted to be doing in ten years. Orenstein said he hoped to be making film documentaries and batted the question back to Barack. In ten years, Barack said, he wanted to be mayor of Chicago.

Back in Chicago after graduation, Barack lived with Michelle on the top floor of the Euclid Avenue house, upstairs from Marian Robinson, as he studied for the Illinois bar exam. As he considered his future, he set out not only to identify opportunities, but to preserve options, including political ones. He wanted no baggage that might later limit his choices or his chances. "Barack thinks about everything. He doesn't do things serendipitously," said attorney Judson Miner, who shared long lunches with Barack that summer of 1991, often at a local Thai restaurant. "He has got one life and he has got to figure out, 'How do I use it effectively? How do I position myself?'" Fresh from the intellectual ferment at Harvard, Barack was discussing with Miner the pros and cons of using the courts as a tool for social change.

Miner, two decades older, had served two years as Harold Washington's corporation counsel, or principal city attorney, and led a small progressive law firm housed in a red-brick townhouse just north of downtown. The firm, then known as Davis, Miner, Barnhill & Galland, made its name in civil rights law while advising nonprofit organizations and doing some general litigation. When he read of Barack's election as *Harvard Law Review* president, Miner had called the law review office. The person who answered essentially told him to take a number. He left a message. Barack telephoned Miner at home that night and surprised him by knowing of his work in the Washington administration. As their conversations unfolded, Miner encouraged him to come to work at the firm, promising that he could choose assignments "that would let him sleep soundly at night." At the same time, it was clear to both men that the activist, anti-establishment nature of the work might carry other costs, two years into what would become the twenty-two-year reign of Mayor Richard M. Daley. Barack "knew full well that the mayor of Chicago was not enamored of us," Miner said, recalling that some people warned Barack against joining the firm. Being labeled an independent Democrat could be a liability, but Barack was sufficiently savvy about Chicago's fractured politics to know that the approach could have the twin benefits of suiting his personality and winning more votes than it would cost him.

Barack signed on at Miner's firm, which represented most of the city's African American aldermen and worked with the Mexican-American Legal Defense and Education Fund. Barack took the side of minority residents in Chicago who challenged Citibank's mortgage practices. He worked on behalf of black voters and aldermen in a St. Louis voting rights case and helped develop a novel legal theory to defend an Illinois redistricting map that had been challenged on grounds of reverse discrimination. For several years, he devoted time to *Barnett v. Daley,* which sought greater representation for African American voters in Chicago. An appellate court said the case tested "the outer limits of minority rights in redistricting situations." Barack also did legal work for the Reverend Arthur M. Brazier's Apostolic Church of God in Woodlawn, as well as a community health network for low-income residents and two nonprofit organizations intent on developing affordable housing. Miner said Barack's efforts were "enormously thoughtful."

As Miner had pledged, the work did feel worthwhile to Barack, and if he did not always sleep soundly, it was more likely due to his tendency to overcommit. While he was working out details with the law firm, he was under contract to write a book that started as a reflection on American race relations and ended as a memoir. He accepted the challenge of registering tens of thousands of new voters and agreed to teach constitutional law at the University of Chicago. And there was his relationship with Michelle, who was not content to be just one item on an endless list. He loved her; it wasn't that. He wanted to be a good partner; it wasn't that, either. He simply wanted to do a lot of things, he wanted to do them well and, it often seemed, simultaneously, a tall order even for Barack Obama.

AS VALERIE JARRETT HAD OBSERVED, he and Michelle were very much a couple, but there was the question of marriage. Not one to wait in silence, Michelle made clear in 1991 that she was ready. "If this isn't leading to marriage, then, you know, don't waste my time," she told him. He usually replied by saying they had a great relationship, why did they need a piece of paper to confirm it? He did not get far with that argument, as anyone who knew Michelle could have told him. "He would sometimes say, 'If two people love each other, what is marriage?'" she recalled. "And I would say, 'Marriage is everything.'" Meanwhile, without telling her, he quietly spoke with her family about his intentions. One night, at a fine dinner for two, ostensibly to celebrate his efforts on the Illinois bar exam, Michelle again raised the question of marriage and began haranguing him for his refusal to commit. Dessert came. On Michelle's plate was a box containing an engagement ring. She was floored, and thrilled. Barack laughed, "That kind of shuts you up, doesn't it?"

THEY WERE MARRIED on October 3, 1992, at Trinity United Church of Christ, the Reverend Jeremiah A. Wright Jr. officiating. It was Barack who first joined the church—motto: "Unashamedly Black and Unapologetically Christian"—near the end of his community organizing days. Trinity offered a sense of community and mission. Anything but staid, it was especially popular with African American professionals, who were variously provoked, entertained, or inspired by Wright's theatrical sermons. One of Barack's signature lines, and the title of his second book, *The Audacity of Hope,* came from Wright—as did trouble for his presidential campaign.

Standing in for their father, Craig walked his sister down the aisle. For the reception, the party moved to the South Shore Cultural Center, formerly the no-Negroes-allowed South Shore Country Club, now owned by the Chicago Park District. In a ballroom facing Lake Michigan, maid of honor Santita Jackson sang Stevie Wonder's "You and I (We Can Conquer the World)," a song Michelle cherished from *Talking Book,* the first record album she owned. It was also the first record album Barack bought with his own money. The bride wore a dramatic white gown. Barack dressed in white tie. The families dined, danced, and got to know each other. Barack's mother, Ann, was there from Indonesia; she was soon to start a job at Women's World Banking, a New York nonprofit that used microfinance to help low-income women establish businesses. Madelyn Dunham, Barack's grandmother Toot, made the trip from Hawaii. "Everybody was delighted with Michelle," said her brother, Charles Payne. "I think people thought Barack was damn lucky to get her."

Family and friends of the bride and groom recognized the strength in each that would help the other. Barack struck Craig as a partner who would appreciate Michelle and earn her respect. Michelle's personality reminded Payne of the inner toughness of Barack's mother and grandmother. For Kelly Jo MacArthur, a colleague of Michelle's at Sidley, the analogy was hydrogen and oxygen: "We understood that together they were going to be so much more than they would have been individually." Harvard law professor David Wilkins recalled the moment he heard that Michelle and Barack were getting married: "I remember thinking to myself, 'That's perfect.' He has somebody who will complement him perfectly, both by being unbelievably supportive and by being unbelievably tough and honest. I said that's what Barack Obama needs. He's going to get every temptation in the world and she is going to ground him."

AT CITY HALL, still in her late twenties, Michelle was one of several staff members with the title of administrative assistant, a moniker that only sounded like a fancy title for secretary. When Jarrett became the commissioner of Planning and Economic Development, Michelle joined her. There, in pursuit of jobs, services, and advancement in neglected neighborhoods, she had money to spend and scissors sometimes just sharp enough to cut red tape. Michelle's job was "operational," as a friend put it. She was a troubleshooter whose interests and assignments ranged widely. She worked on business development, but also on issues connected to infant mortality, mobile immunization, and after-school programs. Her portfolio included black neighborhoods unused to attention from the mayor's office. One question was whom to help. Another was how. An elemental question, said colleague Cindy Moelis, was "whether city government could have a positive impact."

Michelle proved to be flexible and practical, capable of steering her way through a problem, colleagues said. Co-worker Sally Duros recalled Michelle as a "straight shooter" who moved with confidence despite her inexperience. "She was not the type of person who would do you wrong," Duros said, referring to infighting in the bureaucratic vortex of a city powered by politics. "She had a strong value system, a strong sense of what she wanted to do, and so she wasn't going to put up with people who were giving her crap, which is a pretty tough stance to take in City Hall." Duros worked with Michelle on a project designed to improve the distribution of Community Development Block Grants, a program that used federal dollars to attract economic activity to hardscrabble communities. The program was administered downtown, which proved inefficient and ineffective. A better approach, Michelle believed, was to pipe the money directly into the neighborhoods and help recipients avoid the wasteful effects of patronage and graft. "I remember a sense of frustration about the pace of decision making in government and the complexity of the number of characters and actors involved," said David Mosena, Mayor Daley's chief of staff when Michelle was hired. He remained a mentor. "She was 'Let's get this done. Don't tell me stupid stories, don't lie to me, don't BS.' She's got a great laugh and a great smile, but I don't recall her telling a lot of jokes and yukking around the water fountain. She wanted to see things get accomplished."

The city job got Michelle into working-class communities far from the antiseptic corridors of the downtown office towers, and it gave her a taste of the possibilities of government. But it also delivered an education in the obstacles and the infighting that so often inhibited worthy projects. She felt dissatisfied, as she had at Sidley. "It still wasn't enough, because city government is like a corporation in many ways," she said later. Not eighteen months into the job, she was ready to move on. "She wanted to be on her own, wanted direct control, wanted to see the results of her actions," Mosena said. The answer would be an organization called Public Allies.

WHILE MICHELLE WAS WORKING at City Hall, Barack took time to run Project Vote, a drive that added more than 100,000 African American voters to the rolls ahead of the 1992 election. He raised money, hired ten people, recruited seven hundred volunteer registrars, and saturated black radio with the slogan "It's a Power Thing." His goal was to energize Chicago's African American community in ways not seen since Harold Washington's campaigns and help make Carol Moseley Braun the second black U.S. senator elected since Reconstruction. He was calculating where he could make the biggest difference, said his boss, Sandy Newman, who was struck by the way he expanded the scope of the job. Barack raised more money than any of Project Vote's state directors ever had. "It wasn't part of the job description, but it was part of what he did," Newman said. "He did a great job of enlisting a broad spectrum of organizations and people, including many who did not get along well with one another."

For his financial team, Barack turned to John Rogers, a black Princeton graduate, friend of Craig Robinson, and chairman of Ariel Capital, a mutual fund he started. Rogers was joined by John Schmidt, a well-connected white lawyer who had been Richard M. Daley's chief of staff and a candidate for Illinois governor. For grassroots help, he not only developed an array of supporters, but he approached them in ways that made them feel valued. It was no accident that the techniques reflected his community organizing experience. "He went around to each of us individually, sat us down, and said, 'Here's what I'd like to do. It's daunting.' He'd say things like, 'Do you think we should do this? What role would you like to play?' One-on-one is what we call it in organizing. It's such a sign of respect," said Madeline Talbott, chief organizer for Illinois ACORN. "Everybody else just puts out an email and says 'Y'all come.' Barack doesn't do that. He talked to people individually and it's just so different." West Side alderman Sam Burrell called it the most efficient campaign he had seen in twenty years in politics.

There was no doubt that his own political future was on Barack's mind. Asked at the end of 1992 about running for office, he answered, "Who knows? But probably not immediately." He then smiled and said to his interviewer, "Was that a sufficiently politic 'maybe'? My sincere answer is I'll run for office if I feel I can accomplish more that way than agitating from the outside. I don't know if that's true right now." His work at Project Vote earned him attention and contacts. The next year, *Crain's* magazine named thirty-three-year-old Barack to its list of "40 Under 40" rising stars. The magazine noted his passion for social justice, his commitment to the wonky concept of "building institutions," and his decision to teach classes on racism and the law at the University of Chicago. "If you have the chance to go to Harvard Law School, it's no accomplishment to be a partner in a law firm," Barack said. "It's an accomplishment to make a difference."

Despite its praise, the magazine also demonstrated that he might not have the ideal name for the political future he was beginning to imagine for himself. The brief story spelled his name incorrectly three different ways, identifying him as "Borock Oboma" in the first paragraph and "Barock" in the third.

THE IDEA THAT BECAME Public Allies, the organization Michelle would join after leaving City Hall, emerged from the minds of two young women looking to attract members of their generation to public service. Vanessa Kirsch and Katrina Browne polished the concept in November 1991 at a Wingspread conference in Wisconsin, where one invitee was Barack Obama. On the roster of participants, he listed his address as the Robinson bungalow and his profession as "writer." At first, the new organization took a very Washington name, the National Center for Careers in Public Life. But as several participants drove away from the conference in a van, they discussed how young people so often were seen as public enemies. Public Allies was born. They received an early grant from Elspeth Revere at the John D. and Catherine T. MacArthur Foundation and, soon, federal backing for a program that would provide training and public service apprenticeships. After the first class of "Allies" graduated in Washington, D.C., in 1993, Kirsch and Browne looked to start a chapter in Chicago. In search of an executive director, they turned to Barack, who had become a board member. He pointed them toward Michelle and stepped down from the board as the search proceeded.

The job called for creating a mentoring and internship program. The director would build a curriculum, recruit a board, raise money, choose a diverse array of Allies—thirty per year at first, then forty—and find positions for them. Four days a week for ten months, Allies served as apprentices. Some went to City Hall, where Michelle retained her contacts, while others worked with education programs, youth development agencies, economic development projects, and environmental organizations. One lawyer did legal work in a Hispanic neighborhood. Time on Fridays and some evenings was reserved for leadership training sessions and team projects. Jacky Grimshaw, a former Harold

Washington aide, was one of the board members who interviewed Michelle. Grimshaw's first impression: "Boy, she's tall!" Michelle spoke confidently about how to structure and administer the program and how to connect with young people from a wide array of backgrounds. "She was quick to smile. She was very personable. She had that warm personality, which is what we were looking for," Grimshaw said. "We were talking about young persons who needed guidance and we needed a young person to be their leader. She was a perfect fit." Grimshaw also felt sure that anyone admitted to the Chicago program would see that Michelle was direct. There would be no trifling.

As Michelle developed the leadership training and community organizing components of Public Allies, she drew on the ideas of John McKnight and Jody Kretzmann, Northwestern University faculty members who had spotted a flaw in the way outsiders typically perceived the neighborhoods they were trying to help. As they saw it, do-gooders too often failed to appreciate the abilities of people they were trying to help and too rarely drew on them for solutions. Calling their model ABCD, for Asset-Based Community Development, they said solutions needed to be crafted from the inside out and the ground up. Projects should build on neighborhood efforts in order to avoid becoming beholden to outsiders, their theories and their money. A key goal was self-reliance. Only if the project were practical and made sense to the residents would it be sustainable. And only if it were sustainable would it make the neighborhood stronger.

Michelle introduced these concepts to Allies she recruited from across Chicago, adopting a training manual published by McKnight and Kretzmann. Each Ally received a copy during "Core Week," when the concepts were introduced and the coaching and team building began. The manual proposed ways of asking questions and listening, an approach considered preferable to marching into a neighborhood to prescribe and command. It emphasized outreach to residents who had ideas and energy but did not carry the label of "community leader." Successful workers would recognize a suffering neighborhood as a glass half empty, but work with it as a glass half full. They would see assets, in other words, not just deficits.

Kretzmann met for coffee with Michelle as she developed her curriculum. He saw how the theories resonated with her understanding of Chicago's black neighborhoods. Once the Allies were on board, Michelle recognized how much she enjoyed the mentoring and teaching side of the job, recalling the role that elders had played in her own life and the importance of reaching back, just as she had discussed in her Princeton thesis and all those conversations at Harvard. It all fit. "My mom and dad would always say that if just a few people would come back and live in the community, it would make all the difference in the world," Michelle said. "We talked about it a lot."

At each step in her life, Michelle stretched herself in fresh ways, moving from South Shore to Whitney Young to Princeton to Harvard to Sidley to City Hall. The same was true at Public Allies. Most important, she was in charge. The organization was not prestigious, the job was not lucrative, and there was no guarantee of success, but it was hers. "The first thing that was mine and I was responsible for every aspect of it," Michelle said. "It sounded risky and just out there." She described her three-year stint as executive director as the first time in her working life that her talents and her passions converged. In 1995, not two years after starting, she oversaw a budget of $1,121,214, with about half coming from the U.S. government through what had become the AmeriCorps program. Summing up her experience after reaching the White House, she said, "I was never happier in my life than when I was working to build Public Allies."

MICHELLE ATTRACTED young Allies from DePaul University and the University of Chicago and a few from Harvard Law—but also from housing projects such as Cabrini-Green and tough neighborhoods like Little Village and North Lawndale, where the Reverend Martin Luther King Jr. had tried nearly thirty years earlier to expose the wrongs of poverty and discrimination. Some Allies came equipped with only a high school equivalency degree. A few had criminal pasts. Many had trouble at home and little experience with high standards. "She didn't care if you were one of the cool kids. She cared if you were one of the kids who really wanted it," said Jobi Petersen Cates, a member of Michelle's first Public Allies class. "She would pick the one on the edge of her seat. It had nothing to do with intellect or breeding, but that they were itching to get going. That quality of enthusiasm and earnestness was more important than just about anything else." In bringing a wide range of people together, one of Michelle's essential goals was to teach them to walk in unfamiliar worlds, a challenge for sheltered and unsheltered young people alike. "There's nothing funnier," she once said, "than to watch a kid who believes they know it all actually come across some real, tough problems in communities that test every fiber of what they believe." On the flip side, she said, nothing was finer than to see a kid without a high school diploma sit with college graduates and realize that his "ideas are just as good, sometimes even better." Bethann Hester, a white woman who started as an Ally and then joined the staff, recalled that "the most powerful thing she ever taught me was to be constantly aware of my privilege. . . . Michelle reminded me that it's too easy to go and sit with your own. She can invite you in a kind of aggressive way to be all you can be."

If Michelle had only been seeking diversity of palette, she could have chosen well-mannered candidates of varying complexions from comfortable middle-class households. That would have been the path taken by a person "who wants to just look like they're doing well," said Cates, a white Northwestern graduate. But that was not Michelle's approach. "She would always take risks on kids from lower-income neighborhoods—and in Chicago, that correlates with race—just to make sure that they got a chance. She was willing to drive them hard and take extra time, in addition to being executive director, to push these guys. These aren't easy guys to work with." Cates continued, "The people who had privilege coming into the program, she didn't encourage us any less, she didn't push us any less hard. But I got the sense that part of her mission in life was to push all these incredible people not to be left behind, not to let their lives go. She was hard on them, but also didn't kick them out."

Krsna Golden was just eighteen when Michelle recruited him for her first class of Public Allies after meeting him at a leadership awards ceremony. By his own account, he had been in trouble—dabbling in petty crime, running with tough guys, being expelled from school—before straightening up. He was smart, equipped with a big vocabulary and a probing mind, and he was a talker. Michelle complimented him on his ability to parse problems, but she wanted him to come up with solutions. "She has a knack for building as she destroys. If she's addressing one of your weaknesses, she makes it a priority to fill in the gaps with strengths and how, if you apply yourself, you can change," Golden said. "She doesn't let people off the hook . . . but there's a charisma in there that makes you feel like, even if you're in a hard place with her, you're okay. You're still safe, you're still like one of her cubs." Under Michelle's tutelage, Golden won an award that took him to Washington and she helped him travel to Germany on a cultural exchange. He was uncommonly bright, she assured him, but he was in danger of wasting his talents. "She told me, 'Go back to school, go back to school, go back to school.'" *Stanford*, she said, *Stanford*. Two decades later, still smart, still verbal, still thoughtful while cutting hair on the South Side, Golden sometimes wished he had listened and made it past barber college.

Public Allies sought to teach young recruits how to build relationships and achieve results. This happened during their internships, but also at training sessions in the group's downtown offices. It was in the weekly group sessions, Michelle said, "where the magic happened." Sometimes, however, the magic was slow in coming. One night during her third year, a discussion grew so heated that an angry Ally punched a hole in an office door. When Michelle arrived at work the next morning, she did not expel him. Rather, she explained to him that his anger was self-defeating because it removed his ideas from the discussion. "You can't be punching doors here. You lose credibility when you do that. You know what I mean?" she said, according to Leif Elsmo, a long-time colleague. Another day, Michelle sat down with an Ally who was charming but often showed up late, equipped with an elaborate excuse. The young man said he had woken up that morning and taken a drink of booze from the refrigerator. His troubled mother had then asked him to stay home and help her. "I hear that," Michelle replied, "but that can't be how you're defining your choice for the morning. . . . Here are some ways you need to deal with that. This is about you."

It was a tense moment with a kid who was "pretty far gone," said Julie Sullivan, a staff member in the room that day. She said Michelle delivered a message that was equal parts firm and empathetic. "And not in a ridiculous 'Pull yourself up by your bootstraps' way," Sullivan said. "It was realistic and understanding of what people are going through." Michelle did not, however, have polite words for black Allies who tried to use race or upbringing as a crutch, particularly if their pitch included bad-mouthing white people for a lack of understanding. In a page she could have taken from the Shields and Robinson family handbooks, she made clear that young black men had no room for error. A mediocre white kid might be able to skate by on charisma or connections, his competence assumed or his failings forgiven. Less so his black counterpart. Cates, who later worked in City Hall, remembered supervising an African American Ally who did not do his work and resisted earnest efforts to keep him on track. She reported the trouble to Michelle, who "didn't indulge that situation for five seconds. She didn't use kid gloves."

Sullivan was impressed with Michelle's ability to be "understood anywhere" as she crossed back and forth among Chicago's disparate realms. She recalled drives in Michelle's Saab. "We'd go from some burned-out shithole on the West Side, where she's talking to really scary people, and then we'd go downtown to a meeting" with Daley's chief of staff. "She was unafraid to put issues on the table and talk about them clearly. She always had a really, really uncanny combination of unruffled calm and extreme clarity about what needed to happen next, whether it was in the small picture or the big picture. You couldn't not respect her, even if you were mad at her."

When issues of race and class surfaced in Public Allies staff discussions and training sessions, as they always did, Michelle had little tolerance for dogma or meandering debate. Getting from Point A to Point B was her focus, an approach that would become a hallmark of her professional and political life. Paul Schmitz, who ran the Milwaukee office of Public Allies at the time, said Michelle was the person who would say during a discussion, "That's nice, but we've got to get things done."

.   .   .

ONE OF MICHELLE'S TASKS was to find places for the Allies to work. To do so, she drew on a web of relationships that grew with her membership in the 1993 class of Leadership Greater Chicago, an extracurricular networking and education program for promising young leaders in business, government, and other city realms. Valerie Jarrett and John Rogers preceded her in the program. Among those who followed were Barack's close friends Marty Nesbitt and Eric Whitaker; Craig's first wife, Janis Robinson; and future U.S. education secretary Arne Duncan. Michelle persuaded an array of colleagues and friends to talk with Allies, with one eye toward the Allies' edification and another toward their future employment. One of the speakers she imported was Barack, steeped in the ways of community organizing and something of a student of John McKnight's in the 1980s. For all of Barack's talent, some Allies and staff members later laughed ruefully that they had barely noticed him, so dazzled were they by Michelle. To them, he was just Michelle's husband, a likable guy doing some teaching and lawyering somewhere in town.

What Barack brought to the Public Allies training sessions, however, was his knowledge of grassroots organizing and his experience of trying to pry results from City Hall. He often talked about power dynamics. "It was very focused on thinking about how you build constituencies within communities," said Kelly James, who attended the training as an Ally in 1997, after Michelle left the organization, and later took Barack's classes at the University of Chicago Law School. Teaching in Socratic style, he challenged his charges to examine their own thinking and move beyond conventional battle lines, many of them established during the civil rights era. He counseled them to find places where interests intersected and opponents could agree. And, as Michelle always counseled, to focus laser-like on results. Disadvantaged communities cannot be seen as "mere recipients or beneficiaries," Barack said in 1995. "The thrust of our organizing must be on how to make them productive, how to make them employable, how to build our human capital, how to create businesses, institutions, banks, safe public spaces—the whole agenda of creating productive communities. That is where our future lies. The right wing talks about this, but they keep appealing to that old individualistic bootstrap myth: Get a job, get rich and get out."

In a heartbeat, the Ivy-educated couple could have gotten out. They chose to stay, but both began looking for a bigger set of tools. In the end, both chose to work from the inside. For Barack, the answer was politics. In 1995, he decided to run for the Illinois state senate, concluding that a political perch offered leverage that community organizing could not deliver. For Michelle, it was bridge building at the University of Chicago, a privileged and remote institution that tended to see the surrounding South Side black community as an unkempt and threatening backyard. She viewed her role as breaking down barriers between the university and the community. Beyond the sense of purpose, the job paid better, with fewer obligations than Public Allies, where she had served as chief cook and bottlewasher for three nonstop years. And, too, she and Barack wanted children.

The Public Allies job "just wasn't big enough," said board member Sunny Fischer, who hosted a goodbye party at her home, where Michelle grew "a little teary." Barack and Michelle had been guests there before, enthusiastic and witty partners in political conversation with the Fischers and an eclectic array of friends whom they also saw elsewhere in Chicago, including former Weather Underground leaders William Ayers and Bernardine Dohrn. The two had become academics and Hyde Park Little League baseball regulars after years on the lam. Fischer remembered Michelle at the farewell party as "the warmest I've ever seen her." She was thirty-two years old and she felt she had accomplished much, designing the Chicago operation and building it from the ground up. Michelle had loved creating an organization, particularly this one, but Fischer never thought she would stay forever. "I always got the sense," Fischer said, "that there was a restlessness in her, that there was something else she could be doing that had more impact, that could move social change a little faster."

EIGHT

A Little Tension with That

For decades, the relationship of the overwhelmingly white University of Chicago to the surrounding African American community had been unsavory bordering on hostile. It seemed an unlikely place for Michelle to land. "I grew up five minutes from the university and never once went on campus. All the buildings have their backs to the community," she said. "The university didn't think kids like me existed, and I certainly didn't want anything to do with that place." Yet here she was in September 1996 reporting to work on the inside as director of a student community service program—"as fate would have it," she mused, recognizing the irony. She set out to bridge gaps of privilege and race, often finding herself walking in parallel worlds, serving as a kind of translator. The job had its bureaucratic side, but it provided freedom to devise projects that might make a difference. "What I found was that working within the institution gave me the opportunity to express my concerns about how little role the university plays in the life of its neighbors," Michelle said. "I wanted desperately to be involved in helping to break down the barriers that existed between the campus and the community."

The university's neo-Gothic spires had long stood like watchtowers along the green Midway Plaisance, where the first Ferris wheel carved steam-powered circles in the air during the 1893 World's Columbian Exposition. The Midway bequeathed its name to carnivals around the country, and the university, bankrolled in the 1890s by John D. Rockefeller, became a magnet for smart and sober scholarship. The intellectual ferment was recognized with dozens of Nobel Prizes and one of the country's most famous scientific discoveries. In a squash court beneath Stagg Field on December 2, 1942, Manhattan Project researchers produced the first self-sustaining atomic reaction, a precursor of nuclear weapons. It was said only half in jest that modern-day undergraduates would look up from their readings of Hegel and Dostoevsky and declare that the Hyde Park campus was the place "where fun goes to die."

After World War II, the university found itself doubtful about its future in Hyde Park, roughly seven miles south of downtown Chicago. In some ways, Hyde Park was a rare oasis in a segregated city, a place where middle-class black families could aspire to live alongside similarly situated white people. But as the population pressure from the Great Migration grew and barriers fell, administrators feared an influx of low-income African American residents that would repel white faculty and students. The university endorsed restrictive covenants and channeled money to white neighborhood organizations that fought to keep black people out. As Chicago courts stopped enforcing the covenants and the Supreme Court outlawed them in 1948, the university's white leadership gave thought to abandoning the leafy cloisters. "The gutters were full of half-pint whiskey bottles and crime was on the increase," declared one 1950 report, describing a two-block stretch of 55th Street that included 53 bars. By one estimate, 20,000 white people moved out of Hyde Park and neighboring Kenwood in the next six years, while 23,000 nonwhites moved in. Between 1940 and 1956, the nonwhite population went from 4 percent to 36 percent.

University leaders, in the end, chose to stay, but they took radical steps to create a buffer zone. Their method was urban renewal. "Social engineering on a vast and unprecedented scale," wrote University of Chicago historian and dean John W. Boyer. Drawing heavily on federal funding, the administration oversaw plans that displaced hundreds of small businesses and thousands of residents. The largest of the projects led to the demolition of buildings where 4,371 families lived. In all, 2,534 of those families were black, most living on low incomes. "Of those who did not return to Hyde Park, the percentage of blacks was substantially greater than whites," Boyer reported. By 1970, the university and an array of government agencies had spent $100 million on the effort. In place of the old dwellings, the university erected housing unaffordable to most of the black families who had lived there. The goal was to generate real estate prices high enough to "regulate both the number and 'quality' of blacks remaining," wrote historian Arnold R. Hirsch. The project prompted critics to scoff that "urban renewal" really meant "Negro removal." One of the university's most attention-getting opponents was Saul Alinsky, the community organizer whose mobilizing methods influenced Barack.

As the years passed, the University of Chicago endured, but only slowly adapted. On the summer day in 1976 when Boyer, a white man, was awarded his Ph.D., his working-class mother revealed her surprise that he had chosen to study at the university. She had been told by her mother that "people like us don't go there." Boyer explained, "It's not that the university wasn't racist. Of course it was. But it also sent signals to working-class whites—the sense of drawing up the drawbridge, of creating a moat." In racial terms, the leadership and the student body looked nothing like Chicago, much less the South Side. One of the country's most elite universities resided smack in the middle of the largest concentration of African Americans in the country, yet it often seemed to residents that the institution treated its neighbors as a species to be catalogued or, worse, ignored. As late as 1994, soon before Michelle started her job, Barbara Bowman recoiled when someone spoke of the university's "illustrious history" at a campus meeting. The erudite Bowman, an expert in early childhood development and the mother of Valerie Jarrett, could not resist setting the record straight. "You know," she said to the man, "I appreciate what you are saying, but you have to remember that as a black woman I was excluded from the leadership of that 'wonderful' community you are talking about. And so it is very hard for me now to think that it really was all that wonderful back then. In fact, it makes me very angry when you say that it was all that wonderful without recognizing that it excluded *any* black people from positions of leadership."

. . .

THIS TERRITORY WAS NOT unfamiliar to Michelle. She knew something about upper-crust universities from her time at Princeton and Harvard. She also had a snapshot of life on the Hyde Park campus from her mother, who worked as a secretary in the university's legal office in the 1970s, when Michelle was in high school. From the start in September 1996, it was clear to her thirty-two-year-old self that she had work to do. "I know the community does not trust and understand the university, and the university does not trust and understand the community," Michelle said. "Until you can bridge those gaps and hear out both sides and understand why they are afraid, you can't really have a conversation." Her job, director of the University Community Service Center, was a new one that owed its creation to a faculty-student committee that found the university wanting on volunteerism. She aimed to have an impact on nearby neighborhoods, as well as on University of Chicago students. To succeed, she needed to design programs and sell them to her superiors, including Boyer. She also had to find agencies and organizations where students would be welcomed and put to good use.

Michelle built a small staff and set out to increase student awareness of the city's geography, arranging bus tours beyond the Hyde Park campus. She developed a summer internship program infused with lessons from Public Allies and the Asset-Based Community Development approach. Called Summer Links, the project provided ten-week internships that included half-day training sessions on such themes as race relations, welfare reform, affordable health care, and homelessness. Separately, she developed a series of monthly conversations on urban issues, including one timed to coincide with the hundredth anniversary of the U.S. juvenile justice system. The panel included a former juvenile offender, a priest, and a teacher who had worked in a Cook County youth detention center. Barack was on the panel, as was William Ayers, the former Weather Underground leader and federal fugitive, who had recently published a book on juvenile justice. "Students and faculty explore these issues in the classroom, but it is an internal conversation,"

Michelle said. "We know that issues like juvenile justice impact the city of Chicago, this nation and—directly or indirectly—this campus. This panel gives students a chance to hear about the juvenile justice system not only on a theoretical level, but from the people who have experienced it."

Her interest in reaching out to African American residents beyond the campus, however, was largely incidental to the university's focus on its own students. Boyer was looking for ways to attract and satisfy students at a time when the university was struggling. Improvements in the surrounding communities and the residents' attitudes toward the university were welcome, but secondary. When Boyer became dean of the college in 1992, the University of Chicago was accepting nearly 75 percent of applicants. In his first year, 15 percent of the freshman class flunked out or dropped out, a statistic that would have gotten him fired at Harvard or Yale, "like, within two minutes." Soon after university president Hugo Sonnenschein announced plans to increase student enrollment by one thousand, Boyer was glad to see Michelle walk through the door. He reasoned that her concentration on community service would give the college "a broader and more diverse profile, in the sense that our students came here not just to read Shakespeare and take calculus and debate the meaning of life well into the night." Michelle was "convinced that the university was too inward-looking," he said. He called their efforts "a convergence of what she wanted to do and what I was interested in doing."

In Michelle, Boyer saw someone as pragmatic as he was, and as oriented toward results. Smart and tough, he said, persistent without being abrasive, "quite strategic in getting the resources she needed to accomplish her goals." Given the university's racial history, he was pleased to find that she seemed more interested in plotting the future than rehashing the past. He would not have been sympathetic to the argument that the university owed something to black South Side residents because of its history of bigotry, what he called a "reparations mentality." She recognized that the community service program needed to benefit the students and "not just make us into some kind of NGO that would go out and do good in the neighborhood. I wasn't interested in investing money in things that did not have some payoff for the education of our students. My job is dean of the college. I'm not here to save the world, even though I hope the world could be saved."

Michelle expanded the scope of her office during her five years on the job. Many African American students, seeking a campus haven, considered the community service center a gathering spot, said Melissa Harris-Perry, who taught a course on black women's social activism and relied on Michelle and her colleagues to find internships for her students. "They really saw her as an ally and a voice for their interests," she said. Until Michelle arrived, Samuel Speers, associate dean of the university chapel, had served as the primary adviser to the community service center. He recalled her as savvy about navigating the university hierarchy and the politics of the surrounding neighborhoods. "She would wade right in. She's not afraid of conflict, but she also doesn't seek it. You had the sense she had the ear of the university president and the ear of the wider community." Race was never far from the discussion. "You cannot do community-based work in Hyde Park and not engage questions of race," Speers said.

Michelle did not win all of her battles. She argued unsuccessfully that students should get course credit for their volunteer work, a position that Arthur Sussman, who had hired her, considered "toxic" among university faculty. "It was possible that other elite schools were doing it," he said, "but that was not going to be the Chicago way." Overall, Michelle sought to expand the service program while ensuring that neighborhood organizations gained from the collaboration. That lesson stuck with Leif Elsmo, who followed Michelle to the university from Public Allies and worked with her for nearly fourteen years. She taught him to be "sensitive about the promises we made to communities," he said. "We had to fulfill what we said we were going to do, because communities have been failed so many times."

IN 1995, as Michelle was about to welcome her third class of Public Allies and start the job search that would take her to the university, Barack was still doing several things part-time. He enjoyed decent success, but was hardly a player. He taught law at the University of Chicago. He handled public interest cases at Davis, Miner, Barnhill & Galland. He conducted community organizing training sessions, and he served on boards of directors, including the Woods Fund, the Joyce Foundation, and The Chicago Annenberg Challenge. When he published *Dreams from My Father* that year and did a reading at 57th Street Books in Hyde Park, he was the amiable guy from the neighborhood, not a literary star. A grand total of nine people showed up for a reading at Eso Won Books, the leading African American bookstore in Los Angeles. Many years later, the reissued *Dreams* would make Barack and Michelle rich, with several million copies in circulation, but the first printing did not sell enough copies to earn back its $30,000 advance. For all of the buzz about his talents, it was safe to say that Barack's great promise remained unfulfilled. No one felt it more than he did.

Alice Palmer, in 1995, was the state senator from the Illinois 13th Senate District, a swath of South Side turf that included the Obamas' Hyde Park apartment and stretched south and west into tougher working-class neighborhoods. Progressive and well connected, she tended her political garden and faced no foreseeable electoral threat. She spotted a chance to move up the ladder when Representative Mel Reynolds, a black former Rhodes Scholar, became the latest in a string of Chicago politicians to be indicted, in his case for having sex with a sixteen-year-old campaign volunteer and obstructing justice. His conviction and forced exit meant a special election. When Palmer entered the congressional race, Barack declared himself a candidate for her state senate seat, but not before exacting a promise that if she lost, she would not jump back into the senate contest. He also lent his name to her congressional candidacy, an awkward proposition. Her principal opponent was Jesse Jackson Jr., son of a certain other Jesse Jackson, the Operation PUSH leader and two-time presidential candidate, and brother of Michelle's friend Santita Jackson, who had sung at the Obamas' wedding just three years earlier.

Palmer lost the Democratic primary to Jackson, placing third with just 10 percent of the vote. She reiterated that she would not try to keep her senate seat, but her reluctance soon disappeared. With the backing of South Side stalwarts including the elder Jackson and Emil Jones Jr., the Democratic leader of the state senate, she declared that she would run for her old job, after all. "Michael Jordan can come back and so have I," she asserted. A number of her loyalists leaned on Barack to drop out. He refused. The way he saw it, a deal was a deal. After Palmer's team cut corners in collecting signatures to qualify for the ballot, Barack challenged the validity of her petitions and those of the three other Democratic candidates. The board of elections disqualified all four. He was in. The November election against a pair of minor candidates would be just a formality.

Michelle had doubts about the wisdom of a political career. Indeed, she had no truck with politicians or their ways, but she worked hard for Barack's election. "Michelle was determined to run a top-notch campaign, no cheesiness," said Barack's campaign manager, Carol Anne Harwell. "She brought elegance and class to the campaign. She was the taskmaster and she was very organized, even if she didn't know a lot about politics then. When we started collecting petitions, we would set a goal for, say, two hundred signatures that day. There would be a blizzard and we would come back with only a hundred and fifty. Michelle would be furious and we'd have to go out and get the rest." Asked why she went along with Barack's plans despite her misgivings about the profession, she answered, "Because I believe in him."

"How can you impact the greatest number of people? We always debated this," Michelle said, "because my view was, well, you can also impact a lot of people if you're the principal of a high school or a great teacher or a great dad. I wasn't a proponent of politics as a way you can make change." Her mistrust of politics was deeply rooted and would linger long into Barack's political career. "We as a family were extremely cynical about politics and politicians," her brother Craig said. That view was all but inescapable on the South Side in the second half of the twentieth century, a period scarred by schoolhouse inequity, economic neglect, and political corruption that no single politician could fix. Abner Mikva, former Democratic congressman and federal judge, traced Michelle's dissatisfaction to race. "Michelle had a black life in black Chicago," he said. "You can't have any brains and not be influenced in a big way, and pretty negatively."

Beyond her doubts that meaningful change could be produced in the well of the Illinois senate, Michelle worried that Barack would be eaten alive. "I don't trust the people in there," she told interviewer Mariana Cook in May 1996, two months after the primary. "I think he's too much of a good guy for the kind of brutality, the skepticism." Michelle also saw Barack's political aspirations as a threat to the life she wanted for herself—a life fundamentally comfortable, controlled, and private. "When you are involved in politics, your life is an open book and people can come in who don't necessarily have good intent," she said. "I'm pretty private and like to surround myself with people that I trust and love." She wanted to make a difference, sure, but she also wanted a full partner. She saw children in her future, as well as travel and quality time with friends and family. These happened to be among the things Barack had said he wanted when they married, but his entry into politics threatened to create a much different reality. He would be even less available. Gone, in fact. It was one thing for him to surprise her by saying he wanted to go to Bali for a month to work on *Dreams* soon after their California honeymoon. It would be quite another for him to drive three hours to Springfield most Mondays for who knew how many years. And that was if he did not make the jump to Congress or the Senate in far-off Washington. In 1996, Michelle rated the chances as "strong" that Barack would make politics his career. "There is a little tension with that," she acknowledged, but she was trying to keep an open mind. "In many ways, we are here for the ride, just sort of seeing what opportunities open themselves up."

FOR SOMEONE WHO HAD imagined himself running Chicago one day, and maybe the country, the life of a small-time pol in Springfield, Illinois, would seem to hold all the allure of a ten-cent prize at a boardwalk arcade. Yet, his first election behind him, Barack tore into his new work, determined to learn the riddles of power even as he discovered that being a junior member of the minority party gave him virtually no influence. Entrenched senators rolled their eyes at his transparent ambition and his floor speeches, which tended to be lofty and overlong. Some of the fiercest jabs came from black colleagues who mocked his biracial ancestry, his Harvard education, and his home turf in the bourgeois precincts of Hyde Park. To them, he seemed all too eager to accept half a loaf. "He was not any kind of mystery to me," declared Rickey Hendon, a senator from Chicago's suffering West Side. "My friends with all those degrees like to compromise and live in nice rich neighborhoods. They don't see things as they really are. You're not as willing to compromise if you see the poverty all the time." It was a riff that played in different ways depending on the audience. Barack, after all, did tend to see the middle ground as the most likely path to progress, not to mention the functioning of the republic. He was pragmatic. In statewide and national campaigns, that would be seen as a net positive. But in large segments of the black community in the years ahead, the criticism would be rendered in shorthand: Was he black enough?

For all of his pleasure in the power of words, Barack took little satisfaction in scoring rhetorical points if he lost on substance. Sound bites, he said in a 1996 interview, were "dishonest." They masked complexity and disguised "the very real conflicts between groups that are going to have to be resolved through compromise." He had considered the possibilities and limitations of politics for many years before he entered the arena, and he had received no shortage of warnings. Back in Hawaii, former Chicago newsman Frank Marshall Davis advised him that black students emerge from college with an "advanced degree in compromise." A decade later, when Barack gave up community organizing, John McKnight agreed to write a law school recommendation letter, but not before he tacked on a lecture about the price Barack would pay. The cost of surrendering his grassroots role, McKnight predicted, would be the loss of his intellectual integrity. "What you have been doing every day is creating polarities, conflict, and confrontation in order to get to the table. You are a person taking a position that you believe in and that feels a certain way," McKnight told him. "I can tell you that if you get into the heart of politics, the important thing you will be doing is compromise. You will be an architect of compromise."

The discussion had deep roots in African American political history. Modern variants of black political style and substance stretched from the calculations of the Chicago aldermen known as the Silent Six through Whitney Young, the Reverend Martin Luther King Jr. and the Black Panthers, to the post–civil rights era maneuverings of the Congressional Black Caucus and a raft of big-city mayors. Barack and Michelle shared a conviction that racial grievance, however righteous, was not a winning strategy. Results were what mattered most. "We have no shortage of moral fervor," Barack told Hank De Zutter of the *Chicago Reader* in 1995. "The biggest failure of the civil rights movement was in failing to translate this energy, this moral fervor, into creating lasting institutions and organizational structures."

Policymakers could find common ground, Barack argued, if only they could dispense with their partisanship and their invective long enough to discover it. "What if a politician," he told De Zutter as he began his state senate run, "were to see his job as that of an organizer, as part teacher and part advocate, one who does not sell voters short but who educates them about the real choices before them? As an elected public official, for instance, I could bring church and community leaders together easier than I could as a community organizer or lawyer. We would come together to form concrete economic development strategies, take advantage of existing laws and structures, and create bridges and bonds within all sectors of the community."

Barack knew he was making a choice and he could guess how various constituencies might react. He had been leading training sessions and doing some lawyering for the Association of Community Organizations for Reform Now, the grassroots anti-poverty group better known as ACORN. As he entered politics, he alerted ACORN organizer Madeline Talbott that he would have to move toward the political center to be effective. "I may not be as liberal as ACORN members want me to be," he told her. "I may believe some things and do some things that ACORN members believe are too middle of the road." Talbott, inclined to cut him some slack, took his remarks as evidence that he wanted to make a difference and was realistic about what it would take. "He felt the need to give me fair warning, which was unusual. People just thought Barack was so talented even then," she said. Friends sometimes nudged him and said he would be president some day. "He would pooh-

pooh it always and say, 'Don't be ridiculous. I'm just trying to pay off some bills. Leave me alone.' "

THE FRESHMAN SENATOR FOUND his way, partly as a result of the good offices of Emil Jones, a gruff and savvy arm-twister and former city sewer inspector. Although the senior senate Democrat had backed Palmer, he watched with grudging respect as Barack refused to quit the race. In Springfield, Jones saw potential in his eagerness, his work ethic, and his smarts. The freshman struck him as "very aggressive," if a touch naive. "He thought you could press a button and it would be done." Over time, Barack developed a style that was methodical, inclusive, and ever pragmatic. "He wasn't a maverick," said Cynthia Canary, a lobbyist on good-government issues. "There were other legislators I would turn to if I just wanted to make a lot of noise."

Typically spending three nights a week in Springfield, Barack dropped by the ubiquitous cocktail hours that capped the statehouse workday and made friends and occasional allies over golf and poker, leaning across ideological lines to befriend Republicans and some of the more conservative Democrats. Even there, his innate caution came through. One regular at a poker game of legislators and lobbyists described Barack as competitive, yet supremely careful and hard to read. "One night, we were playing and things weren't going very well for me," recalled Larry Walsh, a white state senator. "I had a real good hand and Barack beat me out with another one. I slammed down my cards and said, 'Doggone it, Barack, if you were a little more liberal in your card playing and a little more conservative in your politics, you and I would get along a lot better.' "

Barack, pushed forward by Jones, registered bipartisan successes, negotiating the first ethics reform in Illinois in twenty-five years and brokering a bill that established mandatory taping of interrogations and confessions in death penalty cases. When he was not working, he often had long telephone conversations with Michelle. He remembered storytelling and laughter, "sharing the humor and frustrations of our days apart." Michelle remained unpersuaded. Politics as practiced in Springfield struck her as petty, oily, and, frankly, beneath him. "Barack," she would tell him, "this business is not noble."

MICHELLE GAVE BIRTH to Malia Ann Obama, their first daughter, on July 4, 1998, about eighteen months after Barack started commuting to Springfield. Malia took her middle name from Barack's mother, who had died of cancer in November 1995 at the age of fifty-two. Home after the legislative session ended, Barack described the period after Malia's birth as "three magical months." They sang songs to the little girl and snapped a passel of pictures. But when the legislature resumed work, Barack returned to his weekly commute, two hundred miles each way. The burden of having an often absent husband grated on Michelle, who now had an infant at home and a demanding job at the University of Chicago. Michelle switched to a schedule with fewer hours and lower pay. She welcomed the flexibility, but the workload seemed much the same. "It's like, oh, so you take half a salary and you do the same amount of work," she said. "They don't take anything off your plate." Although the legislature was considered a part-time job, and Barack was usually in Chicago from Thursday to Monday with summers off, he often had evening meetings to attend, legal work to finish, or law school papers to grade. "The strains in our relationship began to show," he said.

Money was becoming an increasing worry for Michelle, despite a joint income that would reach $240,000 in 2000. They were not hurting, but the dollars were going out nearly as fast as they were coming in, paying for a full-time nanny, a mortgage, and student debt. "We didn't pick cheap ones," she once said of their college and law school choices. They paid more each month toward their student loans than they did toward the 2,200-square-foot Hyde Park condominium that they purchased in 1993 for $277,500. Their down payment was about $111,000, with a small assist from Barack's grandmother. And now there was private school and college to think about. Barack continued to care little about money, sometimes forgetting to seek reimbursement for his senate expenses until reminded by an aide. He had no expensive hobbies or tastes and draped his thin frame in a wardrobe of standard-issue suits, business shirts, black sport shirts, and khakis, waiting until his clothes were threadbare to buy anything new. He played golf, but typically on public courses, including the links at the former South Shore Country Club. After he was elected to state office, he sold a black Saab 900S for $2,500 to one of Michelle's former Public Allies, partly to put himself behind the wheel of a more politically palatable American-made car.

IF YOU WANT to be president, it does not take long to realize the stairway to the stars is not in Springfield, even if the Illinois legislature was Abraham Lincoln's first elective office. Barack considered himself burdened by "chronic restlessness," and barely two years into his state senate tenure, he was feeling antsy. The Chicago mayor's office was out. Richard M. Daley won his fourth term in February 1999. His grip on power seemed firm after he swamped U.S. Representative Bobby Rush, whose reputation dated to his past leadership of the Chicago chapter of the Black Panther Party. But Rush's defeat gave Barack an idea. On the eve of a new century, he saw Rush as a 1960s throwback who was not half the congressman his constituents deserved. Against the advice of friends, mentors, and Michelle, he announced that he would challenge Rush, a fellow Democrat. Only after Barack had entered the race in September 1999 did he do any polling. When he did, he quickly learned that Rush, whatever his troubles against Daley when he ran citywide, enjoyed 90 percent name recognition and a 70 percent approval rating in his district. Only one in nine voters had ever heard the name of his challenger, Barack Obama.

In a district that was 69 percent African American and where the median household income was $24,140, Barack promised "new leadership." But he never found his voice, or at least a voice that would connect with working-class black voters who saw no good reason to turn Rush out of office. For all of his brainpower, Barack was wordy on the stump. He struck many preachers, politicians, and business leaders as being too full of himself and in too much of a hurry. Rush and a well-worn challenger named Donne Trotter, a fellow state senator, delighted in attacking Barack for his Hawaiian roots and his bohemian tastes. In this audience, it was not a plus to teach constitutional law at the University of Chicago or to claim the title of community organizer after growing up on a Pacific island. Barack "went to Harvard and became an educated fool. . . . We're not impressed with these folks with these eastern elite degrees," Rush said that year, striking the not-black-enough chord. "Barack is a person who read about the civil rights protests and thinks he knows all about it." Lu Palmer, a black radio host, alluded to Barack's time at Harvard and said, "If you so impress white folks at these elite institutions, and if they name you head of these elite institutions, the *Harvard Law Review,* that makes one suspect." Trotter dispensed with code and asserted that "Barack is viewed in part to be the white man in blackface in our community."

Barack protested that the appeal to street cred stereotypes sold the African American community short and sent a lousy message to black kids that "if you're well educated, somehow you're not keeping it real." Michelle felt the same way, later explaining her frustration with African Americans who "use intellect and race as a way to drive a wedge between certain people in their own community." The attack reminded her of her girlhood: "You talk a certain type of English and then you have to cover that up on your way to school so you don't get your butt kicked. You know, we grew up with that." But even if Barack could find a winning message, which was doubtful, he never had much chance to engage. On October 19, a month after Barack entered the race, Rush's twenty-nine-year-old son Huey—named for Black Panther Party founder Huey P. Newton—was shot during a robbery outside his South Side home. He died a few days later.

Rush was heartsick and Barack had no choice but to curtail his campaigning. A few weeks later, Rush's elderly father died. It was January before the campaign resumed in earnest. By then, Barack had left himself open to criticism that verged on ridicule. He was in the habit of flying to Hawaii for the Christmas holidays with Michelle to enjoy the tropical weather and see his aging grandmother, Madelyn Dunham. Amid campaign demands and a legislative debate about gun regulations, his staff urged him to forgo the trip. But he tried to squeeze the vacation into five days between Christmas and New Year's, vowing to see Toot and "reacquaint myself" with Michelle and eighteen-month-old Malia. On the home front things were going no better than the electoral contest. "Tired and stressed," he said, "we had little time for conversation, much less romance."

While they were gone, Republican governor George Ryan called the Illinois legislature into special session to vote on a gun control bill that had his support and the backing of the Democratic caucus. On the day Barack and Michelle were scheduled to fly back to Chicago, Malia had a high fever. The family stayed put. Barack missed the vote, and the gun bill failed by five votes. Rush and Trotter were quick with criticism, and the *Chicago Tribune* called out Barack and several other politicians by name in a searing editorial that began "What a bunch of gutless sheep."

Barack returned home to the headlines two days later, "a wailing baby in tow, Michelle not speaking to me." Although his absence had not decided the gun bill's fate, he now had to fight the impression that he had been sipping drinks on a Hawaiian beach while the legislature fought to make Chicago's streets safer—at the very time Rush was a public face of the pain of gun violence. Barack, aware that he would lose, woke up every morning with a sense of dread, "realizing that I would have to spend the day smiling and shaking hands and pretending that everything was going according to plan." To compound his misery, President Bill Clinton jetted to Chicago to campaign for Rush and make a commercial reminding listeners of Huey Rush's death. By the time Barack arrived at his election night party, the media had already called the race. He lost by thirty points.

THE THUMPING SENT Barack into a funk, what Springfield aide Dan Shomon called his "morose period." Barack hated the fact that he had been so certain and so wrong. It did not help that he had spent more than he took in, even lending $9,500 to his campaign. The race, he said, left the household "more or less broke." He not only had to ask donors for cash to retire $60,000 in campaign debt, he had to face the people who said "I told you so." Or who bit their tongues and said nothing, which in some ways was worse, for it was easy to imagine their silent pity or disdain. You might attribute defeat to circumstances beyond your control, Barack said, "it's impossible not to feel at some level as if you have been personally repudiated by the entire community, that you don't quite have what it takes, and that everywhere you go the word 'loser' is flashing through people's minds." The defeat bruised his formidable confidence. He began to wonder whether it was all over, this experiment with politics. Maybe he did not have the skills to match his ambition. Maybe Michelle was right when she urged him to find something a little more respectable, a little more lucrative, and a lot more family friendly.

The clouds were slow to part. Hoping it would be "a bit of useful therapy," several friends urged him to go to the August 2000 Democratic National Convention in Los Angeles, where Democrats would send Vice President Al Gore into battle against Texas governor George W. Bush. Although he had set aside that summer for catching up on his legal work and spending time with Michelle and Malia, he decided to go. When he landed at the Los Angeles airport, he made his way to the Hertz counter and handed over his American Express card. "I'm sorry, Mr. Obama, but your card's been rejected," the clerk said. "That can't be right," he replied. "Can you try again?" He had reached his credit limit. On the telephone, he worked out something with American Express, but the week improved little from there. He was not a delegate, and the chairman of the 189-member Illinois delegation said he could not spare a floor pass. To see the show, Barack occasionally accompanied friends into convention center skyboxes, "where it was clear I didn't belong." After watching most of the first two nights of political speeches on television monitors, he decided he was wasting his time. Long before Gore's nomination and acceptance speech, he caught a flight home.

DURING THEIR COURTSHIP and the early years of their marriage, Michelle and Barack had set out to braid their independent lives into a unified whole, finding synergy in the work they did and the ambitions they shared. One of the marriage's strengths, Barack said in 1996, four years after their wedding, was their ability to "imagine the other person's hopes or pains or struggles." Michelle said Barack helped her "kind of loosen up and feel comfortable with taking risks and not doing things the traditional way." Barack, meanwhile, understood Michelle's pull toward "stability and family, certainty." In their different approaches, however, they recognized the potential for friction. "How we approach that tension is going to be really important," Barack said.

One source of strength was the way they pulled together amid early difficulties in starting a family. Julie Sullivan, Michelle's Public Allies colleague, described this period as particularly hard on Michelle and recalled that Barack was "really wonderful," even with his mother dying at the same time. "I've seen that relationship go through some life stresses," Sullivan said, "and they've always just had a really nice way about each other." But as parents, Barack said, they "argued repeatedly" about how to balance their obligations to work and family. At times, Michelle felt she was all but singlehandedly raising Malia and running the household while leading the student community service office. This did not feel like an equal partnership. This was not the life she had expected to lead. She told him more than once, "You only think about yourself. I never thought I'd have to raise a family alone."

On June 10, 2001, Michelle gave birth to daughter Natasha. By that point, on the eve of Barack's fortieth birthday, the downward slide was clear. "My wife's anger toward me seemed barely contained," he said. He had vowed not to be the shirker his father had been. Indeed, his role model was Michelle's father, Fraser Robinson, said his friend Valerie Jarrett. And yet it was as a husband and father that he was most disappointed in himself. Michelle's displeasure forced him to confront the ways he was falling short. His old-school assumptions about gender roles contributed mightily, although he did not see it at first. "As far as I was concerned, she had nothing to complain about," he said. He believed Michelle was being unfair. "After all, it wasn't as if I went carousing with the boys. I made few demands of Michelle—I didn't expect her to darn my socks or have dinner waiting for me when I got home. Whenever I could, I pitched in with the kids. All I asked for in return was a little tenderness. Instead, I found myself subjected to endless negotiations about every detail of managing the house, long lists of the things that I needed to do or had forgotten to do, and a generally sour attitude. I reminded Michelle that compared to most families, we were incredibly lucky. I reminded her as well that for all my flaws, I loved her and the girls more than anything else. My love should be enough, I thought."

When Natasha, known to one and all as Sasha, was just three months old, Barack and Michelle got the scare of their lives. One night, they heard her crying. It was not unusual for her to wake up, but "there was something about the way she was crying," Barack said later. They called the pediatrician, who met them at his office in the morning. Examining Sasha, he correctly suspected meningitis, a potentially fatal inflammation of the membranes surrounding the brain and spinal cord, and immediately sent them to the emergency room. "We were terrified," Michelle said. Sasha, still tiny, underwent a spinal tap. As nurses administered antibiotics, her parents stayed close for three days, "not knowing whether or not she was going to emerge okay," Barack said. "I can't breathe," he told Jarrett when she visited. His world "narrowed to a single point. I was not interested in anything or anybody outside the four walls of that hospital room—not my work, not my schedule, not my future." The antibiotics worked. Sasha recovered. So, too, did their marriage, if more slowly.

IT WAS AT ABOUT this time that Barack most seriously considered an exit from politics. The legislative process felt incremental, the fundraising deadening, the banquets always too long. "The bad food and stale air and clipped phone conversations with a wife who had stuck by me so far but was pretty fed up with raising our children alone." Michelle was openly questioning his priorities, and he wondered if it was time to move on to "more sensible pursuits, like an athlete or an actor who had fallen short of the dream." The door was open at the University of Chicago, where he was teaching popular constitutional law courses. Students loved him, and he enjoyed the mental gymnastics of challenging their exuberant thinking. A tenure-track appointment would connect him more closely to the intellectual life of the Hyde Park campus and deliver lifetime job security. Instead of the long commute to Springfield, he could walk to work. Yet it was an insular world and he was hardly inspired by the legal writing expected of the professoriat. They didn't call it the ivory tower for nothing. Another door led to corporate law, where he could pull down big money in a hurry. Sidley & Austin and any number of other firms would hire him in a flash and gladly pay him a salary deep into six figures. But a decade after he first rejected that path, he saw nothing to suggest that he would find it any less soul-deadening. The same was true of a host of opportunities in business and finance that could have been his for the asking.

Philanthropy, however, caught his eye. The Joyce Foundation, which distributed about $55 million a year to projects connected to such challenges as schools, urban violence, campaign reform, and the environment, was looking for a new president. The job would pay well, it would be close to home, the hours would be manageable, and the work could have an impact. Barack was already on the foundation board, so he knew the players and the mission. He prepared seriously for his interview with board members, working on a strategy with Dan Shomon, his senate aide.

But when he went into the meeting, he was shaking. Shomon said Barack was more fearful that he would get the job than that he would be turned down. Yes, he had been frustrated at times with Springfield and he had felt "completely mortified and humiliated" by the loss to Rush. He was anxious to please Michelle, make time for his daughters, and add some order to his life. But winning the job would mean quitting the legislature. His political career might be over. Board members sensed his uncertainty. One told him, "For God's sake, Barack, this is a great job. But you don't want it." Indeed, he realized, he did not.

Michelle, for all of her frustration, felt his anguish. "It's hard to look at somebody with the talents and gifts of Barack and say, 'Go do something smaller than what you could do,'" she said. Also watching the drama unfold was Maya Soetero-Ng, Barack's half sister, named for poet Maya Angelou the year after the publication of *I Know Why the Caged Bird Sings*. Barack agonized, honestly unsure whether to give politics another chance, Soetero-Ng recalled. "And at the same time," she said, "I think he felt a stirring within and the sense that he was destined for something bigger."

NINE

Just Don't Screw It Up

The University of Chicago brass gathered under a tent with local notables in November 2001 to break ground for a $135 million state-of-the-art children's hospital. Michelle was there in her new role as director of community outreach for the university medical center. Barack dropped by, a local state senator. Through the crisp morning air came the voice of a man on a bullhorn. His name was Omar Shareef, and he was leading a band of protesters who said the university was not giving enough business to African American construction workers. Michelle had only been on the job for a few weeks, but she calculated that this was a community affairs matter. She walked up to Shareef and invited him to talk things over.

Michelle had been on maternity leave after Sasha's birth, giving little thought to her career, when the new job opportunity came up. Susan Sher and Valerie Jarrett, who had opened doors for her at City Hall a decade earlier, proposed her for the role. Sher was the medical center's general counsel and Jarrett sat on the board of trustees. Michelle felt torn about working while the girls were young, but her reluctance freed her to seek a substantial salary and, especially, a flexible schedule. The day of the interview, with no babysitter, Michelle bundled up Sasha, who was still nursing, and took her along. "This is my life," she told hospital president Michael Riordan. Charmed and impressed, he met her terms. She could hardly say no. Not only did the job suit her practical side, it carried the explicit goal of helping South Side communities, a mission largely absent from the University Community Service Center post that she had occupied for the previous five years. It would be her most ambitious job yet. It would also be the last time that her work and her identity would be so independent of Barack.

Michelle saw the largely undefined hospital perch as a way to build on her earlier work and help connect the university with the surrounding neighborhoods. She told colleagues when she was hired that the university hospital, with its staff of 9,500, needed to send people into the community. Borrowing from her Asset-Based Community Development experience, she scheduled staff volunteer days in grittier parts of the city and took trustees and senior staff on field trips. Stepping from a bus at a chosen intersection, the passengers would see in one direction a street of broken-down and boarded-up houses, suggesting decay. Then she would have them turn to see a block of renovated homes with sparkling windows and fresh paint. At her instigation, the hospital supported a Christmas pageant at the Reverend Arthur Brazier's Apostolic Church of God and participated in Bud Billiken Day and the country's oldest African American parade, started in 1929 by *Chicago Defender* publisher Robert S. Abbott. Michelle's father and her uncle Nomenee had belonged to the Billiken club as young children. She also took part in the medical school's summer pipeline program, designed to draw under-the-radar minority students toward science and medicine. Urging them to study hard and recognize where education could take them, her message echoed her work at Public Allies and presaged her efforts as first lady. The heart of her pitch, said a colleague, was an admonition not to be a victim of circumstance.

Explaining her goals for the medical center, Michelle wrote in 2005 that the University of Chicago needed to adjust its priorities. "It's not enough to be at the forefront of medicine if we're not respected in the community," she said, maintaining that the university talked "too much about the negative and we don't embrace all the great assets of the community that surrounds us." Yet she had words of advice for neighboring black residents, too. "The community also has to be open to the new direction and new leadership that is here. And sometimes we have a tough time stepping away from the past." She included herself in both camps: the *we* of the university and the *we* of the black community. Describing herself as "a regular little black girl from the South Side," she said, "Somebody like me, who has feet in both worlds, can help to bridge the gap and create solutions."

WHEN MICHELLE DISCUSSED minority hiring with Omar Shareef, the man with the bullhorn, she brought colleagues from the university. Shareef brought fellow activists. One of his partners, the Reverend Gregory Daniels, was decidedly unimpressed. He complained afterward that the protesters were being fobbed off on underlings "who have jobs to protect or do not have the best interest of blacks at heart." He cited Michelle specifically and demanded that she be removed, claiming that she was working with the university leadership to split the African American community. He called it the "Willie Lynch method," a reference to an apocryphal 1712 story about a Virginia slave master who advocated divide-and-conquer tactics to keep black people in line. Michelle persisted, however, and within a month of the protest, the medical center reached a deal with Shareef's African-American Contractors Association. In return for his promise to end the protests, the university pledged to deliver business to qualified minority-run companies.

Minority contracting was a concern of Michelle's during a stint as head of the Chicago Transit Authority's citizens advisory board—Jarrett was CTA chairman at the time—and it would become a significant part of her portfolio during the seven years she spent at the medical center. She saw the strategy as a way to support businesses run by African Americans, Hispanics, and women, and to pump money directly into surrounding communities. To strengthen the contracting program, she hired the Chicago Urban League's diversity monitor, Joan Archie, a CTA consultant. The hospital made progress and won awards. From the 2002 to 2008 budget years, 42.9 percent of the medical center's spending on new construction went to firms run by minorities or women, a total of $48.8 million, according to university figures. In Michelle's final year on the job, the medical center channeled another

$16.2 million to such firms for goods and services, or 5.7 percent of the overall budget.

Kenneth P. Kates, the hospital's chief operating officer, recalled a meeting where the white owner of a large firm thought he could nod agreeably and ignore the minority hiring requirements. Michelle, however, was "tenacious," he said, and the owner got no more business until he met the hospital's demands. Kates called her a quick thinker who brooked no nonsense yet managed to be collegial. "She would not shy away from taking a position. No matter what it was, you always knew where she stood," Kates said. "She was very good at laying out why she thought she was right. Some people come across as holier than thou. That was not her at all. She never took herself too seriously." After Michelle got to work, he said, the hospital's attention to the black community became "staggeringly different."

Michelle also pushed for greater access to the exclusive University of Chicago Laboratory Schools, which Malia and Sasha attended from an early age. She was among a group of board members convinced that "Lab," a private school coveted by parents across the city, had wrongly reduced its commitment to diversity by race and class and needed to do more. Opponents countered that allocating more slots for diversity would hurt the university's recruiting efforts by limiting spaces for the children of faculty and staff. "Let's just look at the facts," she would say, according to John Rogers, a friend and fellow board member who would later become chairman. "She has this enormous passion to make sure the Lab School remains this diverse, welcoming place for people of color and people of different socioeconomic backgrounds. It took a lot of courage and conviction to push the agenda. Not only to push the diversity, which can be uncomfortable in a public setting, but also the admissions policy."

SMILING AND SHAKING HANDS, Barack worked a Chicago ballroom in the summer of 2003. The event was a fundraiser for Bill Clinton's charitable foundation, but Barack saw it as a chance to talk up his latest quixotic quest: a run for the U.S. Senate. Few people had heard of

Barack at that point, surely not enough to make a cerebral Hawaiian-born man named Barack Obama just the third African American elected to the Senate since Reconstruction. "I saw Barack working the crowd," recalled Geoffrey Stone, a constitutional law scholar and University of Chicago provost. "He was going from person to person, taking their elbows and shaking their hands and looking them in the eye. I was watching this for a while and I thought, 'Ach, what a waste.'"

What chance did he have, this unproven black pol, one of fifty-nine Illinois state senators, a sometime lawyer and law professor who so recently had lost a congressional race by thirty percentage points? It was highly unlikely that he would make it through the primary against a large field of Democrats who were prominent, wealthy, or both. Even if he did, it seemed probable that he would face a moderate Republican incumbent with deep pockets who wielded the advantages of office. Stone found himself standing next to Barack at the shrimp bowl. "Why are you wasting your time on this?" Stone asked him. "Watching you work the crowd like this, it's sort of pathetic. Why don't you make a decision, commit yourself. I think you really could have a career as an academic. I think we'd give you an appointment." In other words, Stone was thinking, *Make something of yourself.*

"He took my elbow," Stone recalled, "and looked me in the eye and said, 'Geof, I really appreciate that. I hear you. I know what you're saying. But I really feel I have a responsibility and a sense of opportunity and I just have to give it a try.' I remember thinking as he turned back to go into the crowd, *What a putz.*"

Much had changed since Barack's jarring defeat in the 2000 congressional race and his flirtation with the Joyce Foundation. He had climbed out of his funk. He had won a third term in Springfield and was driving around the state, learning about places that bore no resemblance to the South Side. Among them were the long reaches of Illinois that lay closer to Memphis and Little Rock than to Chicago. If he were going to build a winning coalition and win statewide office, he would need voters in places like these. He was nothing if not self-critical, and he intently studied his mistakes in the Bobby Rush debacle. He worked on his delivery, which had sometimes come across as wonkish or disdainful. He redoubled his legislative efforts and made the rounds of the pols, preachers, and money people in Chicago who had scoffed at his candidacy. If he decided not to give up on politics, maybe losing to Rush would turn out to be a lucky break, like flunking a midterm with six weeks left until the final. "A wake-up call," said Bill Daley, the mayor's politically minded younger brother. "He didn't seem to get bitter. He didn't turn on people. He engaged people more and worked it. And then he decided to throw the bomb, and rightly so."

Before he could enter the U.S. Senate contest, Barack not only had to convince himself, he had to persuade Michelle. It was late 2002 when Valerie Jarrett hosted a meal among friends to discuss the prospect. She included Marty Nesbitt, a businessman and one of Barack's closest friends, and John Rogers, a childhood friend of Jarrett's and a backer of Barack's as far back as the 1992 Project Vote campaign. Michelle was there, too, of course. She held the most important vote and seemed to be leaving little doubt about how she would cast it. "Walking into that lunch we were resolved we were going to talk him out of this," Jarrett said. "No one thought it was a good idea, Michelle being the most clear that it was a bad idea." Looking back, Michelle recalled her reservations: "It was, gosh, this is going to be painful and hard for me, for us. Let's not go through this again."

Yet Barack was equally resolved. He told the group that he had spotted a golden opening this time and explained why he thought he could top a field that would eventually number seven Democrats and eight Republicans. He laid out his reasoning and acknowledged the risk, especially the blow to his reputation and his prospects if he became a two-time loser. He promised Michelle that it was up or out. "I'm willing to gamble. I know if I lose, I'm probably done," he said. "I have the most to lose and I have confidence that I can win—and I can't do it without you guys."

The friends were sold. "He's really hard to say no to," said Jarrett, who agreed on the spot to be his finance chair. Nesbitt and Rogers, meanwhile, pledged to work their connections to raise money. Early in his deliberations, Barack had toted up the money he thought he could raise. When he added the column of numbers, the figure barely reached

$500,000, roughly what he had raised in losing to Rush in a district with fewer than one-twentieth of the state's population. Barack once mused that Michelle gave a green light to his candidacy "more out of pity than conviction."

For Michelle, getting to yes meant overcoming yet again her doubts about politics and her dislike of political life. She had to trust Barack not to repeat his miscalculations in running for Congress. She was also considering their finances. An improbable victory would mean setting up a second household in Washington when she was already feeling pressed. "I don't like to talk about it, because people forget his credit card was maxed out," she told writer David Mendell. "My thing is, this is ridiculous. 'Even if you do win, how are you going to afford this wonderful next step in your life?' And he said, 'Well, then I'm going to write a book, a good book.' And I'm thinking, 'Snake eyes there, buddy. Just write a good book, yeah, that's right. Yep, yep, yep. And you'll climb the beanstalk and come back down with the golden egg, Jack.'"

The couple took out a second mortgage just to get through the campaign season. On the eve of the Democratic primary in March 2004, the *Chicago Sun-Times* placed Barack's net worth between $115,000 and $250,000. When Michelle joked that losing might not be the worst outcome, friends knew she was not entirely kidding. Michelle said wryly about her role as political wife, "It's hard, and that's why Barack is such a grateful man."

MICHELLE, IN FACT, had been doing a lot of thinking about her life amid the gloom of Barack's losing run for Congress and the dark period that followed. The frustrations crystallized anew after Sasha was born, a period when Barack was traveling the state. She was torn. She felt the familiar tension of wanting to be a good mother and not spread herself too thin. At the same time, she had a sense of purpose, two Ivy League degrees, and plenty of unfulfilled professional drive. She had excelled at work in ways that Barack had not. She had built the Chicago office of Public Allies from scratch, and she had designed and run many components of the University of Chicago's community service program. At the hospital, she inherited a staff of two and would build a twenty-three-member team. It sometimes bothered her that Barack's career always took priority over hers. Like many professional women of her age and station, Michelle was struggling with balance and a partner who was less involved—and less evolved—than she had expected.

Michelle was sometimes in tears "because she couldn't figure out how to juggle everything that she was doing," Barack recalled. Competing visions of herself were at war, he said, "the desire to be the woman her mother had been, solid, dependable, making a home and always there for her kids; and the desire to excel in her profession, to make her mark on the world and realize all of those plans she'd had on the very first day that we met." She was certain that she was performing neither of her main roles well. Yet for all of her frustrations, Michelle was not prepared to leave the workforce and become part of what *The New York Times* dubbed the opt-out generation—educated, accomplished women who quit white-collar jobs to raise their children. Beyond her attraction to professional pursuits, including the chance to preserve her independence and her earning capacity, she doubted she had the temperament to tend children full-time. "Work is rewarding. I love losing myself in a set of problems that have nothing to do with my husband and children. Once you've tasted that, it's hard to walk away," she said. "The days I stay home with my kids without going out, I start to get ill. My head starts to ache."

Michelle realized she was spending an awful lot of energy tugging on Barack to be different: to put his socks in the hamper, hang up his coat, put the butter away, stop smoking, be home with the family. All the while, she was working at the university, running the household, embracing her extended family, and acting as chief organizer of the lives of two small girls. It was exhausting. Through the fog of fatigue, it dawned on her that she was staking too much on Barack changing in ways that seemed increasingly unlikely. He did have a guilty conscience about his absences, he told friends, suggesting that she could probably coax or cajole a few minor adjustments. But she decided the better course was to address what she could hope to control. That meant, first of all, her own frame of mind. "Figuring out how to carve out what kind of life I want for myself beyond who Barack is and what he wants," Michelle said. "I cannot be crazy, because then I'm a crazy mother and I'm an angry wife."

One epiphany came as she stewed over the fact that she was always the one who dragged herself out of bed to feed Sasha. The couple operated on different circadian rhythms, with Michelle usually asleep by 10 p.m., if not earlier, and Barack savoring the quiet apartment into the wee hours, writing, reading, or watching sports. "I am sitting there with a new baby, angry, tired and out of shape," she said. "The baby is up for that 4 o'clock feeding and my husband is lying there, sleeping." It dawned on her that if she escaped to the gym, Barack would have to get up to feed Sasha. So, she started slipping out of the house before dawn to drive to a gym in Chicago's West Loop. By the time she arrived home, Barack would have Sasha and Malia up and fed.

Michelle made peace with the situation, and with Barack. If he was not home because he was out raising money or commuting to a distant job, "it didn't mean he wasn't a good father or didn't care. I saw it could be my mom or a great babysitter who helped. Once I was okay with that, my marriage got better." She said looking back, "The big thing I figured out was that I was pushing to make Barack be something I wanted him to be for me. I believed that if only he were around more often, everything would be better. So I was depending on him to make me happy. Except it didn't have anything to do with him. I needed support. I didn't necessarily need it from Barack."

Her mother's advice helped. "Don't sweat the small stuff. Get up. Get over it. He's a good man. Don't be mad at him," Marian Robinson told her daughter. Reflecting on her daughter's journey, Marian offered a theory about what it took for Michelle to come to terms with her marriage. In Marian's view, Michelle needed to accept the fact that her husband was different from the father she revered. "I just think that's a normal thing that people go through," she said. "The sooner you realize that's the case, the more successful you are."

Barack did some reckoning of his own and saw how unthinking he had been. Although he had lived much of his life in the households of strong women—his mother, his grandmother, and now Michelle—he tended to float above the details, never quite focusing on how certain things got done or where the burden fell. He realized that Michelle was right. The burden most often fell on her, "no matter how much I told myself that Michelle and I were equal partners, and that her dreams and ambitions were as important as my own." His role at home? "Sure, I helped, but it was always on my terms, on my schedule. Meanwhile, she was the one who had to put her career on hold." Whether it was scheduling activities for Malia and Sasha or staying home when the girls got sick or the babysitter cancelled, the task usually fell to Michelle, whatever the implications for her professional life. To some men of his generation, raised in the 1960s and 1970s by women who worked, such observations amounted to commonplaces. Barack, however, was a little slower on the uptake. At the end of what Michelle called "an important period of growth in our marriage," he attributed their endurance to "Michelle's strength, her willingness to manage these tensions and make sacrifices on behalf of myself and the girls." He said he had learned his lesson.

NOT THAT HE WOULD be around much during the Senate campaign. As the race intensified, Barack became less and less available. There was cash to raise, by the million. There were rings to kiss and umpteen hands to shake. Nearly every Sunday, it seemed, he headed to a black church on the South Side or West Side, laboring to build credibility among working-class African Americans who had largely rejected him in the campaign against Bobby Rush. He sounded a lot less Ivy League one day after the Internet bubble had burst, when he talked about U.S. economic troubles during an appearance at Pleasant Ridge Missionary Baptist Church: "We ain't seen no recovery on the West Side. We don't see no recovery in East St. Louis. . . . If there ain't no jobs, there ain't no recovery." The campaign was difficult, and it often seemed that the arrow pointed down. Barack called press conferences that nobody attended. He sat through church services and union meetings where no one acknowledged his presence. He sometimes drove alone downstate, a trip lasting hours, to find just two or three voters waiting for him.

Yet he found himself happy. Really happy. "Freed from worry by low expectations, my credibility bolstered by several helpful endorsements, I threw myself into the race with an energy and joy that I'd thought I'd lost. . . . I felt like working harder than I'd ever worked in my life." Adjustments to the work-life balance, it seemed, would wait.

At first, Barack's six Democratic opponents seemed to pose an array of threats. Dan Hynes was the scion of a prominent Chicago political family close to the Daleys. Blair Hull was a wealthy newcomer who would spend $29 million of his own money on the race. Gery Chico was a former Chicago School Board president who had served as Mayor Richard M. Daley's chief of staff. Joyce Washington was an African American health care executive who threatened to split the crucial black vote. With Hull and Hynes considered the frontrunners, Michelle offered a pithy comment about Illinois politics and the meaning of Barack's candidacy a few days before the Democratic primary. She urged her audience to send a message to the political establishment and to African American children alike. Introducing Barack at the Community Fellowship Missionary Baptist Church, she said, "I am tired of just giving the political process over to the privileged. To the wealthy. To people with the right daddy."

Month by month, the campaign gathered steam, fueled by Barack's legislative success in Springfield, his elbow grease, and, perhaps most of all, his ability to win favor among progressive Democrats, most of them white. Some of the very qualities that doomed his congressional candidacy in a predominantly African American district were now working in his favor. In a stroke of good fortune, it also turned out that his opponents were less formidable than they appeared, with Hynes a lackluster campaigner and Hull undone by divorce records that alleged he had cursed, punched, and menaced his former wife.

In the final weeks, Barack broke through. His campaign husbanded its cash for a burst of television advertising when voters were most likely to be making up their minds. The message, a harbinger of campaigns to come, centered on branding Barack as ethical and upbeat, a skilled legislator who worked across party lines in Springfield and would labor to change the tone in Washington. A new advertising slogan would become his signature: "Yes, we can." At first, Barack did not like the line. It sounded corny. But strategist David Axelrod thought it had a certain simple assertiveness, and Michelle believed it would work with African American voters disenchanted, as she was, with Illinois politics. "She understood before he did that it had some power," said Forrest Claypool, a Chicago politician and consultant who worked in Axelrod's firm. The television ads began running and Barack "took off like a rocket."

On March 16, 2004, Barack swamped the rest of the Democratic field. Surprisingly, given the large field, he piled up 53 percent of the vote and avoided a runoff. He also regained his swagger.

THEN CAME THE BIGGEST BREAK of a very big year: John Kerry, his party's prospective presidential nominee, invited Barack to deliver the keynote speech at the Democratic National Convention in Boston. "We believe he represents the future of the party," Kerry spokeswoman Stephanie Cutter said simply. Barack would get twenty minutes in the brightest of political spotlights just four years after he failed to land a floor pass to the festivities. For a politician who had never won an office higher than state senator—who had *lost* his only race for Congress— the odds of landing the assignment were incalculable. But there he was, putting Kerry's name into nomination against President George W. Bush and pulling his own name, which writer Scott Turow once said "rhymes uncomfortably with Osama," out of obscurity. On July 27, 2004, as he prepared to speak, he had butterflies. Michelle gave him a hug, looked him straight in the eye, and said, "Just don't screw it up, buddy." And they laughed.

Screw it up he didn't. The soaring speech by the unknown politician caught the delegates by surprise, producing paroxysms in Boston's Fleet Center and Democratic households across television land. "This guy's going places!" one newscaster crowed. David Mendell, in the hall for the *Chicago Tribune,* recalled the scene: "Michelle sees this happening and she has tears streaming down her cheeks. I'm sitting in the crowd and a woman next to me is crying, bawling her eyes out. She just keeps screaming, 'This is history! This is history!'"

"Tonight is a particular honor for me because, let's face it, my presence on this stage is pretty unlikely," Barack began. He traced his family history to a village in Kenya and a small town in Kansas. Piecing together bits of his Senate stump speech and the values that drove him into public service, he spoke of the social contract and a politics greater than the partisanship and petty sniping that defined the era.

> If there's a child on the South Side of Chicago who can't read, that matters to me, even if it's not my child. If there's a senior citizen somewhere who can't pay for their prescription and having to choose between medicine and the rent, that makes my life poorer, even if it's not my grandparent. If there's an Arab-American family being rounded up without benefit of an attorney or due process, that threatens my civil liberties. It is that fundamental belief—I am my brother's keeper, I am my sister's keeper—that makes this country work. It's what allows us to pursue our individual dreams, yet still come together as a single American family.

Barack went on to tell the crowd that "there's not a liberal America and a conservative America, there's the United States of America. There's not a black America and white America and Latino America and Asian America. There's the United States of America." He insisted that he was not speaking of "blind optimism." Rather, he was issuing a call to service grounded in the historical argument that progress comes when people fight for it. He wove a sense of optimism for the country into the narrative of his life, borrowing a line passed among black churches, and invoked by his pastor at Trinity United Church of Christ, the Reverend Jeremiah A. Wright Jr. It was the "audacity of hope."

> It's the hope of slaves sitting around a fire singing freedom songs; the hope of immigrants setting out for distant shores . . . the hope of a skinny kid with a funny name who believes that America has a place for him, too. Hope in the face of difficulty, hope in the face of uncertainty, the audacity of hope: In the end, that is God's greatest gift to us, the bedrock of this nation, a belief in things not seen, a belief that there are better days ahead.

The cheers rang on and on. The next day, the circus began. Barack was in demand, for interviews, television appearances, campaign stops, autographs. He was becoming a pop icon. Debra Messing, star of one of the most popular sitcoms on television, *Will & Grace,* soon had a memorable dream on the show: she was showering with the candidate and he was "Ba-racking my world." His Senate gamble—one more shot, up or out—could hardly be paying off bigger. He was famous, and he and Michelle would soon be rich, with the reissue of *Dreams from My Father* and his signature on a $1.9 million contract to write two more books. The looming question was no longer whether he would reach the Senate, which seemed a foregone conclusion. It was whether he would seek the presidency.

IF BARACK WAS a helium balloon, Michelle was the one holding the string. In public, she developed a wry patter designed to affirm his humanity and just maybe keep his ego in check. "Absolutely the messiest person in the household," she said when Oprah Winfrey interviewed them. She called his home office "the hole." When he interjected, she replied, "You had dirty clothes on top of the basket this morning. And I'm just like, 'There's a basket with a lid. Lift it up. Put it in.'" Besides, she would say later, the country needed leaders "who have their feet on the ground." Michelle also tried to put a ceiling on voters' expectations, for their benefit and her husband's. "Barack is not our savior. I want to tell it to the whole country and I will if I get the opportunity," she informed a crowd at Illinois State University. "There are many of us who want to lay all of our wishes, fears and hopes at the feet of this young man, but life doesn't work that way and certainly politics doesn't work that way." It was an observation that would prove prescient.

Michelle played her part on the campaign trail, speaking up for Barack, standing in for him, raising money. She and the girls accompanied him when he went to the summer home of Penny Pritzker to seek the support of the prominent Chicago Democrat, businesswoman, and Hyatt heiress. Very occasionally, the Obamas campaigned as a foursome, an experiment in family togetherness that proved challenging.

Michelle was no more convinced than before that politics was a worthwhile pursuit, at one point that year calling it "a waste of time." But he was in it to win it, as the saying goes, and so was she. On the stump, she vouched for his motives by contrasting her own disdain for the profession with Barack's abiding faith. "I didn't believe that politics was structured in a way that could solve real problems for people, so you can imagine how I felt when Barack approached me to run for state senate," she told the audience at Illinois State. "I said, 'I married you because you're cute and you're smart, but this is the dumbest thing you could have ever asked me to do.' Fortunately for all of us, Barack wasn't as cynical as I was."

In a campaign where Barack's race mattered to voters in myriad ways, Michelle also offered a sturdy defense of his commitment to urban African Americans. The shorthand question confronting the Hawaiian-born, Harvard-educated candidate—*Is he black enough?*—replayed the caricature and the criticism advanced by Barack's opponents in the congressional campaign. Michelle would have none of it. Leaning heavily into her own history, she told a Chicago interviewer, "I'm as black as it gets. I was born on the South Side. I come from an obviously black family. We weren't rich. I put my blackness up against anybody's blackness in this state, okay, and Barack is a black man. And he's done more in terms of meeting his commitments and sticking his neck out for this community than many people who criticize him. And I can say that because I'm *black*."

IN HYDE PARK, Michelle continued to carry the weight of what used to be called homemaking, taking care of the girls' welfare while also pressing forward with her work at the University of Chicago. She started her fourth year at the medical center—her ninth at the university—and continued to build a loyal, tightly knit team. Looking back, she said she loved her work, but it was never easy. "Balancing a full-time job and the round-the-clock needs of my family. Juggling the recital and the conference calls. Making the endless to-do lists that I never got through and often lost. Feeling like I was falling short at work and at home." To make the gears turn at work, she set a standard of efficiency that would become familiar to aides through the years. When, for example, her hospital outreach team proposed a community meeting on a Saturday, cutting into family time, Michelle wanted evidence that the purpose was clear, the scheduling was essential, and the meeting would run on time. "It was never willy-nilly or just to meet," said Leif Elsmo, her longtime deputy. Her colleague Kenneth Kates also recalled the family imperative. Time was valuable and time away from the girls was precious. "The girls came first," he said. "Period."

To make the logistics work, Michelle employed babysitters and paid a housekeeper to corral the flotsam of their busy lives. She also made efforts to look out for herself in other ways. An inveterate list maker, she put herself on her own to-do list, as one aide put it. She also took stock of society's gendered roles. "What I notice about men, all men, is that their order is me, my family, God is in there somewhere. But me is first," Michelle said. "And for women, me is fourth, and that's not healthy." She cared about food and, increasingly, about fashion. She took an occasional trip to a spa. She had hair and manicure appointments with Michael Flowers, better known as Rahni, owner of Van Cleef Hair Salon in downtown Chicago. She first visited the salon with her mother as a teenager, and later took Malia and Sasha. Located in a refurbished church on West Huron Street, the salon was welcoming and busy. Having your hair done at Van Cleef's was a sign of status for black women in Chicago. "A stellar, classy place. If you can, you do, if you know what I mean," said Haroon Rashid, a Van Cleef stylist who founded an organization to support the DuSable Museum of African American History.

Marian Robinson remained a consistent and welcome presence for the Obama family, living less than fifteen minutes away in the Euclid bungalow and working downtown as a secretary. She cut back her hours to help look after the girls on weekday afternoons. Sometimes Michelle took Malia and Sasha to meetings, as did Barack. Dan Hynes recalled seeing Barack at a Saturday morning candidate forum without Michelle. Sasha was two years old, Malia was five. He was "trying to herd these two little kids and they're knocking things over and taking

pamphlets and throwing them. And here he is trying to be this dignified Senate candidate." It was an established household rule, however,
that the girls were not to be trotted out on the campaign trail as props,
although they appeared at ritual election night celebrations. A day or
two after Rod Blagojevich won his second term as Illinois governor in
2002, historian James Grossman bumped into Barack in the produce
section at the Co-Op, a Hyde Park grocery store. Grossman mentioned
that the camera-ready Blagojevich, a sometime Elvis impersonator
who would later land in federal prison on a corruption conviction, had
stood onstage and prompted his small daughter to wave to the crowd.
"If I did that even once," Grossman recalled Barack saying, "I would be
divorced."

It went without saying that Barack's triumphs did not give unalloyed
satisfaction to Michelle. She saw his rise pulling him yet further from
the home life she preferred. Even for Barack, who seemed to delight
in his cascading successes, the victories could be bittersweet. The day
after he scaled the heights in Boston with his convention speech, he
said, "Malia is six years old and, you know, I can't believe it, but a third
of her childhood is over already." When someone asked how much of
her childhood he had missed because of politics, he said, "Too much."

IN YET ANOTHER lucky Barack bounce, Jack Ryan, his Republican
opponent, quit the Senate race because of revelations that he had tried
to pressure his actress wife—Jeri Ryan, who appeared in *Star Trek:
Voyager*—into having public sex with him in nightclubs. That left
Barack without an opponent until the Illinois GOP recruited Alan
Keyes, a sharply conservative black Harvard graduate with no ties to
Illinois. It was a preposterous choice. By the end, Barack was so far
ahead that he had time to cement his star status and earn a some political IOUs by campaigning across the country for other Democrats.

"I don't take all the hype too seriously," Barack said on one of those
trips, acknowledging that he had gotten "some unbelievable breaks." As
a jet chartered by his campaign waited on a nearby tarmac, he insisted
that it was not going to his head. "The attention has come very rapidly

and late. I'm a forty-three-year-old who has worked in obscurity for twenty years on the issues I'm working on now. I'm married with two kids. I've been on the receiving end of bad press. I know what it's like to struggle to pay the bills, know what it's like to lose." He described himself as someone who tried not to get too high when things were going well or too low when the bottom seemed to fall out. "I'm a big believer in not jinxing myself by thinking I've got it made," he added when the plane was airborne. "I get more nervous when things are going well."

Things went well. In fact, they could hardly have gone better. On November 2, 2004, Barack became the country's only black senator and just the third elected since the 1880s. When the votes were counted, Barack had won 70 percent of the vote to Keyes's 27 percent, the largest Senate victory margin in Illinois history. Amid the clamor of his swearing-in ceremony at the U.S. Senate in January 2005, Michelle rolled her eyes in bemusement at the turn their lives had taken. "Maybe one day," she laughed, "he will do something to warrant all this attention."

THE BIGGEST QUESTION the Obamas faced after the Senate victory was where Michelle and the girls would live. It would be difficult for her to move away from Chicago, where she was firmly rooted in her professional life, her family, and her social circle. She looked at houses in the Maryland suburbs, but somehow she could not see herself being happy there. And even though living near the nation's capital would mean more family time with Barack when the Senate was in session, he would often need to make the reverse commute to Illinois, leaving them behind in a city where her network was small. They decided to stay in Hyde Park and find a bigger house—a much bigger one, now that they were flush. Money was pouring in, from the sale of *Dreams*, as well as from Michelle's most recent promotion and raise, which more than doubled her earnings to $273,000 a year. She also joined the board of TreeHouse Foods, which paid her $51,000 in her first full year as a director. In July 2005, the Obamas spent $1.65 million on a red-brick neo-Georgian house with four fireplaces at 5046 South Greenwood Avenue. The home, Michelle said, would be her refuge.

The house purchase, as it happened, was fraught, for Barack had made the mistake of consulting real estate investor Antoin Rezko, a prominent Democratic campaign contributor and future convicted felon who made a habit of befriending up-and-coming Illinois politicians. The house and an adjacent corner lot were for sale by the same owner, but the price of the two together was more than Barack and Michelle wanted to pay. When the Obamas closed on the house in July 2005, Rezko's wife bought the lot on the same day. Seven months later, the Obamas purchased a piece of the empty lot and folded it into their property. Rezko would later go to federal prison for conspiring with Blagojevich to profit illegally from state business, a clandestine scheme under way at the time of the Greenwood Avenue transaction. There was no evidence that the Obamas did anything illegal. They had occasionally dined with the Rezkos. Tony Rezko contributed to Barack's campaigns. Barack called him a friend. But he said he missed the warning signals, including news coverage about shady deals and a political buzz that seemed to foretell Rezko's fall. Barack said of the real estate transaction in 2006, "There's no doubt that this was a mistake. 'Boneheaded' would be accurate. There's no doubt I should have seen some red flags in terms of me purchasing a piece of property from him." New York Times columnist Maureen Dowd asked in print why Obama's "tough, smart and connected" wife, the skeptical and careful one with the Harvard law degree and the eye on the bottom line, did not see trouble coming.

The Rezko incident did no permanent harm to the Obama brand, but it revealed the deep waters into which Michelle would soon plunge. Everything she did would be examined for motive, for plan, for her ability to execute without mishap. She was navigating the political netherworld without a map. Her promotion to vice president of community and external affairs at the University of Chicago raised eyebrows, coming as it did shortly after Barack's election to the Senate. Hospital executives denied to reporters that her elevation had anything to do with his political success. They said the institution was afraid of losing her and that her pay package was in line with the salaries of other vice presidents. This was the first of many times the Obamas would be questioned about their finances and their connections, much to Michelle's frustration. "It's just like, dang, is that what you think? Is that who you think we are? Of all the stuff that we have done over our lifetimes and how Barack has carried himself as a politician, I mean, it's like, is there any basis for that assumption?" she asked in a December 2007 interview with *Chicago Tribune* reporter John McCormick. She was also sensitive to sotto voce suggestions that she was getting ahead professionally because of his success. "The problem is that in this modern day life, where you've got a wife who works—and I've got a job—there is going to be some appearance of something. I can't even think, could I be a babysitter? I really do think about this. What could I do where I would get credit for it completely?"

BY STAYING IN CHICAGO, Michelle found a way to do well and do good without giving up her profession, even if Barack's absences made her life more difficult. Equipped with her new title, she launched the Urban Health Initiative, the most ambitious project of her career. As Valerie Jarrett put it, "We are going to change the way we deliver health care and change life on the South Side of Chicago." It started with a cost-benefit analysis. The university, which estimated that it treated one in ten South Side residents, found that disadvantaged and often uninsured residents were using the emergency room as a primary care clinic. This was not only expensive and time-consuming for patients, who might wait hours to see a doctor for a routine complaint. It was also expensive for the hospital, which calculated that it cost about $1,100 each time a patient walked through the door. Every patient who was running short of insulin or suffering an asthma attack was taking the attention of medical staff trained and equipped to do more complex work. A family doctor or clinic could perform the same service for $100, but one in every four patients who reported to the emergency department had no doctor.

What the hospital saw as a more rational way to allocate resources and expertise, Michelle saw also as an opening to improve options for poorly served residents. The inequity in access to health care was a subject she knew through personal and professional experience. There was her father's long struggle with multiple sclerosis and the haggling that Barack's mother had done with insurance companies as she was dying of cancer. There were relatives with debilitating health problems, limited insurance, and unsteady access to quality care. And, on the flip side, there was the relief she experienced, when Sasha contracted meningitis and Malia suffered an asthma attack, of dialing a doctor, going to a first-rate hospital, and being able to pay.

The scale of Chicago's health care deficit was startling. Among the 1.1 million inhabitants of the sprawling South Side of one of the nation's largest cities, there was no logic to health care, and certainly no system that anyone might recognize as such. Clinics were scattered and family doctors few. Too many patients got too little care until small problems became big ones. Others who were not very sick went straight to emergency rooms. Cook County could barely begin to handle the need. Faced with soaring budget deficits, it started to cut back on public health services. Medicaid helped, but patients and doctors alike often felt shortchanged. As a result, for tens of thousands of the working poor and the unemployed poorer, the concept of a regular doctor and easy access to affordable care was a fantasy. Beyond the simple fact of limited access were the frustrations of seeking care in a part of town where a trip to the doctor often meant waiting in rough weather for an unreliable bus, waiting at a clinic to see an overstretched doctor, and then waiting again for the bus home. Each unpredictable excursion tested the will of the patient, the employer, and those who looked after the children.

In what would become the largest experiment of its kind in the country, the University of Chicago developed the Urban Health Initiative to attract residents to neighborhood doctors' offices or family clinics, a "medical home," where a primary care doctor saw them at nominal cost and tracked their progress and their needs. Clinic staff attended to many problems, from broken fingers and split lips to allergic reactions and chronic maladies. The theory held that if the clinics were nearby and the care first-rate, patients would return more readily for follow-up visits, checkups, and referrals to community hospitals or specialists. Fewer would show up in emergency rooms. People would be healthier. The cost of their ailments would decline. And at the top of the hierarchy, the university medical center could focus on more cases that demanded specialists.

"We have to create a system where people can go. It doesn't exist and we're trying to build it," said Eric Whitaker, a close friend of the Obamas, who departed as director of the Illinois Public Health Department to run the initiative. One partner was the nonprofit Chicago Family Health Center, a group of four clinics where 98 percent of the roughly twenty thousand patients were African American or Hispanic. More than 40 percent were uninsured. The center billed Medicaid and Medicare and collected money from the university, federal grants, and private sources. A sliding-fee scale started at $10 for a visit and lab study. Another partner was the independent Friend Family Health Center, which drew on university money and doctors to expand into the gap created by the new emergency room policy and the closing of two university health clinics. While Friend Family Health, five minutes north of the university hospital, recorded tens of thousands of visits a year, staff members sometimes found it difficult to persuade patients to return for checkups and further care. No-show rates were as high as 50 percent. "People are so used to going to the emergency department. The behavior change is really hard," said Laura Derks, the university's chief liaison to the community clinics.

Michelle increasingly became the face of the project, as well as one of the most high-profile African American figures at the university. She addressed meetings in churches and community centers and spoke with doctors and staff, explaining the university's intentions and plans at a time when skepticism ran deep. "I have seen her in a meeting with the board of trustees, giving a presentation. I have seen her with angry patients and community residents," recalled her friend Susan Sher, the medical center's general counsel.

Reviews of the new urban health project were not entirely positive, and the model was unproven. After Michelle left for Washington, Representative Bobby Rush, who had vanquished Barack in 2000, demanded to know whether the hospital was dumping some of its poorest patients to save money. The Illinois College of Emergency Physicians warned that plans to shrink the emergency department and cut the hospital budget by $100 million would compromise patient safety. In response, the hospital said it was doing no dumping and insisted that time would prove the strategy to be correct.

EARLY IN HIS TENURE as a senator, Barack was already thinking about his next moves. There was really only one, as everybody knew: the presidency. The talk was outlandish, yet also increasingly common. The morning after he was elected to the Senate, reporters in Chicago asked him repeatedly whether he would run for president four years later. As often as they asked, he said no. He called it a "silly question." He declared, "I am not running for president in 2008." He finally said, "Guys, I am a state senator. I was elected *yesterday*. I have never set foot in the U.S. Senate. I have never worked in Washington. And the notion that somehow I am going to start running for higher office, it just doesn't make sense."

The hype never died down, nor did the expectations. He was, plain and simple, a phenomenon. Yet he could always count on Michelle to keep things in perspective. In 2006, his second year in the Senate, he was busy in his three-day-a-week Washington existence and he felt he was making progress on the Senate floor. One day, he called Michelle at home in Hyde Park after a hearing on an anti-proliferation bill that he was co-sponsoring with Senator Richard Lugar, an Indiana Republican who chaired the Senate Foreign Relations Committee. He launched into an exuberant explanation, but Michelle cut him off. "We have ants," she said. "I found ants in the kitchen. And in the bathroom upstairs." She wanted him to pick up ant traps on his way home from the airport. She would do it herself, she said, but the girls had doctor's appointments after school. "Ant traps. Don't forget, okay, honey? And buy more than one. Listen, I need to go into a meeting. Love you." Barack said he wondered as he hung up whether Ted Kennedy or John McCain ever bought ant traps on the way home from work.

TEN

I'm Pretty Convincing

It was late 2006 when Barack, still not two years into his Senate career, approached his brother-in-law to ask a favor. "He comes out of nowhere, like just says, 'Hey, I think I'm going to do this,'" Craig recalled of the conversation in the Obamas' kitchen. "I'm thinking, 'Do what?'" Barack said he was planning a presidential race. "Whoa," Craig thought to himself, "you don't grow up on the South Side of Chicago thinking that somebody's going to walk up to you, who you're related to, and say they're going to run for president of the United States." Handicappers put Barack in the mix for 2008 largely on the strength of his Democratic National Convention speech. Truth be told, his early chances registered somewhere between *improbable* and *not gonna happen,* but Barack and his strategists believed that the 2008 election offered as strong a shot at the presidency as he was going to get. "You will never be hotter than you are right now," David Axelrod wrote in a strategy memo. The advisers concluded that they could develop a message that would resonate, an organization that could compete, and a bankroll that would keep Barack in the game. The last hurdle was Michelle. "Have you talked to your wife about this?" Craig asked. Barack said he hadn't, and added, "You've got to do me a favor. You've got to talk to her because she's not going to go for it." As Craig recalled the conversation, "I was like, you're darn right she's not going to go for it."

For all of the popular excitement surrounding Barack's meteoric rise to the Senate and his place on the national stage, his newfound success had done nothing to make Michelle's life easier except in the ways that money could buy. She was working at the university and doing the lion's share of the work of raising Malia and Sasha, who were then eight and five. Surrounded though she was by friends and relatives, there were days when she felt lonely. Barack was commuting to Washington and somehow had made time to write *The Audacity of Hope*, released in 2006 to strong reviews and stronger sales. Greeted in some places like a rock star, he embarked on a book tour that started to resemble the early stages of a campaign. He was in constant demand on the national lecture and fundraising circuit.

On the plus side, Barack's job appeared secure and he was learning the ropes as Michelle continued her successful run at the University of Chicago medical center. At home, the girls were settled into the routine of a top-notch private school and the embrace of a close group of friends. Marian had retired from the bank to spend afternoons with them. Michelle would later describe the advantages of working down the street from the Lab School: "I've got great access to them, which, you know, you need when you're basically doing it all." As Michelle saw it, a presidential campaign would disrupt even this unsatisfying equilibrium in ways she could barely predict.

Following through on Barack's request, Craig decided to try Marian first, borrowing liberally from the lessons that she and Fraser had imparted to their children. "They talked about passion, talked about doing what's best for everyone. Mom and Dad said you never know when an opportunity is going to arise." Like Michelle, who turned her back on the big money prospects of corporate law because it did not make her happy, Craig had quit investment banking in his late-30s. "I had a Porsche 944 Turbo. I had a BMW station wagon. Who gets a BMW station wagon? It's the dumbest car in the world. Why would you buy a $75,000 station wagon?" Instead, he became a basketball coach and was soon running the program at Brown University. In his pitch to Marian, he asked her to imagine that he had suddenly received an offer from Kentucky, one of the country's most storied hoops programs. Outlandish, yes, but he would accept in a heartbeat, he told her. And here was Barack, a junior senator with huge promise who had a shot at becoming the most powerful man in the world. You shouldn't penalize him, Craig said, for being good at what he does. "Well that's fine," Marian replied, "but I don't think you're going to get your sister to go for it."

MICHELLE WAS at the table when Barack and a small team of advisers gathered in David Axelrod's Chicago office on November 8, 2006, to discuss his prospects. The working theory of his candidacy was developed by Axelrod, a wordsmith and former *Chicago Tribune* political reporter who had done much to propel Barack out of the pack in the 2004 Democratic Senate primary. Amid growing dissatisfaction with George W. Bush's handling of the Iraq War, Axelrod spotted a narrow path to victory for an unconventional presidential candidate who could run against the establishment. The candidate needed to be perceived as a unifier, a problem solver, a change maker, a leader from a new generation. The establishment, in this case, would include Senator Hillary Rodham Clinton, a Wellesley and Yale graduate and former first lady whose husband had developed the richest and deepest Democratic network in modern times. She was trying to make history as the first woman elected president. To compete against an aspiring Republican successor to Bush, Barack would first have to stop the Clintons, and it was clear from the start that this would be the harder task. But Axelrod, David Plouffe, Steve Hildebrand, and other members of Barack's team reasoned that if they could outwork Clinton in the four early states—especially neighboring Iowa, which was rural, midwestern, and 95 percent white—well, anything would be possible. It would be Cassius Clay standing over Sonny Liston, the champion flat on his back on the canvas, stunned by the upstart who trained harder, fought smarter, and performed best when the pressure was on. During his longshot Senate campaign, Barack bought a poster-sized photograph of that very scene and hung it on his office wall.

In Axelrod's conference room, Michelle listened and asked questions, just as she had when Barack launched his Senate campaign after the Bobby Rush debacle. "She was interested in whether it was a crazy, harebrained idea," Axelrod said, "because she's not into crazy, hare-brained ideas." She wanted to know about the finances, about the logistics, about the schedule in a typical campaign week, about what it would mean to their home life and to Barack's relationship to the girls. It was not so long ago that they had struggled to mesh their lives. Now this? Plouffe, who would run the campaign, was meeting Michelle for the first time. "I was impressed by her directness and the no-nonsense focus of her questioning," he said. "She clearly wanted all the facts and I could tell that running was not going to be solely Barack's decision. They would decide together."

When Michelle asked whether Barack could be home every week-end and take Sundays off, Hildebrand nodded his head yes, only to be corrected by Plouffe. "No one had good news for Michelle. There could be no shortcuts," Plouffe recalled. "It would be grueling and then more grueling. The candidate would only be home for snatches of time and when he was, there would be calls to make and speeches to review." During the meeting, Michelle wanted to make sure that Barack, too, knew what was coming. The stakes were high. When he tried to explain something to the advisers, she interrupted to declare, "We're talking about you right now," and he said no more. On his way to the airport, Plouffe called Axelrod, who said he thought Barack wanted to run, "but he's drawn more to the idea of running than actually running. We'll see how he processes the reality of what this will mean, how hard it is, and how long the odds are. Michelle is the wild card. If she is opposed, there is no way this is going to happen. And I can't read yet where she'll come down."

MICHELLE WAS METHODICAL in making decisions. She made lists. She tracked every question, considered every permutation, mapped every-thing that could go wrong. She inclined toward worry. To describe their differences, Valerie Jarrett said Barack was "the kind of person who, the day before the final exam, would open the book, read it and get an A." Michelle, on the other hand, was "the kind of person who, the first day of class when they were discussing dissertations, would plot out how to finish hers." Michelle had said in 1996, when Barack went into politics, that she was trying to learn to be more comfortable with risk, to relinquish some of her need for control. Yet there are no political risks quite like a presidential campaign. An Obama '08 campaign would be a maelstrom and victory would mean giving up her career for four years, maybe eight. It would mean, far more thoroughly than before, seeing her identity attached to Barack's. And, to put it bluntly, it would mean accepting a heightened chance that her husband would be assassinated. "I took myself down every dark road you could go on," she said, "just to prepare myself before we jumped out there."

Michelle had veto power. "The person who was most important in that decision was Michelle," Jarrett said. She framed her exploration of the possibility in two parts. One was logistical. "Okay, how are we going to do this?" she asked herself. "How's this going to look? What am I going to do about my job? How will we manage the kids? What's our financial position going to be? How do we make sure we're still contributing to the college fund? Once I got a sense of how this could work not just for me or him but for our family and the people in our lives, once I had that vision in my head, then I could say, 'Okay, we can do this, I can manage this.' I know what I need things to look like and what resources I need to make sure that all bases are covered."

The other part, more complicated, was the grand conundrum of what would be right for her partner, her family, herself, and—this being the presidency—the country. She saw immediately that running for president was something Barack needed to do or else forever wonder what might have been. And a determination to make a progressive difference had been an essential component of their relationship and their choices from the start. "I've never doubted the mission," she said early in the campaign, "and I've never doubted Barack's ability to carry out the mission." It was the White House, it was his ambition, it was his life. And yet it was her life, too, and the lives of their daughters, their family and friends. "The selfish part of me says, 'Run away! Just say no!' because my life would be better," she said. "But that's the problem we face as a society, we have to stop making the *me* decision and we have to make the *we* and *us* decision." She was in.

"It had taken a little convincing to persuade me that this whole running-for-president thing was a good idea," Michelle explained in late 2007, with the campaign in full swing. "And by 'a little convincing,' I mean it was a lot of convincing, because we had two very young daughters at home, I had a full time job that I loved, and I worried about what it would mean for our family. So it took me a while to get out of my own head, and to set aside my own fears and self interest, and focus on all the good that I believed a man like my husband could do as president." Further, a campaign role for her would not only be expected, but required. "To tell you the truth, I was scared. I was worried that I'd say the wrong thing. I was nervous that someone might ask a question that I didn't know the answer to. And I have a tendency to do that thing a lot of women do, where you get 99 things right, but then you stress and beat yourself up over the one thing you mess up."

The choice Michelle made for her husband was a familiar one, especially to working spouses. Connie Schultz, a sharp-witted *Cleveland Plain Dealer* columnist and winner of the Pulitzer Prize, was in her late forties when she met and married Representative Sherrod Brown, a Democrat from Cleveland. Soon after, he told her that he wanted to run for the U.S. Senate. It was sure to be a brutal race, but he thought he had a chance. She had doubts. "I was really the holdout," Schultz said. "We were in a very new marriage. I was not a political spouse. I knew how you could blow a marriage." As they talked, she came to see that Brown needed to run or forever regret it. As she put it, "The stars had aligned, and I was going to be the big, fat moon in the way." Once Brown entered the 2006 Ohio Senate race, it was only a question of time before Schultz would give up her column, for reasons of ethics, especially, but also of logistics. She made appearances for him, and made sure there were mango slices and carrots in his campaign car. On the bright side, she figured they would share the ride. It would be an adventure, and weren't the best adventures always a bit frightening? She was frightened. After she told her editors that she was relinquishing her column for the duration of the campaign, she opened her journal and wrote in big block letters, "WHAT IS TO BECOME OF ME?"

In Michelle's case, there was one other thing. She insisted, in return for her support, that Barack quit smoking. He was an inveterate smoker and he had tried to quit before. Michelle declared that, this time, it would be for keeps. The results during the campaign would be mixed, but it was not for Michelle's lack of trying. Asked if Barack used a nicotine patch, Craig Robinson laughed and said, "Michelle Obama! That's one hell of a patch right there!" Or, as Barack later joked in a conversation caught on an open microphone, he had a good reason to quit: "I'm scared of my wife."

ON FEBRUARY 10, 2007, the campaign began in brilliant sunshine on the steps of the Old State Capitol in Springfield, where Abraham Lincoln had delivered his "House Divided" speech 149 years earlier. The symbolism was intentional for Barack, who looked for strength and inspiration to the sixteenth president and his struggle for a more perfect union. Michelle stood by his side, bundled against temperatures barely in double digits. Stretching out in front of them, filling the square and flowing into the side streets, was a crowd fifteen-thousand-strong that considered Barack the man who would restore compassion and good judgment to the White House and a measure of humility to American actions abroad. From Springfield, the Obama caravan rolled west across the Mississippi to Iowa, the corn-fed state that more than any other would determine the success or failure of the entire Obama '08 enterprise.

It was difficult to overstate the challenges that Barack faced in becoming a credible candidate, much less a winning one. He was not a polished campaigner during the early going. Energized at first, the candidate was in a funk after only a couple of months on the trail. "Meandering, unmotivated, and hesitant," Plouffe said. He did not like political combat or the shallow necessities of winning the daily news cycle. He needed to build a national organization capable of raising vast sums of money, yet he disliked the care and feeding essential to doing so. He missed the solitary time when he did his best thinking. He missed his family. Arrayed against him, meanwhile, was a deep field led by Clinton, whose political organization had done nothing but win, and former vice presidential nominee John Edwards, a North Carolina trial lawyer who threatened to emerge as Clinton's chief rival. Another obstacle was the perception fueled by much of the national media that Clinton, heir to the best parts of her husband's legacy and beneficiary of his political mind, was a lock to win the Democratic nomination. Viewed through a national lens, it was hard to disagree. For months on end, even after the Obama campaign showed it could raise startling sums, national polls showed Clinton ahead by a cool thirty percentage points.

But Team Obama was making a very different bet, one that required a persistent effort to tune out the doubters, the pundits, and the polls. The Obama forces calculated that they could slow Clinton nationally by beating her locally, in Iowa's first-in-the-nation caucus on January 3, 2008. If they could do that, then deliver strong showings in New Hampshire, South Carolina, and Nevada, they might weaken Clinton's candidacy significantly, possibly fatally, before almost half the country voted on Super Tuesday—the day in early February when her campaign confidently expected to claim the crown. The strategy was audacious, even quixotic, to use words more polite than the ones Barack and his strategists were hearing. One afternoon in October 2007, when Clinton appeared to be lapping the field and Barack's chances looked bleak, one of his most faithful supporters was worried. Abner Mikva, who had served Bill Clinton as White House counsel but wholeheartedly backed Barack for president, had been hearing from friends that the upstart candidacy was doomed. Mikva suspected they might be right, but did not want to believe it. As he discussed the race over lunch at the Cliff Dwellers, his Chicago club, he held out hope on two counts. "Barack is the luckiest politician in America," Mikva said, "and the Clintons always make a mistake."

IOWA, AS IT HAPPENED, all but perfectly fit the needs of the Obama forces. For one thing, the state chose its nominees by caucus, a quirky and complex process that rewarded candidates who cultivated the grassroots and thought two steps ahead—in other words, a community organizer's dream. For another, Iowa caucusgoers were accustomed to giving candidates a good, long look in coffee shops, living rooms, and high school gyms, where they listened and questioned, chewed things over, and questioned some more. In contrast to later primaries, where voters mostly got their information from advertising or the news, Iowans had months to study candidates who offered themselves for close inspection. One October afternoon, Michelle spent more than an hour in an Iowa Falls bookstore, the Book Cellar and Coffee Attic. She delivered remarks, gave interviews to local reporters, and talked with every prospective voter who wanted a word with her. One middle-aged voter, who lived on a farm outside of town, said she was impressed. Asked whether she would caucus for Barack, she said, "Well, I would have to meet him first."

Barack was a senator from neighboring Illinois, which helped with name recognition, knowledge of regional issues, and the logistics of shuttling staff and volunteers into the state. He came across as a fresh voice, and unlike Clinton and the other Democrats, including Senators Joe Biden and Chris Dodd, he had opposed the Iraq War. "I am not opposed to all wars, I am opposed to dumb wars," he said at a Chicago antiwar rally in October 2002, five months before the U.S.-led invasion. The stance earned him a hearing from progressives at a time when the heartland was bearing the brunt of casualties in a war that had cost Republicans control of the Senate in November 2006.

Could a brainy black man become the forty-fourth president of the United States? To do the unthinkable and win Iowa, his advisers believed, Barack would need to show that he was not a one-speech wonder and that he had a sturdy message and a vibrant organization. If he won, he would demonstrate that white voters in middle America would support a black candidate named Barack Hussein Obama. It would be his Good Housekeeping Seal of Approval, helping him not just with many whites who had never backed a minority candidate for president, but with many African Americans disinclined to spend a vote on a black candidate unlikely to win enough white support to become a contender. In other words, a victory in overwhelmingly white Iowa, especially if he could draw a smattering of Republicans and independents, could deliver exactly the validation he needed.

MICHELLE SET OUT to demystify Barack, "to introduce the Obamas the people, not the Obamas the résumés," as she put it. She strode into unfamiliar settings in dozens of cities and towns and returned the questioning gaze of strangers. She urged them to look deeply at her husband, the one who was not white and was not named Washington or Adams or Johnson or Ford or Clinton. Speaking without notes or evident nervousness, she gave her listeners license to share her initial doubts by relating her initial impressions of Barack at Sidley & Austin eighteen years earlier: "I've got nothing in common with this guy. He grew up in Hawaii! Who grows up in Hawaii? He was biracial. I was like, okay, what's that about?" Her stump speech resembled a narrated short story, describing how she learned of their very different upbringings and very similar values, a discovery confirmed one summer afternoon in a sweltering church basement in one of Chicago's poorest neighborhoods. She said it was there, as he spoke with people who felt the world was failing them, that he made plain an individual's obligation to act purposefully in a society too often mean-spirited and unfair. He urged his audience not to settle for the world as it is, but to strive for the world as it should be. "What I saw in him on that day was authenticity and truth and principle," Michelle told her invariably rapt listeners. "That's who I fell in love with, that man." She was saying, *Yes, I know what you're thinking. I know. But hear me out. This is the kind of candidate you said you wanted. He's ready. Are you?* She telegraphed confidence. "I guarantee you," she said one afternoon in the basement of the Rockwell City Public Library, "if I could talk to everybody in this state, they would vote for Barack Obama. I'm pretty convincing."

What began as Barack's quest soon became her own. Everything she said was defined by the goal of getting Barack to the White House, yet Michelle made certain that the message was true to herself and her convictions. She told a story not just of Barack's life, but of her own, always against the daily hum of Chicago's South Side and the people she knew there. To appeal to varied audiences in Iowa, South Carolina, and New Hampshire, she took themes familiar to urban voters and broadened them into conundrums faced by families of modest means across the land. She said people weren't asking for much, just a fair shot at a steady job, affordable health care, good schools, and a secure retirement. The archetype was her father, the blue-collar Chicago water plant worker with multiple sclerosis who managed to support a stay-at-home wife and see his two children reach Princeton. Even the most elemental ambitions seemed increasingly remote to ordinary people, she said, and the decline had come in her lifetime. She pointed to politicians too often cynical and a government and society too often cold. She said, "You can't just tell a family of four to suck it up and make it work."

As for the candidate himself, Michelle declared at a June 2007 women's rally in Harlem, "I am married to the answer!" To her depictions of Barack's achievements at Harvard and his bipartisan efforts in the Illinois legislature, she added the occasional putdown, a familiar tactic from the Senate campaign that hinted at her sense of humor, so often under wraps, and helped show his ordinary-man side. "There's Barack Obama the phenomenon," she said at a Beverly Hills fundraiser in February 2007. "And then there's the Barack Obama that lives with me in my house, and that guy's a little less impressive. For some reason this guy still can't manage to put the butter up when he makes toast, secure the bread so that it doesn't get stale, and his five-year-old is still better at making the bed than he is." She described heart-to-heart talks with Malia and Sasha, often on mornings when Barack was not home, and said, "He's too snorey and stinky, they don't want to ever get into bed with him." *New York Times* columnist Maureen Dowd said such revelations made her "wince a bit." She wrote after the Beverly Hills event, "Many people I talked to afterward found Michelle wondrous. But others worried that her chiding was emasculating, casting her husband—under fire for lacking experience—as an undisciplined child." A reporter asked Michelle about that later. "Barack and I laugh about that," she said. "It's just sort of like, do you think anyone could emasculate Barack Obama? Really now."

As their lives became ever more public, and publicly dissected, Michelle and Barack talked about each other in interviews and on the campaign trail. This was not uncharted territory. Each had discussed their relationship with interviewers and, in Barack's case, shared details in *The Audacity of Hope*. For all of their professional success and their emerging celebrity, they painted themselves as essentially ordinary on the home front, their marriage intact and the two of them feeling good about each other. "She's smart. She's funny. She's honest. She's tough. I think of her as my best friend," Barack said, allowing that maybe he was becoming a better partner. "What I realize as I get older is that Michelle is less concerned about me giving her flowers than she is that I'm doing things that are hard for me—carving out time. That to her is proof, evidence, that I'm thinking about her. She appreciates the flowers, but to her, romance is that I'm actually paying attention to the things that she cares about. And time is always an important factor."

TIME SEEMED in ever shorter supply. Michelle carried two Black-Berry mobile phones, symbols of her split existence. One was for the campaign and one for her job at the University of Chicago, where she worked part-time on urban health issues until she was sucked into the vortex of the presidential race. She began an unpaid leave of absence in January 2008. The job had kept her tethered to a professional pursuit outside of politics, but it was the girls who most thoroughly occupied her thoughts. "I am going to be the person who is providing them with the stability," she said in December 2006. "So that means my role with the kids becomes even more important. What I am not willing to do is hand my kids over to my mom and say, 'We'll see you in two years.' . . . There has to be a balance and there will be a balance."

Michelle took to telling campaign audiences that it was Malia and Sasha whom she thought of first when she woke up and last before she fell asleep. The girls were doing fine, she would say, occupied by school and play dates and the typical busyness of childhood. To keep it that way, Michelle strived mightily for normalcy in a life that was becoming anything but. She instructed the campaign staff to mark certain days as off-limits. When she traveled, roughly once a week, her schedulers tried to place the first speaking engagement in the middle of the day, to give her time to get the girls fed, dressed, and off to school before she hopped a private jet at Chicago's Midway Airport. She kept trips as short as possible and tried to avoid spending the night on the road. When she was away, she relied on her mother and Eleanor Kaye Wilson, fondly called "Mama Kaye," the girls' much-loved godmother. A consultant to nonprofit organizations, Wilson had spent a significant part of her career developing urban education projects, from a welfare-to-work training program to an anti-delinquency project for elementary school children in Chicago housing projects. Wilson was also Marian Robinson's yoga partner. Their instructor was often Marian's youngest brother, Stephen Shields, who ran a studio on the North Side.

Central to Michelle's sanity was the group of friends who, over the years, had become her support group and safety net. Professionals and mothers, they had careers whose fates and fortunes tended to be far removed from the vicissitudes of national politics. Michelle had always had close girlfriends, in high school, at Princeton and Harvard, at City Hall. Linked principally by motherhood, the early gatherings, ostensibly for the benefit of the children, "were for us," Michelle said. "We just shared all those things. And those friendships continued because our girls continued to be friends. Many of those women are still the women that I count on to kick ideas around with, to let my hair down, to vent, to laugh. It's been so important. And I think I had to learn that because Barack traveled. I just realized having some kind of support around, whether it was my mom or a set of friends, was essential to keeping me whole and not so angry or frustrated. Because I could always pick up the phone and somebody would come over with a pizza or we'd just go and have dinner at a friend's and we wouldn't have to cook. And you just share the load."

One of the friends was Sandy Matthews, a children's advocacy group executive married to former Chicago Cubs left fielder Gary Matthews Sr. Another was Yvonne Davila, a publicist and onetime City Hall colleague who lived near the Obamas. She sometimes hosted Malia and Sasha on weekend sleepovers. "We're co-parenting our children. Her kids have toothbrushes at my house," Davila said during the campaign. She described a day when she had felt sure Michelle could use a break. Davila drove over to the house on Greenwood Avenue and swept the girls into the car for an outing. "It's just a silent thing that we as her friends know and do. We've all seen each other through all kinds of things." Good and bad alike, she said.

In the group of friends, Michelle probably spent the most time with

Anita Blanchard and Cheryl Rucker Whitaker, women who rose from modest means to become doctors. Blanchard was an obstetrician; she delivered Malia and Sasha, served on the University of Chicago faculty, and led annual South Side seminars for black girls and their mothers about preparing for adolescence, including matters of reproductive health. Whitaker, a medical doctor from Georgia with a Harvard public health degree, conducted research on hypertension and other chronic illnesses in African American communities. They had children of similar ages to Malia and Sasha, and all attended the University of Chicago Laboratory Schools. The families lived close to one another and the husbands were close friends, as well. While the kids took tennis lessons, the fathers sometimes lolled near the courts, reading the morning papers and shooting the breeze. The group vacationed in Hawaii and on Martha's Vineyard, often joined by Valerie Jarrett, divorced years earlier after a short marriage.

The connections could seem dizzying. Blanchard's husband, Marty Nesbitt, the businessman in the group, chaired the Chicago Housing Authority and worked closely with members of the Pritzker family, later becoming treasurer of the 2008 presidential campaign. Eric Whitaker, raised on the South Side, had run a men's health clinic in nearby Woodlawn and led the Illinois public health department before Michelle and Jarrett recruited him to lead the Urban Health Initiative. Whitaker knew Barack from the basketball courts at Harvard. Nesbitt met Craig Robinson on a basketball recruiting trip, when Princeton coach Pete Carril invited him to watch the Tigers play Ohio State. The two met again in business school, and Nesbitt met Barack while playing basketball at Chicago's East Bank Club. Finally, as medical students at the University of Chicago, Anita Blanchard and Eric Whitaker were mentored by James Bowman, Jarrett's father.

Smart, funny, loyal, down-to-earth, and discreet, they supported one another as they rose to prominence and prosperity. When the campaign began, Cheryl Whitaker asked Barack what he and Michelle needed from the group. "We need you all to be the same," he replied. "I just need to know that if all of this goes south, our friends are still there and that we can still come over and sit in your backyard and we can still come over for dinner." Whenever they could, the friends got together, away from the fray. But it was true that "this running for president thing," as Michelle called it, was altogether different. It astonished them to think that Barack, so recently a state senator, so typically the guy they saw playing Scrabble or basketball or watching ESPN, so essentially a black man in a contest that no black man had ever won, was a genuine contender capturing the nation's attention. "I believe [he] will be president," Jarrett said in July 2007. "It gives me goose bumps and if we continue talking, I'll probably start to cry."

STARTING WITH his first trip to Cedar Rapids on February 10, 2007, Barack had a little more than ten months to win the Iowa caucuses and give himself a chance to claim the Democratic nomination. He assembled an experienced campaign staff that understood Iowa's dynamics in a way that the Clinton team never did. Bill Clinton, deferring to the favorite son candidacy of Senator Tom Harkin in 1992, had not competed in Iowa, while much of Hillary's Washington-based senior staff was slow to recognize the peril. By contrast, virtually every ranking member of Team Obama knew how the first-in-the-nation Iowa contests were won, starting with a willingness to indulge voters their long moment in the spotlight. The needs of the campaign also conveniently dovetailed with the community organizing techniques that Barack and Michelle had studied and adopted—the purposeful personal stories, the one-on-one connections, the principle that grassroots volunteers and voters should not just be asked to follow, but inspired to lead. "Paint the fence!" was one Iowa staff motto, recalling Tom Sawyer's strategy to entice his friends to pitch in, do his work for him, and feel happy about doing it.

Michelle, ever the disciplined student, spent hours reading briefing books, aiming to speak fluently about the Iraq War and the Earned Income Tax Credit, and the contours of the Iowa landscape. On Michelle's first overnight trip to the state, chief of staff Melissa Winter said, "She takes this so seriously because every day not with the girls has to be validated." In a period of thirty-six hours, she traveled to Davenport, Ottumwa, Centerville, Corydon, Lamoni, Indianola, Waterloo, Iowa Falls, Rockwell City, and Fort Dodge. Shaken, she also made an unscheduled stop in Mason City to offer support to a reckless motorcyclist who crashed at high speed into her campaign van and was lucky to be alive.

As the appearances piled up, the staff discovered that Michelle possessed political skills her husband lacked. When a precinct captain in an Iowa town was wavering, many campaign workers preferred Michelle, not Barack, to make the final sale. More than one aide recalled watching as she backed an Iowan against a wall in a high school gym and pressed to know what would seal the deal. They started calling her "the closer." Pete Giangreco, a Chicago political strategist who had worked with the Obamas for years, said of the couple, "He has natural political gifts and he's not a natural politician. She has natural gifts and she's a natural politician. He's rootless, all over the place. She's grounded. People think she's very real. They get where she comes from." This was particularly true of women, the campaign learned, making her role in the duel against Hillary Clinton that much more important. "She connects with women in a really, really powerful way," Giangreco said, "because it wasn't too long ago that 'she was me.'" Jobi Petersen Cates, Michelle's Public Allies recruit and colleague, took the thought one step further. "If you had asked me which one of them would have been in the White House, I'd have said Michelle," Cates said. "Why? Heart. She's a badass."

To succeed in Iowa, the Obama campaign sought to bring thousands of first-time caucusgoers into the mix. They moved beyond the Democratic Party regulars, many of whom had been sewn up by Clinton and Edwards, to court newcomers. They learned their issues, their passions, the names of their children and their dogs. They sat alongside them in church, talked high school sports at the local diner, and invited them to the busy Obama offices that popped up in dozens of storefronts across the state. In that spirit, Michelle put black pen to white notepaper, laboriously writing thank-you notes to Iowa supporters in her neat and unadorned cursive. In the same spirit, far from the spotlight, Barack spoke six times to Douglas Burns, columnist for the *Daily Times*

Herald, circulation six thousand, in Carroll, Iowa. Through Burns and his small-town colleagues across the state, the campaign aimed to reach Iowans whom no number of column inches on the front page of *The New York Times* could persuade. Iowans were the ones who counted most. They were the golden ticket. "It's Iowa or bust," David Axelrod said privately, and for many months in 2007, the smart money was on bust.

Then came the biggest event on the political calendar before caucus night: the Jefferson Jackson Dinner, held November 10 in a downtown Des Moines arena. On his way there, Barack calmly reassured Emily Parcell, the campaign's worried Iowa political director, "I'm a fourth-quarter player. I've got this." Required by house rules to speak without notes, he had been rehearsing. He delivered a fast-paced, energetic performance, painting Clinton as the status quo candidate. "We are in a defining moment in our history," he declared. "Our nation is at war. The planet is in peril. The dream that so many generations fought for feels as if it's slowly slipping away. We are working harder for less. We've never paid more for health care or for college. It's harder to save, and it's harder to retire. And most of all, we've lost faith that our leaders can or will do anything about it." As he worked his way through his campaign pledges, the crowd roared. The media took notice, as did voters.

TEN DAYS LATER, Michelle made her way to Orangeburg, South Carolina, where her singular mission was to persuade skeptical black voters to believe in Barack and his chances. A CBS poll in late 2007 showed that 40 percent of the state's African American voters thought the country was not "ready to elect a black president." Their doubts mattered because the early road to the White House passed through the heart of the old Confederacy. Black voters were likely to cast half of the ballots in the South Carolina primary, sixteen days after Iowa and ten days before Super Tuesday, and Barack needed them. The campaign asked Michelle to make the sale. No one was closer to Barack or had stronger bona fides in the black community. No one told a better story.

To many African American voters, especially women, Michelle herself was a sign that Barack was all right. He had dated white women, but he married a black woman from Chicago. "Had he married a white woman, he would have signaled that he had chosen whiteness, a consistent visual reminder that he was not on the African American side. Michelle anchored him," said Melissa Harris-Perry, who knew the Obamas in Chicago and authored *Sister Citizen: Shame, Stereotypes, and Black Women in America.* "Part of what we as African Americans like about Barack is the visual image of him in the White House, and it would have been stunningly different without Michelle and those brown-skinned girls." As writer Allison Samuels put it, "Michelle is not only African American, but brown. Real brown."

Amid a campaign that had tacked away from explicit talk about race, Michelle's Orangeburg speech could not have been a more direct appeal. The setting itself made a statement: South Carolina State University, a historically black college that made news for lunch counter sit-ins and a 1968 protest against segregation at a bowling alley, a demonstration that ended with three students shot dead by state police. Drawing on themes and convictions that had long animated her, she placed herself, and Barack, firmly in a historical narrative about racism and racial politics in America. She said she stood on the shoulders of Sojourner Truth and Harriet Tubman, Rosa Parks and Mary McLeod Bethune, an honor roll of women "who knew what it meant to overcome." She owed her own opportunities, she said, to "their courage and sacrifice all those years ago" and to the voices of parents, pastors, and elders "who taught me to work hard, dream big and then bring my blessings and my knowledge back to my community." She spoke of her grandfather Fraser, raised just two hours up the road in Georgetown, who taught her that her destiny had not been written before she was born.

Michelle's own success had not been assured, she told her audience, for she, too, had experienced naysaying that could have sapped her soul had she surrendered to it. "From classmates who thought a black girl with a book was acting white. From teachers who told me not to reach too high because my test scores were too low. And from well-meaning but misguided folks who said . . . 'Success isn't meant for little black girls from the South Side of Chicago.'" She had made it, but her life remained out of reach for "too many women, too many little black girls." Reciting details of disparities, Michelle said pay discrimination resulted in black women being paid 67 cents for every dollar a white man earned for doing the same job. Forty-five percent of children from black middle-class families were ending up "near poor," compared with 16 percent from comparable white families. She said, "We know that millions of women over the past decades have been dropped from the welfare rolls and left to fend for themselves without adequate child care. We know that too many black women don't have quality, affordable health care. That we are more likely to die than white women of a whole host of diseases. That we are dying too young, too needlessly. That our babies are dying, too. . . . And we are learning that the dream of giving our children a better life is slipping further out of reach."

Then came the pivot to Barack, first to his story, then to his candidacy and a tribute to those in generations past who "stood up when it was risky, stood up when it was hard." She was asking her audience to do the same, to see Barack in a long line of civil rights luminaries, to trust him and to believe that he would not be defeated and he would not be shot. Months before, uncommonly early in the election cycle, he had started receiving around-the-clock Secret Service protection. "Now I know folks talk in the barber shops and beauty salons," Michelle said, "and I've heard some folks say, 'That Barack, he seems like a nice guy, but I'm not sure America's ready for a black president.' Well, all I can say is we've heard those voices before. . . . Voices that focus on what might go wrong, rather than what's possible. And I understand it. I know where it comes from. . . . It's the bitter legacy of racism and discrimination and oppression in this country. A legacy that hurts us all."

She asked the crowd to overcome the fear—remove the old plastic protecting Grandma's living room furniture, as she put it—and elect her husband. "Ask yourselves, of all the candidates, who will fight to lift black men up so we don't have to keep locking them up? Who will confront the racial profiling and Jena justice that continues to afflict this nation, the voter disenfranchisement that rears its ugly head every few years and the redlining that persists in our communities, keeping prosperity out and hopelessness in? Who will use the bully pulpit of the presidency to call on black men to accept their responsibility and raise their children? Who will refuse to tolerate Corridors of Shame in this country, of all countries? The answer is clear: Barack Obama. . . . So I'm asking you to believe in Barack, but most of all, I'm asking you to believe in yourselves. I'm asking you to stop settling for the world as it is and to help us make the world as it should be."

More immediately, she was inviting black voters—essential, if he were to win—to abandon the Clintons and join them. The next step was up to Barack. If he could win in Iowa six weeks later, these voters might just conclude he had a chance to become president and turn his way for good.

MICHELLE AND THE GIRLS DESCENDED on Des Moines for the final push with an army of relatives, friends, and babysitters. The adults spread out and campaigned while the kids frolicked. It was Michelle's seventeenth trip to Iowa since March. She was bone-tired and on edge. "Exhausted," said Jackie Norris, a campaign aide who often staffed her. "There's an emotional exhaustion that you can never know until your spouse runs for office." Michelle worried that Barack might lose. And yet as the day drew nearer and the odds grew brighter, she worried even more that he might win. What if he did win, she wondered. What would happen to her then?

The night of January 3, 2008, was bitterly cold. Given a chance to see a caucus, the peculiarly democratic phenomenon that had defined the last ten months of his life, Barack headed to a high school in suburban Ankeny. With a Secret Service agent at the wheel, he was accompanied by Plouffe, Jarrett, and two aides. They pulled into the parking lot and were elated to see throngs of people, varying in age and party, ethnicity and class. Barack thought of his late mother, and how she would have appreciated the human tapestry. Afterward, he joined Michelle and Craig, family and friends, at dinner in West Des Moines. He told Plouffe not to call with predictions, only when the results were clear. When the news did arrive, Barack's victory was assured. He would gather 37 percent of the caucus vote, with Clinton slipping into third, a fraction of a point behind Edwards. He won decisively, by eight percentage points, in a state where one year earlier no one had given him a chance. He took the stage, all smiles, at the Hy-Vee Center, with Michelle, Malia, and Sasha beside him, their fashion choices coordinated, a striking family tableau that would soon become familiar.

"Thank you, Iowa!" he called out. "You know, they said this day would never come. They said our sights were set too high. They said this country was too divided, too disillusioned to ever come together around a common purpose. But on this January night, at this defining moment in history, you have done what the cynics said we couldn't do." He thanked the precinct captains, the volunteers, and the campaign staff. He thanked one person by name: "The love of my life, the rock of the Obama family and the closer on the campaign trail. Give it up for Michelle Obama." Thousands of supporters cheered and shouted and grinned from ear to ear. For the Obamas and their growing legion of believers, the moment was electrifying. Tougher days were yet to come, starting five days later in New Hampshire, but there would always be some magic to Iowa.

ELEVEN

Veil of Impossibility

Barack's campaign rocketed into New Hampshire on a high and came crashing down nearly as fast, a victim of its own hubris and a comeback that surprised even his opponents. Hillary Clinton won. The margin was just 7,589 votes, 39.1 percent to Barack's 36.5 percent, and the two candidates each earned nine delegates. But the result reset the narrative and erased the possibility that Barack could knock her quickly out of the race. Amid the gloom in a Concord hotel, it was Michelle who moved among the staff, embraced them one by one, and told them to buck up. Never too high, never too low, was a family mantra. Barack felt blue, but he came to consider the defeat one of the most useful things to happen to his unseasoned campaign. In a long march to the nomination that would toughen them all, Barack faced a political pummeling that was new to him, while Michelle found herself labeled "Mrs. Grievance" on the cover of the *National Review*. Hope might have triumphed over fear in Iowa, but it faced a few other opponents down the road. Washington news reporter Gwen Ifill had been right the year before when she wrote, "The Obamas could not possibly have any idea what awaits them."

In Nevada, eleven days after her New Hampshire victory, Clinton won more votes—if fewer delegates—than Barack, setting the stage for South Carolina, the pivotal battle before Super Tuesday. The pressure was growing and both sides felt increasingly testy. In New Hampshire, where Barack staged large rallies with a triumphant feel, the Clinton troops painted him as condescending during the final debate. During a discussion about likability, he glanced up from his notes and cracked, "You're likable enough, Hillary." Three days later, Bill Clinton disparaged Barack's efforts to distinguish his Iraq War record from Hillary's as "the biggest fairy tale I've ever seen." Spinning the upcoming South Carolina contest, the former president said the candidates were getting votes "because of their race or gender, and that's why people tell me that Hillary doesn't have a chance of winning here." In a state with a sorry history of racially coded language, many African Americans found Clinton's assertion dismissive, at best. "The Clintons are disturbing, telling half-truths and being fearmongers. They're trying to scare white voters away," DeDe Mays, a fifty-nine-year-old black woman, said after attending a multiracial Michelle rally in Hilton Head. "If the Obama camp doesn't do something to counter it, it will probably work."

Michelle did not take kindly to the political punishment that Barack was enduring and she did set out to counter it. She started by lending her name to an unusually pithy fundraising letter. It began, "In the past week or two, another candidate's spouse has been getting an awful lot of attention. We knew getting into this race that Barack would be competing with Senator Clinton and President Clinton at the same time. We expected that Bill Clinton would tout his record from the nineties and talk about Hillary's role in his past success. That's a fair approach and a challenge we are prepared to face. What we didn't expect, at least not from our fellow Democrats, are the win-at-all-costs tactics we've seen recently. We didn't expect misleading accusations that willfully distort Barack's record."

For all of her public protestations that she wanted no seat at the strategy table, Michelle was not shy about speaking up when she believed the Obama campaign was falling short. "If she thinks we're being treated unfairly or doesn't think we're being aggressive enough in debunking attacks, she will say so," strategist David Axelrod said in early 2008. "She does not fold up in the lotus position and start chanting Kumbaya. She's against gratuitous attacks but she's not against defending our position and making sure we don't get punked." Michelle shared this

trait with her brother, Craig, who was talked down by campaign manager David Plouffe when he wanted to fight back harder. As Michelle's
chief of staff, Melissa Winter, said in South Carolina, recalling times
when Michelle was more keen than Barack to go on the attack, "My
girl's tough."

INCONGRUOUS AS IT MIGHT SEEM, Michelle Obama and Bill Clinton
were increasingly measured against one another. She was a recent political recruit—"a conscript," Axelrod said—matched against one of the
most gifted politicians in modern times. Clinton was the commander
in chief while Michelle was still a young lawyer trying to divine her
future. Seventeen years apart in age and vastly different in experience,
they were the history-making spouses of history-making Democratic
presidential candidates, stating their case the best way they knew how.
Both were confident and funny, opinionated and very smart. Both
were Ivy League lawyers with working-class roots. Both had formidable identities independent of their formidable partners. They shared an
ability to please a crowd, although in styles as different as the instru-
ments they played, saxophone and piano. His riffs were showy and
wide-ranging, often roaming exuberantly through complex material;
hers were typically smooth and tart, usually understated, always controlled. His speeches often resembled a State of the Union address as he
ricocheted through Pell grants, health care reform, stem-cell research,
green-collar jobs, Medicare, Iran, the Geneva Conventions, and the tax
code. Hers were more focused, befitting a person who prepared carefully, wasted no words and took her time with the ones she used.

To Michelle, the personal was political. "It isn't just about hope
and inspiration. It is about character, quite frankly," she said in South
Carolina, drawing an implicit contrast with the tumult of the Clinton White House, whose echoes she heard in the attacks on her husband. "I am here, away from my kids, talking like this all over the
country because Barack is different. It is about character." Often asked
how she and Barack were handling the rough-and-tumble, she said
nothing surprised her. "Power concedes nothing without a struggle,"

she said. The line alluded to Frederick Douglass, who said in 1857, "Power concedes nothing without a demand. It never did, and it never will. Find out just what any people will submit to, and you have found out the exact amount of injustice and wrong which will be imposed upon them."

"My fear is that we don't know what truth looks like anymore," Michelle said the day before the January 26 primary, as Bill Clinton campaigned an hour away. "I desperately want change, personally. A change in tone, a change in the tone that creates division and separates us, that makes us live in isolation from one another. Sometimes our politics uses that division as a tool and a crutch. We think we can mend it all up after all the dirt has been thrown, but we can't." Later that day, she directly addressed the former president's allegation about Barack's position on the Iraq War. As a U.S. senator, Hillary Clinton had voted to give President Bush the authority to wage war, while Barack as a state senator had given a speech opposing a U.S. military role. "Well, let me tell you something, I live with the man," Michelle said, her tone combining authority and incredulity. She said Barack had always opposed the war and spoke against it at a risky time for him, when he was launching his run for the U.S. Senate, a detail that "his opponents won't tell you."

Barack walloped the field in South Carolina, taking 55 percent of the vote and beating all projections. Clinton was second with 27 percent. John Edwards, son of a North Carolina millworker, won four in ten white votes, but just 18 percent overall. Barack earned 78 percent of the black vote and 24 percent of the white vote. "Race doesn't matter! Race doesn't matter!" supporters chanted at his victory party. When Bill Clinton commented archly that Jesse Jackson, too, had won South Carolina primaries, a host of pundits and politicians quickly called him out. The January skirmishes made plain that race was bound to surface more widely as the campaign churned onward. Sooner or later, the topic was going to burst into the open, however ebullient the victory party chants.

· · ·

BARACK'S CANDIDACY CAPTURED the hearts of his Democratic supporters in ways unseen since Robert F. Kennedy ran for president forty years earlier. Ally Carragher, a young organizer who joined the campaign in Carroll, Iowa, grew up hearing about Kennedy from her mother, whose eyes sparkled as she told stories from the 1960s. "I know what I will be telling my kids about, and it will be about Obama," Carragher said of the candidate on the eve of Super Tuesday. "What I saw in her eyes is what I feel." A music video capturing that spirit cascaded from giant video screens at Obama rallies and went viral on the Internet when going viral was a relatively new concept. Known as "Yes We Can," the video spliced together Barack's New Hampshire election night speech with scenes of actors and musicians singing the same lines. Its creator was Will.i.am, frontman for the Black Eyed Peas. He said he came up with the concept and the tune because the speech made him think of "freedom . . . equality . . . and truth . . . and that's not what we have today."

The campaign's upbeat call for "change we can believe in" was, in fact, undergirded by a measure of truth telling, and one of the principal tellers was Michelle. Often the more direct of the two Obamas, Michelle did not hesitate to describe the inequities she perceived in the United States at the end of the Bush years, when the Census Bureau estimated that 39.8 million people lived below the poverty line. That meant an individual who earned less than $211 a week and a family of four that collected less than $425. The poverty rate was at an eleven-year high and half the households in the country earned less than $50,303 annually, with corresponding constraints on their access to education and opportunity. The Obamas had recently become wealthy—they reported income of $4.2 million in 2007, almost entirely from book royalties. But Michelle knew the stories behind the numbers through her work on the South Side, her years at Public Allies, and the lives of her own extended family, many of whom were still in the working class or just a decade or two beyond it.

"I look at my life since I was a little girl and things have gotten harder, progressively harder, for regular people. The struggle has been getting worse, not better," she told supporters in Hilton Head, South

Carolina. "And we're still a nation that's a little too mean. I wish mean worked, because we're good at it. Our tone is bad and we've grown to believe that somehow mean talk is tough talk . . . and we reward it. Not just in politics, but we reward it in every sliver of our culture."

The same day, up the road in rural Estill, Michelle carried her message to more than 100 black voters in a storefront office of Obama for America. "This nation is broken," she said. "Our souls are broken and we've lost our way. We have lost our will and the understanding that we have to sacrifice and compromise for one another." Ordinary people were being thwarted again and again, she said, even when their goals were clear and the bar was set. "You reach the bar and they move it. This is true regardless of the color of your skin. This is true regardless of your gender. This is the truth of living in America."

The image of the moving bar, which she used for months, suggested a faceless establishment and a rigged game. In September 2007, she counseled the National Conference of Black Women "to understand what we are up against. You see, for so long, we've been asked to compete in a game where we are given few of the rules and none of the resources to win. And when we do the impossible, when we beat the odds and we play the game better than those who made up the rules, then they do what they do. They change the rules, they move the bar and too many are left behind." *They* were faceless leaders, privileged, unconcerned, or out of touch. The result, she said, was often fear and uncertainty that created a "veil of impossibility." Change would come only when voters became "frustrated and a little angry about the way things are going." In an appeal that could have been pulled from a community organizing handbook, she said "regular folks" needed to talk up Barack's candidacy. They needed to vote their interests and not their fears.

As she toggled between conundrums of race and class, Michelle's campaign message contained both ends of Barack's elemental equation of the world as it is and the world as it should be, the first representing need, the second signifying purpose. For all of the gloom, she always tacked back optimistically to Barack and what he could do for the country. It was Barack Obama, she said, who best represented a step toward fairness, integrity, decency, and dignity—and most represented a break with the established ways. Not Hillary Clinton, not a Republican. "I'm here right now," she said in Hilton Head, "because I think that the only person in this race who has an honest chance of changing the game—not playing it better than those who have played it, but changing the game—is my husband, Barack Obama." She took to ending her speeches with a story about a ten-year-old black girl who approached her in a barber shop in Newberry, South Carolina, birthplace of nineteenth-century AME Church leader Henry McNeal Turner. The girl told Michelle, "If Barack Obama becomes the next president of the United States, it will be historical." Michelle asked what that meant to her. "It means that I can dream of being anything I imagine," the girl replied and began to sob.

"That little girl started to cry, see, because she's 10 and she gets it," Michelle told her audience. "She knows what happens when that veil of impossibility suffocates you, when you live in a country that tells you what you can't do and who you can't be before you even get a chance, when you live in a country that gives education to some and not to all, when you live in a country where politics trumps all reason. That's what's at stake in this election."

KATIE MCCORMICK LELYVELD's phone rang. It was February 18, 2008, and the young press secretary was in Wisconsin on a campaign swing with Michelle, her boss. At the other end of the line were Bill Burton and Dan Pfeiffer, senior members of the campaign's communications staff, calling from Chicago. They had seen the reports and they wanted to know what had gone wrong. Lelyveld, too, had seen the news reports, but did not think anything was amiss. "It's her normal sort of thing," Lelyveld recalled saying. "She doesn't speak in sound bites. She was getting to a bigger point that everybody understood. There's not time in a short broadcast to get there." The Chicago men, already fielding calls from reporters, were worried. When Lelyveld hung up, she flipped the Play button on her ubiquitous pocket recorder and began to transcribe the offending part of the speech.

"Hope is making a comeback," Michelle had said that morning in

Milwaukee, "and, let me tell you, for the first time in my adult life, I am proud of my country. Not just because Barack is doing well, but I think people are hungry for change." *For the first time in my adult life, I am proud of my country.* Fourteen words that would be repeated over and over on the airwaves, dissected by commentators and held aloft by Republican critics as proof positive that Michelle was not the good and decent American patriot that she pretended to be.

The next day, Cindy McCain, wife of Republican candidate John McCain, volunteered, "I'm proud of my country. I don't know about you, if you heard those words earlier. I'm very proud of my country." On Fox News, anti-Obama commentator Sean Hannity told his audience, "To think your country is mean and you have nothing to be proud of, I think that's a big issue." Some critics read into her remarks the idea that she was only proud because Barack, whom she had publicly called "the answer," was winning. Others demanded to know how she could not be proud of a country where she could graduate from Princeton and Harvard, earn a small fortune, and stand a decent chance of taking up residence in the White House. "We've grown up and lived in the same era. And yet her self-absorbed attitude is completely foreign to me," wrote conservative columnist Michelle Malkin, the Oberlin-educated daughter of parents from the Philippines. "What planet is she living on?"

Michelle Obama's remarks that day were not accidental or ad-libbed. She made the same point twice, using nearly identical language several hours apart. Moving from Milwaukee to Madison, the state capital, she said, "Hope is making a comeback. And let me tell you something. For the first time in my adult lifetime, I'm really proud of my country. And not just because Barack has done well, but because I think people are hungry for change. And I have been desperate to see our country moving in that direction and just not feeling so alone in my frustration and disappointment. I've seen people who are hungry to be unified around some basic, common issues and it's made me proud. I feel privileged to be a part of even witnessing this, traveling around states all over this country and being reminded that there is more that unites us than divides us, that the struggles of a farmer in Iowa are no different than what's happening on the South Side of Chicago, that people are feeling the same pain and wanting the same things for their families."

To Michelle's staff and many in her audience, what she said was a commonplace—not remarkable, not meriting the firestorm that followed. What, they wondered, was the big deal? No less respected a figure than Colin Powell, the first African American chairman of the Joint Chiefs of Staff, had written in his autobiography, *My American Journey,* a dozen years earlier, "The army made it easier for me to love my country, with all its flaws." Paul Schmitz, Michelle's former Public Allies colleague, happened to be in the front row in Milwaukee, his video camera rolling. "No one who was there thought they had heard a gaffe. No one leaving there thought, 'Oh, boy, we've got a problem,'" said Schmitz, a white man. "It all made absolute sense. I could have said the same thing. How many people do you know who said, 'A guy with the name Barack Hussein Obama? There's no way. It can't happen.' That was a normal conversation at that time. I think that was common knowledge, that the country really had shown that it had grown up."

Back in Chicago, historian Timuel Black thought nothing of it, certain that Michelle was "expressing a feeling that millions and millions of African Americans feel." Lawyer James Montgomery, who like Black had tasted prejudice, did not think Michelle had misspoken. "That was vintage truth: 'Here I am, my husband is running for president. He is black. And Iowa has just given him a resounding victory,'" said the former civil rights attorney, who lived two doors north of the Obamas in Hyde Park. "I think it really says that deep down in her innards, she had doubts about whether or not a white majority would elect a black president. In her day, she has seen a lot of reasons in Chicago not to be proud of her country."

Inside Chicago headquarters, however, the campaign leadership uttered a collective "Uh-oh." They focused on a broad electorate needing to be persuaded that Barack was safe and sufficiently mainstream. Seen through that prism, Michelle's remarks were unhelpful, to say the least. The damage control started quickly. "What she meant," Burton wrote to reporters, "is that she's really proud at this moment." Barack came to his wife's defense, pointing out her longtime skepticism about politics. He said the comment was misunderstood. "What she meant was, this is the first time that she's been proud of the politics of America. Because she's pretty cynical about the political process, and with good reason, and she's not alone," he said.

At her next public event, two days later in Rhode Island, Michelle herself tried to explain. "I'm proud in how Americans are engaging in the political process," she said. "For the first time in my lifetime, I'm seeing people rolling up their sleeves in a way that I haven't seen." A reporter asked whether she had, in fact, always been proud of her country. "Absolutely," she said. Reflecting on the episode after the caravan had moved on, adviser Robert Gibbs said he was just glad the moment had occurred early in the campaign, and not on the eve of the November election.

REACTIONS TO MICHELLE'S REMARKS exposed a divide in what people were prepared to believe about her. To her fans, she was speaking truth to power, being authentic, keeping it real. She saw problems and identified solutions, using her own narrative of renewed hope to reassure the skeptical and rally the tuned-out. To her foes, she was a naysayer, an ingrate, and a snob who failed to appreciate what the country had done for her and her black Icarus of a husband. The budding anti-Michelle narrative suggested that she was not only divisive, but quite possibly dangerous, maybe treasonous. Her Princeton thesis would be invoked to support that view and so would her membership in Trinity United Church of Christ, with its "unashamedly black and unapologetically Christian" credo. Juan Williams, a black commentator for Fox News, would say later that Michelle has "this Stokely Carmichael in a designer dress thing going." When Michelle greeted Barack onstage at campaign events with a fist bump, a Fox personality asked rhetorically if it was a "terrorist fist jab." Unfounded reports lit up the right-wing blogosphere that Michelle had said bad things about a country run by "whitey."

Michelle dismissed the increasingly fantastical allegations as preposterous, and *The New Yorker* spoofed the emerging caricature on its cover. The cartoon depicted Michelle as an Afro-wearing jihadist in combat boots, a Kalashnikov slung over her shoulder, fist-bumping Barack in the Oval Office. The artist, Barry Blitt, said he was trying to reveal the criticism "as the fear-mongering ridiculousness that it is." The line of attack reached the ears of Malia, who turned ten on July 4, 2008. She asked Barack one day, when Michelle was within earshot, why people on the news were saying that "Mom doesn't love her country." Barack explained that sometimes people in politics say mean things. Malia replied, "Yeah, that's nuts."

Looking for explanations, Michelle's law school friend Verna Williams pointed to the relative novelty in national politics of an accomplished, assertive, professional black woman. She said the critics, so quick to turn to stereotypes, were essentially asking, "How can Michelle Obama be First Lady when she's no lady at all?" Through generations of American history, ladyhood was the province of white women alone. The model political wife in popular memory was obsequious, not to mention white. Making news for anything other than glowing encomiums directed toward the candidate was never the goal. As Marjorie Williams once wrote of Barbara Bush, the tart-tongued wife of George H. W. Bush, "It is one of the chief requirements of her job that she say as few genuinely memorable things as possible." Wives were not expected to say, as Michelle had said already, that the country had gone to war in Iraq because U.S. leaders "were not willing to tell us the truth," or that it would be nice to have someone in the White House "who understands the Constitution, particularly as we have seen it obliterated." In Michelle's case, partisan pushback that might have greeted any assertive political spouse was reinforced by disdain grounded in racial prejudice. The vitriol pooled and eddied in countless Internet comments sections, demonstrating that Michelle was becoming a target in her own right. "You are amazed sometimes at how deep the lies can be," she told *The New York Times*. "I mean, 'whitey'? . . . Anyone who says that doesn't know me. They don't know the life I've lived. They don't know anything about me."

With decisive victories in Wisconsin and Hawaii on February 19, Barack had won ten contests in a row by an average margin of thirty-four percentage points, leaving Clinton ever further behind in the delegate chase. But as she steered toward friendlier ground in Texas and Ohio, the New York senator showed no inclination to quit, telling voters that she was the known quantity, the one who had been close to power, the one they could trust. "This is the choice we face," she said. "One of us is ready to be commander in chief in a dangerous world. One of us has faced serious Republican opposition in the past. And one of us is ready to do it again." Indeed, Clinton would win the Texas and Ohio popular vote, sending the Obamas and much of Barack's high command into a funk as they trudged toward certain defeat seven weeks later in Pennsylvania. Before the Pennsylvania vote, things would get worse, in the shape of the Reverend Jeremiah A. Wright Jr. and the sound of his sermons looping through the mediaplex. The eruption prompted Barack to give his most explicit speech yet on race and racism in American society, a shoal his political strategists had hoped to skirt.

WHO WAS Jeremiah Wright? Barack described him as an inspirational and insightful South Side figure, a deep-thinking pastor who "helped bring me to Jesus and helped bring me to church." He cared about social justice, supported the HIV/AIDS community, developed a church mission in Africa, and delivered the sermon that inspired the title of Barack's second book, *The Audacity of Hope*. Something of a mentor to Barack during his early Chicago years, Wright married Barack and Michelle and baptized Malia and Sasha. On the campaign trail, Michelle would often begin her remarks to African American church audiences by offering greetings from Pastor Wright. But the theatrical, dashiki-wearing character who emerged during the campaign hardly resembled Barack's early portrait. Even allowing for the speedy reduction of Wright to media caricature, it was hard to square Barack's initial description with the shotgun sprays of anti-establishment, anti-government bombast in Wright's sermons.

The campaign staff knew in February 2007 that Wright's presence in the Obama camp created a quandary. He was due to deliver the invocation at Barack's presidential announcement in Springfield, but advisers argued that newly published details of a Wright sermon could swamp coverage of the speech. "Fact number one, we've got more black men in prison than there are in college," Wright preached, according to *Rolling Stone*. "Fact number two: Racism is how this country was founded and how this country is still run! We are deeply involved in the importing of drugs, the exporting of guns and the training of professional killers. . . . We believe in white supremacy and black inferiority and believe it more than we believe in God." Alerted to the magazine article, Barack reluctantly informed Wright that he would not have a speaking part on announcement day. He invited the minister to pray beforehand with the family, which he did.

It was on March 13, 2008, nine days after Barack's draining loss in Texas and Ohio, that Wright emerged as a full-blown campaign problem. The source was an ABC News report, three minutes, twenty-five seconds long, that juxtaposed short excerpts from Wright's sermons with supportive comments from Barack about his twenty years in the Trinity congregation. In a 2003 clip, Wright blamed American authorities for imprisoning excessive numbers of African Americans and expecting citizens "to sing 'God *Bless* America.' No, no, no! God *damn* America! That's in the Bible for killing innocent people. God *damn* America for treating our citizens as less than human! God *damn* America for as long as she acts like she is God and she is supreme."

In another sermon, from September 16, 2001, five raw days after the terrorist attacks on the World Trade Center and the Pentagon, Wright suggested that the attacks were payback for American violence and misdeeds abroad. He pointed out that far more people had died when the United States dropped a pair of atomic bombs on Japan in an effort to end World War II. "America's chickens," he declared, "are coming home to roost." The ABC piece quoted Barack likening his pastor, who had recently retired, to "an old uncle who sometimes says things I don't agree with." It also included Trinity members coming to Wright's defense. "No, I wouldn't call it radical," one woman told the camera crew. "I'd call it being black in America."

The news about Wright—propelled by the video images that became ubiquitous—prompted a new wave of scrutiny of Barack's identity and intentions. At a time when the Clinton campaign was trying to paint him as callow and unelectable, skeptics were asking whether a candidate with a preacher like Wright could be trusted with the keys to the White House. Barack had lost white voters by a large margin in Ohio, and now, as the nomination fight dragged on, Pennsylvania was looming, followed by Indiana and North Carolina. Fresh controversy the campaign did not need. Barack released a statement calling Wright's statements "inflammatory and appalling." But the statement only took him so far. "What you had was a moment where all the suspicions and misunderstandings that are embedded in our racial history were suddenly laid bare," Barack later told Dan Balz of *The Washington Post.* "If we had not handled the Reverend Wright episode properly, I think we could have lost."

MARTY NESBITT WAS in Chicago when he got a call from Barack, who was campaigning in Indiana. Barack reported that he was sitting with Eric Whitaker and Valerie Jarrett and they were holding an empty chair for him. Nesbitt had intended to take that campaign swing, but his wife was about to give birth. He had been following the news. "This Jeremiah Wright thing is a blessing in disguise," he said into the phone. Barack burst out laughing and reported to the others what Nesbitt had said. Nesbitt explained that Wright had created an obstacle, for sure, but one that Barack could remove. He could do it with a speech, often considered by Barack but never delivered, about race in America. Only Barack could give that address, Nesbitt went on, not simply because he identified himself as a black man, but because he had a white mother and a white grandmother and had thought deeply about racial issues for much of his adult life. Nesbitt said that if Barack gave the powerful speech that everyone knew he could give—and that Clinton, as a white woman, could not—it would be "game over." Barack, who had already alerted his advisers, said, "I guess I have to give the speech, then."

Michelle, too, saw the Wright conflagration as a moment when Barack needed to step forward. "The conversation that Barack and I had was, 'This is the opportunity. This is the reason why you're here.

This is why you're in this race, because there is a perspective, a voice, that you can bring to this conversation that is needed and that no one else can do or say," Michelle explained. "What I said to Barack was, 'I know you have it in your head. I know exactly what you want to say to the American people about this and how complex it is.' And this is what leadership is all about. This is the opportunity, and this is just one example of how Barack will have to lead."

Once the decision was made to give the speech in Philadelphia, Michelle made a rare call to campaign manager David Plouffe to ask whether an arena with perhaps a hundred seats for spectators, apart from the media, was big enough. "We need energy and fight and passion, not something that will come across as a dry lecture," Plouffe recalled Michelle telling him. She said Barack needed "to see supportive faces and be boosted." Plouffe reviewed the situation with his colleagues. The campaign stuck with its plan to hold the event at the National Constitution Center. He explained the reasoning to Michelle, who would travel to Philadelphia for moral support, as would Nesbitt, Jarrett, and Eric Holder, the future attorney general. "Michelle was very good in moments like this," Plouffe said. "She didn't raise many questions about the campaign broadly, but when she did, it was with good reason. Once she determined we had worked things through thoroughly, she was generally satisfied, and that was the case now."

AFTER LABORING DEEP into the night to get the words right, Barack delivered the speech on March 18 against a backdrop of American flags stationed onstage like sentinels. With nods toward Abraham Lincoln, the Constitution, and the guiding purpose of his own political quest, he titled the address "A More Perfect Union." It was, in many ways, a speech of translation, the work of a thinking man with a window into many worlds, describing black and white to each other. More significantly, it was a speech of explanation, the product of a politician born with brown skin feeling obligated to describe to a white audience what he was not, and what he was. Barack wove his personal history, and Michelle's, through an account of American history informed by the undeniable fact that an African American man married to a descendant of slaves stood on the threshold of the presidency. The thirty-eight-minute address contained elements of their familiar depiction of the world as it is and the world as it should be, but he added an intermediate step: the world as it was becoming.

There was no doubt, Barack said, that black bitterness and white resentment persisted, fueling mutual anger and a sense of "racial stalemate." But Wright's "profound mistake," he said, was to portray U.S. society as static, as being just as racist as it was when the preacher was coming of age in the 1950s and 1960s, when "segregation was still the law of the land and opportunity was systematically constricted." Those were the times of Jim Crow, Barack reminded his audience, when black people were excluded from labor unions, police departments, and certain neighborhoods, when banks denied loans to black business owners, and the fabric of black families eroded, partly due to the shame and frustration that flowed from the lack of economic opportunity. Those profound injustices weighed black people down, he said, and still informed the views of men and women of Wright's generation—a generation that included, not incidentally, Fraser and Marian Robinson. But where Wright went wrong, Barack said, was in his failure to credit evidence "that America can change."

Barack told worried campaign advisers that he had attended Trinity much less frequently in recent years and did not recall hearing the most inflammatory statements. He nonetheless attempted to explain them, describing Wright's performances as bits of set-piece theater familiar to black congregants across the country. From the pews, he said, worshippers felt free to pick and choose from the rhetorical offerings, just as the faithful do in any religious denomination. "The fact that so many people are surprised to hear that anger in some of Reverend Wright's sermons," Barack said, "simply reminds us of the old truism that the most segregated hour in American life occurs on Sunday morning."

Despite the uproar and the pain, Barack said in Philadelphia that he would not dissociate himself from his pastor. "I can no more disown him than I can disown the black community," he said. "I can no more disown him than I can my white grandmother—a woman who helped raise me, a woman who sacrificed again and again for me, a woman who loves me as much as she loves anything in this world. But a woman who once confessed her fear of black men who passed her by on the street, and who on more than one occasion has uttered racial or ethnic stereotypes that made me cringe. These people are a part of me and they are a part of America, this country that I love." Looking ahead, he counseled the African American community to accept "the burdens of our past without becoming victims of our past." He urged the white community to acknowledge that "what ails the African American community does not just exist in the minds of black people, that the legacy of discrimination, and current incidents of discrimination, while less overt than in the past, are real and must be addressed."

The speech was widely viewed as a political success. It stanched the bleeding caused by the Wright sermons and, for voters willing to be reassured, it offered reason to be so. In Barack's circle, Nesbitt was photographed in the audience, watching silently, a tear trickling down his cheek. Michelle said what Barack "did in his speech was give voice to every emotion I have." She knew better than anyone how Barack had lived the words he spoke, and how he had arrived at them. "I was incredibly proud of what he said. Everything he said spoke to me in so many ways. Every word that he uttered was clarifying and wise and kind and unifying." She predicted that the speech was "only the beginning of a long dialogue that we have to have," and that Barack would lead it, "unlike many before who have just shied away from it because it's hard." Her own view, she made clear: "I'm not afraid of the conversation. I'm desperate for us to have it so that we can move beyond it."

THE OBAMA CAMPAIGN WHEEZED its way, exhausted and disheartened, through the predicted loss in Pennsylvania. The night after the defeat, the high command met around the dinner table at the Obamas' Hyde Park house to focus anew. Still leading in the Democratic delegate count, they saw a new chance in North Carolina and Indiana to do what they had repeatedly failed to do, all the way back to New Hampshire, and put Clinton away. Just as they were building momentum, however, Wright resurfaced with a batch of virulent statements bordering on the bizarre. Barack realized he needed to say something more. He called the performance "appalling" and a "spectacle." It "contradicts everything I'm about and who I am," he said. "I have spent my entire adult life trying to bridge the gap between different kinds of people. That's in my DNA, trying to promote mutual understanding." He said Michelle was "similarly angered." Feeling wounded, betrayed, and mystified, they resigned from Trinity. Barack continued to campaign intently through the firestorm, as did Michelle, who finished a punishing stretch of solo appearances with a speech lasting nearly an hour in Gary, Indiana, late on the night before polls opened. She then jetted to Indianapolis for a final rally with Barack that included a morale-boosting appearance by Stevie Wonder, whose music she had first cherished as a young girl, more than thirty-five years earlier.

Voters in North Carolina broke Barack's way, as did enough Indiana voters to put him within a whisker of a victory there. He did particularly well among African American voters and young people, many of them newly registered. At the end of the night, NBC newsman Tim Russert declared, "We now know who the Democratic nominee will be." The remaining half-dozen primaries were a formality. Clinton had won an estimated 18 million votes and pushed the Obama campaign to the limit, but she could not catch up. On June 3, with voters going to the polls in South Dakota and Montana and so-called super delegates flocking to his candidacy, Barack clinched the nomination. He spoke from a stage in Minnesota, clearly moved by the victory and, he said later, a dawning sense of obligation to win in November.

After the celebration, Michelle flew back to Chicago to be home when Malia and Sasha woke up. The girls were half asleep the next morning when they crawled into bed with her and learned that Barack was going to be the Democratic nominee. "And they're like, 'Ooh, this is a big night for Dad!'" Michelle recalled. "I said, 'Well, do you guys realize what a big deal this is? Do you realize there has never been an African American that has been a presidential nominee?'" Malia answered, "Well, yeah, I can believe that. Because black people were slaves and they couldn't vote for such a long time and of *course* this is a big deal.'"

TRIUMPH ASIDE, the months after the "proud" comments were difficult for Michelle. For all of the accolades from friends and supporters as she emerged on the national stage, she felt misunderstood, at best. The tone of the debate was hurtful and at times hateful. It frustrated her and shook her confidence. More than anything, she told friends and staff, she could not bear the thought that she might be harming Barack's chances. A bevy of reports emerged, fueled by her Wisconsin remarks, that Michelle's campaign trail tone was too negative, too edgy—that she appeared to be, as the simplistic and pernicious stereotype would have it, an angry black woman. Her natural style, some members of the campaign staff thought, was becoming a liability to a black candidate who would need white swing voters to win in November. Strategists concluded that she needed to modify her delivery, but no one wanted to be the bearer of that news. "They were afraid they were going to be shot," said Forrest Claypool, a political adviser involved in the discussions. In the end, several staff members met with her to talk things over. She was furious, but not for the reasons they had anticipated. If her delivery was a problem, she demanded to know, why hadn't someone told her *sooner*? "She was angry that everyone was tiptoeing around the candidate's wife," Claypool said, recalling that she told them, "I can adapt. I want to be an asset to the campaign."

The end of the grueling primary season gave the campaign time to reconsider Michelle's approach, with an eye toward an August relaunch on the grand stage of the Democratic National Convention in Denver. Michelle worked hard at it, following through on her promise. She had never been asked to perform on a stage this big in a moment this important, but her ability to nail a performance had already impressed campaign consultants. Earlier in the primary season, Claypool and John Cooper coached Michelle as she worked through her stump speech. They met in the conference room of the Axelrod firm's headquarters at 730 North Franklin in Chicago. After she delivered the speech, they suggested perhaps two dozen specific improvements in her delivery, such as slowing down in one place or adding emphasis to a particular syllable. "I know that's a lot to absorb. We'll break it out into pieces and we'll go through it," Claypool told her reassuringly. "Okay, let me try it again," Michelle replied. When she finished, Claypool was stunned by how thoroughly she had absorbed the critique and incorporated the changes. "It was flawless. John and I just looked and each other and said, 'I think we're done here.' I've never seen anything like it, ever. She's a pro's pro."

DURING THE LULL after the primaries, Michelle spent more time back in Hyde Park, where the girls finished their year at Lab School and went to after-school activities and sleepovers as Michelle fought to retain a sense of normalcy. Slipping into the rhythms of ordinary family life was next to impossible, not only because of her fame and the demands on her time, but also because of the Secret Service agents who shadowed her around the clock. They set up a command post outside the house. They stationed themselves at school. They organized caravans to ballet classes and soccer matches and kept outsiders at bay. Sasha, who turned seven that year, called them "the secret people."

Michelle had long feared that Barack's prominence could make him a target. Medgar Evers, Malcolm X, and the Reverend Martin Luther King Jr. all fell to assassins' bullets. "It only takes one person and it only takes one incident. I mean, I know history, too," she said. She had met King's widow, Coretta Scott King, a few years earlier. "What I remember most was that she told me not to be afraid because God was with us—Barack and me—and that she would always keep us in her prayers." In agreeing to the presidential race, Michelle made clear to Barack that she expected him to get Secret Service protection. She also wanted to maintain her income and her professional reputation in case he died, given that national politics put him in what she called a position of "high-risk." While there would be "great sympathy and outpouring if something were to happen, I don't want to be in a position one day where I am vulnerable with my children," she told writer David

Mendell. "I need to be in a position for my kids where, if they lose their father, they don't lose everything."

Early in the campaign, Barack's staff printed a sheaf of incendiary material that was circulating on the Internet and delivered it to Senator Richard Durbin, an Illinois Democrat and member of the Senate leadership. Durbin relayed the information to Senate majority leader Harry Reid, starting the process that would establish the Secret Service presence. In May 2007, eighteen months before the general election, Barack began operating behind the cordon, yet it was hard not to fret. He was the target of hatred—sometimes threatening, sometimes merely vile. Many African American supporters, especially, shuddered to think of the instant they would learn that he had been shot. Television newsman Steve Kroft asked Michelle whether she had considered the possibility. "I don't lose sleep over it because the realities are that, as a black man, Barack can get shot going to the gas station," she said. "So, you can't make decisions based on fear and the possibility of what might happen. We just weren't raised that way." The Secret Service became part of the Obamas' lives. Barack's code name was Renegade. Michelle's was Renaissance.

DESPITE THE BARRICADES and restrictions, Hyde Park was a haven, the community where the Obamas felt most at home during the never-ending campaign. The neighborhood spoke to their desires and their values. It also, perhaps inevitably, became a symbol to Republican critics of what was wrong with them. No American president had been elected from a place quite like Hyde Park, home to a university famous for intellectualism, a pair of 1960s Weather Underground radicals famous for being unrepentant, and a bloc of voters famous for choosing John Kerry over the victorious George W. Bush by 19 to 1. Judging by the demonization, the Obamas might as well have lived at the corner of Liberal and Kumbaya. Republican strategist Karl Rove placed Hyde Park alongside Cambridge and San Francisco in a triad of leftist tomfoolery. *The Weekly Standard* recalled Barack's description of former Weatherman Bill Ayers as merely "a guy who lives in my neighborhood" and asked who lives in a neighborhood like that.

In real life, the area more properly described as Hyde Park–Kenwood could not be so easily typecast. The political ethic was proudly progressive on matters of race and social justice, yet the community was anchored by the University of Chicago, an incubator of some of the nation's most prominent conservatives, from Supreme Court justice Antonin Scalia to Nobel Prize–winning free marketeer Milton Friedman. Nation of Islam leader Louis Farrakhan lived within four blocks of the Obamas' $1.6 million home, as did Ayers and his wife, Bernardine Dohrn, a fellow former radical. Yet so did Richard Epstein, a prominent libertarian law professor quick to say that he was friends with Scalia and Ayers and had once tried to hire Dohrn.

To be a Hyde Parker, dozens of residents explained, was to choose to live in a community that considered variations of race, creed, wealth, and politics to be a neighborhood selling point, like bicycle paths or broadband. "I grew up playing with the children of welfare families and the children of Nobel Prize winners and you don't think anything of it," said Arne Duncan, superintendent of Chicago Public Schools and later U.S. secretary of education. "You grow up very comfortable and confident around people who don't look like you and are from very different backgrounds." Mainstream, as mainstream was commonly defined in statistical terms, was not Hyde Park. The average white metropolitan resident in the United States lived in a neighborhood 80 percent white and only 7 percent black. Census tracts in the exurbs and the countryside were often even whiter. By contrast, the 2000 census found that 43.5 percent of the 29,000 residents of Hyde Park proper called themselves white, 37.7 percent black, 11.3 percent Asian, and 4.1 percent Hispanic. Another 3.4 percent answered "other." In economic terms, there was an abundance of six-figure earners, yet one in six residents lived in poverty. The median household income was about $45,000, roughly 10 percent lower than the national average. It was also surely the rare place in the country where an academic and his wife, going through a divorce, would include a clause splitting future winnings if he won the Nobel Prize in economics. One professor and his ex-wife did just that. He won, and sent her $500,000.

The house on Greenwood Avenue that Barack and Michelle bought in 2005 had a lineage that suited the community's modern-day reputation. For seven years in the mid-twentieth century, it was owned by the Hebrew Theological Academy, which ran a Jewish day school there. In 1954, the Hyde Park Lutheran Church purchased the mansion with its four fireplaces and made it the local headquarters of the Lutheran Human Relations Association of America. The Reverend George Hrbek called it home from 1966 to 1971, directing a project designed to counteract racism, principally by raising the consciousness of young white people who visited the house or lived there. At any given time, as many as twenty people bunked in the building, some for weeks, some for years. Hrbek estimated that three thousand people, including waves of divinity students, took part in the training. "If you wanted to deal with racism," he said, "you had to deal with the white community." During the 1968 Democratic National Convention, members of the Chicago Seven stayed in the house. In 1971, four firebombs did minor damage to the outside of the building. When Hrbek learned after the 2008 election that Barack and Michelle owned it, he sent the president a letter saying that their house was "filled with good spirits."

It was nonetheless true that Hyde Park's twentieth-century history had an ugly side even before the University of Chicago's investment in white neighborhood committees and urban renewal. Phoebe Moten Johnson, mother of LaVaughn Robinson and great-grandmother of Michelle, lived in Hyde Park during a paroxysm of harassment and violence intended to terrorize black residents. Between 1917 and 1921, when Phoebe and her family lived at 5470 South Kenwood—six blocks from where Michelle and Barack would live ninety years later—bombs struck fifty-eight homes owned by black families or the white men who sold homes to black people. One week when violence struck her neighborhood, Phoebe was frantic. She mixed water and lye in a kettle and heated it on a wood-burning stove, ready to throw it in the eyes of any white marauders who broke down her door. Friction continued. In the 1940s, it was restrictive covenants. In the 1950s, it was urban renewal. By the 1960s, when some people actually did sing "Kumbaya," the economic divide in Hyde Park prompted a joke that the community, for all of its pride in racial integration, was really a case of "black and white together, standing shoulder to shoulder against the poor."

Author Blue Balliett based her inquisitive, multicultural twelve-year-old protagonists in *Chasing Vermeer* on students at Lab School, where she had taught. Justice John Paul Stevens earned his high school degree there and Langston Hughes had once been artist in residence. "It's a place where you can be who you are and bring any kind of diversity to the table and be celebrated for it," Balliett said of the community. "Kids really can grow up in Hyde Park and never hear a negative conversation about those differences. My son used to say, 'How come we aren't at least Jewish and Christian?'" When he was a boy, social activist Jamie Kalven lived in a third-floor apartment in a home owned by Manhattan Project chemist Harold Urey. At various times, the house was also owned by prizefighter Sonny Liston and jazz pianist Ahmad Jamal. Muhammad Ali once lived nearby. In an outdoor cage, he kept a pair of lions given to him by Mobutu Sese Seko, the corrupt ruler of Zaire. Kalven spoke of the presence in Hyde Park of a roughly equal number of blacks and whites "for whom the fact of living together is no big deal." Which was, in a sense, the big deal.

For Barack, who wanted to be seen during the campaign as distinctive but unthreatening, his chosen turf represented political eclecticism and a sense of possibility that came to be called, with insufficient reflection, post-racial. But the narrative cut both ways as Republicans pushed the argument that the erudite Barack was overly exotic, elitist, and naive. He bodysurfed in Hawaii, he ordered green tea ice cream in Oregon, he wrote his own books, and his name was Barack Hussein Obama. "This is not a man who sees America as you and I do, as the greatest force for good in the world," said Alaska governor Sarah Palin after she became the Republican vice presidential nominee. Valerie Jarrett, who had lived much of her life in the community, begged to differ. "Hyde Park is the real world as it should be," she said. "If we could take Hyde Park and we could help make more Hyde Parks around our country, I think we would be a much stronger country."

THE DEMOCRATIC NATIONAL CONVENTION opened in Denver on August 25, 2008, with Michelle as the keynote speaker on the tone-setting first night. The campaign knew it had work to do to introduce not only Barack but Michelle, whose unfavorability numbers were uncomfortably high. Earlier that month, 29 percent of respondents to an NBC News/Wall Street Journal poll viewed Michelle negatively, including 18 percent who described their feelings as "very negative." Only 38 percent viewed her positively, while 28 percent were neutral and 5 percent did not know her name or were unsure. "It's scary," an undecided voter told the *St. Petersburg Times* after connecting her "proud of my country" comments with her Princeton thesis, which was circulating on the Web. "To think she's going to be whispering in the president's ear when he's in bed."

The campaign saw Denver as a chance to hit the reset button. "It was important to us for a whole range of reasons for her to do well and to address some of these questions that were lingering about her," Axelrod said. "And it was important to us for her to do what she did to explain Barack to people." For Michelle herself, it was a chance to regain her confidence and demonstrate her value on the biggest stage yet. The criticism "really hurt her," Axelrod said, especially as someone accustomed to "excelling and always being prepared and always being able to do the right thing. I think it also gave her a sense of just how exposed she was . . . in this hair-trigger environment." She asked for a draft of her speech more than a month before the curtain went up, then spent weeks refining and practicing it until she knew the words nearly by heart. Her share of the evening began with a six-minute campaign video titled "South Side Girl," borrowing the regular folks frame that she had adopted on the trail. Enveloped by soft voices and soothing music, the film emphasized the themes of family and community and a commitment to give back. Marian served as narrator and Craig and Barack made cameos. No character, however, figured more prominently than her father, Fraser, who had died seventeen years before.

MARIAN: Michelle was especially close to her daddy.
CRAIG: My father was in his 50s and my sister would still sit on his lap and put her head on his shoulder, as she used to do when she was a kid. And that sort of one picture epitomizes their relationship.

BARACK: Her dad was just a sweet man, a kind-hearted man and
somebody who thought everybody should be treated with
dignity and respect. And I think that carried over to Michelle.

MARIAN: Michelle has always reached out to others. It was
something I loved about my husband, too.

CRAIG: Michelle's compassion came from my father and people
came to him with their problems and he always managed to
have people go away feeling better than they did when they
came to talk to him. I'm certain that that's where Michelle gets
her compassion from.

MICHELLE: I think about him every day when I think about how I
raise my kids, because I remember his compassion. I remember
the words, his advice, the way he lived life. And I am trying each
and every day to apply that to how I raise my kids. I want his
legacy to live through them, and hopefully it will affect the kind
of First Lady that I will become, because it's his compassion and
his view of the world that really inspires who I am, who I want
my girls to be, and what I hope for the country.

Michelle's speech, which followed the video and an introduction
by Craig, featured references to Fraser early and late in the narrative.
Three sentences in, she said, "I can feel my dad looking down on us,
just as I've felt his presence in every grace-filled moment of my life."
She declared that she stood on the podium as a sister, a wife, a daughter,
and a "mom." She called her father "our rock" and ended by asking her
audience to devote themselves to Barack's election, "in honor of my
father's memory and my daughters' future," as well as everyone who
labored to build the world as it should be. Beyond telling a story of their
lives that emphasized uplift and hard work, she recognized the eighty-
eighth anniversary of women winning the right to vote and the forty-
fifth anniversary of Martin Luther King's "I Have a Dream" speech.
"I stand here today," she said, breaking through the applause, "at the
crosscurrents of that history, knowing that my piece of the American
dream is a blessing hard won by those who came before me, all of them
driven by the same conviction that drove my dad to get up an hour
early each day to painstakingly dress himself for work, the same con-

viction that drives the men and women I've met all across this country."
She folded into the speech a declaration that she loved her country. The
crowd cheered.

The address was the opening success in what proved to be a happy
week for Democrats, launching the Obamas toward November and
the battle against John McCain, U.S. senator from Arizona, and Palin,
the idiosyncratic governor of Alaska, who wowed the Republican base
but left many others cold. Michelle's poll numbers immediately shot
skyward, rising eighteen points in the Obama campaign's overnight
tracking polls, and they stayed aloft. By October, she drew crowds of
two thousand in Columbus, seven thousand in Pensacola, and eleven
thousand in Gainesville. "Surreal is almost like an understatement,"
her brother, Craig, said. "It's magical is what it is. I mean, it's like going
to sleep and waking up and you're Tinkerbell."

In Akron, eleven days before election day, Michelle no longer mentioned in her stump speech her Ivy League education or Barack's. She
made no reference to his work as a professor of constitutional law, his
eight years in the Illinois senate, or his three-plus years in Washington.
Nor did she mention the stacked deck or the moving bar. What she
said was "We're just regular folks." Before the rally, Michelle dropped
by the local campaign office, where a dozen volunteers were dialing
for voters. Taking a telephone from a supporter, she said cheerily,
"How are you! You're still undecided? That's okay. What can I tell you
about my husband?" In the next few minutes, she did some listening
and some answering, offering a careful rationale for an Obama presidency. "We've been doing the same thing for the last eight years and it
hasn't worked," she said, describing her husband as "a fighter for regular folks, and that's our background." She described her upbringing
as the daughter of working-class parents who did not attend college.
She mentioned Marian, who had retired and was living on a pension,
and Barack's sister Maya, a teacher. She also mentioned Barack's ailing
grandmother Toot, who had long been unable to travel and would die
within a fortnight, two days before her grandson was elected president.
"We're living close to the issues," said Michelle. She added as she hung
up, "That's my pitch. Thank you for letting me go on and on."

. . .

ON ELECTION DAY, Barack and Michelle, joined by Malia and Sasha, voted early at Beulah Shoesmith Elementary in Hyde Park. Michelle went to have her hair done, taking the girls with her, and Barack made the quickest of campaign trips to neighboring Indiana, where a win would be icing and a loss forgettable. He returned in time for an afternoon game of pickup basketball with friends and relatives, then retreated to the house on Greenwood to await results. As polls began to close and votes were counted, Michelle, Barack, Marian, and the girls sat down to dinner with Craig and his family—his second wife, Kelly, and his two children, Avery and Leslie. Marian asked the kids about school, their teachers, their favorite subjects. The television was off, although Michelle and Barack each kept a BlackBerry on the table in front of them. Every so often, one phone or the other would buzz. They would read the message and make no comment. When the pace of buzzing picked up, Barack walked into the kitchen and turned on a small TV. "Well," he said, "looks like we're going to win this thing." Soon after, Michelle answered a call, turned to Barack, and said, "Congratulations, Mr. President."

Barack gave his victory speech in Grant Park, best known until that night as the place where Chicago police battered protesters outside the 1968 Democratic National Convention. As the motorcade headed north along Lake Shore Drive through an unseasonably warm November night, Malia said, "Hey, how come there are no other cars?" Police had stopped traffic in both directions. At that moment, Craig said, it registered with him that voters had actually chosen Barack to be the next president of the United States. As he rode through the city toward the Hyatt hotel where they would await the official results, he told himself that an unfulfilled promise in the Declaration of Independence had finally been borne out, the line that said, "We hold these truths to be self-evident, that all men are created equal."

The crowd in Grant Park, more than 100,000 strong, was delirious with joy when the networks called the election for Barack at 10 p.m. Central Time as polls closed on the West Coast. MyKela Loury wept.

A black woman, she stood alone on a sidewalk within earshot of the cheering throngs. She put her hand to her mouth, then both hands to her temples, her mouth open in a silent gasp. "I'm thinking justice, finally. Fairness, finally," Loury said. "Oh, gosh." The tears came again. "Oh, Jesus." Car horns blared. Supporters shouted and laughed and screamed and hugged one another and laughed some more. So many of Barack's followers had wanted this outcome so badly and yet had dared not believe it would happen. It seemed just possible, in that crystalline instant, that more good things would follow. "We're finally free," Tracy Boykin declared as she headed toward the park with her friend Caron Warnsby, a surgeon. "I'm a doctor, and I don't have to walk in anymore and be a black doctor. She's not the black surgeon, anymore. She's the surgeon. Everything is different." And for that one glorious moment, it was.

Michelle, Barack, and the girls strode onto the stage. As Barack spoke, his family and friends in the wings pinched themselves. Cameras caught Jesse Jackson with tears streaming down his face. He later said he was thinking of Emmett Till, Rosa Parks, Martin Luther King, and the march in Selma. Capers Funnye, one of Fraser's cousins, found Marian and hugged her. "We cried together for her dad, we cried for her granddad, for my mom and all of her siblings who've gone on," Funnye said. "It was a powerful, profound moment. It was an extraordinary moment. There were no words. What could you say?"

Michelle's mother, Marian Robinson, as a young woman in Chicago, where her parents settled after moving from the South.

Michelle's father, Fraser C. Robinson III, shown here in a high school yearbook photo, took classes at the Art Institute of Chicago.

Michelle and her brother, Craig, twenty-one months older, who said they had the "Shangri-La of upbringings" in working-class Chicago.

Kindergarten at Bryn Mawr Elementary in 1970. Michelle is second from the right in the second row from the top.

Michelle as a first-grader on the South Side of Chicago.

Michelle commuted across town to Whitney Young High School, a diverse magnet school, where she was a class officer and a member of the honor society.

Michelle, seventeen years old when she reached Princeton in 1981, struggled at first.

Michelle L. Robinson
7436 S. Euclid Ave.
Chicago, IL 60649
Whitney Young H.S.
January 17, 1964

7436 South Euclid Avenue
Chicago, IL 60649

January 17, 1964

Sociology

Stevenson Hall; Third World Center — Work Study; Third World Center — Governance Board Member; Organization of Black Unity; Third World Center After School Program — Coordinator

Michelle LaVaughn Robinson

There is nothing in this world more valuable than friendships. Without them you have nothing.

Thank-you Mom, Dad and Craig. You all are the most important things in my life.

Majoring in sociology, Michelle said white students often perceived her as "Black first and a student second."

Michelle dated Stanley Stocker-Edwards, a fellow Harvard Law student. She said later, "My family swore I would never find a man that would put up with me."

Michelle and Harvard Law friend Susan Page, appointed U.S. ambassador to South Sudan in the Obama administration.

Michelle visited Barack's family in Hawaii in 1989, the year they met at a Chicago law firm.

Michelle and Barack were married in 1992, by the Reverend Jeremiah A. Wright Jr. at Trinity United Church of Christ in Chicago.

Barack and Michelle visited Kenya, the home country of Barack's father.

"I was never happier in my life," Michelle said, than when building a leadership program at Public Allies in Chicago in the mid-1990s.

In the first apartment she and Barack owned in Chicago, Michelle stands beside a photograph of Judith Jamison dancing Alvin Ailey's iconic work "Cry."

Barack, Michelle, and Malia on election day in 2000. Barack lost the congressional primary to Representative Bobby Rush by thirty points and entered what an aide called his "morose period."

With Sasha in Oskaloosa, Iowa, on July 4, 2007. Michelle curtailed campaign time and her White House schedule to be home for her daughters.

Michelle and Barack strolling down Pennsylvania Avenue during Barack's first inaugural. Designer Isabel Toledo said Michelle made it safe for women to take fashion risks.

Michelle, wearing a Jason Wu gown later donated to the Smithsonian, shares a moment with Barack after dancing at the 2009 inaugural ball.

Michelle in her first official White House photograph, beneath the gaze of Thomas Jefferson.

Delighting in fashion, Michelle took advantage of public occasions to showcase designers and an ever-changing array of styles.

Michelle saw progress when Jacob Philadelphia, age five, told the first African American president, "I want to know if my hair is just like yours." Barack invited him to see for himself.

After she launched Let's Move!, Michelle said, "I'm pretty much willing to make a complete fool out of myself to get our kids moving."

Michelle made the rounds at federal agencies, drawing crowds armed with cell phone cameras. In October 2011, she visited Secret Service headquarters.

Calling Washington her new hometown, Michelle hoped to set an example for disadvantaged children, here visiting Ferebee Hope Elementary School.

After Barack's November 2012 reelection, Michelle launched Reach Higher to expand higher education and training, particularly for low-income students.

Hugs became Michelle's signature gesture, intended as a symbol that the first lady cared. As part of her Joining Forces initiative, she met military families in Minnesota in March 2012.

Michelle increasingly used social media to spread her message. In 2014, she spoke up for Nigerian girls kidnapped by the extremist group Boko Haram.

Michelle, Barack, and Malia at a Team USA basketball game.

Local schoolchildren and White House staff helped Michelle plant the first vegetable garden on the White House grounds since Eleanor Roosevelt's time.

Michelle, in a tug-of-war with Jimmy Fallon, did spoofs and comedy sketches to advance childhood fitness and nutrition.

Posing here with Sesame Street characters in October 2013. Michelle developed partnerships to draw attention to her initiatives, including Joining Forces.

When Barack congratulated the Miami Heat on their latest NBA championship, stars LeBron James and Dwyane Wade did a video about healthy eating with Michelle.

Applause for Michelle, wearing a Michael Kors design, at Barack's State of the Union address to a joint session of Congress in January 2015.

Marian Robinson, standing beside Michelle, moved into the third floor of the White House. "I can always go up to her room and cry, complain, argue," Michelle said. "And she just says, 'Go on back down there and do what you're supposed to do.'"

Michelle and Barack shooting an ad for the 2012 campaign. The win gave them four more years and a greater sense of freedom. Shortly before turning fifty, Michelle said, "I have never felt more confident in myself, more clear on who I am as a woman."

TWELVE

Nothing Would Have Predicted

Michelle never had any doubt that her ascendance to the White House as first lady of the United States—FLOTUS, in Secret Service parlance—was groundbreaking. This was the executive mansion that slaves had helped build and African Americans had helped run, but it had never sheltered a black president or first family. The symbolism alone was stunning. It was evident on the November day, six days after the election, when George and Laura Bush posed with the Obamas outside the White House. And at the inauguration eve concert on the steps of the Lincoln Memorial, where Martin Luther King had delivered his "I Have a Dream" speech. And in Barack's inaugural address on January 20, 2009, in front of an estimated two million people on the National Mall, when he spoke of being the son of a father who, two generations earlier, "might not have been served in a local restaurant." After the swearing-in, where Barack rested his left hand on the velvet-bound Bible used by Abraham Lincoln at his 1861 inaugural, crowds cheered and called out as Michelle and Barack stepped out of their bulletproof limousine to walk hand in hand in the winter sunshine down Pennsylvania Avenue.

Inside the White House, the largely black staff of butlers, housekeepers, and cooks gathered to meet the new first family. "They could not have been kinder to us and warmer to us," Barack said. "And part of it, I suspect, is they look at Malia and Sasha and they say, 'Well, this looks like my grandbaby or this looks like my daughter.' And I think for them to have a sense that we've come this far was a powerful moment for them—and certainly a powerful moment for us." The first night in the mansion, dozens of friends and relatives gathered for a party, no one quite believing what had come to pass. Barack, after asking how to get there, headed upstairs to the residence at 2:30 a.m., following Michelle, who had retired earlier. A signed copy of the Gettysburg Address lay under glass in the Lincoln Bedroom, once Lincoln's office, where Craig and Kelly slept in an elegant eight-by-six-foot rosewood bed after receiving a house tour. One stop was the Truman Balcony and its view south toward the Washington Monument. "My wife and I were just shaking our heads," Craig said.

Not two weeks later, Michelle was speaking at the White House about equal pay for women. Soon, she addressed cheering workers at the Department of Housing and Urban Development and urged them to find "a new level of passion and vigor." A few days after that, she told teenagers at a Washington community health center that she and Barack were "kids like you who figured out one day that our fate was in our own hands." In April, she made a trip to the Capitol to unveil a bust of Sojourner Truth, a freed slave who became a prominent abolitionist and activist for women's suffrage. Born Isabella Baumfree in the late eighteenth century, Truth was sold several times before escaping with one of her children in 1826. She delivered her famous "Ain't I a Woman" speech in 1851. Nearly a century and a half later, she was the first black woman to be honored with a bust in the Capitol. By her very presence at the ceremony, Michelle demonstrated the distance that African Americans had traveled since Martha Washington, accompanied by seven house slaves, took up residence in New York as the wife of the country's first president. Noting that she herself was a descendant of slaves, she called Sojourner Truth "an outspoken, tell-it-like-it-is kind of woman. And we all know a little something about that, right?" She urged her audience, which included Nancy Pelosi, the first female speaker of the House, Hillary Clinton, the new secretary of state, and a bevy of Republican leaders, to reflect on the moment.

"Now," she said, "many young boys and girls, like my own daughters, will come to Emancipation Hall and see the face of a woman who looks like them." Just as no one who looked like the Obamas had graced Emancipation Hall, no one who looked like them had occupied the White House, either, a fact that would influence what Barack and Michelle would do and say, even as they set out unambiguously to be the president and first lady of all Americans.

VIRTUALLY OVERNIGHT, Michelle had become one of the most prominent women in America. Hopes soared among some of her most ardent fans that she would become a White House force in her own right. Her new staff was deluged with invitations to lunches and launches and an endless skein of worthy and not-so-worthy events. The screen was blank and she was free, if one could call it that, to define a role for herself. Yet she soon discovered that her freedom was defined by a tangle of often conflicting expectations and options. What was true for any first lady was doubly so for the first African American first lady, one who carried a significant résumé into the position. She had told delegates to the Democratic National Convention that she stood "at the crosscurrents" of the history of race and gender. Her friend Verna Williams said "in the crosshairs" was more like it. "People are going to be watching every move you make. They're watching you—it's like the Police song."

That first year in the White House, Michelle said later, was about "figuring out the job." There were aides to hire, a household staff to manage, a web of rules—written and otherwise—about how to conduct her affairs. She no longer drove, she no longer went anywhere alone, and even her home was not her own. Meanwhile, she was determined to settle Malia and Sasha into their new lives and support Barack as he confronted two wars and the most serious economic crisis since the Great Depression. Accustomed to control, at times she felt at sea. "It wasn't smooth," said Jackie Norris, her first chief of staff. "It's not smooth for any first lady. It's a hard process."

Michelle had made time, during a campaign that had lasted the better part of two years, to think about the role she might play as first lady. Before reaching Washington, she convened small groups to consider what the job could mean, but she intentionally left the contours vague. When asked in 2007 whether she saw herself more as Laura Bush or as Hillary Clinton, she ducked the comparison. "It is so hard to project out realistically what life will be like for me as a woman, for me as a mother, when Barack becomes president. It's hard to know. What I do know is that given the many skills that I have on so many different levels, I will be what I have to be at the time." The answer was an honest one. It made clear her strong sense of obligation to Malia, Sasha, and Barack. It conveyed flexibility and it also bought her some time. Once she moved into 1600 Pennsylvania Avenue, Michelle's prominent place in the history books was assured by the color of her skin. Surely there was more, much more. But what?

Michelle started out as "risk-averse," in one staffer's words, wrestling with unfamiliar conditions and wary of a misstep. As self-described "mom-in-chief," a term that set some supporters' teeth on edge when they considered her education and skills, Michelle telegraphed that she would leap into no issue or cause before she was ready. She instructed her staff to confine her official working schedule to two days a week at first, later raising it to three. She labored informally on other days while focusing on her family. She operated from the East Wing, the president from the West Wing. Privately, she made clear to her staff that once she chose her course, she would be disciplined about it, conserving political capital while protecting her family time. She said from the outset that her role would be collaborative and measured, always in service to the member of the couple who had been elected—in other words, Barack, who had official duties, constitutional powers, a $400,000 salary, and his sights set on winning a second term. Michelle's first goal, as she had learned the hard way during the campaign, was to do no harm.

Which is not to say that she felt no stress or sense of obligation. Her role may have been unpaid, but she was the same i-dotting, t-crossing Michelle who had stayed up late to finish her high school homework and hated to fall short at anything. "I have a huge responsibility to use this platform in a way that's going to make a difference," she told a student questioner in 2011. "In a way that I feel like I don't want to disappoint my parents, I wouldn't want to disappoint the country. Sheesh, that's a burden. . . . I want to be good at what I do. . . . I want to look back and say I did something good for a bunch of people because I was in this position." The student had asked whether being an African American first lady added to the pressure. Michelle replied that her feelings about the job were "not unique to me because of my race" and reported that other first ladies saw the job in similar terms. "None of us chose the position. You get it because of who you're married to and you don't get a paycheck or a title, but you feel like you want to make the most of it and do some good things." She concluded, to laughter, "Thank you for that question. It's like a therapy session."

IT WAS A TRICKY ROLE, being first lady. There was no script, although there were certainly many models. Modern first ladies were as different in style and substance as their husbands. The woman she succeeded, Laura Bush, had cut a gracious, amiable, and sure-footed figure. She spoke up for the No Child Left Behind education policy and traveled to sixty-seven countries in her husband's second term, playing substantive roles on such issues as political freedom in Burma, women's rights in Afghanistan, and AIDS in Africa. A former school librarian, she was steady and low-key in an administration famous for swashbuckling, her position fortified by the knowledge that she had pushed her husband to stop drinking and save his career. "I'm not here for me, I'm here for George," she told Anita McBride when interviewing her for the job of East Wing chief of staff. "Whatever I do here is to help the president's goals for the country."

An earlier White House occupant, Barbara Bush, Laura's mother-in-law, kept order and fired the occasional verbal dagger on her husband's behalf, while Nancy Reagan combined a steely loyalty and a passion for palace intrigue with a fashion sense that sometimes clashed with the zeitgeist of the 1980s. First ladies were variously known for White House portfolios, real or imagined, and their causes. Lady Bird Johnson had beautification and the War on Poverty, Laura Bush had literacy, Nancy Reagan had the "Just Say No" anti-drugs campaign. Rosalynn Carter attended high-level meetings, taking notes quietly.

"There's no way I could discuss things with Jimmy in an intelligent way if I didn't attend Cabinet meetings," she once said. In the margins of policy papers and memos, the president would sometimes write, "Ros. What think?" The pressure of the White House, meanwhile, weighed on Betty Ford, who had been popping pills and drinking heavily long before the summer day when Richard Nixon resigned and made her husband, former Michigan congressman Gerald Ford, the president. Her poll numbers rose when she discussed on national television an earlier mental breakdown and spoke up for abortion rights, calling *Roe v. Wade* a "great, great decision." She revealed a bout with breast cancer and wore a political button in 1975 urging passage of the Equal Rights Amendment. She said her children probably had smoked marijuana: "It's the type of thing that young people have to experience, like your first beer or your first cigarette." Betty Ford bridged the gap between the presidential cocoon and the rest of the country, wrote author Kati Marton. Americans "saw an open, honest woman talking about issues they were dealing with every day."

As Michelle prepared for the move to the White House, she found herself compared with first ladies from three separate eras, each with a distinctive style. The three—Jackie Kennedy, Hillary Clinton, and Eleanor Roosevelt—could hardly have been more different, illustrating the dilemmas Michelle would face in crafting the style and substance of her own role. Each came to be known best by her first name. Jackie Kennedy was just thirty-one years old when her husband was elected and thirty-four when he died. Her public face was all about style, the arts, and the gauzy image of a new Camelot, fueled by a media bored with the stolid Eisenhower era. John Kennedy himself was only forty-three when he entered the White House, a dashing and philandering father whose two young children would become known to the world in joy and mourning. Hillary Clinton came of age in the tumultuous years after John Kennedy died. A politically minded child of the Chicago suburbs, she was elected president of the Young Republicans before moving to the left in the late 1960s. She graduated from Yale Law School and worked as a lawyer in Little Rock, Arkansas, as her husband climbed the political ranks. Her reputation was rooted in her formidable intellect, her independent career, and her early tendency to speak her mind, or something close to it. She landed in the briar patch with her campaign trail assertion that she was not the type of woman to stay home and bake cookies and, later, with her stewardship of a botched health care overhaul—a policymaking role that Michelle and her team made a conscious decision not to emulate. When she took a more traditional tack and stood by her feckless husband after his most recent sexual affair, this one with White House intern Monica Lewinsky, her popularity grew. Whether due to admiration or sympathy or a combination of the two was a matter for debate.

It was Eleanor Roosevelt, however, who provided the most intriguing point of comparison for Michelle, and the most difficult standard to meet. Brave, singular, a progressive force operating before the media spotlight shone so brightly, Roosevelt created an independent identity while working to shape the thirty-second president's agenda, at one point even seeking a federal job. She held press conferences for women reporters and wrote a popular syndicated newspaper column, "My Day." She joined the Washington, D.C., chapter of the NAACP, supported anti-lynching legislation, and resigned her membership in the Daughters of the American Revolution when the organization refused to allow Marian Anderson to sing at Constitution Hall. Not that she was happy when she arrived at the White House. "The turmoil in my heart and mind was rather great," she wrote in 1933. Rather than be called first lady, she said she preferred "Mrs. Roosevelt." Franklin Roosevelt wrote, in verse, of her predicament:

> *Did my Eleanor relate*
> *all the sad and awful fate*
> *of the miserable lives*
> *lived by Washington wives*

Eleanor often left town. She traveled on her own, sometimes setting out by car and reporting back to her husband on what she found. She was a moral, prodding force in the White House, and she was ahead of her husband and party on matters of poverty, racism, and social justice.

In 1943, Chicago publisher John H. Johnson asked if she would contribute a column to his "If I Were a Negro" series in *Negro Digest,* which predated the launch of his glossy magazines, *Ebony* and *Jet.* "If I were a Negro today, I think I would have moments of great bitterness," she wrote. "It would be hard to sustain my faith in democracy and to build up a sense of goodwill toward men of other races." Although African Americans had been "held back by generations of economic inequality," she continued, "I would know that I had to work hard and to go on accomplishing the best that was possible under present conditions. . . . I would not do too much demanding. I would take every chance that came my way to prove my quality."

The column was a huge success. Johnson reported that his circulation spiked by fifty thousand, doubling the usual press run. "She said, 'If I were a Negro, I would have great bitterness,' and all the northern papers picked that up," Johnson recalled. "But she said, 'But I would also have great patience,' and all the southern newspapers picked that up." Three years after her death, writer Claude Brown dedicated his memoir of life in Harlem, *Manchild in the Promised Land,* to Roosevelt. He cited her support of the Wiltwyck School for Boys, a Hudson River reform school that became a refuge for needy and sometimes troubled or delinquent children. It was Wiltwyck, he said, that turned his life around.

MICHELLE TURNED INITIALLY to what spoke to her, just as she had done during the campaign. One of her first public roles was morale booster. Daughter and granddaughter of government workers, she made a tour of federal agencies, thanking federal employees for their anonymous service to the nation. "Everything you do, every piece of blood, sweat and tears you pour into the work is going to make the difference in our nation, in our planet," she told Environmental Protection Agency workers in February. "Just know that we value you, that America values you," she told Transportation Department staff. She mentioned her uncles who had been Pullman porters and praised their labor union as a "trailblazer in civil rights." At the Agriculture Department, she talked up community gardens, renewable energy, and the expansion of the Children's Health Insurance Program. "We are going to need you in the months and years to come," she said. "The challenges that we face are serious and real and it's going to take quite a long time to get this country back on track." More able to get out and about than her husband, Michelle told a packed auditorium of Education Department workers that she aimed "to learn, to listen, to take information back where possible."

Michelle and her team laid out a series of early priorities. Even then, as she was struggling to find her feet, her concerns had a shape familiar to those who knew her biography. In an echo of her work at Public Allies and the University of Chicago, she spoke up for expanded federal funding of national service programs, illustrated by the Serve America Act signed by Barack in April 2009. During a visit to the Corporation for National and Community Service, she recalled that unpaid internships were beyond her reach as a young woman, "a luxury that a working class kid couldn't afford." Everyone, she said, should have a chance to volunteer and benefit, "regardless of their race or their age or their financial ability."

To spotlight diversity in what she called "my new home town," Michelle explored the vibrant and sometimes troubled Washington in the shadows of the federal government and the downtown tourist attractions. She set out to share her story and the president's with fresh audiences, particularly children of color from less-than-elite backgrounds. She saw her younger self in them, and she wanted to play a role in "opening the doors and taking off the veil." The White House, she said, would be the people's house. "You know, there's a playbook in Washington about what you're supposed to do," her friend Sharon Malone said. "Well, she's not following the playbook. She's doing it the way she wants to do it, by being very involved in the community." On March 19, two months into the first term, Michelle drove across the river to Anacostia High School, located in an impoverished African American neighborhood within sight of the Capitol dome. It would take less than an hour to walk there from, say, Emancipation Hall, but the two worlds rarely intersected. "One of those schools that was basically forgotten," said Roscoe Thomas, dean of students, recalling his first impressions. Michelle gathered students around her and explained that when she began to envision her time as first lady, she realized that she wanted to spend "a whole lot of time outside in the D.C. community." The motivation was her own recollection of how distant the University of Chicago felt to her as a working-class black girl, even though the campus was close to her home. "I never set foot on it. I didn't get to attend any classes. And I think the assumption was . . . that place was different," she said. "It was a college, and it was a fancy college, and it didn't have anything to do with me."

At Anacostia, Michelle talked with girls—and a few boys, to whom she said, "You brothers are lucky, because you got to sneak into this." They were chosen to meet her for a reason. "Each of you has struggled with something, but you've overcome it, you've pushed to the next level. And that for me, that was important. I didn't just want the kids who had already arrived, but kids who were pushing to get to the next place," she said in an echo of what she valued when recruiting for Public Allies. She spoke of her own hard work as an adolescent, and how her mother made clear that Michelle needed to take responsibility if she expected to succeed. "I ran into people in my life who told me, 'You can't do it, you're not as smart as that person.' And that never stopped me. That always made me push harder, because I was like, I'm going to prove you wrong." As intended, the event drew news coverage. It caught the eye of Jasmine Williams, a D.C. public charter school senior who had already asked Michelle to speak at her graduation. "She told them how a lot of people told her she spoke like a white girl," Williams said. "I don't know what that means, but I've been told that, too."

Michelle was just one woman of distinction who ventured into D.C.-area schools that day, part of a White House celebration of Women's History Month. In what would become a template, the East Wing deployed an array of accomplished women, sending them to eleven local schools and welcoming them back to the White House to break bread with Michelle and various girls invited to meet them. That day, the guest list ranged from singers Alicia Keys and Sheryl Crow to gymnast Dominique Dawes, former astronaut Mae C. Jemison, and the first female four-star general in the U.S. military, General Ann E. Dunwoody. When the day was over and the guests had gone home, Michelle told her staff that it was their best event yet. The experience would fuel the East Wing's creation of a mentoring program.

To Michelle, mentoring was a pursuit and a philosophy that infused her agenda throughout the White House years. She drew satisfaction from sharing her stories and she found that they resonated with young audiences, especially African American girls. "She really wanted to think about how to engage young people and to engage young people from all walks of life, not just the expected schools," said Jocelyn Frye, a Washington native and Harvard friend who steered the project as Michelle's policy director. The role seemed to come naturally, and it fulfilled her bedrock determination to reach back. "In every phase of my life, whether I was in high school or Princeton or Harvard or working for the city or working at the hospital, I was always looking for somebody to mentor," Michelle said when she took the project to Detroit in 2010. "I was looking for a way to reach out into my neighborhood and my community and pull somebody else along with me, because I thought, 'There but for the grace of God go I.'"

The program paired twenty high school sophomores and juniors with women who worked in the Obama White House. Michelle wanted the students to experience "substance and fun." They saw Air Force One. They went to Anacostia. They went to the Supreme Court. They accompanied Michelle to see the Alvin Ailey dance company. They met Judith Jamison, the powerful and ethereal dancer who was one of Michelle's childhood heroes. The program was small, but its architecture reflected a determination to invest in activities tethered to a clear purpose. In a realm of infinite options and limited time, there would be no tilting at windmills in Michelle Obama's East Wing. "It's not sufficient to say we're going to do an event on childhood obesity. There has to be a reason for it. It has to have a beginning and an end and be part of a broader strategy," explained Frye, who said of the first Anacostia visit, "We didn't want it to be a one-shot deal, where we appear for a photo and not appear again. She wants us to have a plan, so we don't just go from event to event by the seat of our pants."

OVER IN THE WEST WING, it was difficult to exaggerate the calamities that Barack inherited. There were worries about terrorism during preparations for the inaugural festivities, as if the new president and his family needed any reminder of the perils ahead. Just hours before he took the oath of office, aides updated Barack on intelligence reports that Somali extremists might detonate bombs during his address to the nation. The celebration passed without incident, but the demands of the presidency were soon made plain. The economy, in free fall since the collapse of Lehman Brothers in September, lost an estimated 741,000 jobs in January alone. Another 651,000 jobs disappeared in February and 652,000 in March. The housing market was imploding, causing millions of people to lose their homes or a large chunk of the income they had counted on for retirement. The $236 billion budget surplus at the end of the Clinton years had turned into a $1.3 trillion deficit under George W. Bush, thanks to substantial Republican-inspired tax cuts for the wealthy and a pair of wars, in Iraq and Afghanistan, churning along without end. When Barack took office, 144,000 soldiers, marines, sailors, and airmen were deployed to Iraq. Another 34,000 were stationed in Afghanistan, a figure that would nearly triple on Barack's watch. The threat of terrorism, meanwhile, continued to lurk across an unsettled globe. When Barack Hussein Obama placed his hand on the Lincoln Bible and took the oath, wrote Peter Baker of *The New York Times,* he inherited "a nation in crisis at home and abroad."

The rueful joke told by some Obama supporters was that the country was going to hell, so *of course* they gave the job to a black guy. Being president sometimes felt like standing in a vast maze facing an endless sequence of blind turns leading to one set of choices after another. Each decision blended the consequences of the last one with a mind-bending array of considerations about the ones to come. Politics, principle, and practicalities all factored in, as did the inevitable pronouncements of the commentariat. It was no wonder that Barack liked to turn to ESPN, the sports channel, to escape. Michelle sometimes offered her opinions, not least on personnel. Chicago friend Marty Nesbitt called her the most "do what's right" person in Barack's circle, representing true north. "She's just very pragmatic and straightforward. She doesn't sugarcoat her perspective or dance around the issues. She just calls it like she sees it." Valerie Jarrett, who moved into a West Wing office as a presidential adviser, agreed and said Michelle played an essential role.

"She is completely honest. There are very few people you can say that about. She tells the president exactly what she thinks. She doesn't hold back." Susan Sher added that Michelle tended to speak up about public opinion. "She likes to say, 'This is not what people care about. They care about *this.*'"

That said, Michelle chose her moments. She explained that while she was "honest, absolutely," there were times when a talking-to was not what Barack needed. "In a job like this, the last thing a president of the United States needs when he walks in the door to come home is somebody who is drilling him and questioning him about the decisions and choices that he's made. So, there are definitely times when I may feel something, but I'll hold back because I know he'll either get to it on his own or it's just not time." Living a few steps away from the Oval Office did have its advantages in times of turmoil. "Now I can just pop over to his office," Michelle said, "which sometimes I'll do if I know he's having a particularly frustrating day."

Massachusetts governor Deval Patrick said Michelle's personality helped Barack open up emotionally, providing a space "where he lets himself feel the stuff that goes on in the office and not just think about the stuff and evaluate the stuff and consider his options around the stuff." Patrick, who saw Barack in settings public and private, said the president was empathetic and able to show it behind the scenes, when meeting, for example, with wounded soldiers or victims of a tragedy. But in public, Barack was "very careful emotionally. He's uncommonly analytical and self-contained, in the sense that he is going to let things roll off him that just wouldn't roll off of others." Michelle was able to draw him out. "She's more confident about expressing her emotions, whether grief or anger or frustration or what have you," Patrick said. "Not necessarily publicly, but in company with him, and I think that's helpful for him. She makes him better."

WHILE BARACK FACED the recession, the deficit, the wars, and a hundred other problems, Michelle set out to manage the household. In the residence, there were thirty-six rooms, including five bedrooms on the second floor and six on the third, plus sixteen bathrooms. There was a household staff and an office staff. There were new family routines, a new private school for Malia and Sasha, and new duties, from party planning to official correspondence, plus the care and feeding of everyone who wanted a piece of her day. There was even a new dog, a purebred Portuguese water dog named Bo, promised to the girls as a post-campaign reward. Michelle often felt swamped and was not shy about confessing her unhappiness. She had always relied on her girlfriends for support, yet the challenges of Washington were compounded by having few close friends nearby. Sher, her old friend from City Hall and the University of Chicago, was in the White House counsel's office. Desiree Rogers, the former head of Peoples Gas and ex-wife of John Rogers, was her social secretary. Plus she had Jarrett. "Valerie was the counselor. Valerie was the everything," said Jackie Norris, Michelle's first chief of staff.

To help, the Chicago contingent made frequent trips to the nation's capital, offering reassurance. "Do you still recognize me? Do I still feel like Michelle, or are you tripping?" she would ask when checking in with old friends. In search of equilibrium, the "most unexpected and uniform advice" she received from former first ladies was to go early and often to the presidential retreat at Camp David, about sixty miles north in Maryland's Catoctin Mountain Park. "It's one place you can go where you feel some level of freedom and an ability to breathe," Michelle said. "I think every single first lady felt that was an important resource, an important opportunity, an important thing for the health of the family."

To shore up the home front, Michelle asked her seventy-one-year-old mother to move into the White House, where she could live on the third floor of the residence, help with the girls, and support the first lady. Marian was, to say the least, reluctant. "That I can do without. When you move in, you hear just a little bit too much," she once said. Among other drawbacks, she worried that living in the White House would feel like living in a museum and she did not want to give up her car. She liked to drive. Michelle asked her brother to work on her.

"My sister said, 'You've got to talk to Mom. She's not moving,'" said Craig, who knew that Marian prized her independence and had no use for the rarefied White House air or egos inflated by proximity to power. "She doesn't want grand. She doesn't want great. She would much rather stay home." She was close to relatives and friends and had a routine that suited her. There were shopping trips with her sister, yoga at her brother's studio, and a quiet life at home where she read the newspaper, did crossword puzzles, watched home improvement shows, played the piano, and shoveled her own walk. Her means and her needs were modest.

But she relented. Marian locked the door on the Euclid Avenue house and became an integral part of the Obama household. In Washington, after accompanying Malia and Sasha to school in an SUV driven by the Secret Service, she would often return to the residence and, if Michelle were home, chat with her before heading to her third-floor quarters. At a White House tea, Michelle singled her out, declaring that Marian "has pulled me up when I've stumbled. She's pulled me back when I've run out of line, talking a little too much. She'll snap me up. She really does push me to be the best woman that I can be, truly, as a professional and as a mother and as a friend. And she has always, always, always been there for me. Raising our girls in the White House with my mom—oh, not going to do this," Michelle said, starting to choke up, "is a beautiful experience."

As Marian found her way, she had the advantage of relative anonymity, allowing her to walk out the White House gates and stroll through downtown Washington, maybe stopping at the pharmacy, without creating a fuss. Once, when a passerby remarked that she looked just like Mrs. Robinson, she replied, "Oh, yeah, people say that." And she kept walking. She slipped easily out of Washington, traveling to Chicago or to the Pacific Northwest, where she visited Craig and his family at Oregon State University. Of course, she also sat in the president's box at the Kennedy Center, sometimes joined by her friend Bettie Currie, former White House secretary to Bill Clinton. She flew aboard Air Force One to Russia and Ghana. She met Pope Benedict and Queen Elizabeth. Michelle reveled in her presence and said, "I'm pretty sure the president is happy, too." Barack credited Marian for bringing stories back to the

White House from the outside world because, he said, "she escapes the bubble."

THE BUBBLE IS one of the strangest aspects of the modern presidency and a feature the Obamas especially lamented. In physical terms, the bubble is the security cordon that surrounds the president and his immediate family 24 hours a day, 365 days a year. The Obamas could not go anywhere, ever, without being guarded by gun-carrying Secret Service agents. Eighteen months into his presidency, asked what he missed most, Barack answered, "Taking walks." He regretted being unable to sit absently on a bench in a city park or go alone with his kids to get ice cream. Anonymity, he said, is "a profound pleasure that is very hard to experience now." Beyond the physical cordon, the bubble also came to represent the isolation of life in the White House, which Harry Truman called in his 1947 diary "the great white jail." Truman said the executive mansion was "a hell of a place in which to be alone. While I work from early morning until late at night, it is a ghostly place. The floors pop and crack all night long." In the gloom, he saw the specters of his predecessors. "They all walk up and down the halls of this place and moan about what they should have done and didn't."

Sixty years later, an otherwise simple dinner for two at a D.C. restaurant required a security sweep of the premises and a screening of patrons. A decision to spend a few days outside the capital triggered a far more complex and expensive choreography. Even a stroll through the White House and its grounds posed problems, given the presence of news photographers, staff, and guests in a sprawling mansion that served as government office, tourist destination, and private home. It was surreal. Barack left on trips vertically, from the South Lawn. "Once, someone on my staff e-mailed to tell me that the president was on his way," Michelle said. "But you could already hear the helicopter, so it was like, well, no kidding."

During her first spring in Washington, Michelle approached the Secret Service. She wanted to see the city's glorious cherry blossoms, a simple outing in a season that drew tens of thousands of tourists and residents to the Tidal Basin and more secluded spots. Not so simple, it turned out, for a first lady. She put on a baseball cap and met Cindy Moelis, a Chicago friend from their time at City Hall who ran the White House Fellows Program. With an agent at the wheel, they drove to one destination, but the agent decided the crowds were too thick; Michelle would surely be recognized. They drove instead to a less popular place. The trees were in bloom, and they took a walk. Another time, Michelle was delighted to hear that she could walk to an event at the Corcoran Gallery of Art, only to discover that it was barely across the street from the White House complex. When she went to Target one time, a customer, not recognizing Michelle, asked if she would pull something down for her from a high shelf. She obliged. The first lady told friends that some white people simply did not "see" her, a black woman, when she was out in public and trying to be inconspicuous.

Unlike her husband, Michelle was not trailed by a media pool during her private time. Without him, she could escape, albeit driven and escorted by the Secret Service. She discovered restaurants where she could eat unmolested. She went to the theater and ball games. She visited the homes of friends, who were instructed that informal visits were considered "off the grid" by the Secret Service command, for security reasons. No one was to say where Michelle was headed or when. If word leaked, the excursion might be canceled. Michelle did not like it, not one bit, but she adapted even when her staff told her no. "Just give me the rules. Just tell me. I'll live with it," Michelle said, according to Sher, who was struck by the fresh constraints. "Think of the shock to your system, in an incredibly short time."

How little had changed, even as so much had, in the world of first ladies. In 1789, the first year of the first American presidency, Martha Washington said she felt constrained by the role. "I never goe to any public place, indeed, I think I am much more like a state prisoner than anything else," she wrote to her niece from New York, the temporary seat of government. "There is certain bounds set for me which I must not depart from and as I cannot doe as I like I am obstinate and stay at home a great deal." Asked at a public forum with Laura Bush about Washington's "state prisoner" reference, Michelle said, to laughter, "There are prison elements to it, but it's a really nice prison." Bush interjected, "But with a chef!" Michelle continued, "You can't complain, but there are definitely elements that are confining." In some ways, Michelle quickly discovered, the bubble was a fishbowl and she was the one swimming behind glass. Perceptions could be powerful and criticism withering in a life lived in the public eye. But there were advantages. When she wanted to draw attention to an issue, she knew that pens and cameras would be at the ready.

DURING THE CAMPAIGN, Barack promised Michelle a date night in New York. It would be dinner, a show, just the two of them out on the town. But this was their new life and getting to Broadway was, well, a production. The Obamas, dressed in stylish stepping-out clothes, emerged from the White House in bright sunlight on the afternoon of May 30, 2009. As a pool photographer snapped photos, they strolled hand in hand across the South Lawn to a waiting helicopter, where a marine officer crisply saluted. The chopper took them to Andrews Air Force Base in suburban Maryland, where they boarded a small air force jet to New York. A second helicopter was waiting there to fly them to lower Manhattan, where a motorcade was idling. They climbed into the presidential Cadillac limousine, called "The Beast," a rolling fortress that weighed seven and a half tons, thanks to its titanium and steel armor, its bulletproof glass and its doors, as thick as a commercial airliner's. The vehicle could be sealed from the outside air in case of a chemical weapons attack, and in the trunk it carried a supply of blood with the president's type. As Michelle would joke about their attempts at date nights, "Barack has a 20-car motorcade, men with guns, the ambulance is always there. How romantic can you be?"

Dinner in New York that night, reflecting Michelle's foodie interests and tastes, was at Blue Hill, an upscale locavore haven housed in a former Greenwich Village speakeasy. "Perhaps no other restaurant makes as serious and showy an effort to connect diners to the origins of their food," a *New York Times* food critic wrote in 2006. From the restaurant, the Obamas returned to the waiting motorcade, which included a media contingent—reporters, photographers, video teams—and drove to the Belasco Theatre, where New York police and the Secret Service had cordoned off an entire block of West 44th Street hours before the performance of August Wilson's *Joe Turner's Come and Gone.* The play, set in a northern boardinghouse during the Great Migration, depicted a search for livelihood and identity among dislocated black characters. As theatergoers flowed through metal detectors, the 8 p.m. curtain was delayed for forty-five minutes. Afterward, the Obamas passed throngs of people angling for a glimpse or a snapshot, then made their airborne way back to Washington, the South Lawn, and their permanently lighted, staffed, and secured home. Ticket sales for the show doubled the next day. The theater seats they occupied at the Belasco were unbolted from the floor and offered for sale at a charity auction.

Michelle and Barack had not left New York before the Republican National Committee was criticizing the trip as extravagant and insensitive, with the economy in recession and General Motors days away from declaring bankruptcy. "Have a great Saturday evening," RNC spokeswoman Gail Gitcho scoffed to her digital audience, "even if you're not jetting off somewhere at taxpayer expense." The political quandary the Obamas faced, with reporters recording their every move, would recur throughout their White House tenure. The West Wing foresaw trouble with the New York excursion and released a statement to reporters in Barack's name. "I am taking my wife to New York City," he said, "because I promised her during the campaign that I would take her to a Broadway show after it was all finished." As far as he was concerned, that should have been the end of the story.

"IT's A DERIVATIVE JOB. There's so much there that you're just supposed to do, that everyone's been doing since 1952," Trooper Sanders, an East Wing staff member, said of the role of first lady. To follow the familiar path would be relatively easy, Michelle and her team recognized early on, but it would turn the East Wing into a velvet coffin, comfortable but pointless. A first lady who allowed parties and traditional fare to define her days, Sanders said, would wake up four years or eight years later and say to herself, "I haven't done anything."

Yet Michelle would discover that doing things differently could create its own trouble in hierarchical, tradition-bound Washington. Just as she chose where to play a role, she would choose where not to. Historic preservation, for example, at least in the early going. It was a typical engagement for first ladies, embraced by Hillary Clinton, who created the Save America's Treasures program, and Laura Bush. But Michelle was not particularly interested and felt she brought nothing special to the table, despite a stint on the Chicago Landmarks Commission. When she concluded that it was a cause that could be championed elsewhere in the federal government, she disappointed the leaders of well-connected organizations who had expected more. Similarly, she faced questions about protocol and priorities when she sought to change the tone of the annual Congressional Club First Lady's Luncheon, described by one aide as a "bastion of everything that made us cringe."

The first lady and her staff got a taste of what was to come when a luncheon organizer sent a swatch of fabric from the tablecloths so that Michelle could find a matching dress. Then there was the elevated catwalk, styled like a fashion runway and designed to showcase the guest of honor. Laura Bush walked the catwalk in 2001, her first year in the White House. She "politely declined" thereafter, commenting, "As first lady, I was accustomed to doing almost anything, but this was a bit too much." Bush said the organizers besieged her staff long before the 2002 event, insisting that she use the catwalk. They also asked her to stay for the entire four-hour lunch and honor specific requests about what to say in her remarks. Undeterred, she left the event early that year, hurrying to New Haven to help her daughter Barbara move out of her dormitory room at Yale.

The "constant back-and-forth" over the congressional luncheon invariably reduced someone in her office to tears, said Bush, who reported that in previous years, members of Clinton's staff had cried in frustration, too. Anita McBride sympathized. As Bush's second chief of staff, she alerted Michelle's team to the demands of the social calendar and the choices ahead. She left sample letters for the correspondence office, a list of contacts at every agency, and timelines for all kinds of events, including the annual White House Christmas card, a chore that fell to the first lady's office. She also made sure to mention the challenge of dealing with what Bush called "the Congressional Club ladies." McBride said she told her successors, "This is one of those things that is a have-to-do on the schedule but, you know what, this might be an opportunity to change what the requirements are. There are some have-to-dos, but it doesn't mean the first ladies can't set parameters."

Michelle quickly saw that she was not in Kansas any longer. This was Oz. Or maybe Kafka. Nowhere in her wedding vows did it say "for richer, for poorer, *in the White House* or in health." On the one hand, she wanted to support the political spouses, "because she knows how hard that role is," Norris said. On the other, there was surely a more meaningful option than a fancy lunch. "The one thing that she didn't want to do was just do something because it had been done before." Michelle compromised. She went along with the table linens and the dress, but she also invited the spouses to do a service project. More than 150 wives and husbands joined her on the 100th day of the Obama presidency to fill grocery bags, two thousand in all, at the Capital Area Food Bank.

MICHELLE ARRIVED in London on April 1, 2009, for her first overseas trip as first lady. While Barack held working meetings, she embraced cancer patients at Charing Cross Hospital and took in a ballet at the Royal Opera. Wearing a simple black cardigan and two strands of pearls, she met Queen Elizabeth and promptly broke protocol. Towering above the white-haired monarch, she placed her manicured left hand warmly on Her Majesty's back. It was a natural gesture, but apparently one does not touch the eighty-two-year-old queen, apart from mildly shaking an outstretched hand. The queen did not seem to mind, although gadflies did buzz. It was on a side trip the next day, however, that Michelle unexpectedly found her groove. It happened at the Elizabeth Garrett Anderson School, named for Britain's first female doctor, an advocate of women's suffrage. Ninety percent of the girls came from racial or ethnic minority groups, representing fifty-five languages and count-less challenges overcome. In arranging the event in Islington, Michelle's advisers were looking for a place "the first lady wasn't expected to go," said Trooper Sanders. The team considered what would add value to the president's trip and what would be authentic to Michelle. What they saw at the school was how strongly her own story, anchored in an urban corner of the American Midwest, resonated with teenagers a world away. Michelle saw it, too.

"Nothing in my life ever would have predicted that I would be stand-ing here as the first African-American first lady. I was not raised with wealth or resources or any social standing to speak of. I was raised on the South Side of Chicago. That's the real part of Chicago," she told the girls. "I want you to know that we have very much in common." Echo-ing her remarks at Anacostia High two weeks earlier, she declared that "confidence and fortitude" would win out. "You too, can control your own destiny, please remember that." As she spoke, the girls cheered and Michelle choked up. When she ended her remarks, she surprised them by announcing, "I do hugs." The girls flocked around her and she deliv-ered one embrace after another. Afterward, feeling invigorated, she climbed into her car and said, "I could do that all day."

It was not much of a stretch to say that Michelle had found her métier, in words and gestures. Her story connected with the girls and so did her familiar, affirming embrace. In the White House, a hug would become her signature, natural and abiding, a sign of faith and support. She was not yet certain about the contours of the bully pulpit, nor had she decided which issues to pursue, but a hug was one concrete thing that she could make happen. With a smile, a few words, and an embrace, she would try to convey to thousands of girls and boys that the first lady of the United States believed in them. As for the Elizabeth Garrett Anderson School, she stayed in touch, arranging to meet thirty-five students at Oxford two years later and hosting twelve students at the White House in 2012. On her desk, she kept a photograph of her visit to the school.

Michelle made a point of speaking to young audiences when she visited India, Africa, and Latin America during her first two years in office. East Wing staffers, who asked State Department and National Security Council colleagues how the first lady could be useful, hoped her ability to connect with diverse young people overseas might even deliver a small foreign-policy benefit. At a time when the United States was waging a global competition for hearts and minds, she told university students in Mexico City in April 2010 that the "immense promise" of an Internet-connected generation had persuaded her to make young people the focus of her international efforts. Nearly half of Mexico's population was younger than twenty-five, she noted, while in the Middle East, the figure was 60 percent. She called it a youth bulge and made clear that the status quo would not suffice. "You have an unprecedented ability to organize and to mobilize, and to challenge old assumptions, and to bridge old divides and to find new solutions to our toughest problems," she said. *Organize. Mobilize. Challenge. Bridge.* Through the prism of assets, not deficits. She told her staff, "Don't just put me on a plane, send me someplace and have me smile." She was finding her voice. The challenge was to make it matter.

THIRTEEN

Between Politics and Sanity

For all of the glorious trees and flowers on the eighteen acres of the White House grounds, from Andrew Jackson's southern magnolias to roses of more recent vintage, no one had planted a vegetable garden since Eleanor Roosevelt's time. The idea for a garden and a larger project on children's health came to Michelle in 2007. She was in her kitchen in Hyde Park, starting to imagine ways she might make a difference if Barack actually won the presidency. A garden—simple, satisfying, illustrative. Although she arrived in Washington with little experience with seeds and soil, she intended the garden to be more than a garden. She wanted it to be a national conversation starter "about the food we eat, the lives we lead, and how all of that affects our children." Public elementary school children helped with the planting. The raised beds were visible to passersby beyond the White House fence, she said, "because I wanted this to be the 'people's garden,' just as the White House is the 'people's house.'"

The medium was the message. The new garden became a billboard for Michelle's back-to-basics views on nutrition and fitness, a focus of her White House years. Aides invited the media to cover the planting and advertised the use of the garden's harvest, including honey from a swarm of bees, at White House dinners. White House chefs brewed their own Honey Brown Ale and cooked up a veggie pizza for *Tonight Show* host Jay Leno. The garden became the heart of a glossy book,

American Grown: The Story of the White House Kitchen Garden and Gardens Across America. Written by Michelle and a ghostwriter, the 2012 volume contained dozens of photographs of the first lady, along with suggestions for helping the needy and tips on establishing a community garden. One of the featured gardens, in fact, was at Chicago's Rainbow Beach, the park on Lake Michigan where Michelle rode her bike and attended summer camp. If all went well, she wrote, schools and communities would follow her example and children who had never grown anything would sow, reap, and learn. "For little kids," she said, "the best part is the compost, where they can dig for worms with their hands. They love the idea that a lot of soil is worm poop."

THE GARDEN CREATED an entry point to Michelle's most ambitious and, it turned out, controversial White House initiative, a nutrition and fitness project launched in February 2010. With nearly one in three American children considered overweight and adult obesity rates rising, her goal was to change children's eating and exercise habits nationwide. Her targets ranged from unhealthy school nutrition standards and urban food deserts to restaurant menus and sweet-toothed marketing messages. Amid energetic photo ops that featured her dancing with students and exercising with sports stars, Michelle picked up a telephone in the White House to urge Congress to pass a $4.5 billion child nutrition bill. She also collaborated with pediatricians and corporate food purveyors, as well as media companies that produced programming for children. She called the project "Let's Move!"

The public health implications of fatness were apparent in the nation's expanding waistlines. In one indication of trouble, excessive weight was by far the biggest medical disqualifier in the U.S. armed forces. Between 1995 and 2008, the military counted 140,000 people who failed their entrance physicals because they were overweight. By 2010, half of all volunteers—46.7 percent of men and 54.6 percent of women—were failing a fitness test that required only sixty seconds of push-ups, sixty seconds of sit-ups, and a one-mile run. Further, many recruits had brittle bones because of a diet containing too many fizzy drinks and sugary foods and too little milk and calcium. Obesity and its effects added an estimated $147 billion to the country's annual health costs, according to the Obama administration, and the problems started young. The U.S. Centers for Disease Control calculated that 16 percent of children in 2010 were obese, with many of them developing habits and ailments that would become costly and debilitating in adulthood. A disproportionate number of overweight children were black or Hispanic. It escaped no one's notice that recess and physical education were increasingly rare in U.S. schools, as a result of budget cuts and changed priorities. The CDC reported that only one in twenty-five elementary schools, one in twelve middle schools, and one in fifty high schools offered daily physical education.

On February 9, 2010, in front of a half-dozen cabinet secretaries and a media contingent, Michelle laid out the problem, suggested solutions, and announced a series of partnerships. The American Academy of Pediatrics would develop procedures for measuring body mass index, or BMI, and devise prescriptions for more healthful living. Suppliers pledged to decrease sugar, fat, and salt in food sold to schools and, over the next ten years, double the amount of fruits and vegetables in school meals. The Food and Drug Administration would work with manufacturers and retailers to make food labels more clear, "so people don't have to spend hours squinting at words they can't pronounce to figure out whether the food they're buying is healthy or not," Michelle said. Media companies, including Disney, Scholastic, Viacom, and Warner Bros., would improve public awareness. In a public signal that the project dovetailed with his agenda, Barack that morning signed an order creating a Task Force on Childhood Obesity to review federal policy on nutrition and physical activity. After the Oval Office signing, he turned to Michelle and said, "It's done, honey."

MICHELLE'S REMARKS at the launch were not glib and glossy. Nor were they brief. In a speech that stretched to 5,800 words, she laid out her reasoning. She made plain that she was not blaming kids for eating too many calories or failing to burn them off. It was the role of adults to decide what schools served for lunch, what was available for dinner, and whether time would be set aside for gym and recess. "Our kids don't choose to make food products with tons of sugar and sodium in super-sized portions and then to have those products marketed to them everywhere they turn," she said. "And no matter how much they beg for pizza, fries and candy, ultimately they are not, and should not, be the ones calling the shots at dinnertime." Standing in the ornate State Dining Room, Michelle recalled mealtime in the cramped kitchen on Euclid Avenue. "There was one simple rule: You ate what was on your plate, good, bad or ugly. Kids had absolutely no say in what they felt like eating. If you didn't like it, you were welcome to go to bed hungry."

Michelle drew on her own experience as a working mother, recalling an alarming visit to a Chicago pediatrician who reported that Malia's and Sasha's weight, measured by body mass index, was too high. (Or, as Barack put it when telling the story, Malia was "a little chubby.") The doctor asked what the family ate, prompting Michelle to consider the way they lived their lives, particularly the pace. They always seemed to be racing from work to school to soccer, from ballet to piano to play dates. The parents had deadlines, the kids had homework, each task dueling with other demands, from maintaining friendships and looking after elders to keeping the house in a semblance of order. Comfortably upper middle class, the Obamas had the money to eat well, but too rarely took the time: "There were some nights when you got home so tired and hungry, and you just wanted to get through the drive-thru because it was quick and it was cheap. Or there were the times when you threw in that less healthy microwave option because it was easy." Her family started eating at home more often. They ate more vegetables and fresh fruit and drank more water and skim milk. They stopped keeping unhealthy food in the pantry and declared, as her parents had done, that desserts would largely be a weekend treat.

To emphasize the difficulties of families at varying economic levels, she spoke of "parents working so hard, longer hours, some cases two jobs" and the cost of fruit and vegetables rising 50 percent more than overall food costs since the 1980s. It did not help, she said, that the nation's cities were dotted with food deserts. These were neighborhoods that lacked a decent grocery store, making it harder for shoppers, especially the unemployed and the working poor, to find fresh food. "So this is where we are. Many parents desperately want to do the right thing, but they feel like the deck is stacked against them."

It may have seemed innocuous for a first lady to advocate fitness and healthy eating, but Michelle anticipated criticism. Hoping to inoculate the effort against allegations of government overreach and the inevitable portrayals of her as nanny-in-chief, she said experts did not think the problem would be solved by the government "telling people what to do." Nor was this about "preparing five-course meals from scratch every night. And it is not about being 100 percent perfect 100 percent of the time because, lord knows, I'm not. There is a place in this life for cookies and ice cream and burgers and fries." Money for fruit and vegetables when the country was on the economic skids and teachers and schoolbooks were in short supply? Funding for parks and sidewalks when the nation could not afford health care for its citizens? "These are false choices," Michelle said, "because if kids aren't given adequate nutrition, even the best books and teachers in the world won't help them get where they want them to be. And if they don't have safe places to run and play and they wind up with obesity-related conditions, those health care costs will just keep rising."

She was right to brace herself. For years to come, critics would call her a hypocrite, and worse.

FASHION BECAME a defining element of Michelle's public profile. She delighted in clothes and developed an admiring and covetous following that crossed lines of class and race. She lit up magazine covers, yet nowhere was the phenomenon more pronounced than in the blogosphere. Bloggers raced to identify every designer and off-the-rack selection, often noting the last time she had worn an outfit or which shoes and accessories accompanied it. For five years on Mrs.-O.com, Mary Tomer offered commentary down to the smallest detail, writing in 2009, "For the event, Mrs. O remixed several familiar pieces from her wardrobe. The black and white stripe blouse, last seen at the President and First

Lady's visit to the Capitol City Charter School. As well as the teal cardigan and royal blue patent leather belt, last seen in combination for the National Day of Service. A gray wool blazer and trousers rounded out the multi-layered ensemble (perhaps a cold weather tactic?)." Michelle's range was striking, from bare feet on the South Lawn to a cardigan at Buckingham Palace to kitten heels everywhere, in part to avoid putting Barack, lean and barely two inches taller, in her shadow.

It had been nearly fifty years since a first lady so captured imaginations with her fashion choices. "She has perhaps even surpassed Jackie O. because the world is bigger now than it was then," said designer Thakoon Panichgul. He admired how Michelle dressed "with such confidence," and conceded that it was refreshing to design clothes for someone with "the body of a modern woman today." A body, in other words, that could not be squeezed into a size 2. Talk of Michelle's body, and there was much talk, usually started with her sculpted arms. She earned them in the gym and bore them with pride, opting for sleeveless looks that caused fans to coo and pundits to bark. "She's made her point. Now she should put away Thunder and Lightning," cracked *New York Times* columnist David Brooks to a colleague. Spotting a trend, magazines ran how-to guides and trainers marketed exercise programs, such as *Totally Toned Arms: Get Michelle Obama Arms in 21 Days.*

Michelle went bare-shouldered at Barack's first State of the Union address. She did the same on the cover of *Vogue*. Perhaps most tellingly, she decided to show off her arms in her first official White House portrait, shot in the Blue Room beneath the watchful eye of Thomas Jefferson. She dressed in a black Michael Kors sheath with a double strand of white pearls, her smile broad, her face and hair impeccably styled, her left fingertips resting on a marble table adorned with flowers. She had just turned forty-five when the photo was taken, in the early days of the first term. The image spoke of youth and fitness, the antithesis of many past first ladies. Her blackness was all the more striking in juxtaposition with the painting of the nation's third president, who owned slaves and fathered as many as six children with one of them, Sally Hemings. In 1781, while professing that all men were created equal, Jefferson wrote that black people had a "much inferior" capacity to reason and were "dull, tasteless, and anomalous" when it came to imagination. "Never yet," wrote one of the most erudite of American presidents, "could I find that a black uttered a thought above the level of plain narration; never see even an elementary trait of painting or sculpture." The contrast in the photograph was unintentional, said her press secretary, Katie McCormick Lelyveld, who staffed Michelle that day. "We tried outside, we tried the Red Room, we tried the Green Room, we tried the Blue Room. We tried sitting, we tried standing. We liked this smile the best. We liked this backdrop the best."

IN HER SARTORIAL CHOICES, Michelle was mindful not only of how she would look, but how the fashions would play. Designers learned they could take risks in color, texture, and style when designing for the first lady. Isabel Toledo, born in Cuba, created the shimmering wool lace dress Michelle wore to the inauguration. She called the color lemongrass. "Fashion is what history looks like. For me, that moment in history was a moment of optimism," explained Toledo, who said admiringly that the first lady is "not just covering herself. She cares about what she looks like. She cares about how people perceive her." Twenty-six-year-old Jason Wu, born in Taiwan, designed the ivory chiffon gown that Michelle wore to the inaugural balls. When she donated it to the Smithsonian, she declared it a "masterpiece." Creations by Panichgul, born in Thailand, and Naeem Khan, born in India, found their way into her closet, along with dresses by Peter Soronen and Narciso Rodriguez.

Michelle had aides who helped shop for her couture, while White House lawyers monitored rules governing gifts and favors. Toledo said Michelle paid "several thousand" dollars for the lemongrass creation, a purchase coordinated by high-end Chicago boutique owner Ikram Goldman. Into a lineup rich with costly designer-made duds, some stitched just for her, she folded off-the-rack choices from the likes of J.Crew, Talbot's, and the Gap. More than once, an outfit sold out swiftly when Michelle wore it on television. The same happened with a unicorn sweater worn by Sasha when she was still in middle school. The populist elements to Michelle's selections multiplied when she added an affordable brooch or a wide belt to enliven a workaday ensemble. Telling *Ebony*, "what you wear is a reflection of who you are," she shunned pantyhose as uncomfortable and urged women to choose clothes that made them feel good. She was neither a fashion model nor a performer, but a woman who had been in the workforce for twenty years, half of that as a working mother. Through her choices—the colors, the combinations, the risks—Michelle "gave women the permission, the liberty, to participate" in fashion, said Isabel Toledo's husband, Ruben, an artist and collaborator. Her fans could relate. New York fashion writer Kate Betts titled her book about Michelle's approach to fashion *Everyday Icon*, crediting her with "helping to liberate a generation of women from the false idea that style and substance are mutually exclusive." Betts connected the first lady's style with a gospel of empowerment "that defines style as knowing who you are and being unafraid to show it to the world."

Together, Michelle and Barack delivered "romantic glamor" said Patricia L. Williams, who wrote about race and society for *The Nation*. "She brings a dignity to it. It's not dressing like Rihanna. It's not the entertainment industry, it's not sports. It underscores *lady*." The attention paid to her clothes demonstrated the array of expectations—gendered and otherwise—still attached to the role of first lady. Everywhere she went, even if only to walk Bo on the White House grounds, Michelle knew she might be photographed and examined for fashion flaws. One summer day, she stepped down the stairs of Air Force One to join her family on a walk at the Grand Canyon. It was 106 degrees and she wore shorts—ordinary shorts that came to mid-thigh. The reaction was swift. The first lady wore shorts? In *public*? After NBC's *Today* show discussed the moment on television, 300,000 viewers offered an opinion. At the *Huffington Post*, nearly 13,000 did the same, with 58.6 percent saying she had "the right to bare legs," 16.8 percent saying no, and 24.6 percent answering, "It's not the end of the world, but maybe she should wear longer shorts next time."

Michelle never forgot. Four years later, she called it her biggest fashion regret. Far more considered was her decision to appear on the cover of the March 2009 issue of *Vogue*. Despite the collective misery of the economic recession, she believed it would send a message to African American girls of many shapes and sizes about who they could be when they grew up. Although Michelle sometimes drew criticism when she veered away from American designers, her choices often drew an excited shiver in the commercial fashion world. "Have you seen someone with his hands down and eyes popped out? That was me for a few seconds. Yesterday, I was the third-most Googled person in America. It is unbelievable," said Naeem Khan after seeing Michelle on television in November 2009, wearing one of his lush creations. Steven Kolb, head of the Council of Fashion Designers of America, called Michelle "an incredible booster. Once Mrs. Obama wears a designer, the pride, the enthusiasm, the boasting is a big moment for a designer, particularly a young designer. You can't build a business based on somebody wearing your clothes, but you can capitalize on it."

Disciplined as she was, Michelle suffered a few self-inflicted wounds. One was the day she wore a $540 pair of Lanvin sneakers to volunteer at a Washington food bank. Fashionistas recognized the brand and located the price tag in an Internet minute. Another was the day she donned a $495 pair of Tory Burch boots to pick pumpkins in the White House garden. When Burch's Facebook page crowed that Michelle was wearing his boots, the response reflected the reigning dichotomy. "Wearing them as she walks through dirt to pick a pumpkin. Yeah, she really understands the plight of the common man," someone posted. Others came to her defense, pointing out that taxpayers were not paying for her footwear and, anyway, she was damned if she did, damned if she didn't. "If she went with her head tied in rags and wearing sweat pants, then folks would say she was not representing her position well," a supporter posted. "Some people will complain about heaven being too sunny!"

FIRST LADIES HAD STAGED concerts in the White House since time immemorial. Jackie Kennedy, in the early 1960s, built a portable stage in the East Room and hosted musical evenings and readings, including events for young people. Yet no previous first lady possessed more eclectic tastes than Michelle, who was determined to showcase a wide range of voices. One emblematic night in May 2009 highlighted jazz, the spoken word, and social justice. James Earl Jones recited a passage from *Othello,* while Chicago poet Mayda del Valle delivered a homage to her late Puerto Rican grandmother: "My tongues are broken needles," she said, "scratching through the grooves of a lost wisdom trying to find a faith that beats like yours. What secrets do your bones hold?" Singer and acoustic bass player Esperanza Spalding took the stage, as did Eric Lewis, a rock-jazz pianist who liked to reach into a piano to pluck the wires. For Lewis, it was sweet validation to play in the East Room as the Obamas and Spike Lee looked on. "I was totally surprised she had that kind of candor and sheer taste for something edgy, fast and hip," said Lewis, whose stage name is ELEW. The audience was similarly varied, by Michelle's design. "I love the notion of having members of Congress sitting in the East Room listening to the spoken word," she said. "It's just those incongruencies, making sure the socialites from D.C. are sitting next to the teachers from Anacostia listening to opera. It's that whole mix. You can get so much done and say so much— without saying anything."

Michelle's broader goal, and one particularly connected to the South Side of her upbringing, was to open the White House to children unlikely to drive past the grounds, much less be invited inside. "If I'm giving those experiences to Malia and Sasha, and I think it's important to them, then I can't pretend it's not important for everyone. If they weren't important, the best high schools and grammar schools in the country wouldn't be fighting to make sure they had music," she told *Washington Post* reporter Robin Givhan in 2010. "The more experiences kids have, the more things that they see, the more things that they know to want." In a twist on the traditional White House concert series, Michelle urged stars scheduled to perform for adults at night to conduct workshops for children during the day. "We want to lift young people up. The country needs to be mindful that we have all these diamonds out there, and it would be a shame not to invest in those talents," she said. What united her projects was her determination to support less fortunate people who did not have access to the polished corridors she now walked. These were people whose lives she understood because they were so familiar to her, the ones living in the world as it was, not as it should be.

On the walls of the White House, too, Michelle made clear her tastes in color, design, and social commentary. The first couple's museum borrowings stretched from Degas and Jasper Johns to Mark Rothko and Josef Albers. A colorful 1940s-era oil-on-plywood painting by William H. Johnson called *Booker T. Washington Legend* showed the educator and author of *Up from Slavery* teaching black students. Also among the borrowings were two canvases by Alma Thomas, a black expressionist painter who taught art in Washington public schools and recalled being turned away from museums because of her race. In the White House residence, Michelle hung a painting by Glenn Ligon titled *Black Like Me #2*. It featured a single phrase repeated over and over as if in typeface, the letters gradually becoming blacker toward the bottom of the piece. The phrase came from *Black Like Me,* John Howard Griffin's memoir of darkening his white skin to experience life as a Negro in the Deep South in 1959. The words in the painting read, "All traces of the Griffin I had been were wiped from existence."

FOR THE FIRST TIME in a dozen years, since before Malia and Sasha were born, Michelle and Barack were consistently at home together under one roof. There were no commutes from Chicago to Springfield or to Washington, D.C. They did not even have to leave the building to get to their offices. From a dressing room window in the residence, Michelle could peer across the Rose Garden into the West Wing and see Barack at work. Laura Bush had showed her the window when Michelle visited the White House in November 2008. Barack's office was not far from the girls' new swing set, the pool, and the tennis court. He was routinely home for dinner at 6:30 p.m. and no one had to cook. Many nights, the president stuck around for bedtime before turning back to his work. The family took turns saying grace, always ending with "We hope we live long and strong." Dinner table conversation tended not to focus on the troubles buffeting the republic, but on Malia and Sasha, "what's going on in their lives, and in ours. Some nights, we discuss issues they've heard about in the news," Michelle said. Asked once whether Barack was helpful around the house, she replied, "Even the president of the United States can handle figuring out whether somebody put their writing assignment in their book bag."

There was plenty of space in the residence for childrens' sleepovers on the third floor, and the family could escape to Camp David, where friends would often join them. On weekends in good weather, Barack played golf, most often with lower-level White House aides, and he sometimes coached Sasha's basketball team, the Vipers. The young players thought of him not as the commander in chief, but as Sasha's dad. "This is what dads are supposed to do," he said. "So they take it for granted." He conceded that he had to discourage Sasha from spending so much time on her three-point shot, rather than perfecting skills closer to the basket. One day, the team's head coach was out of commission, so Barack called for his motorcade and headed up Connecticut Avenue to fill in, even though Sasha was on a Colorado ski trip with Michelle and Malia.

Sports mattered in the family, and not only because Barack loved hoops, watched ESPN, and savored those golf outings. Michelle, who lifted weights, jumped rope, did some kickboxing, and played tennis to keep fit, decreed that the girls would each play two sports. "Because it's good for them," she explained. "It's good to practice teamwork, to understand what it means to suffer a loss, to win with grace." Each girl would choose one sport and Michelle would choose the second one. "I want them to understand what it feels like to do something you don't like and to improve, because in life you don't always get to do the things you want." Her choice for them was tennis, as an activity that could sustain them for a lifetime. "When they started, the racket was bigger than Sasha," Michelle related. "She was frustrated because she couldn't hit the ball. Malia didn't understand why I was making them play. But now they're starting to get better and they actually like it. And I'm like, 'Mom was right!'"

The Obama kids would grow up with their feet on the ground, if their parents had their way. Michelle forbade the housekeepers from making the girls' beds. She expected Malia and Sasha, three years apart in age, to learn how to do laundry and honor limits on screen time. Also, no cell phones before they turned twelve. They attended Sidwell Friends, the celebrated private school in Northwest Washington that Chelsea Clinton attended. "They don't have any excuse not to be outstanding students. We're counting on them to do that," Michelle said. Malia and Sasha were also expected to appreciate lives less privileged than their own. In their teenage years, Barack said, the girls needed to learn about working for minimum wage, "to feel as if going to work and getting a paycheck is not always fun, not always stimulating, not always fair." When Malia lamented one aspect or another of her curious life, Michelle responded, "You want to see hardship? You want to see struggle? You don't have it, kid. Having the president as your father is way down on the list of tough."

The technology had changed and the family lived at a fancier address, but the messages recalled the lessons of Michelle's childhood, even if Marian felt sure that her daughter was a tougher taskmaster than she had been. Michelle, in mom-in-chief mode, instructed the nation's children and her own children alike. "You can't think you can be a jerk and lazy and trifling now and that one day you're going to wake up and just be great, right? . . . I tell my girls this now. 'Make up your bed today so that you know how to make up your bed when you're twenty. Clean up your room now so that when you go to college, you don't live like a pig. Do your homework now, not because you have to, but because you need to be in the practice of sitting down and finishing what you start.'"

By the same token, Michelle worked to preserve kid-friendly routines. The girls often escaped the White House to spend time at their friends' houses, especially as they grew older. They snapped selfies. They went to sleepaway camp. They went on family vacations to Martha's Vineyard in the summer and Hawaii at Christmas. Malia learned to drive. When they had to ride somewhere with their father, they found the presidential motorcade "a complete embarrassment." What they craved was normality, or as much normality as the first family's impossibly rarefied life could deliver. What was true for the children was true for the parents. "I think in our house we don't take ourselves too seriously, and laughter is the best form of unity, I think, in a marriage," Michelle said. "So we still find ways to have fun together, and a lot of it is private and personal. But we keep each other smiling, and that's good." Barack agreed. He spoke of the stress-relieving pleasure of conversations with his daughters. He once said, "What I value most about my marriage is that it is separate and apart from a lot of the silliness of Washington, and Michelle is not a part of that silliness."

In 2010, Barack published a children's book, *Of Thee I Sing,* in the form of a letter to his daughters. It started, "Have I told you lately how wonderful you are?" He interwove their potential with the story of the United States, delivering a notably multicultural portrait of America. He chose thirteen distinctive individuals as models of particular traits. Jane Addams for kindness, Jackie Robinson for bravery, Georgia O'Keeffe for creativity, Martin Luther King for perseverance. He invoked Vietnam memorial designer Maya Lin and farmworkers' organizer Cesar Chavez, as well as George Washington and Abraham Lincoln. To honor differences, he quoted Sitting Bull: "For peace, it is not necessary for eagles to be crows."

BARACK HAD ANOTHER brutal year in 2010. The economy was lagging, job creation was not nearly catching up with the losses of the recession, and unemployment stood at 9.6 percent. On January 19, the eve of his first anniversary as president, Democrats lost the Senate seat that had been occupied by Ted Kennedy for forty-six years before his death in August 2009. With it went the sixtieth vote needed by Democrats to overcome a filibuster. Against the odds, and against the counsel of some of his closest advisers, including chief of staff and future Chicago mayor Rahm Emanuel, Barack pressed ahead with his bid to reform the jury-rigged U.S. health insurance system and expand coverage to millions of Americans who could not afford a quality plan. It was a monumental undertaking and it was messy. Tens of millions of Americans younger than sixty-five, the age when Medicare took effect, had no health coverage. Millions more had coverage that paid for little actual care. Still others, afflicted with illnesses and ailments known in insurance-speak as "preexisting conditions," were unable to change jobs for fear of losing coverage that would be difficult to regain. A single-payer system was not in the cards, not with Republicans in revolt, not with rampant skepticism about the federal government's abilities, not with the private-sector oxen certain to be gored. The House and the Senate found a way forward. The result, which Barack signed with twenty-two pens on March 23, 2010, was sausage. But it was easily the most ambitious expansion of the safety net since the creation of Medicare in 1965. Barack said that day in a raucous East Room ceremony that the law enshrined the principle that everyone should have "some basic security" in tending to their health. If it could survive the Supreme Court and the Republicans—no sure thing—it might just be a step toward the more level playing field that Barack and Michelle were determined to help create.

White House jubilation had barely ebbed when an explosion on the Deepwater Horizon oil platform killed eleven workers and sent oil pouring into the Gulf of Mexico. The calamity showed just how unpredictable the president's job could be. For twelve weeks, the public watched on live video as the underwater well defied public and private efforts to cap it. Barack could do little but watch impotently as an estimated 210 million gallons of oil spilled into the gulf and damaged communities still recovering from Hurricane Katrina. Nationally, the president's approval ratings had dropped to 45 percent, down from 62 percent when he took office less than two years earlier. "The left thinks he did too little; the right too much," wrote *The New York Times* shortly before the November 2010 midterm elections, which could hardly have gone worse for the president. Democrats lost control of the House and surrendered six seats in the Senate, making Barack's legislative ambitions immeasurably harder to achieve. "A shellacking," he conceded at a press conference the next day. He acknowledged that his relationship with the American people had become "rockier and tougher."

It was true that Barack had stirred much of the country when he stood on the Capitol steps as the first African American taking the oath of office. But for many others, the honeymoon was over before it began. A passel of Republicans saw obstructionism as their ticket to Valhalla. Mitch McConnell, a dour Kentucky Republican, said on becoming Senate minority leader in 2011, "The single most important thing we want to achieve is for President Obama to be a one-term president." In rhetorical flights of fancy, opponents painted Barack variously as a socialist, a tyrant, a tribal African, a Muslim. Bugbears all. Most definitely *other*. That was the point. Nor did the disparagement come only from the fledgling Tea Party or the political fringe. Newt Gingrich, former Republican Speaker of the House and future presidential candidate, said Barack suffered from a "Kenyan anti-colonialist mentality." Mike Huckabee, a repeat presidential candidate and Fox News host, said the president's views were shaped by his childhood in Kenya, a country Barack did not visit until after college. John Sununu, a former New Hampshire governor and White House chief of staff to George H. W. Bush, was most succinct of all: "I wish this president would learn how to be an American."

Popular talk radio and television hosts devoted endless airtime to the anti-Barack cause, stoking doubt that morphed into disdain. Forty-five percent of Republicans in 2011 believed the president was born in another country, and they did not mean Hawaii. This was snake oil, the height of ridiculousness. Hawaiian authorities and news organizations had delivered multiple forms of proof that he was, indeed, born in Honolulu. These included his standard birth certificate, the one his fellow Americans used to get a driver's license or a passport, as well as the August 13, 1961, edition of *The Honolulu Advertiser*. On the list of recent births was "Mr. and Mrs. Barack H. Obama, 6085 Kalanianaole Hwy., son, Aug. 4." But the reality-deniers who became known as birthers refused to concede. Like southern state troopers in the Jim Crow era, they demanded to see Barack's papers, in this case his long form Certificate of Live Birth, stored in state files and not ordinarily made public.

On April 27, 2011, Barack strode into the White House press room and announced the release of the long form document. All the information, of course, checked out. "I know that there's going to be a segment of people for which, no matter what we put out, this issue will not be put to rest," he said. "But I'm speaking to the vast majority of the American people, as well as to the press. We do not have time for this kind of silliness." In character, the chairman of the Republican National Committee promptly blasted the president for wasting time on the birther question. "Unfortunately," Reince Priebus said in the tone of mock dudgeon reserved for such occasions, "his campaign politics and talk about birth certificates is distracting him from our No. 1 priority—our economy."

RUNNING FOR PRESIDENT, Barack said he sometimes felt like a Rorschach inkblot because so many voters saw what they chose to see. The same could be said of Michelle. Polls showed that she was quite popular despite the nation's polarization. Her favorability numbers typically ranged from the mid sixties to the low seventies, significantly higher than Barack's, which increasingly ducked into the low forties. She was not easily characterized and yet public reaction was often binary. Adore. *Abhor.* Respect. *Reject.* Warm, wise, and embracing. *Haughty, petty, and disdainful.* Criticism was expectable from anti-Obama partisans who could not bear a Democrat, especially these Democrats, in the White House. Some of the vitriol could be traced to racism and sexism or, at a charitable minimum, a lack of familiarity with a black woman as accomplished and outspoken as Michelle. "Just as an assertive woman is so frequently labeled aggressive, an audacious Black woman runs the risk of appearing, well, there is not another way to say it, uppity," journalist Gwen Ifill wrote in 2007 after traveling with the future first lady.

Criticism also emerged from people who viewed Michelle positively but asked why, given her education, her experience, and her extraordinary platform, she did not speak or act more directly on a host of progressive issues, whether abortion rights, gender inequity, or the structural obstacles facing the urban poor. Where was Michelle the take-charge hospital executive? Where was Michelle the strong-minded advocate who had been so pointed and forceful, so comfortable speaking truth to power, on the campaign trail in 2007 and early 2008? The Michelle, for example, who said of women in April 2007 that "we do what we can, in spite of the fact that we're not getting the kind of support we need from government and society as a whole. . . . We've essentially ignored the plight of women and told them to go figure it out."

The East Wing registered the criticism early, said chief of staff, Jackie Norris. "We heard it from women's groups. 'You're making her look like eye candy. She's so great, why is it that all we're ever hearing about is fashion?' People wanted us to do more, be out there more, be more aggressive, be more in the community." Through a feminist lens, which often meant white middle-class feminism, "mom-in-chief" sometimes seemed a synonym for copout. Writer Linda Hirshman said Michelle navigated the difficult waters of race and gender with "superbly canny, disciplined perfection," but observed that doing so required Michelle to imitate "a warm and fuzzy, unthreatening, bucolic female from some imaginary era from the past."

There was some truth to the idea that the politics of the job required Michelle to come across as warm and unthreatening, not just because she was the first lady, but because she was the first black first lady. A false step risked death by a thousand tweets. It was also significant, and readily apparent to people who knew her well, that Michelle cared deeply about her responsibilities as a mother. Part of what she meant by mom-in-chief was that Malia and Sasha really did come first. But managing her choices and accounting for the perceptions was like playing a game of three-dimensional chess. Rebecca Traister, author of *Big Girls Don't Cry,* admired Michelle for shattering "all kinds of molds of innocuous, feminine first-ladyhood." Yet she felt Michelle had been forced to surrender much of her identity to White House convention and her husband's career. "The stuff that was hers has been erased. It's not about, 'Does she have a job?' It's about, 'Does she have herself?' It's like somebody in a cage. You know that she knows it all, but what has to be presented to the world is this incredibly reduced version of who she is."

As Traister appreciated, to suggest that Michelle was melting into the White House draperies was to understate what she was doing and saying, and why. It also failed to account for the multiple meanings that Michelle's role tended to hold for African American women. Black women had been in the workforce since slavery, but their experiences were largely ignored in debates about how women should balance career and family. Part of the reason was economic. Until recently, few black women had the combination of financial security and family stability required to consider staying home. In mainstream popular culture, black women had more often been featured raising other people's children—notably, white people's children—than their own. "What's frequently missing from the discussion of black women is their role as loving mothers, beloved wives, valued partners, cherished daughters, cousins, relatives," said Columbia law professor Patricia J. Williams. She recalled long periods when black women were "relentlessly taxonimized as mammy rather than mom." On the other hand, she said, Michelle "defies stereotypes" and "expands the force field of feminism in ecumenical and unsettling ways."

Brittney Cooper, a scholar of black women's history, took similar issue with a critique of Michelle as a "feminist nightmare," in the words of a provocative *Politico Magazine* headline. "My message to white feminists is simple: Lean back. Way back. And take your paws off Michelle Obama," Cooper wrote. "Black women have never been the model for mainstream American womanhood." Michelle, in her view, should be left to decide for herself where to invest her energies. This also happened to be Michelle's opinion. "Part of what we fought for is choice," she said, "not just one definition of what it means to be a woman."

The public debate was mirrored in social media and kitchen table conversations, where a racial divide was similarly evident. In a 2011 poll, nearly eight in ten black women said they personally identified with Michelle. Eighty-eight percent said she understood their problems, according to the survey by *The Washington Post* and the Kaiser Family Foundation. Eighty-four percent of black men agreed, compared with just 51 percent of white women and 44 percent of white men. Only 2 percent of black women said she was not a good role model. One reason that African American women defended Michelle's emphasis on her family, said National Public Radio host Michel Martin, was "a feeling of relief and sympathy that at least one of their community, broadly defined, has the opportunity to protect her children, to cherish her family life, and to even have some personal time to shop and exercise and look good."

AS THE WHITE HOUSE GLARE intensified, friends were as important as ever, maybe more so. "We work hard to make them laugh. Their lives are so serious," said Cheryl Whitaker, who visited from Chicago from time to time and joined Michelle on family vacations. Beyond the friends who visited and those who decamped to Washington, Michelle resumed her friendship with her Princeton roommate, now Angela Kennedy Acree, a senior attorney representing indigent clients in the D.C. public defender's office. At a time when she felt she had few confidants in Washington, she also became close to Sharon Malone, who knew something about the challenge of balancing career, motherhood, and the ambitions of a famous spouse. Malone was a prominent obstetrician-gynecologist married to Eric H. Holder Jr., chosen by Barack as the first African American attorney general of the United States. Malone, who bore the primary responsibility for their household and the daily lives of their three children, did not opt out of her job as Holder moved from assignment to demanding assignment. "I have worked too hard to be where I wanted to be, not to pursue it to the fullest," she said.

Malone was raised in Mobile, Alabama, the youngest of eight children. This was the Deep South during the final paroxysms of Jim Crow. Her father was a farmer, her mother a maid. Neither could vote. In 1963, her older sister Vivian tried to enroll in the all-white University of Alabama and became a central player in a scene that became famous as Governor George Wallace's "stand in the schoolhouse door." As the news media watched on a sweltering June day, deputy U.S. attorney general Nicholas Katzenbach, supported by a federal judge and a commitment from President Kennedy, escorted Malone and James Hood to the Tuscaloosa campus. Wallace yielded, but not before he complained that U.S. government measures to allow African Americans to attend the university were "illegal and unwarranted."

The month that Malone took up her studies, she appeared on the cover of *Newsweek*. Two years later, she became the first black graduate in the university's 134-year history. When Lyndon Johnson signed the landmark Voting Rights Act of 1965 to preserve "the decency of democracy," he invited Malone to the ceremony and presented her with one of the signing pens. Later that year, in Chicago to receive an award from the local NAACP, one of her hosts was the Reverend Carl Fuqua, the organization's executive director, who had presided over Fraser and Marian Robinson's wedding. "Once your sister stands in the face of the governor . . . , it broadens your horizons," Sharon Malone said. "I knew I was going somewhere and wouldn't be sitting on a porch in Mobile, Alabama."

Sharon Malone graduated with honors from Harvard in 1981 and, after a stint at IBM, attended Columbia University Medical School. She considered present-day African Americans to be "survivors of a 300-year legacy" and, like Michelle, gave much credit to her parents. "That's the part that amazes me, that you can grow up where everything negates your humanity and yet you're able to keep intact and impart that to your children. The confidence to be who we are." Malone and Holder married after meeting at a 1989 fundraiser for the Concerned Black Men charity. Holder met Barack at a dinner party hosted by Ann Walker Marchant, a cousin of Valerie Jarrett's, and when Barack decided to run for president, he offered to help. Malone approved, although she counted Barack's chances of victory as zero. "I'm forever colored by my experiences growing up in the segregated South," she said. "I grew up in an era where neither of my parents could vote. And the notion that we would elect an African-American, I honestly didn't believe it."

MICHELLE CAME TO personify vim and vigor. She jumped rope double Dutch and starred in a jumping jack contest with more than four hundred kids. She played flag football in New Orleans and she ran across the lawn while carrying water jugs, an effort to persuade children to drink up. She won a push-up contest on daytime television with Ellen DeGeneres and staged a sack race in the White House with late-night comedian Jimmy Fallon. She did a dance step with middle school kids in Northwest Washington, D.C., showing off the choreography of her friend Beyoncé Knowles. It was a marketing campaign, pure and simple. "As you can see, I'm pretty much willing to make a complete fool out of myself to get our kids moving," Michelle said in late 2011, near the end of the second year of the Let's Move! campaign. "But there is a method to my madness. There's a reason why I've been out there jumping rope and hula hooping and dancing to Beyoncé, whatever it takes. It's because I want kids to see that there are all kinds of ways to be active. And if I can do it, anybody can do it." As she would say in the second term, offering insight into her philosophy of progress, "You have to change attitudes before you can change behavior."

The response was not always cheerful. "MO is a complete imposter like her husband," one *Washington Post* reader wrote during the Obamas' trip to India in 2010. Others disparaged her clothes, her nutrition efforts, and her now infamous comments about being proud of her country. Sarah Palin mocked and misrepresented her on reality television in 2011 as the former Alaska governor shopped for cookie makings. "Where are the s'mores ingredients?" she asked as the camera rolled. "This is in honor of Michelle Obama, who said the other day we should not have dessert." Palin was not finished. She said in a talk show appearance, "Instead of a government thinking that they need to take over and make decisions for us according to some politician or politician's wife's priorities, just leave us alone, get off our back, and allow us as individuals to exercise our own God-given rights to make our own decisions and then our country gets back on the right track."

Representative James Sensenbrenner, a Republican from Wisconsin, was caught discussing Michelle's body in unflattering ways not once, but twice. At a church event, he commented about her "big butt." Soon afterward, he was overheard on his cell phone at an airport saying, "She lectures us on eating right while she has a large posterior herself." He apologized. Meanwhile, one year after the launch of Let's Move!, Rush Limbaugh told his listeners, "It doesn't look like Michelle Obama follows her own nutritionary, dietary advice. . . . I'm trying to say that our first lady does not project the image of women that you might see on the cover of the *Sports Illustrated* swimsuit issue." This would be the portly radio host who sometimes called her "Michelle My Butt."

The criticism got uglier. In the global village that was the Internet, where anyone could be a town crier, Michelle was likened to Dr. Zira, the chimpanzee physician from *Planet of the Apes,* and a Wookiee in the *Star Wars* series. A California rodeo clown joked over the loudspeakers in 2013 that *Playboy* had offered $250,000 to Mitt Romney's wife, Ann, to pose in the magazine. He went on to say that the White House was upset about it because *National Geographic* only offered Michelle Obama $50 to pose for them. A Virginia school board member relayed an email that showed a group of bare-breasted African women doing a tribal dance. The text said it was Michelle's high school reunion. A Republican former chairman of the South Carolina Election Commission posted a comment on Facebook, after a gorilla escaped from the zoo, "I'm sure it's just one of Michelle's ancestors—probably harmless." The Republican speaker of the Kansas House of Representatives forwarded a Christmas email depicting Michelle as the Grinch and alluding to the taxpayer-borne costs of her travel: "I'm sure you'll join me in wishing Mrs. YoMama a wonderful, long Hawaii Christmas vacation—at our expense, of course."

Michelle listened. She heard. She bit her tongue.

FOURTEEN

Simple Gifts

There was no fanfare in Michelle's address to the Women's Conference in Long Beach, California, in October 2010. Hers was a solitary voice in a vast arena. The lights were dim and all eyes were trained on her as she quietly explained why American society had an obligation to military families. It was a new interest of hers, one she developed on the campaign trail when she met women whose stories "took my breath away." Michelle considered herself wise about women's concerns. "Reading about, thinking about, talking about and living these issues my entire life," as she put it. But here was a group of women—wives of soldiers, sometimes soldiers themselves—whose experiences were new to her. These were women bearing the weight of wars in Iraq and Afghanistan that would leave more than 6,600 Americans dead, upwards of 50,000 wounded, and an estimated 250,000 bearing the residual effects of traumatic brain injury, principally from roadside bombs. In all, well over two million U.S. military personnel had cycled through the war zones in the decade since 9/11.

While they were away from home, typically for twelve months or more, their families were on their own. Michelle met women whose husbands were on their third, fourth, or fifth deployment. Women who were moving every couple of years, uprooting their children or interrupting their careers and education because of a transfer. Women who struggled to keep a toehold in the middle class. Women who worried that their husbands might die. "A good day," one told her, "is when a military chaplain doesn't knock on my door." It was a revelation. "Many of these women were younger than I was," Michelle said. "They had far less support and far fewer resources than I ever had. And every day, they were confronting challenges that I could barely even imagine."

The speech introduced Joining Forces, an East Wing initiative in support of military families. The launch was still months away, but Michelle and her aides saw the conference, organized by Maria Shriver, wife of California governor Arnold Schwarzenegger, as a chance to get the tone right. They were finding it difficult. "You don't want to preach at people like you're telling them what to do," said Jocelyn Frye, her domestic policy adviser. "And particularly with military families, you want to make sure you're not overdramatizing the issue or pandering." Military families—and wounded soldiers, in particular—too often found themselves treated as victims when what they wanted was awareness and respect. Frye worried that the speech would not go well. The team discussed style as well as substance during the run-throughs. "We were going back and forth. And then she practiced it and virtually every concern I had went away. She just knew how to hit it—to make it lighter where it needed to be lighter, to make it less aggressive where it felt aggressive." It was not the first time that Frye had seen Michelle elevate her game. She said the first lady would set a standard for herself, then exceed it. "Some of it has to do with a very good sense, an almost uncanny sense, of understanding the tone and mood for everything we do," said Frye. She also credited clarity of purpose. "It's an ongoing conversation, not only about the substantive issue, but what her role could be in that issue."

Michelle often saw herself as a woman talking to women about matters that, more often than not, fell to women to accomplish. When she spoke of expanded health insurance, she described it as a benefit to the women who typically bore responsibility for family health care decisions. When she talked about children's nutrition, ditto. And it was the same thing when she appealed to the fourteen thousand female listeners at the Women's Conference, her largest audience since the campaign. She asked them to put themselves in the shoes of military women, wondering aloud how to find balance when one partner is in a dangerous job half a world away, and how to crack the glass ceiling: "Try doing that when you don't live anywhere long enough to get promoted or gain seniority in your job." She pointed to a study that indicated military spouses made $10,500 less annually than their civilian counterparts, yet military families made time for community service at far higher rates than the general population. What she wanted to give military spouses, she said, were opportunities to use their skills "and the support they need to juggle their responsibilities."

Michelle suggested that government could help. But, sounding a note that echoed the Let's Move! approach and the playbook that said officialdom was never the complete answer, she said a little girlfriend-to-girlfriend assist would make a difference. "You see," she said, "this is what we do for each other as women. . . . We show up. We show up at the door with some food. We show up at the door with some chocolate. And if things are really bad, we show up at the door with a bottle of wine, right? We take that shift in the carpool. We say, 'Hey, send the kids over to my house right now. I'll take them off your hands for a day, a night, a weekend, whatever you need.'" The soldiers and their families were doing their part to defend the country and help the world. "It's not enough just to feel grateful," she said, the closest she came to an admonishment. "It's time for each of us to act."

JOINING FORCES WAS NOT glamorous. Much of the early work, in fact, was mundane, a matter of tedious bureaucratic troubleshooting. At the time of its April 2011 launch, for example, one in three military spouses worked in professions that required state licenses, perhaps a nursing or teaching credential. When a soldier was transferred, it often took months before his wife could work. Yet fewer than a dozen states had regulations on the books to correct the problem. Or, when the army moved a soldier from, say, Fort Drum, New York, to Fort Benning, Georgia, would his daughter's new high school grant credit for a history class taken in New York? "At this point, it has affected millions of kids," said navy captain Brad Cooper, imported from the Defense

Department to manage one stage of the project. "There's not a voice for this. It often can't rise above the noise."

Lieutenant Colonel Jason Dempsey, an infantry officer and West Point graduate recently back from Afghanistan, served as something of a coach and translator, explaining military culture to the first lady and a staff largely inexperienced in such matters. "The families just don't have a sense that anybody else understands what they're going through," he said near the end of his assignment as a White House fellow. "They don't want a pity party. They don't want people to just give them a free car." The military community, he knew, was ever watchful for false sincerity, particularly in service to political ambition. Michelle and her partner, Jill Biden, a college English professor, army mother, and wife of the vice president, were willing to do something to help. Yet in the East Wing's eyes, the military bureaucracy was moving too slowly. "Was the first lady frustrated? Absolutely, and rightly so," said Jackie Norris. "She felt like she wanted to do more than a public service announcement that raises visibility. She saw this as 'How can I do something that's more sustainable?'"

Yet Michelle did not want to run the policy herself. That was not her role, and as everyone around her recognized, such a strategy could create as many problems as it might solve. What she could do, she reasoned, was to use her voice and her convening power. Dempsey, in visits to sometimes skeptical Pentagon brass, argued in favor of the project's potential and defended Michelle's authenticity. "Listen," he recalled saying, "you're right that this is not necessarily going to be perfect, it's not going to be all-encompassing, and we're not going to solve all of everybody's problems. But you know what? This is the first and only time that the first lady of the United States has been interested in this issue. . . . Any first lady can come in and choose any issue—autism, hunger. This first lady has decided she's going to dedicate her time to the needs and concerns of the military community, so we've got to take full advantage." He said Michelle was quick to understand the complexities and careful to tread lightly. "Very cognizant that she doesn't have all the answers," he said.

As the program developed, the White House staff labored to understand mental health needs, a significant and growing concern of veterans and their families. They collected pledges from medical schools to improve the training of doctors and nurses in treating veterans. They wrangled promises from American companies to hire veterans returning home to unemployment rates higher than those faced by civilians. Michelle appealed directly to the nation's governors, asking them to make professional credentials more portable and find ways to help soldiers translate their military skills into civilian licenses, and jobs. Little noticed by commentators inclined to dismiss her work as mere mom and apple pie was the fact that many returning military personnel belonged to the nation's hard-pressed working class. In 2012, roughly 80 percent of the nation's active duty military lacked a college degree. Among enlisted men and women, the figure was 93 percent. Joining Forces working groups asked how to help veterans find steady jobs in such roles as drivers or meter readers, then reached out to utilities, delivery companies, and large retailers. "It was in the discussions we had, who we needed to help," said Matthew McGuire, a senior Commerce Department official who had known the Obamas in Chicago. "We cared about everyone who was coming home, of course, but we knew that the gunnery sergeant with just a high school degree was going to need more help reentering the civilian labor market than the commander of a nuclear submarine who went to the Naval Academy."

Michelle took note of the hardships and the country's economic and political divide in remarks in Fort Bragg, North Carolina, six weeks into Barack's presidency: "I think many people were like me, not realizing so many of our military families are living right at the poverty line. Not realizing that it is hard for spouses to get jobs when they move, or that they can't often transfer credits and finish their education, and they're struggling with the high cost of quality and affordable childcare." Barack, echoing the order he issued when Michelle launched Let's Move! the year before, issued a presidential directive to federal agencies demanding coordinated improvements in the way military families were treated. Michelle publicly promised to tell Barack what she had learned at roundtables around the country.

For all of the personal connection that Michelle felt to the families, Joining Forces also fulfilled her goal of boosting Barack's agenda. As a U.S. senator, Barack had served on the Veterans Affairs Committee, chairing town hall meetings in Illinois, proposing legislation, and quietly visiting wounded warriors in military hospitals, something he would continue to do as president. During the presidential campaign, he not only criticized the decision to wage a preventive war in Iraq, but blasted the Bush administration for failing to live up to the country's obligation to veterans, especially the wounded. "We've heard rhetoric that hasn't been matched by resources," he told a gathering at a Houston VFW hall in February 2008. In time, the Veterans Administration in Barack's administration would have its own grievous failings, but Michelle worked on the issue, and her focus also served an electoral purpose. Military votes could be helpful against a Republican candidate in 2012. In a toss-up state like Virginia, North Carolina, or Colorado, it could even make the difference between a win and a loss.

ON JANUARY 8, 2011, a wild-eyed shooter named Jared Loughner opened fire at an outdoor political event in Tucson, killing six people, including a federal judge, and piercing the brain of Representative Gabrielle Giffords, a Democratic member of Congress. Giffords, remarkably, survived. While it was not immediately clear why Loughner targeted Giffords at one of her trademark Congress on Your Corner gatherings, the national conversation turned to the bitterness of American political discourse. Four days later, Barack spoke before thousands of people in the University of Arizona field house and, in cadences that echoed the best of his political speeches, urged Americans to listen to one another more carefully and deepen their capacity for empathy. "Let's use this occasion to expand our moral universe," he said in an address that could be filed in the category of Obama essentialism. "We recognize our own mortality and we are reminded that in the fleeting time we have on this earth, what matters is not wealth or status or power or fame. But, rather, how well we have loved and what small part we have played in making the lives of other people better. And that process of reflection, of making sure we align our values with our actions—that,

I believe, is what a tragedy like this requires." Barack quoted scripture as Michelle sat in the front row, next to Giffords's husband, astronaut Mark Kelly. As the president announced that Giffords had opened her eyes for the first time since the shooting, Michelle gripped Kelly's right hand with her left and cupped her right hand reassuringly on his forearm. As the crowd cheered and everyone stood, she gave him a hug. It was a natural gesture, simple and warm.

The shooting got the country's attention only partly because Loughner fired thirty-one shots in less than thirty seconds from a 9mm Glock 19, a semi-automatic handgun widely available for legal purchase. Giffords herself owned one. Other madmen had done the same, and worse. The Tucson case also hit home because of who was shot. The six dead and the 12 wounded offered stories and symbols that would have made Norman Rockwell pull out his palette. The federal judge. The congressional aide. The church volunteer who tried save his friend. The retired marine, wounded as he tried in vain to shield his wife. And, perhaps most of all, nine-year-old Christina Green, a swimmer, a dancer, a gymnast, an A student recently elected to the student council. Improbably, she was born on September 11, 2001. "She saw all this through the eyes of a child, undimmed by the cynicism or vitriol that we adults all too often just take for granted," Barack said. "I want to live up to her expectations. I want our democracy to be as good as Christina imagined it." After he ended his remarks, a choir sang "Simple Gifts," a nineteenth-century Shaker song also performed during his inauguration.

Michelle and Barack pictured their children in Christina, who was just three months younger than Sasha when she died. Seeing a role for herself as a mother who had a platform as first lady, Michelle wanted to make a public statement. She wrote a letter and taped a video, but the West Wing preferred the president to take the lead, and to be seen as taking it. The video was never released. The day after Barack's speech in Tucson, the White House did release, in Michelle's name, an "open letter to parents." As parents, she said, the assault and its aftermath "makes us think about what an event like this says about the world we live in—and the world in which our children will grow up. . . . The question my daughters have asked are the same ones that many of your children will have—and they don't have easy answers." In echoes of the lessons of her childhood, she urged parents to teach their children "about the values we hold dear, about finding hope at a time when it seems far away." And, too, ways of "assuming the best, rather than the worst, about those around us."

AS SHE CAST her mind over the possibilities for her White House years, Michelle told her staff that the goal was to "move the ball." That meant building something enduring, leaving a legacy. Yet in a role that was forever neither-nor, she had neither a big budget nor a large staff, and turnover was frequent. Anything she wanted to build, the East Wing would have to piece together on its own. "It's not up to her to go from cabinet department to cabinet department saying, 'I'm working on this, I'm doing this, you need to help me.' They don't work for her," said Katie McCormick Lelyveld, her press secretary. Michelle searched for allies and dispatched her aides to do the same. For Let's Move! she wanted support from doctors, business leaders, parents, the president's cabinet—and "certainly, West Wing oomph," Lelyveld said. The staff reached out to federal agencies and courted mayors and governors, inviting them to the White House or onto stages across the country, where they could stand with a first lady consistently more popular than her beleaguered husband. "The power she has," said Norris, "is that most people want to make the first lady happy."

To get the word out, Michelle turned to celebrities, none more prominent than Beyoncé Knowles, a performer with a big voice and a flashy stage presence. With her husband, Shawn Carter, better known as the rapper Jay Z, she was savvy in the ways of music and marketing. Beyoncé reconfigured her song "Get Me Bodied" to create "Move Your Body," a catchy, kid-friendly tune: "A little sweat ain't never hurt nobody. Don't just stand there on the wall! Everybody just move your body." A video staged as if done by a high school flash mob, would register vast numbers of views—more than 30 million by early 2015. Separate videos of Beyoncé doing the dance at P.S. 161 in Harlem and Michelle dancing the Dougie at Alice Deal Middle School in Washington garnered millions more. Soon, schools and public health departments across the country did their own versions. Michelle's staff admitted, somewhat sheepishly, to practicing the dance step in the carpeted confines of the East Wing.

Michelle drew on tennis champion Serena Williams, and other big names from the professional sports ranks. Gymnasts Dominique Dawes and Gabby Douglas. Quarterbacks Drew Brees and Colin Kaepernick. Ice skater Michelle Kwan. Basketball player Grant Hill. Runner Allyson Felix. She also included Cornell McClellan, the Obamas' longtime personal trainer, who moved from Chicago to lead workouts in the White House gym. Barack named McClellan to the revamped president's fitness council, which became the President's Council on Fitness, Sports and Nutrition in honor of Let's Move! Michelle also matched famous chefs with school kitchens and did her own turns on television cooking shows.

Nearly four years into the project, Michelle corralled the Miami Heat into making an irreverent video in praise of healthy eating. When the team visited the White House to celebrate its latest NBA title, head coach Eric Spoelstra staged mock interviews with all-star Heat players Dwyane Wade and Ray Allen, while in the background, LeBron James held up a backboard and hoop. Michelle darted in and dunked, then did a guttural laugh worthy of a preening young street hoops player. Later, Michelle and the players nonchalantly munched apples. This was not Jackie Kennedy's White House. Or Hillary Clinton's. "LOL LOL I love her," one netizen wrote in response to the video, which got big play on television and the Web. Another posted, "That is so funny. . . . Mrs. O is a cool lady." But there were many other reactions, too. Among the more printable ones: "Disgusting is putting it mildly. Not very dignified. She's still got that fat ass." And "Too many monkeys." Plus "God she makes me sick."

THE SECRET SERVICE RECORDED significantly more threats against Barack than against any of his predecessors. The risk accounted for the ubiquity of the security bubble and justified the fact that Barack had received Secret Service protection earlier than any previous presidential candidate. The seriousness of threats was sometimes difficult to assess, but on a November night in 2011, the danger was all too real and the performance of the Secret Service none too impressive. That night, a gunman named Oscar R. Ortega-Hernandez, believing that Barack "had to be stopped," parked his car on Constitution Avenue and fired a Romanian-made semi-automatic rifle at the White House residence, hitting the building at least seven times.

A bullet pierced the antique White House glass but was stopped by a layer of bulletproof glass that protected the residence. Another bullet lodged in a wooden windowsill on the Truman Balcony. When Ortega-Hernandez opened fire at about 8:30 p.m. on a Friday night, only Sasha and Marian were home. Michelle and Barack were away and Malia returned to the residence about an hour later, escorted by her security detail. Although several Secret Service officers felt sure they had heard shots, as did others nearby, a supervisor told his colleagues to stand down, apparently believing a car had backfired. It would be four days before the agency realized that shots had hit the White House. When Michelle learned of the shooting from an assistant White House usher, not the Secret Service, she was "aghast—and then quickly furious," Carol Leonnig of The Washington Post reported. Michelle later challenged the Secret Service chief directly. Not only had the Secret Service failed to recognize or stop the attack, but bullets fired from seven hundred yards away had slammed into a part of the residence the Obamas used often. They sat outdoors on the Truman Balcony on warm days and mild nights. They entertained there. And, on the other side of the bulletproof glass, the Yellow Oval Room was Michelle's favorite room in the house.

Not quite three years later, in September 2014, an Iraq War veteran named Omar Gonzalez jumped a White House fence on Pennsylvania Avenue and raced past the North Portico into the building, carrying a knife. He could have run up the stairs to the residence, but darted instead toward the East Room and then the Green Room before he was tackled. An investigation showed that the Secret Service did not release a guard dog and had no swift way to lock the White House doors.

A loud warning alarm had been disconnected at the request of White House ushers, who protested that it often malfunctioned.

PLAYERS FROM THE FOOD, retail, and restaurant industries trekked to the White House to ask what they could do for their overweight country. They heard the same message Michelle delivered to a Grocery Manufacturers Association conference, when she had said, "Step it up." "We need you not just to tweak around the edges, but to entirely rethink the products that you're offering, the information that you provide about these products and how you market those products to our children," Michelle told the conference. The companies needed to reformulate their recipes, she said, and reshape their marketing to tout the benefits. "What it doesn't mean is taking out one problematic ingredient, only to replace it with another. While decreasing fat is certainly a good thing, replacing it with sugar and salt isn't. And it doesn't mean compensating for high amounts of problematic ingredients with small amounts of beneficial ones. For example, adding a little bit of Vitamin C to a product with lots of sugar, or a gram of fiber to a product with tons of fat, doesn't suddenly make those products good for our kids."

Michelle's work led to commitments by the likes of Olive Garden and Red Lobster, restaurant chains that catered to the middle class, to make their meals less salty and more healthy. General Mills and Kraft were among the many companies that promised to reduce calories in their foods. Subway would join the mix, promising to provide healthier options for kids—fruit instead of cookies, skim milk and water instead of soda—while spending $41 million over three years to market the new selections. Walmart, the retailing behemoth working assiduously to reform its image, announced that it would sell more fresh fruit and vegetables, remove trans fats from packaged food, and cut the sodium content of processed foods by 25 percent. The East Wing calculated that Walmart's decision would shape the behavior of its suppliers and spark changes throughout the industry.

Implicit in Michelle's call for better behavior was the fact, welcomed by the industry, that the government would not be imposing new regulations. Her efforts relied on calculations of mutual self-interest, specifically an East Wing bet that voluntary corporate efforts would produce better results than any attempt to mandate rules on, say, nutritional content or marketing to children. The corporate side of the program was coordinated through a new nonprofit, Partnership for a Healthier America (PHA), established alongside Let's Move!, although technically independent. Members of the partnership, including Walgreens, Hyatt, and a bevy of hospitals and health care providers, found it useful to be associated with nutrition and good health—an issue that the first lady described as one of her passions. When announcements were made, Michelle was often on hand with a smile and plenty of praise. The White House saw it as a win-win. "PHA works with the private sector to create meaningful commitments, and ensures that when those commitments are made that credit is given where credit is due," the partnership's website said of its strategy. PHA has no interest in forcing industry to meet unrealistic benchmarks. The goal is to maximize the potential of the private sector to achieve success. We want the private sector with us because, quite simply, we will not succeed without it."

Nutrition advocates doubted that business conglomerates would move far enough and fast enough without public prodding—in other words, without formal rules and regulations. Research had shown that advertising influenced children's desire for foods high in sugar, salt, and fat. But when Congress developed guidelines designed to limit marketing that targeted children, lobbyists from the food and media industry—some working for companies that publicly backed Let's Move!—killed them. The lobbyists complained that the provisions, although voluntary, were sweeping and unscientific, despite the endorsement of the American Academy of Pediatrics, among others. The White House blamed Congress for backing down. Senator Tom Harkin, an Iowa Democrat, pointed a finger at 1600 Pennsylvania Avenue, although not directly at the East Wing. "The White House got cold feet," Harkin said. "It sort of undermines everything that the first lady was doing."

Popular interest in healthier food was already growing when the Obamas arrived in Washington. Companies had been changing tack for good business reasons. As far back as 2005, McDonald's added salads to its menu. But the first lady's efforts gave the national dialogue a boost. From the White House garden to Let's Move!, from the new nutrition standards to the inspiration for countless school gardens, and even the cajoling of American businesses, the needle was beginning to move.

MICHELLE RECEIVED almost unfailingly positive attention in the mainstream media. One exception was a private trip she took with Sasha to Spain in August 2010—private to the extent that anything could be private, when an air force jet and a Secret Service detail were required. "A Modern-Day Marie Antoinette" blared a headline in the *New York Daily News*. (That would be the Marie Antoinette ever known as having said of starving French peasants, "Let them eat cake," although historians doubt she actually said it.) For Michelle, the trip was a getaway in support of Anita Blanchard, one of her close Chicago friends, whose father had recently died. The genesis of the trip was a birthday promise that Blanchard and her husband, Marty Nesbitt, had made to their children. Each child, upon turning ten, could choose a trip to take. It was Roxanne Nesbitt's turn to celebrate and she picked Spain, where Michelle and her friends would stay in an opulent hotel on the Costa del Sol.

Members of the White House staff spotted trouble. They knew the optics would be bad on a fancy foreign trip in the middle of an economic slump and the tough 2010 election season. Michelle listened, but she said the trip was important to her. She was going. Sure enough, Spanish media were all over the story, and quickly. Photographs appeared of Michelle strolling through Marbella, Ronda, and the Alhambra, later paying a courtesy call with Sasha on King Juan Carlos I and Queen Sofia in Majorca, where she shared an elegant lunch of turbot and gazpacho. The visuals and accompanying stories were instantly troublesome. The Obamas paid hotel expenses and the equivalent of first-class airfare for Michelle and Sasha, an arrangement that predated this presidency, but those costs were minimal next to the share footed by taxpayers, who paid for her traveling staff and the large Secret Service contingent dictated by security concerns. A conservative watchdog group filed a Freedom of Information Act request and estimated later that the four-day vacation cost the federal treasury more than $467,000. Asked about the expense in a time of austerity, White House press secretary Robert Gibbs replied, "The first lady is on a private trip. She is a private citizen and is the mother of a daughter on a private trip. And I think I'd leave it at that."

It was the New York date night all over again, but this time with a considerably higher price tag. There were other trips as well. Skiing with the girls in Colorado, sightseeing and theater with them in New York, a vacation in France, a safari in South Africa. Each time, a scribe or a critic would calculate the cost of operating an air force Boeing 757, which ran to $11,351 an hour, plus other expenses. Traveling with security and being ferried by a U.S. government plane was a fact of first family life, and it had been for many years. George Bush made 77 visits to his ranch in Crawford, Texas, during the eight years of his presidency, spending at least part of 490 days there; he went 187 times to Camp David, where the corresponding number of days was 487. What should a first lady do?

Anita McBride, who wrestled with such questions as Laura Bush's chief of staff, said foreign vacations with hefty price tags might best be left for later in life. When Laura Bush went out of town with her friends, the destination was likely to be a national park. "You have temporary custody of the job," McBride said. "It's probably best to find the least controversial ways to get your down time.... It's just not worth it." Michelle's staff, whose job was to deflect the flak, was painfully alert to the dilemma. "She would fly United if she could, but she can't," Lelyveld said. "At a certain point, she just wants to go on an educational trip with her girlfriends and her kids. The question is, should she not make this trip because of the financial and personnel footprint? Where do you draw the line?"

THE SEAS MAY HAVE PARTED to allow Barack to win the first time, but when the reelection campaign got under way in 2011, the tide was high and the waters were rough. Economic growth was barely above flat and the budget deficit seemed stuck on a number with too many zeroes to count. During the summer of 2011, unemployment was running at 9 percent, higher than any incumbent president had faced on election day since before World War II. Six million people had been out of work for twenty-seven weeks or more, according to the Bureau of Labor Statistics. The national unemployment rate was 9.1 percent; for African Americans, it was 16.7 percent. A survey by NBC News and *The Wall Street Journal* fifteen months before the 2012 election concluded that 73 percent of Americans thought the country was on the wrong track. For the first time, a slight majority disapproved of the job Barack was doing overall, while 59 percent disapproved of his handling of the economy. He received higher marks—50 percent approval—on foreign policy. If there were any source of solace, it was that only 13 percent of Americans approved of the performance of Congress, where the House was run by Republicans.

Barack turned fifty on August 4, 2011, dancing with Michelle as Stevie Wonder performed in the East Room. The very next day, credit agencies downgraded U.S. debt for the first time in history, citing political gridlock in Washington. The deficit would drop, of course, when economic activity picked up. Yet Barack and the economists who contended that higher federal spending would speed the recovery—and that austerity would delay it—were stymied by Republicans who insisted that the deficit was too high to justify the outlay. The GOP also had political reasons for thwarting jobs bills and stimulus packages: If the economy improved and more Americans thought the country was moving in the right direction, Barack would get credit. And that would threaten the Republicans' cherished goal of defeating him in November 2012.

The brickbats came from all sides. Barack was rebuffed in his effort to reach a grand bargain on spending and taxes with House Speaker John Boehner, an Ohio Republican saddled with limited vision and an unruly caucus. When word emerged that Barack had offered major concessions and still come up short, growing numbers of Democratic supporters saw the president as callow, particularly after he agreed to extend the Bush-era tax cuts for the wealthiest Americans. Meanwhile, to their consternation, immigration reform had gone nowhere;

the cap-and-trade program to slow climate change was doomed; the Guantánamo prison was still open; and the fate of Barack's signature achievement, the Affordable Care Act, remained in the hands of the Supreme Court and its 5-to-4 conservative majority. The stock market was a bright spot, at least for the 50 percent of Americans with investments, climbing far above its recession lows. But even there, August 2011 provided bad news. The S&P 500 index was down 5.7 percent for the month, its fourth straight decline. The economy added no new jobs in August, raising fears of a double-dip recession.

On the plus side, Barack's unpopular bet on the Detroit auto industry was paying off. He helped bring an end to Muammar Qadhafi's mercurial tenure in Libya without risking American troops. He won the biggest gamble of his presidency when the navy's SEAL Team Six dropped into a compound in Pakistan and killed al Qaeda leader Osama bin Laden, architect of the 9/11 attacks and the most hunted man in the world. As Vice President Joe Biden would say on the campaign trail, arguing for a second Obama term, "Bin Laden is dead and General Motors is alive." And yet August 2011 would also prove to be the deadliest month of the Afghan war, now in its tenth year. Sixty-six American service members died, including thirty aboard a Chinook helicopter shot down by Afghan fighters.

This was not the record that Barack had expected to carry into the 2012 election, when he aimed to become only the second Democrat since Franklin Roosevelt to be elected to two full terms. Bill Clinton was the other. When they returned to Martha's Vineyard for their summer vacation in August, Michelle and Barack discussed the possibility of losing. Barack was determined to persevere. "He felt strongly that he had done a lot of hard work trying to get the economy on track," strategist David Axelrod said. "The notion of surrendering that to the next guy to come in and be the hero, that was not a scenario he was excited about."

Nor did it take an advanced degree to guess whose company Barack would keep in the history books if he lost or quit. It would not be Lincoln or Roosevelt or even Reagan, but the one-termers, Jimmy Carter and George H. W. Bush. A 2012 triumph by a Republican would feel an awful lot like repudiation. What's more, it would threaten Barack's fragile accomplishments, most clearly health care reform. Yes, he was frustrated and worn down, but defeat would not do. Barack and Michelle were nothing if not competitive. Scrabble or the presidency, they hated to lose.

MICHELLE WAS READY again to do her part, maybe more ready than ever. The girls were settled, the household was humming, and her initiatives were gathering speed. As she told a group of reporters in early 2011, "I have better clarity about what my role is going to be. Our agenda is clearer. We know who we are, we know where we're going." She had learned what to expect from the political fray, as well. She was a target, but she was considerably more popular than Barack. In August, as his numbers were drifting toward new lows, an Associated Press poll found that 70 percent of Americans had a favorable impression of Michelle. Even Republican-minded Fox News put her favorability at 62 percent in October, with just 28 percent of respondents viewing her unfavorably. Among Democrats, women, and African Americans, the positives were higher.

One of Michelle's essential political tasks was to energize voters who had backed Barack before. He needed their money, their energy, and their votes. The campaign was positioning him as a defender of the middle class at a time of rising and increasingly visible economic inequality. A new Gilded Age, it sometimes seemed. "A nation cannot prosper long when it favors only the prosperous," Barack had said in his inaugural address. Using every news medium short of smoke signals, Michelle sought to reassure voters that he was worthy and remind them why they should care. Her message echoed her speeches from early in the 2008 campaign and her conversations with Barack about fairness and purpose twenty years earlier in Chicago.

On September 30, 2011, the final day of the fundraising quarter, a lovely autumn day, Michelle spoke to donors dining on lobster in Port Elizabeth, Maine. On the eve of her visit, the state Republican Party chairman predicted that Barack would lose Maine's four electoral votes. "People who work with their hands are going to vote Republican. They understand the grand experiment didn't work," Charlie Webster told the *Portland Press Herald*. Michelle, who had been raising millions for Obama 2012 and the Democratic Party, recognized the campaign as a political battle. Despite her feelings about the profession, and her less than intensive effort in the 2010 midterm elections, she was all in. She wasted no time before telling her well-heeled audience how the other half lived, and not just people who worked with their hands. She cited stories of "businesses that folks are trying to keep afloat" and "doctor's bills that they cannot pay" and the "mortgage that they can no longer afford." She said, "These struggles aren't new. For decades now, middle-class folks have been squeezed from all sides. The cost of things like gas and groceries and tuition have been rising continuously, but people's paychecks just haven't kept up. And when this economic crisis hit, for so many families the bottom just fell out."

Fairness, a quality she had consistently considered since her youth, lay at the center of the debate and the president's agenda, she said. It was the idea that "everyone, *everyone*, gets a fair shake and does their fair share." Voters choosing between Barack and a Republican would be making a decision between "two very different visions." There was the helping hand from Barack, who she said had a knack for remembering personal stories. And there were the other guys, the GOP candidates, whom she never identified by name or party. "It's about whether we as a country will honor that fundamental promise that we made generations ago, that when times are hard, we don't abandon our fellow citizens. We don't let everything fall apart for struggling families. Instead, we say, 'There but for the grace of God goes my family.' Instead, we remember that we're all in this together."

The language, the tone, the themes; it was vintage Michelle. She offered a pointed defense of Barack's priorities, from the benefits of a jobs bill to the misery that would follow if "folks"—meaning congressional Republicans—repealed the Affordable Care Act. "Today we need to ask ourselves, will we let them succeed? Will we let insurance companies deny us coverage because we have preexisting conditions like breast cancer or diabetes? Or will we stand up and say that in this country, we will not allow folks to go bankrupt because they get sick?

Who are we? Will we let insurance companies refuse to cover basic preventative care, things like cancer screenings and prenatal care, that saves money and saves lives?"

Seven times in the speech, she asked who Americans are as a people. "Will we be a country that tells folks who've done everything right but are struggling, 'Tough luck, you're on your own?' . . . Will we be a country where opportunity is limited to a few at the top? Or will we give every child a chance to succeed, no matter where she's from or what she looks like or how much money her parents have? Who are we?" She ended her speech with a patented call and response. "So, let me ask you one final question: Are you in?" she asked. "Yes!" the audience shouted. "Really, I need to hear this. Are you in?" "*Yes!*"

Ten days later, far from Maine, feminist pioneer Gloria Steinem watched Michelle work an audience of progressive women in Manhattan. Many of them, she said, arrived none too happy. They wished Barack were driving a harder bargain with Republicans. "You can imagine the feeling in a New York room," Steinem said. "Well, by the end of her speech, people were standing and cheering and ready to go to work. It was a transformation." In fact, Michelle became accustomed to pushing back against progressive critics, sometimes in Barack's presence, sometimes not. At a small New York fundraiser in 2012, she told a group of women donors who had paid $20,000 a ticket, "I'm tired of all the complaining. My husband has worked his heart out to get a lot of things done for this country, up against a bunch of folks on the other side who will do anything to get in the way. So just stop it! He needs your help, not your complaints!" After Michelle departed, Axelrod stayed behind to reassure the donors and "make sure everything was okay."

AN ALTOGETHER DIFFERENT CROWD gathered to hear Michelle that year in Woodlawn, on Chicago's South Side, a few blocks from the apartment where she had lived as a baby. The setting was a community room connected to a beauty salon. The neighborhood was dicey— there had been shootings—and it was nighttime. Each time a woman entered, someone made sure the door to the street locked behind her.

Michelle's voice emerged from a speakerphone, rallying women across the country to work for Barack's reelection. The Woodlawn women, all of them African American, were thrilled. "So happy for her and her mother and her children because they are women, black women, in the White House. Living it, eating it, feeling it," said Hope Hundley, an ophthalmic technician. "I never felt that much about a first lady."

Hundley reveled in Michelle's remarks that February night and her big-time role in Washington. "I love him," she said of Barack, "but that's my sister girl." She explained: "We have that fellowship with all the girlfriends we jump rope with, but there's always one sister girl. . . . It's the sister girl connection where they feel you, you feel her. . . . You can pick up the phone and they're already on the phone." Hundley had never met Michelle, yet she loved her confidence, the example she was setting, the mold she was breaking. A few days earlier, Michelle had drawn criticism for taking an expensive ski trip to Aspen, Colorado, something most Americans could not afford. "I was like, 'Girl, go ski. Girl, wear your arms out. Put your stilettos on, on a good day; put your gym shoes on, on a better day. Let your hair down. 'How can you touch Queen Elizabeth?' Guess what? She's gonna do it again." Hundley said Michelle was facing "that hatin' racism" as a black first lady. But she felt sure that she remained a steady force "even in the midnight hours" when Barack was facing obstacles and opponents and demons galore. "I can see her saying, 'Come on, baby, you can do it. Come on. Come on, baby. Just do it one more time. Go back in there tomorrow and get 'em.'"

MICHELLE LIKED CONTROL. She put herself in positions where the chances of mistake or surprise were minimal. When speaking in public, she rehearsed and often used a teleprompter, as Barack did. Her staff was extremely cautious about material dispatched in her name, even though her campaign email appeals brought in more money than Barack's. When two society wannabes crashed the first state dinner, a startling breach of security and protocol, the blame fell partly on the East Wing and social secretary Desiree Rogers, a Chicagoan who was not long for the job. Michelle was upset because the incident embarrassed the White House and drew a spotlight to an avoidable miscue. She made her expectations clear to her aides, who worked fiercely and creatively to avoid unforced errors, target her message, and protect her brand. For media access, White House aides most often chose outlets where the audience was desirable, the questions predictable, and the tone forgiving. They also became expert at winning slots on comedy shows, talk shows, and kids' programs, all the while posting cheerful photographs and videos on White House and campaign social media accounts.

Through the years, the strategy meant granting precious few audiences to the correspondents who covered her for the daily print media, the ones who followed her most closely and knew her work best. Among the group were Robin Givhan, a Pulitzer Prize–winning *Washington Post* culture critic; Krissah Thompson from the *Post*; Darlene Superville from the Associated Press; and *New York Times* correspondent Rachel Swarns, who wrote a serious book about Michelle's ancestry. Beyond limiting interviews and unscripted media sessions with the first lady herself, the East Wing worked hard to limit access to staff members, friends, and former colleagues. This was true even when the prospective sources had positive things to say, which they almost always did. Michelle "frowns on people who speak out of school," said Jackie Norris. "She expects of her friends that they will check in and have conversations and make sure that it's good for her." The people in Michelle's extensive orbit tended toward loyalty, and they toed the line.

Above all, the goal was to promote Michelle's agenda and Barack's reelection. "I'm not a big fan of the press about myself, period, so I can't say there's a huge upside," Michelle said early in her political life. Despite the straight-ahead press she got from reporters who took her seriously—and the professionals did—she often felt that the Michelle Obama portrayed in print bore little resemblance to her actual self. In 2009, she offered praise to a group of African American publishers who visited the White House. "You know our story, our images, our journey," Michelle said as she and Barack welcomed them. "Our paths are not foreign to you and we are reminded of that when we read our story in your stories. It feels different. I often say I finally recognize myself when I read your papers." Not that the experience made her any more willing to talk with Givhan, Thompson, Superville, or Swarns, all of whom were African American.

Michelle's prominence, and the popular fascination with her story, led to news coverage that told her things about her lineage that she had not known. Swarns and colleague Jodi Kantor, working with a genealogist, traced a branch of Michelle's family back to slavery. They reported that she had a white ancestor, a slave owner's son named Charles Marion Shields, who had a child with the family's young slave, Melvinia Shields. The Obamas, who had been hosting a large family Thanksgiving dinner each year at their home in Hyde Park, moved the gathering to the White House in 2009. That year, Michelle handed out copies of the family tree sketched by *The New York Times*. Later, in a rare session with reporters, she reflected on the course of history and her position as the first African American first lady. "My great-great-great-grandmother was actually a slave," she said. "We're still very connected to slavery in a way that's very powerful. . . . That's not very far away. I could have known that woman."

THE OPENING WORDS of a front-page *New York Times* story in January 2012 represented the kind of story Michelle hated. It began, "Michelle Obama was privately fuming, not only at the president's team, but also at her husband." Written by Jodi Kantor, the piece offered an advance look at the reporter's new book, *The Obamas*, billed rather extravagantly as the inside story of a White House marriage. Kantor said in the article that Michelle was "mastering and subtly redefining the role." But the piece also suggested an edgier tale about "strains" and "tensions" between the first lady and the president's advisers. Not necessarily news for the ages, but catnip to a certain Washington audience. By coincidence, Michelle had scheduled a broadcast interview to help Gayle King, a Chicago friend, in her first week as a host of *CBS This Morning*. The CBS show aired the day after Kantor's book appeared. "I never read these books," Michelle told King. But she said she had learned some details and signaled that she thought Kantor had overplayed her material. Her own sensitivities were clear. "I guess it is more interesting to imagine this conflicted situation here, and a strong woman, you know," Michelle said. "But that's been an image that people have tried to paint of me since, you know, the day Barack announced. That I'm some angry black woman." Visibly irritated, she continued, "Who can write about how I feel? Who? What third person can tell me how I feel?"

The East Wing had long known that Kantor's book was coming. She had been granted access to a number of key players, although Michelle declined to be interviewed for the book. Weeks before publication, the White House asked former communications director and Democratic strategist Anita Dunn to evaluate what Kantor was reporting and consider how to respond. Staff members lined up people to defend the first lady. When the book emerged, the West Wing press office pointedly labeled Kantor's work "an overdramatization of old news." Aides worked their phones and keyboards aggressively, telling reporters and producers where they thought the writer had gone wrong. More than a few people in the Obama camp, present and former staff members alike, noted that the generally upbeat book contained neither bombshells nor biting critique and questioned the wisdom of the public relations strategy. If anything, the staff's fusillade drew extra attention to a book that the East Wing would have preferred no one read.

CRITICS ON THE RIGHT were all too eager to add stories, real and invented, to their own Michelle narrative, which bounded wildly down media lane. She was elitist! She was socialist! She was a militant! She was a hypocrite! "We have a name for Michelle: Moochelle," Rush Limbaugh crowed after Michelle returned from Spain. "Mooch, mooch, Moochelle Obama. That will tick 'em off, won't it, Snerdly?" Limbaugh's shtick had earned him a fortune and he was quick to recognize a crowd-pleasing label when he saw it. As used by denizens of the right, "Moochelle" suggested many things. A fat cow, perhaps, or a leech. It encompassed big government, the welfare state, big-spending Democrats, and black people living on the dole. The term harked to the market-worshipping Ayn Rand, whose *Atlas Shrugged* was something of field guide for the anti-government Tea Party and its mainstream Republican courtiers. Rand disparaged the "moochers," who supposedly lived off the hard work of the producers. Paul Ryan, a Republican congressman from Wisconsin who used to give *Atlas Shrugged* as a Christmas gift, said in 2010 that the United States was developing "a majority of makers versus takers." By 2012, Ryan was the nominee for vice president, and "makers against takers" was a Republican talking point. The man who selected Ryan was Mitt Romney, who reaped great riches largely by putting capital to work for him. Romney finished off his own wounded duck candidacy with comments about "the 47 percent," Americans who, in his view, believed that "government has a responsibility to care for them" and would undoubtedly vote for Barack. Michelle would have pointed things to say about the Romney-Ryan worldview when she addressed the Democratic National Convention in Charlotte in September.

BEFORE MICHELLE REACHED Charlotte, she paid a visit in June to Nashville and the annual African Methodist Episcopal Church national conference to do some tending of black voters. It was Orangeburg 2007 revisited, except this time she was not introducing Barack, but asking her audience not to give up on him. The slaves were not freed nor the vote granted in a day, she said, as she reached into the pantheon to speak of Rosa Parks on a Montgomery bus, Ernest Green at Little Rock's Central High, and Oliver Brown in Topeka, where he gave his name to *Brown v. Board of Education,* the case that ended, as she put it, "the lie of 'separate but equal.'" It was easy to feel "helpless and hopeless," she said, but "history has shown us that there is nothing, *nothing,* more powerful than ordinary citizens coming together for a just cause." Her speech reflected years of conversations with Barack and her friends about the questions she had been asking herself for much of her life. "I mean, what exactly do you do about children who are languishing in crumbling schools, graduating from high schools unprepared for college or a job? And what about the 40 percent of black children who are overweight or obese? ... What about all those kids growing up in neighborhoods where they don't feel safe, kids who never have opportunities worthy of their promise? What court case do we bring on their behalf? What laws do we pass for them?"

Michelle asked her audience, thousands strong, to start by voting and getting friends and relatives to vote, and then to do more. Follow the news, she said. Start an email list and send people articles about important issues—"and then call them to make sure they've read them." Talk to people in barber shops and church parking lots about political doings in City Hall and Washington. Go to City Hall and "ask what they're doing to fight hunger in their community." Show up at school board meetings. Run for office. It is entirely okay, she assured her listeners, to discuss policy and politics in church: "To anyone who says that church is no place to talk about these issues, you tell them there is no place better. No place better. Because ultimately, these are not just political issues, they are moral issues."

Michelle had always told audiences that she and Barack felt an obligation to reach back, counting themselves among "those to whom much is given," a reference to Luke 12:48, the parable of the faithful servant. In Nashville, she offered a rare look into her religious thinking, drawing connections among faith, politics, and racial uplift. The legacy of Jesus Christ, she said, summons people to do as he did, "fighting injustice and speaking truth to power every single day. He was out there spreading a message of grace and redemption to the least, the last and the lost. And our charge is to find Him everywhere, every day, by how we live our lives."

Creating the world as it should be was not a sporadic thing, she said: "Living out our eternal salvation is not a once a week kind of deal. And in a more literal sense, neither is citizenship. Democracy is also an everyday activity." It is hard to climb the mountain, she continued, when "the problems we face seem so entrenched, so overwhelming that solving them seems nearly impossible. But during those dark moments, I want you to remember that doing the impossible is the root of our faith. It is the history of our people and the lifeblood of this nation."

When Michelle finished, to thunderous applause, churchgoers

thronged to the rope line, hoping to clasp her hand, take a photo, grab a few seconds to wish her God's grace. Once she had retreated to her motorcade and her flight home, a church bishop stepped onstage and announced that the Supreme Court, that very morning, had voted to uphold the Affordable Care Act. He asked for a hallelujah and an amen. The crowd erupted in cheers. Microphone in hand, he called for an organist and started singing a gospel song, "Victory Shall Be Mine."

THE DEMOCRATIC NATIONAL CONVENTION opened on September 4, five days after Mitt Romney accepted the Republican nomination in Tampa. In the months before the Democrats met, Barack's position among voters had strengthened. Even with the economy struggling and unemployment at 8.3 percent, he was running even or better with the enigmatic Romney, who ditched his moderate Massachusetts record in hopes of attracting conservative Republicans, then found himself in an awkward straddle as he tried to move toward the middle. The GOP convention was a muddle, epitomized by the odd sight of eighty-two-year-old actor Clint Eastwood spending eleven excruciating prime-time minutes having a conversation onstage with an empty chair. He said he was talking to an invisible Barack Obama. In the most scripted of events, it was improv and it bombed. More important, the convention failed to dispel the image of Romney as a sheltered son of privilege and the Republican Party as an exceedingly white, overly male bastion, all *noblesse* and no *oblige*. As the curtain fell in Tampa and attention turned to Charlotte, the Democrats could hardly have asked for a better foil. Barack's political luck—"my almost spooky good fortune," he once called it—was holding.

"The way we thought about the convention, the first night was going to be about connecting Obama to the middle-class experience," David Axelrod explained later. The lineup included Deval Patrick, the Massachusetts governor who had spent his boyhood on Chicago's South Side, and keynote speaker Julian Castro, a thirty-seven-year-old San Antonio mayor who said his grandmother "cleaned other people's houses so she could afford to rent her own." There was Tammy Duckworth, a former army helicopter pilot who had been shot out of the sky and grievously wounded in Iraq; and Lilly Ledbetter, whose fight for equal pay made her a progressive symbol. But all were essentially warm-up acts for Michelle, who was tasked with telling Barack's story and making people feel it. "I wanted her to dominate that first night because I knew she would do well. But even I was shocked at how well she did," Axelrod said. "Meryl Streep could not have done it better." He was not alone. On Fox News, Chris Wallace called her delivery "masterful," while Chuck Todd said on NBC that Michelle "owned this convention in a way that no speaker owned the convention in Tampa."

Introduced by Elaine Brye, a science teacher, Air Force ROTC member, and mother of four military children, Michelle touched the stations of the family cross. Her father, climbing the stairs slowly and borrowing money to pay his share of her Princeton bills. Barack's white grandmother, riding the bus to her bank job and training male colleagues who were promoted while she hit the glass ceiling; the men earned "more and more money while Barack's family continued to scrape by." Barack and Michelle in Chicago as young marrieds, paying more toward their student loans than toward their mortgage, "so young, so in love, and so in debt." Barack as father, "strategizing about middle school friendships," and as president, reading letters about hardship. He had been tested "in ways I never could have imagined. I have seen first hand that being president doesn't change who you are. It reveals who you are." For good measure, nearing their twentieth wedding anniversary, she said she loved him more than when they married and more than she had four years earlier.

Threaded through stories designed to make the first family seem modest and recognizable was the idea that Barack, as Michelle liked to say during the 2008 campaign, "gets it." This time, the contrast was with Romney, who once tried to connect with Detroit voters by saying that his wife, Ann, "drives a couple of Cadillacs." Ann had once expressed their sense of economic distress by reporting that they made it through Mitt's college and graduate school years only by selling stocks his auto executive father had given him. The policy contrast was just as stark. "Women," Michelle said, "are more than capable of making our own choices about our bodies and our health care." Helping others is more important than getting ahead yourself and "success doesn't count unless you earn it fair and square." Everyone in the country should have an equal opportunity, she declared, "no matter who we are or where we're from or what we look like or who we love."

Most pointedly, in the context of rugged individualism run amok, Michelle uttered a single, charged line that simultaneously challenged Republican actions and reasserted the principles that had long animated her work: "When you've worked hard and done well and walked through that doorway of opportunity, you do not slam it shut behind you. No. You reach back, and you give other folks the same chances that helped you succeed." By the end, the Democrats in Charlotte were on their feet, cheering and remembering and believing all over again. It was just one speech, but the stakes were high and Michelle was giving people a reason to think. Nielsen reported that 26 million people had watched. The next day, after the positive reviews were in, *New Yorker* humorist Andy Borowitz posted a mock convention schedule:

DEMOCRATS REVISE CONVENTION SCHEDULE

CHARLOTTE (The Borowitz Report)—The Democratic National Convention today released a dramatically revised schedule for the night of Wednesday, September 5th:

8:00: Call to Order by First Lady Michelle Obama

8:10: National Anthem, performed by Branford Marsalis (saxophone), Michelle Obama (vocals)

8:15: Pledge of Allegiance to Michelle

8:20: Former President Bill Clinton introduces video of Michelle Obama

8:25: Video replay of last night's speech by Michelle Obama (on loop until 10:58)

10:58–10:59: Remarks by Vice-President Joe Biden

10:59: Benediction by the Reverend Michelle Obama

.   .   .

BEFORE THE POLLS OPENED on election day, Michelle and Barack were all but certain they would win. Reports of early votes matched or exceeded the campaign's rigorous projections, and virtually every national poll showed Barack ahead of Romney, who had not been able to capitalize on an awful October 3 debate performance by the president that set Democratic nerves ajangle. The night before the final triumph, Barack and Michelle returned to Iowa one last time, a pilgrimage as much as a rally. By the time she introduced him, after a performance by Bruce Springsteen, twenty thousand people were standing in the cold night air to cheer them. This was where the road to the White House had begun nearly six years before, and they were on the verge of a new triumph. Michelle said it would be the last time they would be onstage together at a campaign rally and recalled the early days, "back when I wasn't so sure about this whole process." She revisited the greatest hits of the first term and introduced "my husband, the love of my life, the president of the United States, Barack Obama."

For Barack, who had poured enormous energy into the campaign, tears came to his tired eyes as he talked about the support Iowa had given him. He threw in a patented wisecrack, too. "You've seen a lot of me these last six years and, you know what? You may not agree with every decision I've made. Michelle doesn't. There may have been times when you've been frustrated at the pace of change. I promise you, so have I." But he said there were fights yet to be won and led the crowd in one last call and response, a refrain from the 2008 campaign: *Fired up? Ready to go! Fired up? Ready to go!* With that, he worked the rope line and headed to Chicago to await the results. The next day, Barack collected 332 electoral votes to Romney's 206. He won the popular vote by five million, swamping his oblivious opponent, who was so sure of victory that he had not prepared a concession speech.

FIFTEEN

I Am No Different from You

Nine days after she performed in the 2013 inaugural festivities in Washington, D.C., someone shot Hadiya Pendleton. She was fifteen years old, a cheerful girl sheltering against a Chicago winter rain with a dozen friends less than a mile from the Obamas' house. The young South Side shooter was aiming at someone else, but it didn't matter. A bullet caught Hadiya in the back and killed her, a heartbreakingly random act of violence in a city that had recorded 506 homicides in 2012. Such violence was only the most final of the obstacles that disproportionately afflicted black teenagers, and it revealed the stacked deck. Nearly fifty years after the Civil Rights Act, options for African American young people in Chicago were fewer, schools were worse, and their lives were more perilous than those of their white counterparts, whatever Barack's reelection said about progress. Hadiya was an honor student, a volleyball player, a majorette, and a member of the praise dance ministry at her church. She had good-hearted friends, devoted parents, and a godmother who described her as the kind of kid who had to be told, "Slow down, you can't do everything." Michelle had never met Hadiya, but she flew to Chicago to attend her funeral. She met the slain teenager's mourning friends and wondered what on earth she could say to them. The moment affected her deeply as she considered their future and her remaining years in the public eye. "Hadiya Pendleton was me and I was her," the first lady said later. "Hadiya's family did everything right, but she still didn't have a chance."

Countless children lacked equal chances in the modern-day United States, especially black children. Michelle had always said so. Her views were reflected in her mentoring work, her approach to White House cultural events and the talks she gave in neighborhoods like Anacostia. She sometimes referred to society's responsibility to help young people "fulfill their god-given potential." As she told Valerie Jarrett at Hadiya's funeral, she wanted to reach back and lift up and make a difference, not just an appearance. Entering the second term, with Barack's final election behind them, the Obamas concentrated more directly on issues of fairness. Soon, Michelle would adopt a new mission, aiming to push disadvantaged teenagers like Hadiya's friends toward college, an initiative she called Reach Higher.

Michelle spoke out more in the second term and addressed a greater variety of topics important to her. In addition to the standard tools—a targeted interview or a newspaper column—she often did something short or catchy, perhaps a photograph to her 1.2 Instagram followers, a video, or a tweet to the million-plus followers of her @FLOTUS Twitter account. In November 2013, she tweeted her support to a group that pushed immigration reform with a public fast on the National Mall. "As families begin to gather for Thanksgiving, I'm thinking of the brave #Fast4Families immigration reform advocates. We're with you.—mo." (A tweet signed "—mo" signified that it came from her, not from her staff.) The day after Thanksgiving, Barack and Michelle visited the protesters and listened to their stories. One critic tweeted back at her, "Michelle Obama thinks she's still occupying the deans office at Harvard." Another typed, "@FLOTUS Politicizing Thanksgiving with your stupid immigration garbage? LMFAO. Pathetic."

In December 2013, Michelle defended the embattled Affordable Care Act and encouraged families, specifically black families, to sign up for health insurance. "We shouldn't live in a country this rich, right, where people are choosing between their rent or their medicine, where kids aren't getting the immunizations they need," she said on the Reverend Al Sharpton's radio show. She joked during an Oval Office publicity session that mothers should "make it a Christmas treat around the table to talk about a little health care. Ring in the New Year with new coverage!" A few months later, the Islamic extremist group Boko

Haram—a phrase loosely translated as "Western education is a sin"—
kidnapped more than two hundred girls from a school in northern
Nigeria. Amid an unsuccessful international campaign to win the girls'
release, Michelle tweeted a photograph that showed her with a sad face
holding up a hand-lettered sign that read #BringBackOurGirls.

Abroad, on a 2014 trip to China benignly described by the East Wing
as a goodwill tour focused on children and education, Michelle made
assertive remarks about Internet freedom, minority rights, and the
importance of questioning and criticizing a nation's leaders. In a country where the government heavily censored the Internet and hounded
the political opposition, she said at Peking University, "Time and again,
we have seen that countries are stronger and more prosperous when
the voices and opinions of all their citizens can be heard." She called
freedom of worship and open access to information "the birthright of
every person on this planet." And she used her own life, and Barack's,
as an example of the power of the civil rights movement. She also
endeared herself to her Chinese audience by doing tai chi, jumping
rope, feeding pandas, and going sightseeing with Marian, Malia, and
Sasha, to the Great Wall, the Forbidden City, and Xi'an, home of the
terra-cotta warriors. On her last day, she pointedly dined at a Tibetan
restaurant in Chengdu to show solidarity with a persecuted ethnic
minority. Around her neck, her host draped a *khata*, a ceremonial white
scarf. A White House photographer was on hand to ensure that the
images went public.

YET, WAS IT ENOUGH? Was Michelle doing all she could? It was a
nagging question that came not from the Republican right, which had
essentially written her off, but from reasoned voices in her own corner.
After she presented the Academy Award for Best Picture to *Argo* by live
feed from the White House, Courtland Milloy, a black *Washington Post*
columnist, wrote that Michelle "ought to be under consideration for a
seat on the Supreme Court, not recruited as a presenter in some Hollywood movie contest." Noting that she often said she was standing
on the shoulders of the greats who preceded her, including Sojourner

Truth, he asked whether her own shoulders would be "broad enough for future generations of women and girls to stand on? Or just good to look at?" Milloy said she was frittering away an opportunity. "Enough with the broccoli and Brussels sprouts—to say nothing about all the attention paid to her arms, hair, derriere and designer clothes. Where is that intellectually gifted Princeton graduate, the Harvard-educated lawyer and mentor to the man who would become the first African American president of the United States?"

"I HAVE NEVER FELT more confident in myself, more clear on who I am as a woman," Michelle said a few months before she turned fifty. She had said she intended to live life "with some gusto," and there was evidence she was doing so in public and private, even in the gilded cage of the White House. She pitched Let's Move! by doing a spoof called "The Evolution of Mom Dancing" with Jimmy Fallon, a scene that would be viewed more than 20 million times on YouTube. She and the girls tagged along when Barack visited Ireland and Germany, ducking into a pub one day for lunch with Bono, the charismatic U2 singer and activist. She celebrated her fiftieth birthday in January 2014 with a girl-friends' getaway at Oprah Winfrey's Hawaiian estate and a White House party for hundreds of friends and acquaintances. Beyoncé and Stevie Wonder performed. John Legend sang "Happy Birthday." Barack, who had tweeted on their twentieth anniversary that Michelle was "the love of my life and my best friend," delivered a toast that left guests misty-eyed. Michelle, he said, had made him a better man.

Despite the trappings of Washington and her star turns in designer dresses, Michelle managed to come across to most Americans as authentic. From the self-examination as she answered questions to the humor she showed with a look or an inflection, people felt they could relate to her. High school basketball star Jabari Parker said after volunteering at a Let's Move! event in Chicago, "She's almost like everyday people. She wasn't trying to big-time anybody. She was really cool, down to earth." More than two-thirds of Americans had a favorable impression of the first lady, although conservative Republicans disliked her by a margin of about two to one. Arne Duncan, the education secretary and a longtime friend from Hyde Park, spent family time at the White House and traveled with her to advance an ambitious and controversial schools agenda. After conceding that he was biased, he said, "What you see is what she is. There are no airs, there's no fanciness. She can talk to policymakers, she can talk to parents, she can talk to children. She is absolutely comfortable in every environment. . . . And she just tells the truth."

Support from African American women remained sky-high. Robin Givhan, who graduated from Princeton one year after Michelle and covered her for the *Washington Post,* noted the first lady's ability to win admiration and affection from black people at both ends of the socioeconomic spectrum. She earned working-class respect by paying homage to her forebears, taking pains not to put on airs, and encouraging black young people to excel. "She underscores that she is no different from so many other black folks," said Givhan, who observed that Michelle also earned admiration from more successful African Americans who "know the microscope she's under and admire that she's done it so well. She has made them proud by showing the wider world that their ilk—educated, focused, ambitious, family-oriented—exists."

The reelection helped her confidence and her mission. Together, she and Barack had battled the opposition in a mean, messy, billion-dollar campaign and triumphed straight up. They were happy that the good guys had won, of course, but they also saw the victory as validation of their White House work and evidence that the November 2008 election was not a historical accident. Had they fallen short in 2012, "they thought people would be able to say it was a fluke," said John Rogers, their longtime Chicago ally. Michelle's friend Cheryl Whitaker said the win was something to savor: "He's not the first black president anymore. He's the president. She's the first lady."

Yet in the second term, as in the first, Republican leaders on Capitol Hill practiced obstruction as a savage art, barely bothering to disguise their determination to run out the clock on the Obama presidency. Following the December 2012 rampage that killed twenty schoolchildren and six adults in Newtown, Connecticut, Barack pushed a package of gun measures in Congress that would expand background checks and

ban high-capacity magazines. The proposals had overwhelming popular support, and posed no threat to the lawful owners of the roughly
300 million guns in circulation in the United States. Michelle backed
them publicly, telling a Chicago audience after Hadiya Pendleton's
death, "Right now, my husband is fighting as hard as he can and engaging as many people as he can to pass common-sense reforms to protect
our children from gun violence." Despite majority support in the Senate, the rules fell short of the sixty votes needed to break a filibuster and
the effort died. "A pretty shameful day for Washington," Barack said in
disgust. Not ninety days into the new term, the defeat foretold arduous
years ahead. So much for his hope, expressed on the campaign trail,
that a November 2012 victory would "break the fever" of the Republican opposition.

NOT LONG AFTER the second term got under way, Michelle made a
point of publicly praising the first NBA player to come out as gay: "So
proud of you, Jason Collins! This is a huge step forward for our country. We've got your back!—mo." In December 2013, when ABC news
reporter Robin Roberts came out, Michelle tweeted, "I am so happy for
you and Amber! You continue to make us all proud.—mo." And when
University of Missouri defensive end Michael Sam announced in February 2014 that he was gay, she tweeted, "You're an inspiration to all of
us, @MikeSamFootball. We couldn't be prouder of your courage both
on and off the field.—mo."

Gay rights resonated with the first lady. As Barack struggled to
explain what he believed while calculating what he could afford to say,
Michelle spoke up for equality for lesbian, gay, bisexual, and transgen-
der people. In 2007, at a California forum, she had spoken of the ways
the country was segmented, leaving Americans isolated, "sometimes by
fears, sometimes by ignorance, sometimes by resources." She argued
that values of decency and honesty united the nation, "I don't care
what race, what political party or sexual orientation." Still earlier, in
2004, gay activists in Chicago had been surprised and pleased when she
attended a fundraiser for the Lesbian Community Cancer Project. She

did not simply greet people and move out the door. She stuck around. "It wasn't like it was busting out with politicians," said Jane Saks, a lesbian friend and occasional workout partner. "I don't think it was, 'Am I for being gay or not?' It was, 'These people are working for progress.' I think she knew a lot of us." In the mid-1990s, Michelle took aside eighteen-year-old Public Allies member Krsna Golden, who considered himself "very homophobic" at the time. When he was assigned a gay roommate at a Public Allies retreat, he chose to sleep on a colleague's couch, instead. Michelle told him calmly that she understood his feelings but felt disappointed. "You have to be more open-minded," she said. "This is something you have to grow past."

Michelle had gay friends and colleagues and paid attention to issues that affected and afflicted the gay community, from parenting and workplace rights to HIV/AIDS. Starting as a teenager in the early 1980s, she spent hours with her Chicago hairdresser, Rahni Flowers, a gay man who was still doing her hair during the 2008 campaign, countless appointments later. He said he told her early about his sexuality because she gave him "that feeling of openness and a very sensible curiosity. She's more concerned with me being a good, kind, giving human being." During Michelle's time at Trinity United Church of Christ, the Reverend Jeremiah A. Wright Jr. endorsed the creation of an HIV ministry, a rare move for a black pastor at a time when many African American churches in Chicago were bitterly anti-gay. Michelle knew people who died of the disease, including a Public Allies colleague, and on a trip to Kenya, she and Barack made a public show of taking HIV tests to reduce the stigma of the test and the illness. In the White House, she considered the Obama administration a force for progress on LGBT rights. She hired as East Wing communications director Kristina Schake, a prominent defender of gay marriage who became an adviser on the issue.

For his part, Barack did an awkward dance, particularly on same-sex marriage. His support could not have been more clear in 1996 when he answered a questionnaire from *Outlines*, an LGBT newspaper in Chicago. On a one-page, typewritten letter that bore his signature, he said, "I favor legalizing same-sex marriages, and would fight efforts to prohibit such marriages." He also said, "I would support and co-sponsor a state civil rights bill for gays and lesbians." Lest there be any doubt, he voiced firm support that year in a separate survey from IMPACT Illinois, a Chicago political action committee. The survey quoted from a proposed resolution that called marriage "a basic human right" and declared that "the state should not interfere with same-gender couples who chose to marry and share fully and equally in the rights, responsibilities and commitment of civil marriage." Barack's handwritten response: "I would support such a resolution."

Those were the most positive public statements Barack would make for sixteen years. In the interim, even as he worked in the Illinois state senate to fight discrimination against the LGBT community, his answers on civil marriage ranged from "undecided" in 1998 to "I am not in favor of gay marriage" in 2007. He said his opinions were "evolving." More than a few aides thought the principal factor in his evolution was the increasingly forgiving political landscape. Finally, in May 2012, pushed by events and reassured by public opinion, Barack told Robin Roberts in a nationally broadcast interview—before she came out publicly as gay—that same-sex couples should be allowed to marry. Recalling dinner table conversations, he said it "doesn't make sense" to Malia and Sasha that the same-sex parents of their friends should be treated differently from other couples. The television moment was "cathartic" for the president, said political adviser David Axelrod. "For as long as I've known him, he has never been comfortable with his position on this." Michelle had always urged Barack's gay supporters to be patient, telling them the moment would come, if more slowly than they wanted. When Barack left the residence for the Roberts interview, Michelle told him, "Enjoy this day. You are free."

Greeting guests in June 2014 at the annual White House Pride celebration, Barack enthusiastically listed his administration's LGBT achievements, including the appointment of eleven openly gay federal judges. He talked about changing attitudes and joked that the marriage of *Modern Family* characters Mitch and Cam in an episode that drew 10 million viewers "caused Michelle and the girls to cry. That was big." Michelle, standing beside him, agreed.

. . .

MICHELLE'S STAFF SCHEDULED her for three workdays a week, a practice that dated to 2009, and they tried not to schedule events after roughly 5 p.m. She worked informally on other days, plus times when the demands of her role intervened. On Fridays, at her request, she received her briefing book for the following week and studied it assiduously. She asked for bios and photos of the people she would meet, including notations about their families and interests and whether she had met them before. One of her central goals was to put people at ease. For formal events, she always reviewed her written remarks in advance and often made changes. Unlike Barack, she was not comfortable being handed a speech a few minutes before the lights went up. Her tendency, as ever, was to overprepare. She was an early riser and her predawn emails to her aides, if she felt they had fallen short, could be blistering. She set a high bar for herself and she expected excellence from her staff—and Barack's. "When she thought he was being ill served, that would be communicated. Sometimes through him, sometimes through Valerie Jarrett, and in those unlucky moments when she summoned you to a meeting to explain things," said Axelrod. "When she was unhappy, that pall hung over the West Wing."

Escaping the media pool that followed her husband, Michelle came and went quietly from the White House to see friends and visit restaurants and the gym. Malia and Sasha were teenagers now, and they increasingly had their own plans. They also had Secret Service agents to escort them and Michelle's assistants to help coordinate their schedules. Their parents talked wistfully about how the girls were growing up fast. At home, Michelle and Barack often walked the dogs together—Bo had a new playmate, Sunny—and, in warm weather, the Obamas spent casual time together on the Truman Balcony. "Just kind of hanging out and reading the paper and catching up on the news and all that good stuff," she said. Michelle continued to pay attention to fitness. She was often spotted at a gym outside the White House grounds: "I want to be this really fly 80-, 90-year-old."

Michelle and Barack, who rarely went out to dinner in Washington, started holding private dinners in the White House residence. No motorcade, no hassle, and a limitless pool of prospective guests happy to spend an evening in the residence, with drinks, creative food, lively conversation—and music from Barack's jazz playlists in the background. The unpublicized gatherings included notables from the worlds of art, letters, business, media, and, less often, politics. Not sure what to expect, one couple passed through White House security at 6 p.m., figuring they would be out the gate and on their way home by nine o'clock. It was well after midnight when the gathering ended. A guest who went to dinner on a different night did not make it back to his hotel until 2:30 a.m.

Marian remained a steady and steadying presence. "Not long on pretense," as Michelle put it. "The first one to remind us who we are." Michelle said her mother gave her "endless amounts of time just to talk and talk and talk and talk." Or, as she explained when she hosted the annual White House Mother's Day tea five years into Barack's presidency, "There is no way I would be standing up straight on my feet if it weren't for my mom, who is always there to look after our girls, to love them and be mad at me when I'm disciplining them, which I still don't get. . . . She's like 'Why are you so mean?' But that's what grandmas are for. But, especially, she's been that shoulder for me to lean on. I can always go up to her room and cry, complain, argue. And she just says, 'Go on back down there and do what you're supposed to do.'"

WHERE MICHELLE BELIEVED she could make the greatest difference was in the lives of young people. She spoke to elite audiences from time to time, including the high-profile White House interns, who were already well on their way. When they won seats at the table, she informed them in no uncertain terms, they had a responsibility to speak for people less privileged. And if they were not willing to risk their power, as she put it, they should step aside for someone who would. Far more often, however, Michelle chose to speak to disadvantaged teenagers, particularly from minority communities. Drawing on the narrative of her own upbringing and a cold-eyed assessment of current conditions, she shared tactics and conclusions that flowed from her own experience, all but willing them across the finish line. She implored students on society's bottom rungs to concentrate on the factors they could control. Implicit in her message was the fact that no one, including a well-intentioned president, could remove the vast structural obstacles and equalize the odds any time soon. They should not wait for the cavalry to rescue them, she was saying. There was no cavalry.

"The only reason that I am standing up here today is that back when I was your age, I made a set of choices with my life. Do you hear me? *Choices*," Michelle told several thousand Chicago schoolchildren in March 2013. "Although I am the first lady of the United States of America—listen to this, because this is the truth—I am no different from you. Look, I grew up in the same neighborhoods, went to the same schools, faced the same struggles, shared the same hopes and dreams that all of you share." Her message was fundamentally conservative and it negated the cardboard critique that she and Barack encouraged victimhood, favored government solutions, and played to racial hostility. Nor was she calling for collective action or protest. She was addressing young people as individuals and imploring them to pursue a path to success, one step at a time. Then, if all went well, they could reach back and help others as they climbed. It was a formula that had worked for Michelle, who braced them for the difficulties ahead. "You will get your butts kicked sometimes and you will be disappointed. And you will be knocked down, and you have to get back up. There will be people hating on you. . . . Can you handle that? As you improve your lives, are you going to be afraid? Are you going to be afraid, and then retreat back into what's comfortable?"

Barack, too, used his own story to instruct African American students. Two weeks before Michelle spoke in Chicago, his motorcade pulled up at Hyde Park Academy High School, where Michelle's uncle, Nomenee Robinson, had been a student leader sixty years earlier. To an audience of black teenagers, Barack confessed to getting stoned, getting drunk, neglecting his schoolwork, and being angry about his absent father. He urged them to get serious about their studies and craft "a backup plan in case you don't end up being LeBron or Jay Z." The startling part of his message, in one young man's eyes, was less what

Barack accomplished in high school than what he did wrong. "Are you talking about *you*?" the boy asked uncertainly, unable to reconcile the story with the fact that the storyteller was the president of the United States.

Soon after their Chicago visits, Michelle and Barack delivered graduation speeches two days apart at historically black colleges. Their remarks emphasized personal responsibility, an element of what was sometimes called respectability politics. Michelle spoke on May 17, 2013, at Bowie State University, founded in January 1865 by the Baltimore Association for the Moral and Educational Improvement of Colored People. She told of slaves who risked their lives to read and write. She noted schools burned to the ground and black students jeered, spit upon, and ostracized just for seeking an education. She recalled the Little Rock Nine and six-year-old Ruby Bridges, who integrated a New Orleans school in 1960, then spent the year being taught alone when white parents refused to allow their children to be taught alongside her. (Photographs of the little girl being escorted to school by white federal marshals inspired Norman Rockwell to paint *The Problem We All Live With*, a canvas later displayed in the Obama White House, where Barack welcomed Bridges and paid homage to her.) Each of the protagonists in Michelle's speech had suffered and forged ahead. Yet in modern-day America, she pointed out, only one in five African Americans between the ages of twenty-five and twenty-nine possessed a college degree. Michelle made no more than a glancing reference to the failure of government and society to address the nation's stark inequities. Rather, she focused on individuals and their choices. "When it comes to getting an education, too many of our young people can't be bothered," she said. "Today, instead of walking miles every day to school, they're sitting on couches for hours playing video games, watching TV. Instead of dreaming of being a teacher or a lawyer or a business leader, they're fantasizing about being a baller or a rapper."

Two days later, on May 19, Barack delivered the commencement address at Morehouse College in Atlanta. He spoke of policy in ways that Michelle did not. He described underfunded schools, violent neighborhoods, and the dearth of opportunities for more than the fortunate few. He said society has a collective responsibility "to advocate for an

America where everybody has a fair shot in life." In sync with Michelle, he also invoked the importance of individual decisions. He guessed that each one of the graduates had been told by an elder that "as an African American, you have to work twice as hard as anyone else if you want to get by." He recalled periods in his youth when he dismissed his own failings as "just another example of the world trying to keep a black man down," but he asked the students to look to the tribulations overcome by their black forebears, including some of the greats: "They knew full well the role that racism played in their lives, but when it came to their own accomplishments and sense of purpose, they had no time for excuses."

"THERE'S A LOT WRONG HERE," writer Ta-Nehisi Coates commented after studying the Obamas' speeches that graduation season. Coates believed that the United States had never properly reckoned with the consequences of slavery or the government's role in racial oppression. In his view, Michelle and Barack did not sufficiently acknowledge or address the causes of inequality in low-income, largely segregated neighborhoods. He said Barack was a "remarkable human being" who was "better read on the intersection of racism and American history" than any of his predecessors. Yet he saw the president becoming "the scold of 'black America.'" If the dreams of many black kids did not extend much past LeBron and Jay Z, Coates said, one cause was the limited cultural exposure in "impoverished, segregated neighborhoods. Those neighborhoods are the direct result of American policy."

THE DISCUSSION WAS NOT NEW. The debate over uplift and personal responsibility had a history in the black community that dated to the nineteenth century. What was sometimes painted in shorthand as Booker T. Washington versus W. E. B. Du Bois became by the end of the twentieth century a tangled knot of questions about who was to blame for the problems of the black underclass. The questions persisted—indeed, they intensified—during Barack's presidency. Was black disadvantage a product of institutional racism and the cumulative discrimination suffered by African Americans at the hands of a white-ruled society? Was it modern-day inattention to the grotesque inequality of opportunity in U.S. cities? Was it a failing by a segment of the black community that looked too readily to others for deliverance, or at least a helping hand? To the Obamas, it was pieces of each of these. Barack reported in 2014 that "some thoughtful and sometimes not so thoughtful African-American commentators have gotten on both Michelle and me, suggesting that . . . we're engaging in sort of up-by-the-bootstraps Booker T. Washington messages that let the larger society off the hook." Invoking Malcolm X and the Reverend Martin Luther King Jr., he argued that there is "no contradiction" between calls for greater personal responsibility and an acknowledgment that some troubles in the black community "are a direct result of our history."

To do something meaningful was the challenge. Harvard professor Randall Kennedy asserted in the summer of 2014 that Barack fell woefully short. On "critical matters of racial justice," Kennedy said, "he has posited no agenda, unveiled no vision, set forth no overarching mission to be accomplished." The president "might work on black issues behind the scenes," wrote Kennedy, the brother of Michelle's friend, Angela Kennedy Acree. "But he won't be caught promoting them out front, not even now, when he is free of the burden of seeking reelection." It was Eric Holder, the attorney general, who had spoken most assertively, painting the United States as "a nation of cowards" on racial matters.

During the first term Barack had confided that he could not talk as openly about race as he wanted. And shortly before he moved into the White House, he had a revealing conversation with Jim Montgomery, a black trial lawyer and Hyde Park neighbor who dropped by with celebratory champagne. As Montgomery recalled it, he told Barack while they were making small talk that he wanted to discuss domestic policy when the president-elect had a moment. Barack asked what he had in mind. Montgomery explained, "When you get ready to spend these billions of dollars on infrastructure and all this jazz to create jobs, make sure there is a provision in there for some set-asides and some employment for black people.' He says, 'Jim, you ain't gonna ever change. If I did something like that, white folks would go crazy.'" In the same period, a wealthy white woman on Chicago's North Shore shared that very worry with Montgomery: "Jim, I'm concerned. Is he just going to be a president for the black people?" Montgomery replied with a point about electoral math. The onetime civil rights lawyer from the South Side told her, "You will find that Barack is going to be the whitest president you've ever seen."

One year into the second term, Barack launched an effort to help young black and Latino men through a mentoring program called My Brother's Keeper, underwritten by $200 million in starter pledges from foundations and corporate entities. Why young black men? He cited the "plain fact" that there are "groups that have had the odds stacked against them in unique ways that require unique solutions; groups who've seen fewer opportunities that have spanned generations." Earlier, he had argued for expanded Head Start programs and universal preschool, but this was not Great Society 2.0. My Brother's Keeper was a modest public-private partnership that consciously echoed the model of Let's Move! and Joining Forces. In the wake of protests against the treatment of African Americans by police and prosecutors, Barack announced that My Brother's Keeper would expand. Adding his name to a project specifically designed to help black people was a second-term sign that Barack felt liberated—in his ever cautious and pragmatic way—to be a president explicitly for African Americans, as well as for all Americans.

THE REUTERS DAYBOOK, a catalog of upcoming events in Washington, announced the screening of a Muppets film at the White House, part of Michelle's effort to draw attention to military families: "Joint Chiefs of Staff Chairman Gen. Martin Dempsey and Kermit the Frog participate." The March 2014 exchange between the frog, the general, and the first lady featured plenty of cornball humor and drew laughs, with Kermit saying to the assembled families, "I may not be a Marine, but I am marine life. I salute you." The media spread the word, boosted by entertaining photos and video, and Michelle notched a small win. Ditto in October 2014, when she did a six-second Vine video, dancing with a purple-and-white turnip in a riff on the song "Turn Down for What." In less than a month, viewers looped through the video more than 34 million times.

Laughs were fewer when Michelle engaged in an unusually public fight over nutrition standards with congressional Republicans who sought to dilute the policy at the heart of Let's Move!. She was not shy about defending the regulations she had lobbied Congress to pass four years earlier and her promise to "fight until the bitter end" showed that the issue was not as benign as some critics suggested. When the House of Representatives approved the Healthy, Hunger-Free Kids Act by a vote of 264–157 in 2010, it started a process designed to promote healthier school meals at a time when 31 million children bought school lunches each day, including 20 million low-income students subsidized by the federal government. The new law expanded access to the program and tightened nutrition regulations to include more whole grains, fruit, and vegetables and less salt, sugar, and fat. The measure also encouraged use of school gardens and locally grown produce, while setting a deadline for improving the healthiness of food sold in school vending machines. When skeptics complained that the costs would weaken school finances, Michelle and a raft of public-interest groups countered that the expenses were manageable and justified, given the stakes. "When we send our kids to school," Michelle said, "we have a right to expect that they won't be eating the kind of fatty, salty, sugary foods that we're trying to keep from them when they're at home."

That brought the wrath of adult naysayers, not to mention an array of students who took to YouTube and Twitter using the hashtag #ThankYouMichelleObama to complain that new meals created by school cooks tasted awful or left them hungry. It was a significant sign of her stature in the national debate that Michelle became the focus of criticism. Never mind that Congress had approved the approach by bipartisan vote or that the Department of Agriculture developed the rules based on independent recommendations from the nonpartisan health arm of the National Academy of Sciences. Michelle was the face of the program, so she took the heat. But backing down unless absolutely necessary was not her style. "I know that kids occasionally grumble about eating healthier food," she said. "But, look, that is to be expected because, frankly, that's what kids do, including my own kids. They want what they want when they want it, regardless of whether it's good for them or not. And when they don't get what they want, they complain. . . . It's our job to say, 'No, you cannot have a candy bar for breakfast.' And, 'Yes, you have to eat some vegetables every day.' And, 'No, you can't sit around playing video games all day. Go outside and run.'"

By 2014, about 90 percent of schools across the country reported being in compliance with the rules, some through gritted teeth. What followed, however, was a revolt among members of Congress, assisted by the School Nutrition Association, a trade organization backed by corporations that did billions of dollars in business with school cafeterias. The battle was already brewing in 2011, when lobbyists persuaded Congress, over the objections of the Obama administration, to count an eighth of a cup of tomato paste in pizza sauce as the equivalent of a half cup of vegetables. Michelle took to the opinion pages of *The New York Times* three years later to defend the nutrition standards. Referring to the pizza squabble, she said, "You don't have to be a nutritionist to know that this doesn't make much sense." She also challenged an effort by the potato lobby and federal legislators to expand access to white potatoes for millions of participants in the Women, Infants and Children program. Potatoes are fine, said the first lady, who often described french fries as her favorite food. But research showed that many women and young children in the supplemental nutrition program were already getting enough starch and potatoes—which they could purchase with food stamps, if they chose—and not enough "nutrient-dense fruits and vegetables."

What really bothered Michelle, however, and prompted her to make repeated calls to individual senators, was the attempt to waive the school nutrition rules. Such efforts, she said, went against science and good sense and did a disservice to parents, who were "working hard to serve their kids balanced meals at home and don't want their efforts undermined during the day at school." Not incidentally, she argued that obesity was now contributing to $190 billion in higher annual health costs. She insisted that the $10 billion spent by taxpayers on school lunches should not pay for "junk food for our children." The heart of her argument rested on the needs of impoverished children. She noted that millions of disadvantaged kids relied on school meals as their main source of nutrition and cited research that well-fed children do better in school. "We simply can't afford to say, 'Oh, well, it's too hard, so let's not do it,'" she said.

MICHELLE CONTINUED to work on Let's Move! and on Joining Forces. She called homelessness among military veterans "a stain on the soul of the nation." She helped enlist local leaders to work on the problem as federal authorities delivered more money for housing vouchers. Drawing attention to women who served in Iraq and Afghanistan, she said it was "just wrong" that their 11.2 percent unemployment rate was five points higher than men from the same wars, and more than double the rate of civilian women. She also took tentative steps to add a new project to her portfolio. Early in the White House years, she had envisioned a larger international role for the second term, but with the girls in school, Barack under pressure, and the optics of foreign travel a potential political liability, she looked for issues closer to home and her heart. Her message was direct and her tone was raw when she spoke up for a $50 million public-private partnership that would deliver after-school programming to urban kids in Chicago. The fate of black teenagers was on her mind. Her voice caught in her throat as she recalled a private scene from Hadiya's funeral, when it was "hard to know what to say to a roomful of teenagers who are about to bury their best friend." She declared that adults have a "moral obligation" to provide children with safe neighborhoods, cultural opportunities, and classrooms without "crumbling ceilings and ripped-up textbooks."

Following the Newtown shootings and Hadiya's death, Michelle discussed gun violence with friends and staff, but did not make urban violence or gun laws or after-school programs a significant part of her agenda. Rather, she turned to higher education and patterns of unequal access to college. In her Chicago speech, she repeated a conviction that had been a constant in her thinking and Barack's. It was the view that disparate outcomes in minority communities had less to do with the young residents' aptitudes than with the disparate opportunities they were afforded. Growing up in South Shore in the 1960s and 1970s, she felt safe, she took part in a range of engaging activities, and she had adults who pushed and supported her. "And that, in the end, was the difference between growing up and becoming a lawyer, a mother and first lady of the United States—and being shot dead at the age of fifteen."

Through a new East Wing project called Reach Higher, she set out to encourage young people from low-income families to attend college or training schools and to persevere long enough to get a degree. The need was clear: Only one in ten young people from low-income backgrounds typically earned a bachelor's degree by age twenty-five, while roughly half from high-income families did. Following the formula of Let's Move! and Joining Forces, the project supported Barack's agenda, in this case his effort to construct a smarter, more skilled workforce. In 1990, the United States ranked first in the world in the percentage of college graduates in the 25-to-34 age group. By 2014, the country had fallen to 12th. Noting that education would influence the nation's economic future and rates of upward mobility, Barack tried to set the nation's sights on regaining the top position by 2020. His project was called North Star.

Michelle and Barack had long talked publicly about the obstacles to higher education for disadvantaged students and the struggles many of them faced when they got there. They saw the disparities during their own climbs through college and, more recently, in the experiences of Malia and Sasha, who attended Sidwell Friends, where the 2014–2015 tuition was $36,264 per student. Students in the girls' circle not only received a first-rate education, but valuable practice in taking college admission exams, which Barack described as standardized tests that are "not standardized." Unequal access to preparation, he said, "tilts the playing field. It's not fair and it's gotten worse."

A few months earlier, Michelle had watched a new film, *The Inevitable Defeat of Mister and Pete*. Partly funded by singer Alicia Keys, it was a story that made her cry not only when she watched it, but when she thought back on its most poignant scenes. The movie depicts the struggles of two young boys largely fending for themselves in a Brooklyn housing project while their mothers are behind bars. By the time the credits rolled, Michelle had decided to screen the film in the White

House to advance the initiative that would become Reach Higher. "Because there are millions of Misters and Petes out there who are just struggling to make it," she said, vowing that the film would be the guidepost for her remaining time as first lady.

At the White House screening in January 2014, on the eve of a gathering of university presidents to discuss ways to improve college access, Michelle spoke soberly and directly, explaining her plan to use her pulpit. She would tell adults that kids needed schools to teach them, programs to support them, and universities "to seek them out and give them a chance and then prepare them and help them finish their degrees once they get in." However much her progressive critics might urge her to play a more active role, Michelle said there was little she could do personally, on the policy or spending front. "The one thing I can bring to this is the message that we can give directly to young people."

To young people all around the country, Michelle set out to be booster, coach, advocate, and role model. She was the mom-in-chief, and she wanted them to see their rocky path through childhood as a strength, not a weakness. Life was tough, sure, but they were still standing. Resilience, as she liked to tell Malia and Sasha, was a response learned through experience. She set out to deliver reassurance and practical advice to teenagers who doubted that they had what it takes, just as she had done at Anacostia High, the Elizabeth Garrett Anderson School, Hadiya Pendleton's funeral, and a hundred other places all the way back to the offices of Public Allies. She had proven that she belonged at one unlikely destination after another, that she *was* supposed to be there. So, too, were they.

MICHELLE FLEW TO Atlanta one day in September 2014 to tell her story and repeat her mantra at Atlanta's Booker T. Washington High School, opened in 1924 as the first public high school in Georgia built for African American children. Standing at a lectern in the school gymnasium as her prepared remarks scrolled through twin teleprompters, Michelle said that she had faced challenges getting her education and she recognized that many Washington High students had confronted worse, from financial hardship and tumult at home to the wounds of drugs and guns. She said their tribulations were "advantages," and their successes demonstrated courage and grit. She urged the ninth and tenth graders to make a plan to advance themselves and instructed the eleventh and twelfth graders to study for college assessment tests. She told them all to ask for help, not once but often. "Are you listening to me?" she asked the hundreds of students who packed the bleachers and stood in front of the stage. "Do you hear what I'm telling you, because I'm giving you some insights that a lot of rich kids all over the country—they know this stuff and I want you to know it, too, because you have got to go and get your education. You have got to!"

MTV personality Sway Calloway flew in from New York to emcee the event. He told the students to look lively because his reports would appear on MTV, BET, and Nickelodeon. He said the first lady "could be anywhere on this planet today, literally, but she chose to come to your high school." Calloway's presence offered evidence of the way that Michelle and her staff had promoted her programs on their own terms, to the audiences they coveted. Michelle made no time for questions from news reporters, but she gave risk-free one-on-one backstage interviews to Calloway and LGBT media figure Tyler Oakley, whose upbeat conversation with her registered 1.2 million YouTube views in just ten days.

To the students in the gym, Michelle spoke of racism and Jim Crow. She invoked Booker T. Washington and the school's most famous alumnus, Martin Luther King Jr., who graduated from Morehouse, a ten-minute walk away. She said the two men had bequeathed to the students a legacy of progress and a responsibility to better themselves and their families. "There is absolutely no excuse," she told the teenagers. "If there's anybody telling you that you're not college material— anyone—I want you to brush 'em off. Prove them wrong." She might as easily have been talking about the legacy that her grandparents passed to her parents and that Fraser and Marian Robinson passed to her and to Craig. Ever the South Side girl, Michelle was passing it on, too. "I love you all," she said. "God bless. Keep working hard."

Epilogue

Nearly six years into her White House life, Michelle took to the campaign trail in late 2014 as Democrats fought to retain their Senate majority. Barack seemed beleaguered, his hair ever grayer and his favorability numbers in the low forties, at least twenty points lower than his wife's. Many candidates calculated that a campaign rally with the president would be a net loss, but coveted a visit from Michelle. In more than a dozen states from Florida to Maine to Colorado and three trips to Iowa, she became Barack's proxy, talking up the things that were going right and criticizing Republican behavior that "just wastes time and wastes taxpayer dollars. In fact, it's gotten so bad, they're even trying to block the work that I do on childhood obesity. And that's really saying something." Barack made a ripe target. Demonized in ever more fantastical ways, he seemed unable to find a response that worked, even to persuade fellow Democrats. In November, the country was in such a sour mood that only 36 percent of voters bothered to cast ballots, the lowest figure since 1942. Republicans surged gleefully into control of the Senate, leaving the forty-fourth president ever more isolated.

Michelle carried on with her projects, but her public and private reflections sometimes took on a valedictory tone. As attention shifted to the election of Barack's successor, she told friends that she intended to stay in Washington until Sasha graduated from high school in 2019, if that's what Sasha wanted. Despite her Chicago roots and the friends and family still living on the South Side, Barack set his sights on New York, at least as one of their future homes. If it came to that Michelle reckoned that she could be more anonymous there than in Chicago, an appealing thought after the White House fishbowl. She said she looked forward to staying fit, traveling to beautiful places, and, one day, being a grandmother. At an event with Laura Bush, who appeared to be carving a satisfying post-politics life in Dallas, Michelle said she saw in the Bush family "a level of freedom" that comes when the spotlight shifts. "There is more that you're able to do out of office, oftentimes, than you can do when you're in office." Working on a memoir likely to fetch millions of dollars, she told friends that she would have much to say when she no longer had to worry quite so much about the consequences. Privately, she once mused that when she left the White House, she would be just like Barbara Bush. She paused for comic effect as her guests conjured the unlikely image. Because you'll start wearing three strands of pearls? one perplexed friend asked. No, Michelle laughed, because I'll be able to say whatever the hell I want.

Michelle had once called herself a "statistical anomaly," a black woman who had climbed from the Chicago working class into elite American society. Her place in history reflected the distance she and the country had traveled since January 1964. Opportunities had multiplied and paths had grown smoother. And yet she remained, in so many ways, an exception that proved the rule. More than a half century after her birth, the odds remained daunting for the vast majority of the 41 million people in the United States who identified themselves as African American. There were yawning gaps between blacks and whites in household income, home ownership, college completion rates, and net worth, not to mention disparities in incarceration rates and levels of confidence in the legal system. Michelle herself said in May 2014, "We know that in America, too many folks are stopped on the street because of the color of their skin." The idea of the country being post-racial would have been laughable were it not so depressing. Michelle belongs to a generation, said historian Marcia Chatelain, that sees "incredible amounts of change and incredible amounts of stagnation." When the first lady considered the stacked deck and grew impatient, Barack would remind her that they were "playing a long game here, and that change is hard and change is slow and it never happens all at once. But eventually we get there, we always do."

One day in the Oval Office, very quietly, so quietly that Barack had to ask him to repeat it, a five-year-old black boy named Jacob Philadelphia asked the president a question. He said, "I want to know if my hair is just like yours." Barack invited him to see for himself and, standing beside his desk, leaned down. As Jacob reached up to touch his hair, a White House photographer snapped a picture. For more than five years, the photo hung in the West Wing as dozens of others were swapped out. Michelle described the scene to an African American church audience in Nashville, offering it as a sign that progress does come, however glacial, however imperfect. "I want you to think," she said, "about how children who see that photo today think nothing of it because that is all they've ever known, because they have grown up taking for granted that an African American can be president of the United States." She once reflected, while hosting a White House workshop to celebrate the rise of 1960s Motown music, that "something changed when little girls all across the country saw Diana Ross on *The Ed Sullivan Show*." Just maybe, she thought, something was changing, too, as little girls and boys across the country saw Michelle Obama in the White House.

Michelle devoted countless hours to her work on obesity, education, and military families. She hoped her projects, and the messages behind them, would endure. And yet the power that she invoked most often in her public life was the symbolic power of her trajectory—the fact that she made it from Richard J. Daley's unforgiving Chicago all the way to Princeton, to Harvard, to prosperity and a measure of professional fulfillment, and then to the gleaming pulpit that was the White House. That was why she told her story so often to students who felt marginalized and unsure. It was why she emphasized discipline, persistence, and decency—and why she gave out all those hugs. One day, explaining "why, as first lady, I do this," she told a high school audience in Washington that she urged them onward "because this is all I can be for you right now, is just this model of an alternative." Could she do more? That was the lingering question of her final stretch in the White House and the years to come.

"WE HAVE A BLACK FAMILY in the White House. Amazing!" said Maya Angelou at a BET awards ceremony after Michelle introduced her. To Michelle, Angelou was a hero and muse whose affirming words "lifted me right out of my own little head." After the poet's death in 2014, the first lady spoke of what she had learned about authenticity and self-worth from the writer, dancer, singer, teacher, and short-order cook from Stamps, Arkansas. She said Angelou, born in 1928, "celebrated black women's beauty like no one had ever dared to before— our curves, our stride, our strength, our grace." In an era when black women faced "stifling constraints," Michelle said, Angelou "serenely disregarded all the rules. . . . She was comfortable in every inch of her glorious brown skin."

In her eulogy, delivered at a memorial service in Winston-Salem, North Carolina, Michelle painted herself anew as "a little black girl from the South Side of Chicago." She described her feelings of loneliness in Ivy League classrooms and "long years on the campaign trail where at times my very womanhood was dissected and questioned." It pleased her when people called her authentic. And when they did, she thought of Angelou. She said the poet's work allowed her and many others "just to be our good old black-woman selves. She showed us that, eventually, if we stayed true to who we are, then the world would embrace us."

Acknowledgments

This book, much like the Obama presidency, got its start in Iowa. In 2007, Michelle Obama rolled from Davenport to Iowa Falls to Fort Dodge to Rockwell City, telling her story and talking up her husband's candidacy. She spoke of Barack's life and her own, and asked listeners to believe in him the way she did. I followed her through Iowa and, as the campaign gained momentum, I watched her in New York and Texas, South Carolina and Indiana, and, in the final days of the race, Ohio. Before and after the election, I explored Michelle's history and her Chicago career while spending considerable time writing about Barack's own trajectory. For those early forays from *The Washington Post*'s Chicago bureau, I am grateful to the *Post* editors who humored me and to the politics-writing colleagues who made me wiser.

As I watched at close range, it became clear that Michelle merited a book that placed her at the center of her own narrative, not simply as the wife of the famous Barack, nor simply as first lady. When I embarked on the project, two friends at the *Post* steered me to Andrew Wylie and Scott Moyers. After Scott returned to Penguin, Andrew proved savvy and steadfast, the shrewdest ally a writer could want. Thanks to Jacqueline Ko at the Wylie Agency for answering many questions. At Knopf, Erroll McDonald believed in the idea from the start and, through thick and thin, never wavered. I am grateful to Knopf's talented team, who guided the book to the finish, including Nicholas Thomson, Cassandra Pappas, Claire Bradley Ong, and Carol Devine Carson.

At Northwestern University, where I have been fortunate to teach since leaving the *Post*, I gained greatly from the labors of a lively and dedicated team of undergraduate researchers. Rhaina Cohen and Yvonne Kouadjo came to know Michelle's story almost as well as I did, adding details and smart thinking to chapter after chapter. I was fortunate to have Benjamin Purdy's considerable contributions for two years and, in the homestretch, the work of Emily Jan, who paid particular attention to the photographic record; plus Ashley Wood and Yoona Ha. Many thanks to two deans of Northwestern's Medill School of Journalism, Bradley Hamm and John Lavine, and former associate dean Mary Nesbitt. Their support and flexibility contributed mightily to my ability to finish this project in something short of a light-year. As I completed the book, the Hutchins Center for African and African American Research offered a welcome haven and access to Harvard's libraries.

So many colleagues at Northwestern offered conversation and words of encouragement. Heartfelt appreciation to Medill friends Cecilia Vaisman, Ava Greenwell, Rick Tulsky, Jack Doppelt, Judy McCoy, Emily Withrow, Kari Lydersen, Charles Whitaker, and Louise Kiernan. Also Stephan Garnett, Alex Kotlowitz, Beth Bennett, Josh Meyer, Loren Ghiglione, Mei-Ling Hopgood, Karren Thompson, Douglas Foster, and many other terrific colleagues and students. Beyond Medill, I was pleased to be able to turn for guidance on Chicago history and culture to Northwestern professors Henry Binford, Mary Pattillo, and Darlene Clarke Hine.

Dozens of people shared their stories and their wisdom about Michelle and Barack Obama and the world they inhabit. For their reflections and their trust, I thank them. I owe a deep debt to reporters and media figures who asked thoughtful questions of the Obamas, some as long as twenty years ago, others quite recently. Their work enriched the narrative immeasurably. A special shout-out to colleagues who opened their notebooks and shared unpublished interviews, including Michael Powell of *The New York Times*, Scott Helman of *The Boston Globe*, David Mendell and John McCormick, late of the *Chicago Tribune*, and Lauren Collins of *The New Yorker*.

This book would not be the same without the rigor and sage advice of friends who broke into their busy lives to read the manuscript. For that, I thank Robin Givhan, Rachel Swarns, David Remnick, Peter Baker, Kevin Merida, and Dexter Filkins. Each of them not only plowed through the evolving biography but kept up helpful and long-running conversations along the way. Martha Biondi, expert in the history of campus politics, graciously read the Princeton and Harvard chapters. Any errors of fact or interpretation, naturally, are mine alone.

Truth be told, there was never a day when I did not look forward to working on this project and solving one riddle or another. Countless times, a kind word or a generous suggestion from a friend was a welcome balm. I much appreciate support from those who spoke and those who mostly listened, including Bill Hewitt, Krissah Thompson, Geraldine Baum, David Von Drehle, John Rogers, Elizabeth Shogren, Cathy Lasiewicz, Mellody Hobson, Chris Westefeld, John Audley and Andrea Durbin. I am grateful to Russ Canan, Sheryll Cashin, Blaine Harden, Margot Singer, Connie Schultz, Esther Fein, Steve and Rena Reiss, Tom Ricks, Masha Lipman, Joe Day, John Westefeld, John Heilemann, and Steve Mufson. In Evanston, I thank Andrew Johnston—so generous with his expertise about photography—Tracy Van Moorlehem, Deb Turkheimer, Dylan Smith, Dylan Penningroth, Ian Hurd, and all the Lincoln and Nichols friends. Special thanks to Mike Klearman, who always managed to talk of this project with a gleam in his eye.

Every so often, a thick envelope of news clippings would arrive from my mother, Katherine Day Slevin, who first lived in Washington in the 1930s and remembers cutting through the White House grounds to get from Pennsylvania Avenue to the National Mall. Well into her nineties, my mother has a keen eye for details that reveal character, a trait she shared with my late newsman father, Joseph R. Slevin. To the two of them, and their generous spirit, I owe more than I can convey. I thank my siblings, Michael Slevin, Jonathan Slevin, and Ann Peck, for their love and encouragement, and Ann Masur for being a laser-eyed reader of the manuscript and a great support to our family. A bevy of Slevins, Masurs, and their kin offered invariably lively conversation and good cheer.

I recognized how much this project had become part of our family's life when Kate asked a question at dinner one summer evening in 2013: "Does anyone know what's happening July seventeenth?" Without hesitating, six-year-old Milo said, "Michelle Obama's half-birthday?" He was right about the date, although Kate had a different event in mind. Isaac and Milo learned their facts and asked thoughtful questions, even as they surely wondered when I would finally finish. Their older brother, Nik, was unfailingly enthusiastic while cheering from a greater height and distance. Kate Masur contributed a historian's expertise and a scholar's sensibility. Ever smart and stalwart, ever cool under pressure, a great reader and a greater friend, she sharpened my thinking and rallied the troops, staying true to the end.

Notes

INTRODUCTION

4   "Maybe you feel like no one has": Michelle Obama, Academies of Anacostia graduation, June 11, 2010.

5   "We live in a nation": Michelle Obama, remarks to the National Congress of Black Women, September 30, 2007.

5   "So the world has": "Running Mates: Michelle Obama One on One," *Good Morning America*, ABC News, May 22, 2007.

5   "So many people have no idea": Verna Williams, interview with author.

5   "the balance between": Michelle Obama, remarks at University of California–Merced, May 16, 2009.

5   "You do not want": Trooper Sanders, interview with author.

6   "I think that girl was": Michelle Obama, *106 and Park*, BET, November 13, 2013.

1 | CHICAGO'S PROMISE

7   "The gutsiest guy": Dan Maxime, interview with author.

8   "What would my father think": Michelle Obama, Harlem, June 26, 2007.

8   "the glue": Capers Funnye, interview with author.

8   "I remember his compassion": *South Side Girl*, Democratic National Committee video, August 26, 2008.

9   "I could calculate": Richard Wright, *Black Boy*, p. 252.

9   "depressed and dismayed me": Ibid., p. 261.

9   "I knew that this machine-city was": Ibid., p. 262.

9   overcrowding forced many black schools: St. Clair Drake and Horace R. Cayton, *Black Metropolis: A Study of Negro Life in a Northern City*, p. 202.

10 In one direction was a library named for: Ibid., p. 379; and Adam Green, *Selling the Race: Culture, Community, and Black Chicago, 1940–1955*, pp. 58–59.

10 "The capital of black America": Nicholas Lemann, *The Promised Land: The Great Migration and How It Changed America*, p. 64.

11 "And they risked serious reprisals": John Paul Stevens, "The Court and the Right to Vote: A Dissent," *New York Review of Books*, August 15, 2013.

11 "The whites in power": Rachel L. Swarns, *American Tapestry: The Story of the Black, White, and Multiracial Ancestors of Michelle Obama*, pp. 156–160.

11 "a young man destined for better things": Ibid., p. 79.

11 "He wanted a different kind of life": Ibid., p. 80.

11 He set up pins: Ibid., pp. 92–93.

12 James moved: Ibid., p. 83.

13 The policy, known as redlining: Beryl Satter, *Family Properties: Race, Real Estate, and the Exploitation of Black Urban America*.

13 three-fourths of Chicago's black population: Arnold R. Hirsch, *Making the Second Ghetto: Race & Housing in Chicago, 1940–1960*, pp. 4–5.

13 they charged rents far higher: Ibid., p. 29.

13 Three black infants died: Drake and Cayton, p. 202.

13 By 1945, more than half of the Black Belt: Ibid., p. 206.

13 "They faced what other African American families faced": Barack Obama, speech, Washington, September 18, 2007.

13 LaVaughn again took up housecleaning: Swarns, p. 93.

13 John, who died as a baby: Nomenee Robinson, interview with author.

14 "separated, without dependants [*sic*]": Swarns, p. 97.

14 She relied especially on two older women from Georgetown: Swarns, p. 100.

14 the first African American woman: Scott Young, Moody Bible Institute, email, April 26, 2013.

14 "Everything educational, they got it": Swarns, p. 100.

15 "I just loved that little toy": Nomenee Robinson, interview.

15 "Don't you dare go out there again": Ibid.

15 His mother knew the location: Nomenee Robinson, interview.

16 named for a friendly Italian woman: Swarns, p. 101.

16 "He happened to hear me screaming": Nomenee Robinson, interview.

16 He left that chore to his wife: Craig Robinson, *A Game of Character: A Family Journey from Chicago's Southside to the Ivy League and Beyond*, p. 27.

16 He worked on the horse-drawn cart: Nomenee Robinson, interview; Michelle Obama, *American Grown: The Story of the White House Kitchen Garden and Gardens Across America*, p. 12.

16 "We had to be hustlers": Nomenee Robinson, interview.

16 In the mid-1940s: Ibid.

17 "Her style was very open": Richard Hunt, interview with author.

17 "escaping and coming to the land of the free": Ibid.

17 "The teachers might suggest": Ibid.

17 "You'd hardly know he was around": Reuben Crawford, interview with author.

17 He saw Fraser: Nomenee Robinson, interview; family remembrance prepared for Fraser Robinson's memorial service, Chicago, March 10, 1991.

17 "He was secure with himself.": Nomenee Robinson, interview.

18 "Make your own little list": Nelson Algren, *Chicago: City on the Make*, pp. 45–46.

18 "We were taught the history": Charlie Brown, interview with author.

19 "faced with abhorrence of everything": Margaret T. G. Burroughs, "What Shall I Tell My Children Who Are Black?" Chicago: M.A.A.H. Press, 1968.

19 At first, she thought: Margaret Taylor Burroughs, *Life with Margaret: The Official Autobiography*, pp. 72–73.

19 "An agitator by profession.": Richard Hofstadter, *The American Political Tradition and the Men Who Made It*, p. 135.

19 "When you lived in Chicago back then": Brown, interview.

20 "If one word": Bernard Shaw, interview with author.

20 "You *had* to do better": Crawford, interview.

20 "an absolute conviction": Funnye, interview.

21 He "encouraged striving": Ibid.

21 Eldridge Cleaver and Anne Moody: Adam Green, p. 198.

21 "I couldn't get Emmett Till": "The Murder of Emmett Till," http://www.pbs.org/wgbh/amex/till/sfeature/sf_remember.html.

22 One thought running through her head: The Rev. Jesse Jackson Sr., "Appreciation: Rosa Parks," *Time*, October 30, 2005.

22 once you put money in a bank: Nomenee Robinson, interview.

22 It was an initiative of the Dining Car Workers: National Register of Historic Places registration form, National Park Service, October 2011.

22 In the immediate postwar years: James R. Grossman, Ann Durkin Keating, and Janice L. Reiff, eds., *The Encyclopedia of Chicago*.

22 The complex opened: National Register of Historic Places registration form, National Park Service, October 2011.

23 "the opening of a new frontier": Mary McLeod Bethune, "Chicago's Parkway Gardens Symbol of Growing Economic Unity and Strength," *Chicago Defender*, December 9, 1950.

23 He wanted not only to provide: Richard M. Leeson, *Lorraine Hansberry: A Research and Production Sourcebook*, p. 6.

23 "hellishly hostile": Lorraine Hansberry, *To Be Young, Gifted and Black*, p. 51.

24 "it is a play that tells the truth": Anne Cheney, *Lorraine Hansberry*, p. 55.

24 "We ain't never been that poor": Lorraine Hansberry, *A Raisin in the Sun*, p. 143.

24 "one of America's greatest stories": Scott Feinberg, "Tonys: A Moment in the Sun for 'A Raisin in the Sun' Nominee LaTanya Richardson Jackson," *Hollywood Reporter*, May 27, 2014.

24 Fraser joined the army: Andrew Robinson, interview.

25 "You fell out for formation": Joe Hegedus, interview with author.

25 He was awarded a good conduct medal: U.S. Army records.

25 He would complete his service: U.S. Army records.

25 As African Americans continued to migrate: Christopher Manning, "African Americans," in Grossman, Keating, and Reiff, eds.; Nicholas Lemann, p. 70.

2 | SOUTH SIDE

26 They broke up: Marian Robinson, unpublished interview with Scott Helman, 2008.

26 "philosopher in chief": Marian Robinson quoted in Craig Robinson, *A Game of Character: A Family Journey from Chicago's Southside to the Ivy League and Beyond*, p. xi.

26 "If it can be done": Jim Axelrod, "In the Family," *CBS Sunday Morning*, March 1, 2009.

27 "I come from a very articulate": Michelle Obama, "Reaching Out and Reaching Back," *InsideOut*, University of Chicago Office of Community and Government Affairs, September 2005.

27 they would raise seven children: Michelle Obama, remarks to National Council of La Raza, July 23, 2013, New Orleans.

28 As adults, they both learned to read: Rachel Swarns, *American Tapestry: The Story of the Black, White, and Multiracial Ancestors of Michelle Obama*, pp. 150–151.

28 "The women in my family were dressmakers": Scott Helman, unpublished interview with Marian Robinson, 2008.

28 He then found work as a plasterer: Swarns, p. 88.

28 With Purnell and his sister: Ibid., p. 72.

28 "When I finally came to Chicago on May 9, 1930": Dempsey Travis, *An Autobiography of Black Jazz*, p. 240.

29 "You learn to sleep through jazz": Laura Brown, "Michelle Obama: America's Got Talent," *Harper's Bazaar*, October 13, 2010.

29 "By calling a chef, drummer and jazz aficionado": Robinson, p. 16.

29 He was denied better jobs and pay: Susan Saulny, "Michelle Obama Thrives in Campaign Trenches," *New York Times*, February 14, 2008.

29 "I had a father who could be very angry about race": Marian Robinson, unpublished interview with Michael Powell, 2008.

30 "Segregation and poverty have created": National Advisory Commission on Civil Disorders, pp. 1–2.

30 "All of us know what those conditions are": Lyndon Baines Johnson, speech, The White House, July 27, 1967, http://millercenter.org/president/speeches /speech-4040.

31 "This difference has its source": Pierre de Vise, *Chicago's Widening Color Gap*, p. 18.

31 In raw numbers: Ibid., pp. 75–76.

32 "Statistically, Woodlawn had become": John Hall Fish, *Black Power / White Control: The Struggle of the Woodlawn Organization in Chicago* (Princeton, N.J.: Princeton University Press, 1973), p. 13; and interview with author.

32 going "way out south": Timuel Black, interview with author.

32 With no children of their own: Robinson, p. 5.

32 "People here are dedicated": Sel Yackley, "South Shore: Integration Since 1955," *Chicago Tribune*, April 9, 1967.

32 Leonard was a commercial artist: "His Designs on Shower Curtains Led to Success," *Chicago Tribune*, April 14, 1966.

32 "I had the best childhood ever": Leonard Jewell, interview with author.

33 One of the very few stay-at-home mothers: Mariana Cook, interview with Barack and Michelle Obama, 1996.

33 "There were good schools": Ta-Nehisi Coates, "American Girl," *Atlantic,* January 2009.

33 "the Shangri-La of upbringings": Robinson, p. 7.

33 "We are here because the Savings and Loan": Taylor Branch, *At Canaan's Edge: America in the King Years, 1965–68,* p. 516.

34 "I *still* have faith in the future.": Ibid., pp. 501–509.

34 "I wish I were an Alabama trooper": Jeff Kelly Lowenstein, "Resisting the Dream," *Chicago Reporter,* May 2006.

34 "I have never in my life": Branch, pp. 509–511; Lowenstein, "Resisting the Dream."

35 "We should have known better,": Branch, p. 558.

35 "cracked a beguiling": Ibid.

35 "We are all, let us face it": Ibid., p. 523.

35 "Daley had a special weak spot": Leon Despres, *Challenging the Daley Machine: A Chicago Alderman's Memoir,* p. 45.

36 At its height, the Chicago machine: Adam Cohen and Elizabeth Taylor, *American Pharaoh: Mayor Richard M. Daley—His Battle for Chicago and the Nation,* p. 157.

36 "You couldn't cut": Ibid., p. 146.

36 "We gave out jobs": Flynn McRoberts, "Chicago's Black Political Movement: What Happened?," *Chicago Tribune,* July 4, 1999.

36 "blunted by the taste": Ibid.

36 "You went along with things": Mitchell Locin and Joel Kaplan, "'I Never Did Think I Would Ever Be Really Involved in Politics'—Eugene Sawyer," *Chicago Tribune,* February 1, 1989.

37 "There are no virgins": William E. Schmidt, "Chicago Nears Choice for Mayor as Race Issue Flares," *New York Times,* February 27, 1989.

38 "the beginning of the good": Dan Maxime, interview with author.

38 "felt local politics was the most important": Marian Robinson, unpublished interview with Powell, 2008.

38 "a visiting kind": Marian Robinson, unpublished interview with Helman, 2008.

39 "If I had to describe": Craig Robinson, interview with author, 2007.

39 "Everything that I think about": Kristen Gelineau, "Would-be First Lady Drifts into Rock-Star Territory, Tentatively," Associated Press, March 30, 2008.

39 "It was almost": Robinson, p. 12.

39 impossibly contoured blonde Malibu Barbie: Michelle Obama, remarks at a memorial service for Maya Angelou, June 7, 2014.

39 and a black Barbie imitation: Rosalind Rossi, "Obama's Anchor," *Chicago Sun-Times,* January 21, 2007.

39 "I liked everything Barbie": Michelle Obama, North American Aerospace Defense Command, December 24, 2012.

40 "the standard for perfection": Michelle Obama, remarks at memorial service for Maya Angelou, June 7, 2014.

40 "taught me how to throw": Michelle Obama, speech to the International Olympic Committee, Copenhagen, Denmark, October 2, 2009.

40 "kind of a tomboy": Grace Ybarra, "Michelle Obama Gets Kids Moving," *Sports Illustrated Kids,* June 25, 2013.

40 "a gift I shared": Michelle Obama, speech to International Olympic Committee.

40 The children were limited: Saulny, "Michelle Obama Thrives."

40 When the weather: Robinson, p. 11.

40 During football season: Ibid., p. 8.

40 Once earned $7 a day: Barack Obama, presenting the Presidential Medal of Freedom, November 20, 2013.

40 Craig once said: *Chicago Tonight,* WTTW, April 30, 2010.

41 "and after school": Michelle Obama, *American Grown: The Story of the White House Kitchen Garden and Gardens Across America,* p. 15.

41 "I guess she figured": Harriette Cole, "From a Mother's Eyes," *Ebony,* September 2008.

41 "Just like Sasha": Ibid.

41 told a co-worker: Jacquelyn Thomas, interview with author.

41 "Her mom told the teacher": Saulny, "Michelle Obama Thrives."

41 emphasized effort and attitude: Elizabeth Brackett, *Chicago Tonight,* WTTW, October 28, 2004.

42 When they finished: Robinson, p. 70.

42 how much they regretted: Scott Helman, "Holding Down the Obama Family Fort: 'Grandma' Makes the Race Possible," *Boston Globe,* March 30, 2008.

42 "We told the kids": Marian Robinson, interview with Helman, 2008.

42 "written from the black perspective": Robinson, p. 58.

42 "Now, you've got to remember": Craig Robinson, remarks at "Coming Back: Reconnecting Princeton's Black Alumni," Princeton University, October 18, 2014. The Black Panther Party was founded in 1966.

43 He dismissed the 1963 March: Kevin Merida, "A Piece of the Dream," *Washington Post,* January 16, 2008.

43 "I am not advocating": Jackie Robinson column, *Chicago Defender,* March 14, 1964.

43 "Before Malcolm X": Ta-Nehisi Coates, "The Legacy of Malcolm X: Why His Vision Lives On in Barack Obama," *Atlantic,* April 2, 2010.

44 "repeated acts of self-creation": Barack Obama, *Dreams from My Father,* p. 86.

44 "If you think about it": Remnick, *The Bridge,* pp. 233–234.

44 Fraser also spent: Robinson, p. 53.

44 "I liked it because": Robinson, p. 12, and Laura Brown, "Michelle Obama: America's Got Talent."

44 "my mother would not": Ta-Nehisi Coates, "American Girl."

44 Late on a summer night: "Northwestern Dorms Bar Negro Students," *Chicago Defender,* August 14, 1943; "N.U. Keeps Jim Crow in Dorms," *Chicago Defender,* September 11, 1943; "Northwestern Sued for $50,00 in Dorm Ban," *Chicago Defender,* December 11, 1943.

45 "She was friendly, but": Betty Reid, interview with author.

45 Michelle said both sides: Rosemary Ellis, "A Conversation with Michelle Obama," *Good Housekeeping*, November 2008, www.goodhousekeeping .com/family/celebrity-interviews/michelle-obama-interview.

45 She remembered enduring: Michelle Obama, Google+ Hangout with Kelly Ripa, March 4, 2013.

45 "a basic foundation": Rosemary Ellis, "A Conversation with Michelle Obama."

45 "to explore and find": Robinson, p. 77.

46 "about how Fraser": Ibid., p. 155.

46 "That love for one another": Ibid., pp. 6–7.

46 Craig recalled their parents: *A Salute*, p. 68.

46 "a mother who": Michelle Obama, "Be Fearless," in Editors of *Essence* Magazine, *A Salute to Michelle Obama* (New York: Essence Communications, 2012), p. 36.

46 She and her brother: Rosalind Rossi, "Obama's Anchor: As His Career Soars Toward a Presidential Bid, Wife Michelle Keeps His Feet on the Ground," *Chicago Sun-Times*, January 21, 2007.

46 "didn't overdo the praise": Robinson, p. 70.

46 "But there was a whole lot": Elizabeth Brackett, *Chicago Tonight*, WTTW, October 28, 2004.

46 "You follow people": Marian Robinson, unpublished interview with Powell, 2008.

46 "If it sounds like": Cole, "From a Mother's Eyes."

47 She attended: Michelle Obama, remarks in Topeka, Kan., May 17, 2014.

47 "That's where we got": Coates, "American Girl."

47 "resented it when I couldn't say": Ibid.

47 "More important, even": Lauren Collins, "The Other Obama: Michelle Obama and the Politics of Candor," *New Yorker*, March 10, 2008.

47 "by ear, day by day": Cole, "From a Mother's Eyes."

3 | DESTINY NOT YET WRITTEN

49 "Thus began a conversation": Craig Robinson, *A Game of Character: A Family Journey from Chicago's Southside to the Ivy League and Beyond*, p. 58.

49 If they experienced animosity: Ibid., p. 59.

49 No one can make: Ibid., pp. 58–60.

49 "When you grow up as a black kid": Craig Robinson, interview with author, 2007.

50 Purnell Shields, Michelle's maternal: Michelle Obama, remarks to National Council of La Raza, July 23, 2013.

50 "They might not like": Grace Hale, interview with author.

50 "Very smart, but very quiet": Ibid.

50 "She had very strong values": Jacquelyn Thomas, interview with author.

51 If he had been born white: William Finnegan, "The Candidate: How the Son of a Kenyan Economist Became an Illinois Everyman," *New Yorker*, May 31, 2004.

51 "a discontent about him": Shailagh Murray, "A Family Tree Rooted in American Soil," *Washington Post*, October 2, 2008.

51 "not always enjoyable": Robinson, pp. 103, 14–15.

51 "On one visit": Ibid., pp. 14–15.

51 "His whole demeanor": Capers Funnye, interview with author.

51 "He was wrestling": Nomenee Robinson, interview with author.

52 "didn't exactly spew love": Andrew Robinson, interview with author.

52 Nomenee went to India: Paul Grimes, "Galbraiths Fete Mrs. Kennedy at Formal Dinner on Her Last Day in India," *New York Times*, March 21, 1962.

52 died a prosperous man: Andrew Robinson and Nomenee Robinson, interviews with author.

53 "veil of impossibility": Michelle Obama, remarks in Orangeburg, S.C., November 20, 2007.

53 "did not let it carry over": Marian Robinson, unpublished interview with Michael Powell, 2008.

53 "An ice house!": Sterling Stuckey, interview with author.

53 "Parents were trying": Rachel Swarns, panel discussion, Northwestern University History Department, October 19, 2012.

53 "We want you to": Rachel Swarns, *American Tapestry: The Story of the Black, White, and Multiracial Ancestors of Michelle Obama*, p. 108.

53 "the mothers and the fathers": Michelle Obama, Whitney Young film screening, White House, August 27, 2013.

54 "We didn't think of it": Deval Patrick, *A Reason to Believe: Lessons from an Improbable Life*, p. 22.

54 "From that position": Ibid., p. 119.

54 "I was surrounded by adults": Ibid., p. 32.

54 "The true gift": Deval Patrick, interview with author.

54 "They did not want": Patrick, p. 17.

55 At that point: Robinson, p. 28.

55 "Lunch on school days": Finnegan, "The Candidate"; Michelle Obama, *American Grown: The Story of the White House Kitchen Garden and Gardens Across America*, p. 13.

55 "If the TV broke": Lauren Collins, "The Other Obama: Michelle Obama and the Politics of Candor," *New Yorker*, March 10, 2008.

55 "Are we rich?": Robinson, pp. 29–30.

56 He would even make time: Craig Robinson, book-tour discussion, Dominican University, April 27, 2010.

56 "A smart man learns": Jim Axelrod, "Craig Robinson, First Coach," CBS, March 1, 2009.

56 "If you disappointed": Craig Robinson, interview with author.

56 "I never had any": Craig Robinson, *Good Morning America*, March 4, 2010.

56 "Unofficial counselor to family": Robinson, p. 147.

56 "Fraser was the type of person": Grace Hale, interview with author.

57 He would shave: Robinson, p. 73.

57 "That's where I went": Nomenee Robinson, interview with author.

57 "Before he got really sick": Laura Brown, "Michelle Obama: America's Got Talent," *Harper's Bazaar,* October 13, 2010.

57 but by 1965: Michelle Obama, speech to Democratic National Convention, August 26, 2008.

57 "I never knew my father": Michelle Obama, remarks in Grinnell, Iowa, December 31, 2007.

58 He took pride: *Rickey Smiley Show,* RadioOne, February 7, 2014.

58 "When you have a parent": Holly Yeager, "The Heart and Mind of Michelle Obama," *O: The Oprah Magazine,* November 2007.

58 "Here's a guy": Dan Maxime, interview with author.

58 "thought he had the greatest": Jim Axelrod, "First Coach."

58 "To have a family": Craig Robinson, interview with author.

58 A favorite destination: Michelle Obama, *American Grown,* p. 15.

59 "I was going through my cursing": Darlene Superville, "First Lady: Not Surprised by Reaction to Oscars," Associated Press, March 1, 2013.

59 One warm day: Robinson, pp. 60–61.

60 "He said, 'You guys can't'": Leonard Jewell, interview with author.

60 As Michelle propelled herself: Robinson, p. 35.

60 "Michelle works harder": Rebecca Johnson, "The Natural," *Vogue,* September 2007.

60 "strong, strong, strong": Leonard Jewell, interview with author.

61 "We had so much": Ibid.

61 "really does hate to lose": Judy Keen, "Candid and Unscripted, Campaigning Her Way," *USA Today,* May 11, 2007.

61 "She would practice": Karen Springen, *Chicago,* October 2004. Reprinted at www.chicagomag.com as "First Lady in Waiting," June 22, 2007.

61 To soothe Craig's nerves: Robinson, p. 84.

61 If the game was close: Ibid., p. 81.

61 running 50 meters in: Results sheets from Illinois Senior Olympics, per staff member Deborah Staley, Springfield, Ill.

61 "If I can't do it fast": Yeager, "Heart and Mind."

61 put in some time: Grace Ybarra, "Michelle Obama Gets Kids Moving," *Sports Illustrated Kids,* June 25, 2013.

61 "Tall women *can*": Yeager, "Heart and Mind."

62 "represented those women": Judith Jamison, *Dancing Spirit: An Autobiography,* p. 132.

62 "I think to myself": Peter Bailey, "Young: 4th Black Leader to Die Since 1963," *Jet,* April 1, 1971.

62 "drew on his decency": Michelle Obama, Whitney Young film screening, White House, August 27, 2013.

62 "force you outside": Ava Greenwell, interview with author.

62 "probably the finest ever": Chicago Urban League newsletter, May/June 1975.

63 "We are delighted": Ibid.

63 "in such a way that": Bernarr E. Dawson, memorandum, Whitney Young High School archive.

64 "Whitney Young was built": Jeffrey Wilson, interview with author.

64 "It was a grand experiment": Ibid.

65 "I'm fixin' to go": Ibid.

65 Sometimes, to get a seat: Geraldine Brooks, "Michelle Obama and the Roots of Reinvention: How the First Lady Learned to Dream Big," *More*, October 2008.

66 plagued by construction defects: Kathy Burns, "South Shore High: Flaws Mar 'Architect's Jewel,'" *Chicago Tribune*, July 20, 1969. Bernard Judge, "Witness Tells of Vast Waste at School Site," *Chicago Tribune*, March 7, 1970.

66 "the outsider, the racial minority": Robinson, p. 79.

66 "My sister always talked": Craig Robinson, speech to the Democratic National Convention, August 26, 2008.

66 "I signed up for every activity": Michelle Obama, speech to Martin Luther King Jr. Magnet School, Nashville, Tenn., May 18, 2013.

66 She earned extra money: Michelle Obama, Corporation for National and Community Service remarks, May 12, 2009, Washington, D.C.

67 "She badgered and badgered": Yeager, "Heart and Mind."

67 "She sat on his desk": Marian Robinson, unpublished interview with Michael Powell, 2008.

67 In addition to her job: Lynn Sweet, "The Obamas and Their Jobs," *Chicago Sun-Times*, August 14, 2008.

67 "because that's who I saw": Katie Couric, "Michelle Obama: Your First Lady," *Glamour*, November 2009.

67 "I'm sure it was psychological": Richard Wolffe, "Barack's Rock," *Newsweek*, February 25, 2008.

67 "She saw I never studied": Elizabeth Brackett, *Chicago Tonight*, WTTW, October 28, 2004.

67 "She'd study late": Marian Robinson, unpublished interview with Michael Powell, 2008.

68 tasked her with hiring: Aaron Payne papers, University of Illinois–Chicago archives.

68 "They said, 'Go to Spiegel'": Reuben Crawford, interview with author.

68 Another beneficiary was: Murrell Duster, interview with author.

68 She earned two degrees: Teresa Fambro Hooks, "18th Annual Chicago Film Fest Opening Honors the Primos," *Chicago Defender*, August 1, 2012.

68 She was a regular: Grace Hale, interview with author; Murrell Duster, interview with author.

68 a civil rights lawyer: Maureen O'Donnell, "Ida B. Wells' Grandson Took On Machine," *Chicago Sun-Times*, February 17, 2011.

68 "They talked about everything": Murrell Duster, interview with author.

69 "People reacted as if": Robinson, p. 95.

69 "It's like I say": Marian Robinson, unpublished interview with Scott Helman, 2008.

69 Other colleges: *Chicago Tonight*, WTTW, April 30, 2010.

69 "It might as well": Craig Robinson, remarks at "Coming Back: Reconnecting Princeton's Black Alumni," Princeton University, October 18, 2014.

69 His father's offer: Robinson, p. 96.

69 Craig, who later learned: Michelle Obama, speech to Democratic National Convention, September 4, 2012.

70 "It made me mad": Michelle Obama, speech at Booker T. Washington High School, Atlanta, Ga., September 8, 2014.

70 Michelle applied to Princeton: Theresa Fambro Hooks, "Weeklong Drama Festival at Chicago Ensemble Theater," *Chicago Defender,* November 16, 2006.

70 "long, long": Marian Robinson, unpublished interview with Michael Powell, 2008.

4 | ORANGE AND BLACKNESS

71 "Of 11,602 aspirants": Alan Sipress, "Class of 1985 Stands as Most Selective Ever," *The Daily Princetonian,* June 4, 1981.

71 "not merely as a means": William Bowen address, September 13, 1981, Princeton archives.

72 "I sometimes feel": Ibid. Former first lady Jacqueline Kennedy Onassis requested that "Ithaka" be read at her 1994 funeral.

72 Michelle Robinson reached: Michelle Obama, remarks at White House, January 16, 2014.

72 "When I first got in": "Obama Speaks with MSNBC's Mika Brzezinski," MSNBC, November 13, 2007.

72 She slept with her: Michelle Obama, remarks, Eastern Kentucky University graduation, May 12, 2013.

72 "I remember being shocked": Rebecca Johnson, "The Natural," *Vogue,* September 2007.

72 Michelle sometimes felt: Michelle Obama, remarks at Bell Multicultural High School, November 12, 2013.

73 "struggling just to keep": Michelle Obama, speech to Martin Luther King Jr. Magnet High School, Nashville, Tenn., May 18, 2013.

73 "a world that existed": Craig Robinson, *A Game of Character: A Family Journey from Chicago's Southside to the Ivy League and Beyond,* p. 105.

73 standing at a pay phone: Ibid., pp. 113–114.

74 He later said that: Ibid., p. 124.

74 "As a freshman": Marvin Bressler, interview with author.

74 "infamous for being racially": Michelle Robinson, "Princeton-Educated Blacks and the Black Community," (senior thesis, Princeton University, 1985), p. 26.

74 "Princeton is actively seeking: Princeton University records.

74 The class of 1985: The class of '85 statistical reference comes from Princeton University records.

75 "double-consciousness": W. E. B. Du Bois, *Souls of Black Folk.*

75 "I grew up around": Hilary Beard, interview with author.

75 "My experiences at Princeton": Michelle LaVaughn Robinson, "Princeton-Educated Blacks and the Black Community," senior thesis, Princeton University, 1985.

76 Brown was horrified: Brian Feagans, "Color of Memory Suddenly Grows Vivid," *Atlanta Journal-Constitution*, April 13, 2008.

76 "one of the funniest": Ibid.

77 "There were those black students who": Ruth Simmons, interview with author.

77 "I didn't want this Third World place": Robin Givhan, interview with author.

77 "I wanted to create a differne social": Sharon Holland, interview with author.

78 "some of the best of times": Ibid.

78 "She took time to talk": Hilary Beard, interview with author.

78 "a program that would": Czerny Brasuell, interview with author.

78 "because of the isolation": Ruth Simmons, interview with author.

78 "You learned about politics": Craig Robinson, remarks at "Coming Back: Reconnecting Princeton's Black Alumni," Princeton University, October 18, 2014.

78 "She was generally": Kenneth Bruce, interview with author.

79 "As a black student:" Lauren Ugorji, interview with author.

79 She was pictured in: *Daily Princetonian*, February 26, 1985.

79 To raise money: Sally Jacobs, "Learning to be Michelle Obama," *Boston Globe*, June 15, 2008.

79 "because she is so tall:" *Daily Princetonian*, February 26, 1985.

79 "If I drove, I would": Hilary Beard, interview with author.

79 "Her thoughts were never": Ibid.

80 "Michelle's always been very vocal": Lauren Collins, "The Other Obama: Michelle Obama and the Politics of Candor," *New Yorker*, March 10, 2008.

80 "You need to make sure": Jodi Kantor, "The Obamas' Marriage," *New York Times Magazine*, October 26, 2009.

80 punched in the stomach: Michelle Obama, remarks to D.C. College Application Program graduates, Washington, D.C., June 21, 2014.

80 "a place of peace and calm": Tamara Jones, "Michelle Obama Gets Personal," *More*, January 31, 2012.

81 "That family more nearly": Marvin Bressler, interview with author.

82 "Across the board": Kenneth Bruce, interview with author.

82 "There were the beginnings": Sharon Holland, interview with author.

82 "The question that bothered me": Lauren Ugorji, interview with author.

83 One year later: William G. Bowen and Derek Bok, *The Shape of the River: Long-Term Consequences of Considering Race in College and University Admissions*, p. 5.

84 But Powell also cited: Ibid., p. 8.

84 "We created a community": Sarah Brown, "Obama '85 Masters a Balancing Act," *Daily Princetonian*, December 7, 2005.

84 "We couldn't afford": Collins, "The Other Obama."

84 "giggled and laughed": Rosalind Rossi, "Obama's Anchor: As His Career Soars Toward a Presidential Bid, Wife Michelle Keeps His Feet on the Ground," *Chicago Sun-Times*, January 21, 2007.

84 "We were three black": Karen Springen and Jonathan Darman, "Ground Support," *Newsweek*, January 29, 2007.

85 "terrorized and humiliated": Randall Kennedy, *The Persistence of the Color Line: Racial Politics and the Obama Presidency,* pp. 182, 16.

85 "My dad reacted": Ibid., p. 183.

85 "We were expected": Mark Bernstein, "Identity Politics: Why Randall Kennedy '77 Writes About Racial Loyalty, Betrayal and Selling Out," *Princeton Alumni Weekly,* April 2, 2008.

86 "They created a family": Randall Kennedy, interview with Brian Lamb, March 3, 2002.

86 "What are the important": Suzanne Alele application file, Princeton University.

87 "Suzanne was the spirit": Czerny Brasuell, interview with author.

87 "always made decisions": Michelle Obama, interview with author, 2007.

87 She was invited: Suzanne Alele obituary, *Princeton Alumni Weekly,* October 24, 1990.

87 valedictorian of her class: Joan Quigley, "Homecoming," *Princeton Alumni Weekly,* December 8, 2010.

88 "I felt guilty to even ask": Michelle Obama, Corporation for National and Community Service remarks, May 12, 2009.

88 "Being in the woods": Eric Schmidt, "Fresh Air Fund Offers Off-Season Adventures," *New York Times,* June 16, 1985.

89 "Average kids with a chance": Geoffrey Canada, newyorktimes.com, video, 2006, https://www.youtube.com/watch?v=Ca9rd4aA_t0&feature =related.

89 "one of my heroes": Michelle Obama, remarks at University of California–Merced graduation, May 16, 2009.

89 "I liked the hayride": "Fresh Air Fund Opens Up New Views of Family and Community," *New York Times,* May 19, 1985.

89 "The first time": "Voices Ring Out at a Fresh Air Camp," *New York Times,* August 11, 1985.

89 "You learn a lot: "Wishes and Goals at Camps for City Children," *New York Times,* August 10, 1986.

90 It was an "illusion": William Julius Wilson, *The Declining Significance of Race: Blacks and Changing American Institutions,* p. 21.

90 Wilson's drives: William Julius Wilson, interview with author.

91 "Before a group can enter": Quoted in Michelle Robinson, "Princeton-Educated Blacks," p. 8.

91 From Andrew Billingsley's: Ibid., p. 7.

91 "They discuss problems": Ibid., pp. 8–9.

91 The "White cultural": Ibid., p. 3.

91 "may be attributed to": Ibid., p. 54.

92 "black underclass": Wilson, p. 2.

92 Black graduates could: Michelle Robinson, "Princeton-Educated Blacks," p. 55.

92 her major conclusion: Ibid., p. 53.

92 Noting that the university: Ibid., p. 62.

92 As for her own views: Ibid., p. 3.

92 "It is conceivable": Ibid., p. 3.

93 Howard Taylor, a sociology: Esther Breger, "All Eyes Turn to Michelle Obama '85," *Daily Princetonian*, November 5, 2008.

93 "Do you become the wealthiest person": Kenneth Bruce, interview with author.

93 "One of the points": Michelle Obama, interview with author, 2007.

93 "It is incumbent on us": Ibid.

94 "We teased them about": *South Side Girl,* Democratic National Convention, August 26, 2008.

5 | PROGRESS IN EVERYTHING AND NOTHING

95 pressed ahead: Michelle Obama, remarks to D.C. College Access Program graduation, June 21, 2014.

95 "It is Monday morning": Scott Turow, *One L: The Turbulent True Story of a First Year at Harvard Law School,* p. ix.

96 "feeling like you were": Ibid., p. 277.

96 "I almost didn't apply": Robert Wilkins, interview with author.

96 "The black community": Verna Williams, interview with author.

97 numbering 170 among: *Harvard University Fact Book,* http://oir.harvard .edu/fact-book.

97 It was certainly a contrast: William G. Bowen and Derek Bok, *The Shape of the River: Long-Term Consequences of Considering Race in College and University Admissions,* p. 5.

97 "a lifesaver for me": Verna Williams, interview with author.

97 " 'What are you going to do' ": Ibid.

97 The 575: Michelle Deakin, spokesperson, Harvard Law School, email exchange with author.

97 "caught up in all that goes": Jocelyn Frye, interview with author.

97 With her friends: Verna Williams, interview with author.

98 "Parents know their children": Kevin Murphy, "Actress Rashad Delivers Cosby's Message," *Capital Times* (Madison, Wisc.), September 19, 2006.

98 "She was not the person": Verna Williams, interview with author.

98 "The thing about law": Jocelyn Frye, interview with author.

99 "She is saying something": Verna Williams, interview with author.

99 "Michelle always, everything she wrote": Charles Ogletree, interview with author.

99 she volunteered as an editor: Michelle Robinson, Harvard Law School yearbook, 1988; *BLJ* 1986 issue.

99 "All the talk and the debates": David Remnick, *The Bridge: The Life and Rise of Barack Obama,* p. 187.

100 The goal was to produce: BLJ document; interview with Ginger Chavers McKnight, a former BLJ editor, with author.

100 "the most race-conscious": Remnick, *The Bridge*, p. 200.

100 "I've worked at the Supreme Court": "Dreams of Obama," *Frontline*, January 2009.

100 "pride in her color and her race": Derrick Bell, "The Civil Rights Chronicles," *Harvard Law Review*, November 1985, p. 13.

101 "defy and transcend": Ibid., p. 14.

101 "We have made progress": Ibid., p. 16.

101 "What is impossible": Ibid., p. 30.

101 "a legal system which": Derrick A. Bell, "Who's Afraid of Critical Race Theory?" *University of Illinois Law Review* 893 (1995): 900.

102 "the spotlighted few": Bell, "Civil Rights Chronicles," p. 11.

102 "the patterns of racial": Wilson, *The Declining Significance of Race*, p. 120.

102 "History gets made through": Fox Butterfield, "Old Rights Campaigner Leads a Harvard Battle," *New York Times*, May 21, 1990.

102 "This is a university": Ibid.

102 "Even liberal white scholars": Vincent Harding, "Equality Is Not Enough," *New York Times*, October 11, 1987.

103 "time for re-evaluation": Victor Bolden, "Black Lawyers Host Constitutional Conference," *Harvard Law Record*, September 18, 1987.

104 "We were trying to search": Robert Wilkins, interview with author.

104 "The absence of minorities": Michael Sudarkasa, "Verna Williams: Providing a Spark, a Light . . . a Beacon," *BLSA Memo*, Summer 1988, p. 7.

105 "In the name of tradition": Michelle Robinson, "Minority and Women Law Professors: A Comparison of Teaching Styles," *BLSA Memo*, Summer 1988, p. 30.

107 "to understand that": Charles Ogletree, interview with author.

107 "Part of the reason why": Michelle Robinson, "Minority and Women Law Professors."

107 "Students come to me": Ibid.

108 "to shake students out": Ibid.

108 "strong on what her opinions": David Wilkins, interview with author.

108 "You can't begin to": Karyn E. Langhorne, "Bureau Commemorates 75 Years of Legal Aid," *Harvard Law Record*, April 29, 1988.

109 "A large number of": Ibid.

109 One was a matter: Harvard Legal Aid Bureau records.

109 "experienced the tactical": 75th Annual Report of the Harvard Legal Aid Bureau, 1988.

109 "a commitment to her father": "Michelle Obama's Commitment to Public Service Began at HLS," *Harvard Law Bulletin*, 2008.

109 "People looked at her": Ilene Seidman, interview with author.

110 "It was less a thoughtful": Mariana Cook, interview with Barack and Michelle Obama, 1996.

110 "There was a real sense": Robert Wilkins, interview with author.

110 "You guys, this is": Areva Bell Martin, interview with author.

111 "We were treated like celebrities": Ibid.

111 "Yes, you're privileged": Ibid.

111 "My personal experience": Karen W. Arenson, "Princeton Honors Ex-Judge Once Turned Away for Race," *New York Times,* June 5, 2001.

112 "There's no other black student": Jocelyn Frye, interview with author.

112 "We had—and we should": Ibid.

113 "something more, not a social club": Verna Williams, interview with author.

114 At least one faculty: Robert Wilkins, interview with author.

114 "The majority of young people": Stefan Fatsis, "Arias Urges 5,500 Harvard Graduates to Help Ease Suffering," Associated Press, June 9, 1988.

114 He lamented the low: "Bok Assails Gap in Pay in Vital Jobs," *New York Times,* June 10, 1988.

115 "Harvard Law School is a hard place": David Wilkins, interview with author.

6 | FINDING THE RIGHT THING

116 More money than her parents combined: Michelle Obama, remarks, November 2, 2009, Washington, D.C.

117 "I have been asked": Flynn McRoberts, "Chicago's Black Political Movement: What Happened?," *Chicago Tribune,* July 4, 1999. Metcalfe's words were written for him by Vernon Jarrett, *Chicago Tribune* writer and future father-in-law of Valerie Jarrett, the Obamas' friend and adviser.

117 Washington received just: Andrew H. Malcolm, "A Matter of Blacks and Whites," *New York Times,* March 27, 1983.

118 "His picture was everywhere": Barack Obama, *Dreams from My Father,* p. 147.

119 "so obviously a quality candidate": Alan Greene, interview with author.

120 Michelle's assignments as a young: Lynne Marek, "The 'Other Obama' Honed Her Skills at Sidley Austin," *National Law Journal,* June 23, 2008.

120 for example, reading storyboards: Mary Hutchings Reed, interview with author.

120 "I knew Michelle was frustrated": John Levi, interview with author.

120 "She was very at ease": Mary Hutchings Reed, interview with author.

120 "A lot of people come": Nate Eimer, interview with author.

120 Michelle volunteered: Levi, interview.

121 "There was always a bit": Steven Carlson, interview with author.

121 Despite what she described: Suzanne Malveaux, "The Obamas," CNN, January 1, 2009.

121 For one thing: Barack Obama, "My First Date with Michelle," *O: The Oprah Magazine,* February 2007.

121 It was the ears: Michelle Obama, *The Oprah Winfrey Show,* January 19, 2005.

121 "probably just a black man": Holly Yeager, "The Heart and Mind of Michelle Obama," *O: The Oprah Magazine,* November 2007.

121 "But he walked into": Mariana Cook, interview with Barack and Michelle Obama, 1996.

121 "Well, Barack grew up": Ibid.

122 "I'm going to focus": Cassandra West, "Her Plan Went Awry, but Michelle Obama Doesn't Mind," *Chicago Tribune,* September 1, 2004.

122 a pattern she chose: Michelle Obama, *106 and Park*, BET, November 19, 2013.

122 "My family swore": Michelle Obama, remarks in Harlem, June 26, 2007.

122 the couple quietly married: David Maraniss, *Barack Obama: The Story*, p. 162.

122 At the time, laws prohibiting: Ibid.

122 His younger sister: Michelle Obama, remarks at Maya Angelou memorial service, June 7, 2014.

122 "This is no picnic for": Barack Obama, *Dreams*, pp. 47–48.

123 Madelyn worked: Michelle Obama, speech to Democratic National Convention, September 4, 2012.

123 "too old and too troubled": Barack Obama, *Audacity of Hope*, p. 346.

123 "Well, he ended up pretty": Charles Payne, interview with author.

123 "You know, I got my": Michelle Obama, campaign rally, Akron, Ohio, October 24, 2008.

123 "Indifferent" was how he recalled: Barack Obama, *Dreams*, p. 98.

123 smoked so much pot: Maraniss, *Barack Obama*.

123 "I rebelled," he once said: Barack Obama, speech to Northwestern University commencement, 2006.

124 "She cut me off": Barack Obama, *Dreams*, p. 95.

124 "A few miles from Pasadena": Ibid., p. 98.

124 "leaving your race at the door": Ibid., p. 97.

124 "seemed indistinguishable from": Ibid., p. 98.

124 "We always just thought": Charles Payne, interview with author.

124 "uttered racial or ethnic": Barack Obama, "A More Perfect Union," speech in Philadelphia, April 2008.

125 "a big, dark woman": Barack Obama, *Dreams*, p. 102.

125 When Barack told Regina: Ibid., p. 104.

125 "Oh Barack": Ibid., p. 105.

125 He went to one cloth-napkin lunch: Newton Minow, interview with author.

125 "Barack Obama, One L!": Remnick, *The Bridge*, p. 193.

126 "I was impressed by his": Laurence Tribe, unpublished interview with David Remnick.

126 "in every way you can": Suzanne Malveaux, CNN, January 1, 2009.

126 "When I first met him": Rosemary Ellis, "A Conversation with Michelle Obama," *Good Housekeeping*, November 2008, www.goodhousekeeping.com/family/celebrity-interviews/michelle-obama-interview.

126 "He is very persistent": Ibid.

126 "I said, okay, we'll go": Malveaux, CNN, January 1, 2009.

126 "I was sold": Ibid.

126 "In her eyes": Mariana Cook, interview with the Obamas, 1996.

127 "terrifyingly random": Barack Obama, *Audacity of Hope*, p. 329.

127 He said he would like: Ibid., p. 332.

127 To impress him: Michelle Obama, *Rachael Ray Show*, September 17, 2012.

127 which Fraser and Marian had bought: Cook County property records.

128 "For someone like me": Barack Obama, *Audacity of Hope*, pp. 332–333.

128 "cruddy": Liza Mundy, *Michelle: A Biography*, p. 138.

128 His only pair: Michelle Obama, speech to Democratic National Convention, 2012.

128 "He loved that car": Mundy, p. 138.

128 he considered working: Barack Obama, *Dreams*, p. 142.

128 The project descended: Peter Slevin, "For Clinton and Obama, a Common Ideological Touchstone," *Washington Post*, March 25, 2007.

129 "a basic belief in": Mike Kruglik, interview with author.

129 although his supervisor: Gregory Galluzzo, interview with author; and Slevin, "For Clinton and Obama."

129 he worked with African American: Barack Obama, *Dreams*, p. 170.

129 "this dual sense": Ibid., p. 157.

129 "He said that all too often": Michelle Obama, speech to Democratic National Convention, August 26, 2008.

130 "It was how he felt about": Michelle Obama, speech at Christ Church College, University of Oxford, May 25, 2011.

130 "We gave it a month, tops": Rebecca Johnson, "The Natural," *Vogue*, September 2007.

131 "you sort of felt sorry": M. Charles Bakst, "Brown Coach Robinson a Strong Voice for Brother-in-Law Obama," *Providence Journal*, May 20, 2007.

131 "She's very accomplished": Bill Reynolds, "Welcome to Obama's Family," *Providence Journal*, February 15, 2007.

131 "She found that he never": Suzanne Malveaux, CNN, January 3, 2009.

131 "A little bit": Elizabeth Brackett, *Chicago Tonight*, WTTW, October 28, 2004.

131 "When she asked me": Chuck Klosterman, "First Coach," *Esquire*, February 1, 2009.

131 "Confident without being cocky": Johnson, "The Natural."

132 "The fact that I've been": Fox Butterfield, "First Black Elected to Head Harvard's Law Review," *New York Times*, February 6, 1990.

132 "If Suzanne or I": Amanda Paulson, "Michelle Obama's Story," *Christian Science Monitor*, August 25, 2008.

132 "how I would want to be": Michelle Obama, interview with author, 2007.

133 Doctors at the University: Craig Robinson, *A Game of Character: A Family Journey from Chicago's Southside to the Ivy League and Beyond*, pp. 153–54.

133 "Would you just stop it": Ibid., p. 155.

133 "As the casket was lowered": Barack Obama, *Audacity of Hope*, p. 332.

133 "Can I go to the family reunion": Debra Pickett, "My Parents Weren't College-Educated Folks, So They Didn't Have a Notion of What We Should Want," *Chicago Sun-Times*, September 19, 2004.

133 "Just like that": Michelle Obama, North Carolina A&T commencement, May 12, 2012.

7 | ASSETS AND DEFICITS

134 "I don't want to be": Susan Sher, interview with author.

134 Not wanting to let her: Valerie Jarrett, interview with author, 2007.

134 "He wanted to kick": Ibid.

135 "Valerie, put yourself in": Cal Fussman, "Valerie Jarrett: What I've Learned," *Esquire*, May 2013.

135 "Everybody in my mother's": Timuel D. Black Jr., *Bridges of Memory: Chicago's First Wave of Black Migration*, p. 579.

135 Barbara recalled that: Ibid., p. 581.

135 "My grandmother always": Ibid., p. 593.

136 Showing up for work: Valerie Jarrett, remarks at National Medical Fellowships ceremony, Chicago, November 2008.

136 "My wife and I decided": Death notice, University of Chicago, September 29, 2011.

136 "We said, 'Let's look'": Black, p. 575.

136 "Because she didn't know": Ibid., p. 578.

136 "Because it was so hard": Ibid., p. 592.

136 "In order to compete": Ibid., pp. 581–582.

137 Well into adulthood: Joe Heim, "Just Asking: Valerie Jarrett on Giving Bad Advice, Shyness, and the Value of Loyalty," *Washington Post*, December 7, 2014.

137 "I had a great office": Fussman, "Valerie Jarrett."

137 "there was no reason to be happy": Abner Mikva, interview with author.

137 "She was a political novice": Valerie Jarrett, interview with author, 2007.

138 "before they were married": Ibid.

138 "It just seemed incredible": Jay Newton-Small, "Michelle Obama's Savvy Sacrifice," *Time*, August 25, 2008.

138 "ultimately you're not going": Jim Axelrod, "First Coach," CBS, March 1, 2009.

138 "Don't you want to pay": Newton-Small, "Michelle Obama's Savvy Sacrifice."

138 One was a Coach: Rebecca Johnson, "The Natural," *Vogue*, 2007.

138 "City government, in addition": Michelle Obama, interview with author, 2007.

139 "We all thought Barack": Charles Payne, interview with author.

139 Barack informed Mikva: Abner Mikva, interview with author.

139 In ten years, Barack said: Bruce Orenstein, interview with author.

139 Barack lived with Michelle: Barack Obama, interviewed by *Parade*, June 22, 2014.

140 Barack telephoned Miner: Judson Miner, interview with author.

140 "that would let him": David Remnick, *The Bridge: The Life and Rise of Barack Obama*, p. 220.

140 Barack "knew full well": Judson Miner, interview with author.

141 "The outer limits of minority": *Barnett v. Daley*, 32 F.3d 1196 (1994).

141 Barack also did legal work: Judson Miner, memorandum to author, July 2007.

141 Miner said Barack's efforts: Miner, interview with author.

141 "If this isn't leading to marriage": Debra Pickett, "My Parents Weren't College-Educated Folks, So They Didn't Have a Notion of What We Should Want," *Chicago Sun-Times*, September 19, 2004.

141 "He would sometimes say": "Barack Obama Revealed," CNN, August 20, 2008.

141 Meanwhile, without telling her: Ibid.

142 "That kind of shuts you": Carol Felsenthal, "The Making of a First Lady," *Chicago,* January 16, 2009.

142 first record album: Barack Obama, remarks at the Presidential Medal of Freedom ceremony, Washington, D.C., November 24, 2014.

142 Barack's mother, Ann: Janny Scott, *A Singular Woman: The Untold Story of Barack Obama's Mother,* p. 303.

142 "Everybody was delighted": Charles Payne, interview with author.

143 "We understood that together": Felsenthal, "The Making of a First Lady."

143 "I remember thinking to myself": David Wilkins, interview with author.

143 She worked on business development: Carol Felsenthal, "Yvonne Davila, Close Friend of Michelle Obama, Could Be in Trouble," *Chicago,* December 2012.

143 "whether city government": Cindy Moelis, interview with author.

143 "She was not the type": Sally Duros, interview with author.

144 "I remember a sense of frustration": David Mosena, interview with author.

144 "It still wasn't enough": Geraldine Brooks, "Michelle Obama and the Roots of Reinvention: How the First Lady Learned to Dream Big," *More,* October 2008.

144 "She wanted to be on her": David Mosena, interview with author.

145 "It wasn't part": Sandy Newman, interview with author.

145 "He went around to each": Madeline Talbott, interview with author.

145 the most efficient campaign: Gretchen Reynolds, "Vote of Confidence," *Chicago,* January 1993.

145 "Who knows?": Ibid.

145 "If you have the chance": Veronica Anderson, "Forty Under 40: Here They Are, the Powers to Be," *Crain's Chicago Business,* September 27, 1993.

146 Vanessa Kirsch and Katrina Browne: Wingspread conference agenda, November 1991.

146 On the roster of participants: Wingspread conference participant list, November 1991.

146 But as several participants: Paul Schmitz, *Everyone Leads: Building Leadership from the Community Up,* p. 17.

146 One lawyer did legal: Eric Krol, "Service to Community Helps Pay the Way Toward College Education," *Chicago Tribune,* April 29, 1994.

147 "Boy, she's tall!": Jacky Grimshaw, interview with author.

147 Each Ally received a copy: Leif Elsmo, interview with author.

147 The manual proposed ways: John P. Kretzmann and John L. McKnight, *Building Communities from the Inside Out: A Path Toward Finding and Mobilizing a Community's Assets,* 1993.

148 "My mom and dad would always say": Michelle Obama, speech to Democratic National Convention, 2008.

148 "The first thing that was mine": Geraldine Brooks, "Michelle Obama and the Roots of Reinvention."

148 "It sounded risky and just": Richard Wolffe, "Barack's Rock," *Newsweek*, February 25, 2008.

148 She described her three-year stint as executive: Ibid.

148 In 1995, not two years after: Jeremy Mindich, "AmeriCorps: Young, Spirited and Controversial," *Chicago Tribune*, April 9, 1995.

148 "I was never happier": Michelle Obama, speech to the Corporation for National and Community Service, Washington, D.C., May 12, 2009.

148 "She didn't care": Jobi Petersen Cates, interview with author.

149 "There's nothing funnier": Michelle Obama, speech at a Greater D.C. Cares event, June 16, 2009.

149 "the most powerful thing": Christi Parsons, Bruce Japsen, and Bob Secter, "Barack's Rock," *Chicago Tribune*, April 22, 2007.

149 "who wants to just look": Jobi Petersen Cates, interview with author.

150 "She has a knack": Krsna Golden, interview with author.

150 "where the magic happened": Michelle Obama, speech at a Greater D.C. Cares event, June 16, 2009.

150 "You can't be punching": Leif Elsmo, interview with author.

150 "I hear that": Julie Sullivan, interview with author.

151 "didn't indulge that situation": Jobi Petersen Cates, interview with author.

151 "We'd go from some": Julie Sullivan, interview with author.

151 "That's nice, but we've": Paul Schmitz, interview with author.

152 "It was very focused on": Kelly James, interview with author.

152 "The thrust of our": Hank De Zutter, "What Makes Obama Run?," *Chicago Reader*, December 8, 1995.

153 She viewed her role: Michelle Obama, speech at University of California–Merced commencement, May 16, 2009.

153 "just wasn't big enough": Sunny Fischer, interview with author.

8 | A LITTLE TENSION WITH THAT

154 "I grew up five minutes": Holly Yeager, "The Heart and Mind of Michelle Obama," *O: The Oprah Magazine*, November 2007.

154 "As fate would have it": Michelle Obama, speech to University of California–Merced commencement, May 16, 2009.

154 "What I found": Ibid.

155 The university endorsed restrictive covenants: Arnold R. Hirsch, *Making the Second Ghetto: Race and Housing in Chicago, 1940–1960*, pp. 144–145.

155 "The gutters were full": John W. Boyer, *A Hell of a Job Getting It Squared Around: Three Presidents in Times of Change; Ernest D. Burton, Lawrence A. Kimpton, and Edward H. Levi*, p. 112.

155 By one estimate: Ibid., p. 116.

155 "Social engineering on a vast": Ibid., p. 131.

155 "Of those who did not return": Ibid., p. 130.

156 By 1970, the university: James R. Grossman, Ann Durkin Keating, and Janice L. Reiff, eds., *The Encyclopedia of Chicago*, p. 848.

156 "regulate both the number": Hirsch, p. 170.

156 "people like us": John Boyer, interview with author.

156 "I appreciate what you are saying": Timuel D. Black Jr., *Bridges of Memory: Chicago's First Wave of Black Migration*, p. 583.

157 She also had a snapshot: Arthur Sussman, interview with author.

157 "Until you can bridge those": Michelle Obama, interview with author, 2007.

157 Called Summer Links: Summer Links and Jennifer Nanasco, "Close-up on Juvenile Justice: Author Former Offender Among Speakers," *University of Chicago Chronicle* 17, no. 4 (November 6, 1997).

157 "students and faculty explore": Ibid.

158 Improvements in the surrounding communities: Arthur Sussman and John Boyer, interviews with author.

158 In his first year, 15 percent: John Boyer, interview with author.

158 "a broader and more diverse profile": Ibid.

158 "convinced that the university": Ibid.

158 "not just make us into some kind of NGO": Ibid.

159 Many African American students: Melissa Harris-Perry, interview with author.

159 "You cannot do community-based": Samuel Speers, interview with author.

159 "It was possible that other elite schools": Arnold Sussman, interview with author.

159 "We had to fulfill": Paul Schmitz, *Everyone Leads: Building Leadership from the Community Up*, p. 245.

160 A grand total of nine: Robert Draper, "Barack Obama's Work in Progress," *GQ*, November 2009.

160 Many years later: Jeff Zeleny, "As Author, Obama Earns Big Money and a New Deal," *New York Times*, March 20, 2009.

161 "Michael Jordan can come": Thomas Hardy, "Jackson Foe Now Wants Old Job Back," *Chicago Tribune*, December 19, 1995.

161 "She brought elegance and class": David Remnick, *The Bridge: The Life and Rise of Barack Obama*, p. 283.

161 "Because I believe": Michelle Obama, unpublished interview with Scott Helman, 2007.

161 "How can you impact": Scott Helman, "Early Defeat Launched a Rapid Political Climb," *Boston Globe*, October 12, 2007.

161 "We as a family": Liza Mundy, "A Series of Fortunate Events," *Washington Post*, August 12, 2007.

161 "Michelle had a black": Abner Mikva, interview with author.

162 "I don't trust the people": Mariana Cook, interview with Barack and Michelle Obama, May 1996.

162 "When you are involved in politics": Ibid.

162 It was one thing for him to surprise her: Draper, "Barack Obama's Work in Progress."

162 "There is a little tension with that": Cook, interview with the Obamas, May 1996.

163 "He was not any": Remnick, *The Bridge*.

163 "the very real conflicts": Joe Frolik, "A Newcomer to the Business of Politics Has Seen Enough to Reach Some Conclusions About Restoring Voters' Trust," *Cleveland Plain Dealer*, August 3, 1996.

163 Back in Hawaii: Barack Obama, *Dreams from My Father*, p. 97.

163 "What you have been doing": John McKnight, interview with author.

164 "We have no shortage": Hank De Zutter, "What Makes Obama Run?," *Chicago Reader*, December 8, 1995.

164 "What if a politician": Ibid.

164 "I may not be": Madeline Talbott, interview with author.

165 The freshman struck: Emil Jones, interview with author.

165 "He thought you could press": Remnick, *The Bridge*, p. 299

165 "He wasn't a maverick": Cynthia Canary, interview with author.

165 "One night, we were playing": Larry Walsh, interview with author.

165 "sharing the humor": Barack Obama, *Audacity of Hope*, p. 339.

166 "this business is not": Carol Felsenthal, "The Making of a First Lady," *Chicago*, January 16, 2009.

166 "three magical months": Barack Obama, *Audacity of Hope*, p. 339.

166 "It's like, oh": Geraldine Brooks, "Michelle Obama and the Roots of Reinvention: How the First Lady Learned to Dream Big," *More*, October 2008.

166 "The strains in our relationship": Barack Obama, *Audacity of Hope*, p. 339.

166 Money was becoming an increasing: Barack and Michelle Obama, IRS Form 1040, 200.

166 "We didn't pick": Michelle Obama, unpublished interview with Scott Helman, 2007.

166 They paid more: Ibid. See also Michelle Obama, speech to Democratic National Convention, September 4, 2012.

166 Their down payment: Ray Gibson, John McCormick, and Christi Parsons, "How Broke Were the Obamas? Hard to Tell," *Chicago Tribune*, April 20, 2008.

166 with a small assist: Maggie Murphy and Lynn Sherr, "The President and Mrs. Obama on Work, Family and Juggling It All," *Parade*, June 20, 2014.

167 After he was elected: Malik Nevels, interview with author.

167 Barack considered himself: Barack Obama, *Audacity of Hope*, p. 3.

167 he quickly learned: Ibid., p. 105.

168 "went to Harvard and became": Ted Kleine, "Is Bobby Rush in Trouble?," *Chicago Reader*, March 17, 200.

168 "If you so impress white": Ibid.

168 "Barack is viewed": Ibid.

168 "if you're well educated": Ibid.

168 "You talk a certain type": David Mendell, *Obama: From Promise to Power*, pp. 190–191.

169 "Tired and stressed": Barack Obama, *Audacity of Hope*, p. 340.

169 "What a bunch": "Philip, Criminals Win Again," *Chicago Tribune*, December 31, 1999.

169 "a wailing baby in tow": Barack Obama, *Audacity of Hope*, p. 106.

169 "realizing that I would": Ibid.

169 The race, he said: Ibid., p. 354.

170 "it's impossible not to": Ibid., p. 107.

170 "a bit of useful": Ibid., p. 355.

170 "I'm sorry, Mr. Obama": Ibid.

170 "imagine the other person's hopes": Mariana Cook, interview with Barack and Michelle Obama, 1996.

171 "How we approach": Ibid.

171 "I've seen that relationship": Julie Sullivan, interview with author.

171 But as parents: Barack Obama, *Audacity of Hope*, p. 336.

171 "You only think about": Ibid., p. 340.

171 "My wife's anger": Ibid.

171 He had vowed: Ibid., p. 346.

171 Indeed, his role model: Valerie Jarrett, interview with *Frontline*, www.pbs .org/wgbh/pages/frontline/government-elections-politics/choice-2012/the -frontline-interview-valerie-jarrett.

171 "As far as I was": Ibid.

171 "After all, it wasn't as if": Ibid.

172 "We were terrified": Michelle Obama, speech, Dwight D. Eisenhower Executive Office Building, Washington, D.C., September 18, 2009.

172 "not knowing whether": Barack Obama, remarks, Bipartisan Health Care Summit, Washington, D.C., February 25, 2010.

172 "I can't breathe": Valerie Jarrett, interview with *Frontline*, PBS, posted on the show's website, but this comment was not included in the broadcast. See www.pbs.org/wgbh/pages/frontline/government-elections-politics/choice -2012/the-frontline-interview-valerie-jarrett.

172 "narrowed to a single": Barack Obama, *Audacity of Hope*, p. 186.

172 "The bad food and stale air": Ibid., p. 4.

172 "more sensible pursuits": Ibid.

173 Shomon said Barack: Dan Shomon, interview with author.

173 "completely mortified and humiliated": Barack Obama, interviewed by David Remnick, American Magazine Conference, Phoenix, Ariz., November 2006.

173 "For God's sake": Helman, "Early Defeat Launched a Rapid Political Climb."

173 "It's hard to look": Ibid.

173 named for poet Maya Angelou: Michelle Obama, remarks at Maya Angelou memorial service, June 7, 2014.

173 "And at the same time": Helman, "Early Defeat."

9 | JUST DON'T SCREW IT UP

174 She walked up: Susan Sher, interview with author.

174 "This is my life": Valerie Jarrett, interview with author, 2007.

175 She told colleagues when: Susan Sher, interview with author.

175 Stepping from a bus: Kenneth Kates and Susan Sher, interviews with author.

175 The heart of her pitch: Rosita Ragin, interview with author.

175 "It's not enough to be": Michelle Obama, "Reaching Out and Reaching

Back," *InsideOut,* University of Chicago Office of Community and Government Affairs, September 2005.

176 "Somebody like me": Michelle Obama, "Reaching Out."

176 "who have jobs to protect": Annah Dumas-Mitchell, "Officials to Contractors: Blacks Won't Be Cheated," *Chicago Defender,* November 29, 2001.

176 In return for his: LaRisa Lynch, "AACA and University of Chicago Hospitals Reach Agreement to Increase Black Participation in Construction Employment Opportunities," *Chicago Defender,* December 6, 2001.

176 Minority contracting was: Chicago Transit Authority documents, obtained through Freedom of Information Act.

176 To strengthen the contracting: Joan Archie, via John Easton, University of Chicago communications department.

176 From the 2002 to 2008: University of Chicago statistics.

177 "She would not shy away": Kenneth Kates, interview with author.

177 "Let's just look at the facts": John Rogers, interview with author.

178 "I saw Barack": Geoffrey Stone, interview with author.

179 "He didn't seem": William Daley, interview with author, 2007.

179 "Walking into that lunch": Valerie Jarrett, interview with author, 2007.

179 "It was, gosh": Michelle Obama, interview with author, 2007.

179 "I'm willing to gamble": Valerie Jarrett, interview with author, 2007.

179 When he added the column: Barack Obama, *Audacity of Hope,* p. 100.

180 roughly what he had raised: Federal Election Commission, campaign finance reports.

180 "more out of pity": Barack Obama, *Audacity of Hope,* p. 5.

180 "I don't like to talk": David Mendell, *Obama: From Promise to Power,* p. 152.

180 On the eve: Scott Fornek, "Barack Obama," *Chicago Sun-Times,* March 1, 2004.

180 "It's hard, and that's why": William Finnegan, "The Candidate: How the Son of a Kenyan Economist Became an Illinois Everyman," *New Yorker,* May 31, 2004.

181 "because she couldn't figure": *New Day,* CNN, June 23, 2014.

181 "the desire to be": Barack Obama, *Audacity of Hope,* p. 341.

181 She was certain: Ibid., p. 341.

181 "Work is rewarding": Rebecca Johnson, "The Natural," *Vogue,* September 2007.

181 He did have a guilty: Dan Shomon, interview with author.

181 "Figuring out how": Cassandra West, "Her Plan Went Awry, but Michelle Obama Doesn't Mind," *Chicago Tribune,* September 1, 2004.

182 "I am sitting there": Holly Yeager, "The Heart and Mind of Michelle Obama," *O: The Oprah Magazine,* November 2007.

182 "it didn't mean he wasn't": Johnson, "The Natural."

182 "The big thing I figured out": Yeager, "Heart and Mind."

182 "Don't sweat the small": Michelle Obama, remarks at the Women's Conference, Long Beach, Calif., October 23, 2007.

182 "I just think that's": Marian Robinson, unpublished interview with Scott Helman, 2008.

183 "no matter how much": Barack Obama, *Audacity of Hope,* p. 340.

183 "Sure, I helped": Ibid., p. 341.

183 "an important period": Yeager, "Heart and Mind."

183 "Michelle's strength, her willingness": Barack Obama, *Audacity of Hope,* p. 341.

183 "We ain't seen no": Barack Obama, remarks at Pleasant Ridge Missionary Baptist Church, 2003. Videotape by Bruce Orenstein and Bill Glader.

184 "Freed from worry": Barack Obama, *Audacity of Hope,* pp. 5–7.

184 "I am tired": Lauren W. Whittington, "Final Days for Fightin' Illini," *Roll Call,* March 9, 2004.

184 In a stroke of good fortune: Frank Main, "Hull's Dirty Laundry on the Line," *Chicago Sun-Times,* February 28, 2004.

185 "She understood": Forrest Claypool, interview with author.

185 "We believe he represents": Monica Davey, "A Surprise Senate Contender Reaches His Biggest Stage Yet," *New York Times,* July 26, 2004.

185 "rhymes uncomfortably": Scott Turow, "The New Face of the Democratic Party—and America," *Salon,* March 30, 2004.

185 "Just don't screw it up": Barack Obama, *Audacity of Hope,* p. 359.

185 "This guy's going": "Dreams of Obama," *Frontline,* January 20, 2009.

185 "Michelle sees this happening": Ibid.

186 a line passed among: Elizabeth Taylor, "There Has Always Been . . . This Hopefulness About the Country," *Chicago Tribune,* October 29, 2006.

186 "It's the hope of slaves": Barack Obama, speech to the Democratic National Convention, July 27, 2004.

187 "Absolutely the messiest": *Oprah Winfrey Show,* January 19, 2005.

187 leaders "who have their feet": Yeager, "Heart and Mind."

187 "Barack is not our savior": Suzanne Bell, "Michelle Obama Speaks at Illinois State U," *Daily Vidette,* October 26, 2004.

188 "a waste of time": Debra Pickett, "My Parents Weren't College-Educated Folks, So They Didn't Have a Notion of What We Should Want," *Chicago Sun-Times,* September 19, 2004.

188 "I didn't believe that politics": Bell, "Michelle Obama Speaks at Illinois State U," 2004.

188 "I'm as black as it gets": Elizabeth Brackett, *Chicago Tonight,* WTTW, October 28, 2004.

188 "Balancing a full-time": Michelle Obama, remarks to Women's Conference, Long Beach, Calif., October 26, 2010.

189 "It was never willy-nilly": Leif Elsmo, interview with author.

189 "The girls came first": Kenneth Kates, interview with author.

189 she put herself: Katie McCormick Lelyveld, interview with author.

189 "What I notice about": Johnson, "The Natural."

189 "If you can, you do": Haroon Rashid, interview with author.

189 "trying to herd these two": Carol Felsenthal, "The Making of a First Lady," *Chicago,* January 16, 2009.

190 "If I did that even": James Grossman, interview with author.

190 "Malia is six years": David Mendell, "Barack Obama: Democrat for U.S. Senate," *Chicago Tribune,* October 22, 2004.

190 In yet another lucky: Rick Pearson and John Chase, "Unusual Match Nears

Wire: Obama, Keyes Faceoff to Have Place in the Books," *Chicago Tribune,* November 2, 2004.

190 "I don't take all the type": Barack Obama, interview with author, 2004.

191 "I'm a big believer": Ibid.

191 "Maybe one day": Jeff Zeleny, "New Man on the Hill," *Chicago Tribune,* March 20, 2005.

191 She also joined the board: Bob Sector, "Obama's 2006 Income Drops," *Chicago Tribune,* April 17, 2007.

192 "There's no doubt": Barack Obama, interview with author, 2006.

192 "tough, smart and connected": Maureen Dowd, "She's Not Buttering Him Up," *New York Times,* April 25, 2007.

193 "The problem is that": Michelle Obama, unpublished interview with John McCormick.

193 "We are going to change": Valerie Jarrett, interview with author, 2007.

193 A family doctor: James Madera, then University of Chicago Hospitals president, interview with author.

194 In what would become: Harlan Krumholz, Yale University, interview with author.

195 "We have to create": Eric Whitaker, interview with author.

195 "People are so used to going": Laura Derks, interview with author.

195 "I have seen her": Yeager, "Heart and Mind."

196 In response, the hospital: James Madera, interview with author.

196 One day, he called: Barack Obama, *Audacity of Hope,* pp. 326–327.

10 | I'M PRETTY CONVINCING

197 "He comes out of nowhere": Craig Robinson, book-tour discussion, Dominican University, April 27, 2010.

197 "you don't grow up on": Ibid.

197 "You will never be hotter": Dan Balz and Haynes Johnson, *The Battle for America 2008,* p. 30.

197 "Have you talked to your wife?": Cynthia McFadden, *Nightline,* ABC, October 8, 2012.

198 "I've got great access to them": *Larry King Live,* CNN, February 11, 2008.

198 "They talked about passion": Craig Robinson, Dominican University, April 27, 2010.

198 "I had a Porsche": Pete Thamel, "Coach with a Link to Obama Has Hope for Brown's Future," *New York Times,* February 16, 2007.

199 "Well that's fine": Craig Robinson, Dominican University.

199 "She was interested in whether": Gwen Ifill, "Michelle Obama: Beside Barack," *Essence,* November 5, 2008.

200 "I was impressed by her": David Plouffe, *The Audacity to Win: The Inside Story and Lessons of Barack Obama's Historic Victory,* p. 12.

200 "No one had good news": Ibid.

200 "We're talking about": Jodi Kantor and Jeff Zeleny, "Michelle Obama Adds New Role to Balancing Act," *New York Times,* May 18, 2007.

200 "but he's drawn more": Plouffe, *Audacity to Win,* p. 13.

200 "the kind of person": Cal Fussman, "Valerie Jarrett: What I've Learned," *Esquire*, April 22, 2013.

201 Michelle had said in 1996: Mariana Cook, interview with Barack and Michelle Obama, 1996.

201 "I took myself down": Ifill, "Michelle Obama."

201 Michelle had veto: McFarland, *Nightline*.

201 "The person who was most": Valerie Jarrett, interview with author.

201 "Okay, how are we going to do this?": Michelle Obama, interview with author, 2007.

201 "I've never doubted the mission": Ibid.

201 "The selfish part of me": Ibid.

202 "It had taken a little convincing": Michelle Obama, remarks at the Women's Conference, Long Beach, Calif., October 23, 2007.

202 "I was really the hold out": Connie Schultz, interview with author.

203 "Michelle Obama! That's one": Kantor and Zeleny, "Michelle Obama Adds New Role to Balancing Act."

203 "I'm scared of": "Obama Hasn't Smoked in Years, Scared of My Wife," Associated Press, September 23, 2013.

203 a funk after only: Plouffe, *Audacity to Win*, p. 59.

203 "Meandering, unmotivated, and hesitant": Ibid., p. 138.

204 "Barack is the luckiest": Abner Mikva, interview with author.

205 "Well, I would have to": Author interview with voter.

205 when the heartland was bearing: Peter Slevin, "Midwest Towns Sour on War as Their Tolls Mount," *Washington Post*, July 14, 2007.

206 "I guarantee you": Michelle Obama, remarks in Rockwell City, Iowa, October 9, 2007.

207 "You can't just tell": Robin Roberts, *Good Morning America*, ABC News, May 22, 2007.

207 "I am married to": Michelle Obama, remarks in Harlem, June 26, 2007.

207 "There's Barack Obama the phenomenon": Maureen Dowd, "She's Not Buttering Him Up," *New York Times*, April 25, 2007.

207 "He's too snorey": Tonya Lewis Lee, "Your Next First Lady?" *Glamour*, September 2007.

207 "Many people I talked to afterward": Dowd, "She's Not Buttering Him Up."

207 "Barack and I laugh about that": Raina Kelley, "A Real Wife, In a Real Marriage," *Newsweek*, February 16, 2008.

208 "What I realize as I get older": Lynn Norment, "The Hottest Couple in America," *Ebony*, February 2007.

208 She began an unpaid: John Easton, spokesman, University of Chicago Hospitals, July 17, 2014.

208 "I am going to be the person": David Mendell, *Obama: From Promise to Power*, p. 381.

209 A consultant to nonprofit: President's Commission on White House Fellowships, website.

209 Their instructor was often: Sandra Sobieraj Westfall, "5 Things to Know about Grandma-in-Chief Marian Robinson," *People*, January 20, 2009.

209 "We just shared all": Kelly Wallace, "What's a Hui and Why Michelle Obama Can't Live Without Hers," *iVillage,* November 5, 2012.

209 "It's just a silent thing": Yvonne Davila, interview with author.

210 Blanchard was an obstetrician: "Meet Dr. Anita Blanchard: A Doctor with a Mission," *InsideOut,* University of Chicago, September 2005.

210 Nesbitt met Craig Robinson: Marty Nesbitt, interview with author.

210 He met Barack: Ibid.

210 "We need you all to be": Harriette Cole, "The Real Michelle Obama," *Ebony,* September 2008.

211 "I believe [he] will be president": Valerie Jarrett, interview with author, July 5, 2007.

211 "She takes this so seriously": Melissa Winter, interview with author, 2007.

212 Shaken, she also made: Peter Slevin, "Michelle Obama in Iowa Accident," *Washington Post,* October 9, 2007.

212 "He has natural political": Pete Giangreco, interview with author.

212 "If you had asked me which": Jobi Petersen Cates, interview with author.

213 Through Burns and his small-town: Peter Slevin, "A Tiny Iowa Paper and One Very Big Name: Obama," WashingtonPost.com, January 3, 2008.

213 "It's Iowa or bust": Plouffe, *Audacity to Win,* p. 17.

213 "I'm a fourth-quarter player": Chelsea Kammerer, interview with author.

213 not "ready to elect a black president": Peter Wallsten and Richard Faussett, "For Black Skeptics, Obama Cites Iowa," *Los Angeles Times,* January 7, 2008.

214 "Had he married a": Remnick, *The Bridge,* p. 502.

214 "Michelle is not only African American": Allison Samuels, "What Michelle Means to Us," *Newsweek,* November 21, 2008.

215 "Ask yourselves, of all the candidates": Michelle Obama, speech in Orangeburg, S.C., November 25, 2007. "Jena justice" refers to a sequence of racially charged incidents in Jena, Louisiana. A white prosecutor's decision to charge five black Jena High School students with attempted murder in the December 2006 beating of a white student led to protests by demonstrators who argued that the charges were excessive and represented a pattern of unequal treatment of black residents. Authorities later filed reduced charges. Five students pleaded guilty to misdemeanor simple battery. One student pleaded guilty to second-degree battery and received jail time. Mary Foster, "Jena 6 Case Nears Conclusion," Associated Press, June 25, 2009.

216 "There's an emotional exhaustion": Jackie Norris, interview with author.

11 | VEIL OF IMPOSSIBILITY

218 "The Obamas could not possibly": Gwen Ifill, "Michelle Obama: Beside Barack," *Essence,* November 5, 2008.

219 "because of their race or gender": Alec MacGillis, "A Margin That Will Be Hard to Marginalize," *Washington Post,* January 27, 2008.

219 "The Clintons are disturbing": DeDe Mays, interview with author.

219 "In the past week or two": Michelle Obama, Obama campaign letter, January 24, 2008.

219 "If she thinks we're being": Lauren Collins, "The Other Obama: Michelle Obama and the Politics of Candor," *New Yorker,* March 10, 2008.

220 "My girl's tough": Melissa Winter, interview with author, 2008.

220 She was a recent political: David Axelrod, interview with author.

220 "Power concedes nothing": Michelle Obama, speech in Estill, S.C., January 2008.

221 "My fear is that we don't know": Michelle Obama, speech in Hilton Head, S.C., January 2008.

221 "Well, let me tell you something": Ibid.

221 Barack earned 78 percent of black: David Plouffe, *The Audacity to Win,* p. 163.

222 "I know what I will be telling": Ally Carragher, interview with author.

222 "freedom . . . equality . . .": Will.I.Am, "Why I Recorded 'Yes We Can,'" *Huffington Post,* February 3, 2008.

222 "I look at my life": Michelle Obama, speech in Hilton Head, S.C.

223 "This nation is broken": Michelle Obama, speech in Estill, S.C.

223 "You reach the bar": Ibid.

224 "That little girl started to cry": Michelle Obama, speech in Hilton Head, S.C.

224 Katie McCormick Lelyveld's phone rang: Katie McCormick Lelyveld, interview with author.

225 "To think your country": *Hannity & Colmes,* Fox, March 8, 2008.

225 "We've grown up and lived": Michelle Malkin, "Michelle Obama's America—and Mine," *Augusta Chronicle,* February 21, 2008.

225 "Hope is making a comeback": Michelle Obama, speech in Madison, Wisc., C-SPAN.

226 "The army made it easier": Colin Powell, *My American Journey,* p. 62.

226 "No one who was there": Paul Schmitz, interview with author.

226 "expressing a feeling that": Timuel Black, interview with author.

226 "That was vintage truth": James Montgomery, interview with author.

226 "What she meant" Burton wrote: Michael Cooper, "Comments Bring Wives into Fray in Wisconsin," *New York Times,* February 20, 2008.

227 "What she meant was, this is the first time": "Obama Defends Wife's Remark on Pride in Country," Associated Press, February 20, 2008.

227 "I'm proud in how Americans are": "Michelle Obama Seeks to Clarify 'Proud' Remark," Associated Press, February 21, 2008.

227 Reflecting on the episode: Robert Gibbs, interview with author, 2008.

227 "Stokely Carmichael in a designer dress": *The O'Reilly Factor,* Fox, January 26, 2009.

228 The cartoon depicted Michelle: *New Yorker,* July 21, 2008.

228 "as the fear-mongering": Nico Pitney, "Barry Blitt Defends His New Yorker Cover Art of Obama," *Huffington Post,* July 13, 2008.

228 "Mom doesn't love her country": Rosemary Ellis, "A Conversation with Michelle Obama," *Good Housekeeping,* November 2008.

228 "How can Michelle Obama be": Verna Williams, "The First (Black) Lady," *Denver University Law Review* 86 (June 1, 2009).

228 "It is one of the chief requirements": Marjorie Williams, "Barbara's Backlash!," *Vanity Fair*, August 1992.

228 "who understands the Constitution": Michelle Obama, speech in Iowa, 2007.

228 "You are amazed sometimes": Michael Powell and Jodi Kantor, "After Attacks, Michelle Obama Looks for a New Introduction," *New York Times*, June 18, 2008.

229 "This is the choice we face": Patrick Healy and Jeff Zeleny, "Wisconsin Hands Obama Victory, Ninth in a Row," *New York Times*, February 20, 2008.

229 "helped bring me to Jesus": Obama, Obama for America statement, March 14, 2008.

230 "Fact number one": Ben Wallace-Weld, "Destiny's Child," *Rolling Stone*, February 22, 2007.

230 The source was an ABC News: Brian Ross, ABC, March 13, 2008.

231 "What you had was a moment": Dan Balz and Haynes Johnson, *The Battle for America 2008: The Story of an Extraordinary Election*, p. 201.

231 "This Jeremiah Wright thing": Marty Nesbitt, interview with author.

231 "The conversation that Barack and I had": Cash Michaels, "Wright Episode Was 'Opportunity' to Lead, Says Mrs. Obama," *New York Amsterdam News*, April 18, 2008.

232 "We need energy and fight": Plouffe, *Audacity to Win*, p. 212.

232 "Michelle was very good in moments like": Ibid., p. 213.

233 Barack told worried campaign: Ibid., p. 208.

234 What Barack "did in his speech was give": MacKensie Carpenter, "Michelle Obama Wows Them at CMU," *Pittsburgh Post-Gazette*, April 3, 2008.

234 "I was incredibly proud": Michaels, "Wright Episode."

235 He called the performance "appalling": Barack Obama, remarks in Winston-Salem, N.C., April 29, 2008.

235 "And they're like, 'Ooh, this is a big night'": Rosemary Ellis, "A Conversation with Michelle Obama," *Good Housekeeping*, November 2008.

236 It frustrated her and shook: David Axelrod, interview with author.

236 "They were afraid they were going": Forrest Claypool, interview with author.

236 "She was angry that everyone was tiptoeing": Ibid.

237 "Okay, let me try it again": Ibid.

237 "It only takes one person": David Mendell, *Obama: From Promise to Power*, p. 382.

237 "What I remember most was": Michelle Obama, speech in Orangeburg, S.C., November 2007.

237 "great sympathy and outpouring": Mendell, p. 382.

238 Durbin relayed the information: Richard Durbin, interview with author.

238 "I don't lose sleep": *60 Minutes*, CBS, February 2007.

239 Yet so did Richard Epstein: Richard Epstein, interview with author.

239 "You grow up very comfortable": Arne Duncan, interview with author, 2008.

239 The average white metropolitan resident: Mary Pattillo, interview with author.

239 He won, and sent her: Ellen Warren, "Economist Gets Nobel, but Ex-Wife Is the Real Winner," *Chicago Tribune*, October 20, 1995.

240 During the 1968 Democratic National Convention: George Hrbek, interview with Rhaina Cohen.

240 In 1971, four firebombs: "Firebombs Damage Hyde Park Church," *Chicago Tribune*, June 21, 1971.

240 "filled with good spirits": Hrbek, interview with Rhaina Cohen.

240 She mixed water and lye: Rachel Swarns, *American Tapestry: The Story of the Black, White, and Multiracial Ancestors of Michelle Obama*, p. 63.

240 "black and white together": Comment attributed to comedians Mike Nichols and Elaine May.

241 "It's a place where you can be who you are": Blue Balliett, interview with author.

241 In an outdoor cage: Jamie Kalven, interview with author.

241 "for whom the fact of living together": Ibid.

241 "If we could take Hyde Park": Valerie Jarrett, interview with author, 2008.

242 "It's scary": Alex Leary, "It's Michelle Obama's Time of Opportunity," *St. Petersburg* (Fla.) *Times*, August 25, 2008.

242 It was important to us for a whole range": David Axelrod, interview with author.

244 Michelle's poll numbers: Plouffe, *Audacity to Win*, p. 301.

244 "Surreal is almost like": Kristen Gelineau, "Would-be First Lady Drifts into Rock-Star Status, Tentatively," Associated Press, March 30, 2008.

244 "How are you!": Michelle Obama, campaign office visit, Akron, Ohio.

245 "Congratulations, Mr. President ": Craig Robinson, *A Game of Character: A Family Journey from Chicago's Southside to the Ivy League and Beyond*, p. 243.

245 As he rode through the city: Ibid., p. 244.

246 "I'm thinking justice": MyKela Loury, interview with author.

246 "We're finally free": Tracy Boykin, interview with author.

246 thinking of Emmett Till: David Remnick, *The Bridge: The Life and Rise of Barack Obama*, p. 558.

246 "We cried together": Capers Funnye, interview with author.

12 | NOTHING WOULD HAVE PREDICTED

247 "They could not have been kinder": *The Tom Joyner Radio Show*, August 27, 2013.

248 "My wife and I": Craig Robinson, interview with author, 2009.

248 "many young boys and girls": Michelle Obama, remarks at the U.S. Capitol, April 28, 2009.

249 "in the crosshairs": Verna L. Williams, "The First (Black) Lady," *Denver University Law Review* 86 (June 1, 2009).

249 "People are going to be watching": Verna Williams, interview with author.

249 "figuring out the job": Michelle Obama, remarks to reporters, White House, January 13, 2010.

249 "It wasn't smooth": Jackie Norris, interview with author.

250 "It is so hard to project": Robin Roberts, *Good Morning America,* ABC News, May 22, 2007.

250 "I have a huge responsibility": Michelle Obama, remarks at Georgetown University, Washington, D.C., November 11, 2011.

251 "I'm not here for me": Anita McBride, interview with author.

252 "There's no way I could discuss things": Kati Marton, *Hidden Power: Presidential Marriages That Shaped Our Recent History,* p. 232.

252 "It's the type of thing that": Ibid., p. 209

252 "saw an open, honest woman": Ibid.

253 "The turmoil in my heart": Ibid., pp. 61–62.

253 "Did my Eleanor relate": Ibid., p. 64.

254 "If I were a Negro today": Eleanor Roosevelt, "If I Were a Negro," *Negro Digest,* October 1, 1943.

254 "she said, 'If I were'": John Johnson, oral history, TheHistoryMakers .com.

254 "Everything you do, every piece of blood": Katherine Boyle, "EPA: Agency Is at Center of President's 'Highest Priorities,' First Lady Says," *E&E News PM,* February 26, 2009.

254 "trailblazer in civil rights": Michelle Obama, remarks at the U.S. Department of Transportation, February 23, 2009.

254 "We are going to need you": Michelle Obama, remarks at the U.S. Department of Agriculture, February 19, 2009.

255 "to learn, to listen, to take": Michelle Obama, remarks at the U.S. Department of Education, February 2, 2009.

255 "a luxury that a working class kid": Michelle Obama, remarks at the Corporation for National and Community Service, May 12, 2009.

255 "my new home town": Michelle Obama, speech at Washington Mathematics Science Technology High School graduation, June 3, 2009.

255 "opening the doors": Michelle Obama, remarks at Anacostia High School, March 19, 2009.

255 "Well, she's not following": Lois Romano, "White House Rebel," *Newsweek,* June 20, 2011.

255 "One of those schools": Roscoe Thomas, interview with author.

256 "I never set foot on it": Michelle Obama, remarks at Anacostia High School, March 19, 2009.

256 "You brothers are lucky": Ibid.

256 "She told them how a lot of people": Robin Givhan, "Speaking Not of Pomp, but Circumstance," *Washington Post,* June 4, 2009.

256 When the day was over: Michelle Obama, remarks at the White House, November 2, 2009.

257 "She really wanted to think": Jocelyn Frye, interview with author.

257 "In every phase of my life": Michelle Obama, speech at Detroit Institute of Arts, May 27, 2010.

257 "substance and fun": Ibid.

257 "It's not sufficient": Jocelyn Frye, interview with author.

258 Just hours before: Peter Baker, "Inside Obama's War on Terror," *New York Times Magazine,* January 5, 2010.

258 lost an estimated 741,000: "The Employment Situation: March 2009," U.S. Bureau of Labor Statistics.

258 and 652,000 in March: "The Employment Situation: May 2009," U.S. Bureau of Labor Statistics.

258 "a nation in crisis": Peter Baker, "Obama Takes Oath and Nation in Crisis Embraces the Moment," *New York Times,* January 21, 2009.

258 "She's just very pragmatic": Marty Nesbitt, interview with author.

259 "She is completely honest": Valerie Jarrett, interview with author.

259 "She likes to say, 'This is not what people'": Susan Sher, interview with author.

259 "In a job like this": Cynthia McFadden, "The Contenders: Family Ties," *Nightline,* ABC News, October 8, 2012.

259 "Now I can just pop over": Oprah Winfrey, "Oprah Talks to Michelle Obama," *O, The Oprah Magazine,* April 2009.

259 "where he lets himself feel": Deval Patrick, interview with author.

259 In the residence: Details from whitehousemuseum.org.

260 "Valerie was the counselor": Jackie Norris, interview with author.

260 "Do you still recognize me?": Robin Givhan, "One Lady, One Year, a Whole Lot of Firsts," *Washington Post,* January 14, 2010.

260 "It's one place you can go": Michael Scherer and Nancy Gibbs, "Find Your Space, Find Your Spot, Wear What You Love," *Time,* June 1, 2009.

260 "That I can do without": Holly Yeager, "The Heart and Mind of Michelle Obama," *O: The Oprah Magazine,* November 2007.

260 "My sister said": Rachel L. Swarns, "An In-Law Is Finding Washington to Her Liking," *New York Times,* May 4, 2009.

261 There were shopping trips: Eli Saslow, "From the Second City, an Extended First Family," *Washington Post,* February 1, 2009.

261 In Washington, after accompanying Malia: Oprah Winfrey, "Oprah Talks to Michelle Obama," *O: The Magazine,* April 2009.

261 "has pulled me up": Michelle Obama, remarks at Mother's Day tea in White House, May 7, 2010.

261 As Marian found her way: Katherine Skiba, "First Grandma Keeps a Low Profile," *Chicago Tribune,* March 8, 2010.

261 "Oh, yeah, people say that": Susan Sher, interview with author.

261 "I'm pretty sure": Michelle Obama, remarks at Mother's Day tea in the White House, May 7, 2010.

262 "she escapes the bubble": *Oprah Winfrey Show,* May 2, 2011.

262 "A profound pleasure": Michael D. Shear, "Obama Tries Diplomatic Outreach to Israeli Public," *Washington Post,* July 9, 2010.

262 "They all walk up": "Harry S. Truman's Diary Book," January 6, 1947. Truman Presidential Library and Museum, www.trumanlibrary.org/diary /transcript.htm.

262 "Once, someone on my staff": Oprah Winfrey, "Oprah Talks to Michelle Obama," *O, The Oprah Magazine,* April 2009.

263 "Just give me the rules": Susan Sher, interview with author.

263 "I never goe": Peter Henriques, *Realistic Visionary: A Portrait of George Washington*, p. 101.

264 "There are prison elements to it": Michelle Obama and Laura Bush, remarks in Dar es Salaam, Tanzania, July 2, 2013.

264 "Barack has a 20-car motorcade": *Late Night with Jimmy Fallon*, NBC, February 22, 2013.

264 "Perhaps no other restaurant": Frank Bruni, "Food You'd Almost Rather Hug Than Eat," *New York Times*, August 2, 2006.

265 The theater seats they occupied: Randy Kennedy, "The Obamas Sat Here: Theater Seats to Be Auctioned," NewYorkTimes.com, September 25, 2009.

265 "It's a derivative job": Trooper Sanders, interview with author.

266 "bastion of everything": Jackie Norris, interview with author.

266 "As first lady": Laura Bush, *Spoken from the Heart*, p. 288.

266 The "constant back-and-forth": Ibid.

266 She left sample letters: Anita McBride, interview with author.

267 "This is one of those things": Ibid.

267 "because she knows": Jackie Norris, interview with author.

268 "Nothing in my life": Michelle Obama, speech to the Elizabeth Garrett Anderson School, April 2, 2009.

268 "I could do that all day": Trooper Sanders, interview with author.

268 On her desk: Joanna Sugden, "'She made us all feel that our goals are achievable,'" *Times* (London), January 9, 2012.

269 "You have an unprecedented ability": Michelle Obama, speech in Mexico City, April 14, 2010.

269 "Don't just put me on a plane": Trooper Sanders, interview with author.

13 | BETWEEN POLITICS AND SANITY

270 no one had planted: Michelle Obama, *American Grown: The Story of the White House Kitchen Garden and Gardens Across America*, p. 28.

270 She was in her kitchen: Ibid., p. 24.

270 "about the food we eat": Ibid., p. 9.

270 "because I wanted this": Ibid., p. 31.

271 "For little kids": Ibid., p. 107.

271 Amid energetic photo ops: Jocelyn Frye, interview with author.

271 Between 1995 and 2008: "Too Fat to Fight: Retired Military Leaders Want Junk Food Out of America's Schools," www.missionreadiness.org/2010/too -fat-to-fight.

271 Further, many recruits: Michelle Obama, *American Grown*, p. 174.

272 Obesity and its effects: U.S. Department of Agriculture news release, February 9, 2010.

272 The CDC reported: Mark Fainaru-Wada, "Critical Mass Crisis: Child Obesity," ESPN.com, March 26, 2009.

272 "It's done, honey": Sheryl Gay Stolberg, "Childhood Obesity Battle Is Taken Up by First Lady," *New York Times*, February 10, 2010.

273 "Our kids don't choose to make": Michelle Obama, speech at the White House, February 9, 2010.

273 "a little chubby": *Parents,* March 2008.

273 "There were some nights when you got home": Michelle Obama, speech at the White House, February 9, 2010.

273 Her family started eating: Michelle Obama, *American Grown,* p. 17.

274 "For the event, Mrs. O": Mary Tomer, www.Mrs-O.com, March 3, 2009.

275 "She has perhaps even surpassed": Kate Betts, *Everyday Icon: Michelle Obama and the Power of Style,* p. 107.

275 "She's made her point": Maureen Dowd, "Should Michelle Cover Up?," *New York Times,* March 8, 2009.

275 trainers marketed: Rylan Duggan, *Totally Toned Arms: Get Michelle Obama Arms in 21 Days* (New York: Grand Central Life & Style, 2010).

276 "Never yet": Thomas Jefferson, *Notes on the State of Virginia,* 1781.

276 "We tried outside": Katie McCormick Lelyveld, interview with author.

276 "Fashion is what history looks like": Isabel Toledo, interview with author.

276 Toledo said Michelle paid: Ibid.

276 The same thing happened: Rheana Murray, "ASOS to Restock Sasha Obama's Beloved Unicorn Sweater," *New York Daily News,* November 21, 2013.

277 "what you wear": "First-Lady Style," *Ebony,* September 2008.

277 "gave women the permission": Ruben Toledo, interview with author.

277 "helping to liberate": Betts, p. x

277 "that defines style": Ibid., p. xiii.

277 "romantic glamor": Patricia J. Williams, interview with author.

277 After NBC's *Today* show: Lisa Orkin Emmanuel, "Michelle Obama's Shorts Are Latest Style Flap," Associated Press, August 20, 2009.

277 "It's not the end of the world": Ann Strzemien, "Michelle Obama's Shorts: Does the First Lady Have the Right to Bare Legs?," *Huffington Post,* September 13, 2009.

277 Four years later: Michelle Obama, *106 and Park,* BET, November 19, 2009.

278 she believed it would send: Katie McCormick Lelyveld, interview with author.

278 "Have you seen someone": Rachel Dodes, "Naeem Khan on Designing Michelle Obama's 'Priceless' First State Dinner Dress," *Wall Street Journal,* November 25, 2009.

278 "an incredible booster": Steven Kolb, interview with author.

279 "I was totally surprised": Robin Givhan, "To Showcase Nation's Arts, First Lady Isn't Afraid to Spotlight the Unexpected," *Washington Post,* July 21, 2010.

279 "I love the notion of having members": Givhan, "To Showcase Nation's Arts."

279 "If I'm giving those experiences": Ibid.

279 "We want to lift young people up": Laura Brown, "Michelle Obama: America's Got Talent," *Harper's Bazaar,* October 13, 2010.

280 The first couple's museum: Carol Vogel, "A Bold and Modern White House," *New York Times,* October 7, 2009.

280 Also among the borrowings: Holland Carter, "White House Art: Colors from a World of Black and White," *New York Times,* October 10, 2009.

280 Laura Bush had showed: Laura Bush, *Spoken from the Heart,* p. 426. Barbara Bush had shown the window to Hillary Clinton, who showed it to Laura Bush, p. 166.

281 "what's going on in their lives": Michelle Obama, *American Grown,* pp. 213–214.

281 "Even the president": Yungi de Nies, *Good Morning America,* ABC, April 15, 2010.

281 "This is what dads are": Andy Katz, interview with Barack Obama, *Good Morning America,* ABC, March 12, 2012.

281 did some kickboxing: Oprah Winfrey, "Oprah Talks to Michelle Obama," *O: The Oprah Magazine,* April 2009.

281 When they started: Sally Lee, "Michelle Obama's New Mission," *Ladies' Home Journal,* August 2010.

282 "They don't have any excuse": Michelle Obama, *106 and Park,* BET, November 19, 2013.

282 "to feel as if going to work": Maggie Murphy and Lynn Sherr, "The President and Michelle Obama on Work, Family, and Juggling It All," *Parade,* June 22, 2014.

282 "You want to see hardship?": *Nightline,* ABC News, October 8, 2012.

282 "You can't think you can be a jerk": "The First Lady Mentors in Denver," video, www.whitehouse.gov, January 10, 2010.

282 "a complete embarrassment": *Larry King Live,* CNN, February 9, 2010.

282 What they craved was normality: Michelle Obama, appearance with Jimmy Fallon, *Tonight Show,* NBC, February 2014.

283 "I think in our house": Nia-Malika Henderson, "Michelle Obama's Unfolding Legacy," *Washington Post,* February 9, 2011.

283 "What I value most": Jodi Kantor, "The First Marriage," *New York Times,* November 1, 2009.

283 "Have I told you lately": Barack Obama, *Of Thee I Sing: A Letter to My Daughters,* 2010.

284 signed with twenty-two: Sheryl Gay Stolberg and Robert Pear, "Obama Signs Health Care Overhaul Bill, with a Flourish," *New York Times,* March 23, 2010.

284 "The left thinks he did too little": Peter Baker, "The Education of President Obama," *New York Times,* October 17, 2010.

285 "The single most important": Major Garrett, "Top GOP Priority: Make Obama a One-Term President," *National Journal,* October 23, 2010.

285 "Kenyan anti-colonialist": Robert Costa, "Gingrich: Obama's 'Kenyan, Anti-Colonial Worldview,'" *National Review,* September 11, 2010.

285 "I wish this president": Richard A. Oppel Jr., "After Pressing Attacks on Obama, Romney Surrogate Later Apologizes," The Caucus blog, *New York Times,* July 17, 2012.

285 Forty-five percent of Republicans: Michael D. Shear, "Citing 'Silliness,' Obama Shows Birth Certificate," *New York Times,* April 28, 2011.

286 "Just as an assertive woman": Gwen Ifill, "Michelle Obama: Beside Barack," *Essence*, November 5, 2008.

286 "we do what we can": Kate M. Grossman, "Michelle in the Game: 1st Fundraiser adds $750k Fundraiser to Husband's Campaign," *Chicago Sun-Times*, April 17, 2007.

287 "We heard it from women's groups": Jackie Norris, interview with author.

287 "superbly canny, disciplined": Michelle Cottle, "Leaning Out: How Michelle Obama Became a Feminist Nightmare," *Politico*, November 21, 2013.

287 "all kinds of molds of innocuous": Rebecca Traister, interview with author.

288 "What's frequently missing:" Patricia J. Williams, interview with author.

288 "My message to white feminists": Brittney Cooper, "Lay Off Michelle Obama: Why White Feminists Need to Lean Back," *Salon.com*, November 29, 2013.

288 "Part of what we fought for": Jesse Washington, "Michelle Obama: The Person and the Persona," Associated Press, August 18, 2012.

288 In a 2011 poll: Krissah Thompson and Vanessa Williams, "Kindred Spirits," *Washington Post*, January 24, 2012.

288 "a feeling of relief": Michel Martin, "What I've Left Unsaid: On Balancing Career and Family as a Woman of Color," *National Journal Magazine*, July 26, 2014.

289 "We work hard to make": Cheryl Whitaker, interview with author.

289 "I have worked too hard": "Sharon Malone: The First Lady of Justice," *Essence*, December 16, 2009.

289 "illegal and unwarranted": George Wallace, speech, June 11, 1963, Alabama State Archives, www.archives.state.al.us/govs_list/schooldoor.html.

290 Later that year: "Women's Benefit Council Honors Pretty Vivian Malone," *Chicago Defender*, October 2, 1965.

290 "Once your sister stands": Toni Locy, "D.C. Politics Beckons, Repels Holder; Racial Tensions Have Chilling Effect on Prosecutor's Ambitions," *Washington Post*, December 21, 1996.

290 "That's the part that amazes me": Isabel Wilkerson, "Holding Fast," *Essence*, September 2012.

290 Malone and Holder: Ibid.

290 "I'm forever colored by my": "Sharon Malone: The First Lady of Justice," *Essence*, December 16, 2009.

291 "As you can see": Michelle Obama, speech to Partnership for a Healthier America in Washington, D.C., November 30, 2011.

291 "You have to change": Michelle Obama, remarks in conversation with Laura Bush and Cokie Roberts, August 6, 2014, Washington, D.C.

291 "MO is a complete imposter": Comments on Washingtonpost.com following an article by Emily Wax, "Michelle Shakes It Up During Visit to India," *Washington Post*, November 9, 2010.

291 "Instead of a government thinking": Neil Katz, "Sarah Palin: Americans Have 'God-Given Right' to Be Fat?" CBSnews.com, November 30, 2010.

291 At a church event: Daniel Bice, "Sensenbrenner Apologizes to First Lady over 'Big Butt' Remark," *Milwaukee Journal-Sentinel*, December 22, 2011.

291 "It doesn't look like Michelle Obama": Dana Milbank, "Limbaugh's Anti-Michelle Binge," *Washington Post,* February 27, 2011.

292 "The White House is upset": Cynthia Lambert and Sarah Linn, "Rodeo Clown Apologizes for Racist Joke About Michelle Obama," *San Luis Obispo Tribune,* September 18, 2012.

292 The text said it was Michelle's: Jenee Desmond-Harris, "More Nat'l Geographic First Lady Jokes: School Board Member Fired," Theroot.com, May 31, 2013.

292 A Republican former chairman: Katrina A. Goggins, "Ex-SC Official Apologizes for Roast Remark," Associated Press, June 17, 2009.

292 "I'm sure you'll join me": Scott Rothschild, "Speaker O'Neal apologizes for Forwarding an Email That Calls Michelle Obama 'Mrs. YoMama,'" *Lawrence Journal-World,* January 5, 2012.

14 | SIMPLE GIFTS

293 "more than 6,600 Americans dead: Hannah Fischer, "U.S. Military Casualty Statistics," Congressional Research Service, February 5, 2012.

294 "A good day": Michelle Obama, the Women's Conference, Long Beach, Calif., October 26, 2010.

294 "You don't want to preach": Jocelyn Frye, interview with author.

294 "We were going back": Ibid.

294 When she spoke of expanded health insurance: Michelle Obama, *Keepin' It Real with Reverend Al Sharpton,* December 19, 2013.

295 "It's not enough just": Michelle Obama, Women's Conference, 2010.

295 "At this point": Bradley Cooper, interview with author.

296 "The families just don't": Jason Dempsey, interview with author.

296 "She felt like she wanted to": Jackie Norris, interview with author.

296 "you're right that": Jason Dempsey, interview with author.

297 Michelle appealed directly: Michelle Obama, remarks to National Governors Association, February 25, 2013.

297 roughly 80 percent: "2012 Demographics: Profile of the Military Community," Department of Defense, pp. 40–41.

297 "It was in the discussions": Matthew McGuire, interview with author.

297 "I think many people were": Reginald Rogers, "First Lady Visits Fort Bragg, Vows Support for Military Families," American Forces Press Service, March 13, 2009.

298 "We've heard rhetoric that": Barack Obama, Houston, February 29, 2008.

298 "Let's use this occasion to expand": Barack Obama, Tucson, January 12, 2011.

299 She wrote a letter: Susan Sher, interview with author.

299 "makes us think": Michelle Obama, open letter to parents, January 13, 2011.

300 "move the ball": Sheryl Gay Stolberg, "After a Year of Learning, the First Lady Seeks Out a Legacy," *New York Times,* January 14, 2010.

300 "It's not up to her": Katie McCormick Lelyveld, interview with author.

300 "The power she has": Jackie Norris, interview with author.

301 Michelle's staff admitted: Jocelyn Frye, interview with author.

301 "LOL LOL": "The Miami Heat at the White House: Healthy Tips from NBA Champions," YouTube, comments section, 2014.

301 The Secret Service recorded: Carol D. Leonnig, "Secret Service Fumbled Response After Gunman Hit White House Residence in 2011," *Washington Post,* September 28, 2014.

302 When Michelle learned: Ibid.

303 A loud warning alarm: Carol D. Leonnig, "White House Fence-Jumper Made It Far Deeper into Building Than Previously Known," *Washington Post,* September 29, 2014.

303 "We need you not just to tweak around": Michelle Obama, remarks to Grocery Manufacturers Association, March 16, 2010.

303 The East Wing calculated: Katie McCormick Lelyveld, interview with author.

304 "PHA works with": Partnership for a Healthier America, 2014 website.

304 "The White House got cold feet": Matea Gold and Kathleen Hennessey, "First Lady's Food Effort Stumbles," *Los Angeles Times,* July 21, 2013.

306 A conservative watchdog group: Dave Boyer, "First Lady's Spanish Vacation Cost Taxpayers $467K, Critics Estimate," *Washington Times,* April 27, 2012.

306 "The first lady is on a private": Lynn Sweet, "Michelle Obama at Luxury Spanish Resort: Gibbs Asked About 'the Appearance' of Trip," *Chicago Sun-Times,* August 5, 2010.

306 George Bush made 77 visits: Brian Montopoli, "487 Days at Camp David for Bush," CBSnews.com, January 16, 2009.

306 "You have temporary custody": Anita McBride, interview with author.

306 "She would fly United": Katie McCormick Lelyveld, interview with author.

307 The national unemployment rate: Shaila Dewan, "Zero Job Growth Latest Bleak Sign for Economy," *New York Times,* September 2, 2011.

307 If there were any source of solace: NBC/Wall Street Journal poll, August 2011.

308 "He felt strongly that he had done": David Axelrod, interview with author.

309 "I have better clarity": Nia-Malika Henderson, "Legacy in the Making," *Washington Post,* February 9, 2011.

309 In August, as his numbers were drifting: Katherine Skiba, "First Lady Set for Big Campaign Role," *Chicago Tribune,* September 1, 2011.

309 Even Republican-minded: Fox News poll, August 2011.

310 "People who work with their hands": Tom Bell, "First Lady Visits Maine Today," *Portland Press Herald,* September 30, 2011.

310 "These struggles aren't new": Michelle Obama, remarks in Portland, Maine, White House transcript, September 30, 2011.

311 "You can imagine the feeling": Nancy Benac, "First Lady a Not So Secret Campaign Weapon," Associated Press, September 29, 2011.

311 At a small New York fundraiser: David Axelrod, *The Believer,* p. 5.

311 Axelrod stayed behind: David Axelrod, interview with author.

312 "I love him": Hope Hundley, interview with author, February 22, 2012.

312 brought in more money: Mark Halperin and John Heilemann, *Double Down: Game Change 2012,* p. 35.

313 "frowns on people": Jackie Norris, interview with author.

313 "I'm not a big fan of the press": Rosemary Ellis, "A Conversation with Michelle Obama," *Good Housekeeping*, November 2008, www.goodhouse keeping.com/family/celebrity-interviews/michelle-obama-interview.

313 "Our paths are not foreign to you": Hazel Trice Edney, "White House Cele brates Black Press Week," *Washington Informer*, March 26, 2009.

314 That year, Michelle handed out copies: Capers Funnye, interview with author.

314 "My great-great-great grandmother": Robin Givhan, "We've Gotten a Lot Done, Michelle Obama Says of Year One as First Lady," *Washington Post*, January 14, 2010.

314 "Michelle Obama was privately fuming": Jodi Kantor, "First Lady's Fraught White House Journey to Greater Fulfillment," *New York Times*, January 7, 2012.

315 "I guess it is more interesting": Gayle King, *This Morning*, CBS, January, 11, 2012.

315 "We have a name for": "Obama Tells You to Sacrifice While Moochelle Vacations in Spain," *Rush Limbaugh Show*, August 10, 2010.

316 who used to give: Katherine Mangu-Ward, "Young, Wonky and Proud of It: Wisconsin Republican Paul Ryan Makes Waves," *Weekly Standard*, March 2003.

316 "the 47 percent": David Corn, "Romney Tells Millionaire Donors What He REALLY Thinks of Obama Voters,"*Mother Jones*, September 17, 2012.

316 "she paid a visit in June": Michelle Obama, remarks to African Methodist Episcopal Church General Conference, June 28, 2012.

318 "my almost spooky": Barack Obama, *Audacity of Hope*, p. 118.

318 "cleaned other people's houses": Julian Castro, Democratic National Con vention, September 4, 2012.

319 "I wanted her to dominate": David Axelrod, interview with author.

319 "drives a couple of Cadillacs": Felicia Sonmez, "Romney: Wife Ann Drives a Couple of Cadillacs," Washingtonpost.com, February 24, 2012.

319 Ann had once expressed: Jack Thomas, "Ann Romney's Sweetheart Deal," *Boston Globe*, October 20, 1994.

321 "back when I wasn't so sure": Michelle Obama, remarks in Des Moines, Iowa, November 5, 2012.

15 | I AM NO DIFFERENT FROM YOU

322 "Slow down, you can't": Jennifer Delgado, Bridget Doyle, and Jeremy Gorner, "Teen's Killing Ignites Widespread Outrage," *Chicago Tribune*, Jan uary 31, 2013.

322 "Hadiya Pendleton was": Michelle Obama, remarks in Chicago, April 10, 2013.

323 "fulfill their god-given potential": Michelle Obama, remarks at Michelle Nunn for Senate rally, Atlanta, Georgia, September 8, 2014.

323 she wanted to reach back: Ari Shapiro, "We Have to Do More: Michelle Obama's Next Four Years," NPR, April 12, 2013; Philip Rucker and Krissah

Thompson, "An Increasingly Activist Michelle Obama?," *Washington Post,* April 10, 2013.

323 "We shouldn't live in a country this rich": Michelle Obama, *Keepin' It Real with Reverend Al Sharpton,* December 19, 2013.

323 "make it a Christmas treat": Michelle Obama, remarks at the White House, December 18, 2013.

324 "ought to be under consideration": Courtland Milloy, "Michelle Obama's Oscars Appearance Was an Unbecoming Frivolity," *Washington Post,* February 27, 2013.

325 "I have never felt more confident": Maggie Murphy and Lynn Sherr, "Michelle Obama on the Move," *Parade,* August 15, 2013.

325 "with some gusto": "Oprah Talks to Michelle Obama," *O: The Oprah Magazine,* April 2009.

325 Michelle, he said, had made him: Katherine Skiba, "Michelle Obama's 50th: 'Such a Fun, Fun Party,'" *Chicago Tribune,* January 19, 2014.

325 "She's almost like": Colleen Kane, "Parker Meets Michelle Obama, Speaks to Youth During Busy Week," *Chicago Tribune,* February 28, 2013.

325 More than two-thirds of Americans: Bruce Drake and Seth Motel, "Americans Like Michelle Obama, Except for Conservative Republicans," Pew Research Center, February 10, 2014.

326 "What you see is what": Arne Duncan, interview with author.

326 "She underscores that she is no": Linton Weeks, "The Cultish Appeal of Michelle Obama," NPR.org. February 19, 2014.

326 "they thought people": John Rogers, interview with author.

326 "He's not the first black president": Cheryl Whitaker, interview with author.

327 "Right now, my husband:" Michelle Obama, remarks in Chicago, April 10, 2013.

327 "A pretty shameful day": Barack Obama, remarks in the Rose Garden, April 17, 2013.

327 As Barack struggled to explain: Michelle Obama, "The World as It Should Be," *The Advocate,* August 27, 2008; Michelle Obama, remarks to the Gay and Lesbian Leadership Council, Democratic National Committee, New York, June 26, 2008.

327 "sometimes by fears": Michelle Obama, Women's Conference, October 23, 2007, Long Beach, Calif.

328 "It wasn't like it was busting out": Jane M. Saks, interview with author.

328 "You have to be more open-minded": Krsna Golden, interview with author.

328 "that feeling of openness": Kerry Eleveld, "It's Not Just About the Hair," *The Advocate,* August 27, 2008.

328 On a one-page, typewritten: Tracy Baim, "Obama Changed Views on Gay Marriage," *Windy City Times,* January 14, 2009.

329 "in a separate survey from IMPACT Illinois": Ibid.

329 same-sex couples should be allowed to marry: Barack Obama, interview with Robin Roberts, ABC News, May 9, 2012.

329 "For as long as I've known him": Jo Becker, *Forcing the Spring: Inside the Fight for Marriage Equality* (New York: Penguin, 2014), p. 296.

329 "Enjoy this day": Ibid.

329 "caused Michelle and the girls": Barack Obama, remarks, White House Pride Celebration, June 30, 2014.

330 "When she thought he was:" David Axelrod, interview with author.

330 "Just kind of hanging": Michelle Obama, *Live with Kelly and Michael*, April 21, 2014.

330 "I want to be this really fly": Maggie Murphy and Lynn Sherr, "Michelle Obama on the Move," *Parade*, August 15, 2013.

331 "Not long on pretense": Jonathan Van Meter, "Leading by Example," *Vogue*, April 2013.

331 "endless amounts of time": Michelle Obama, remarks at Mother's Day Tea, White House, May 9, 2013.

331 "There is no way": Michelle Obama, remarks at Mother's Day Tea, White House, May 12, 2014.

332 "The only reason that I am standing": Michelle Obama, remarks in Chicago, April 10, 2013.

332 "You will get your butts": Michelle Obama, remarks at Georgetown University, November 8, 2011.

333 "Are you talking about": David Remnick, "Going the Distance: On and Off the Road with Barack Obama," *New Yorker*, January 27, 2014.

333 a canvas later displayed: DeNeen L. Brown, "Iconic Moment Finds a Space at White House," *Washington Post*, August 29, 2011.

333 "When it comes to getting an education": Michelle Obama, speech at Bowie State University commencement, May 17, 2013.

334 "just another example": Barack Obama, speech at Morehouse College commencement, May 19, 2013.

334 "There's a lot wrong here": Ta-Nehisi Coates, "How the Obama Administration Talks to Black America," *Atlantic*, May 20, 2013.

335 "some thoughtful and sometimes not so thoughtful": Remnick, "Going the Distance."

335 "critical matters of racial justice": Randall Kennedy, "Did Obama Fail Black America?," *Politico Magazine*, July/August 2014.

335 "nation of cowards": Eric Holder, remarks on Black History Month, Washington, D.C., February 18, 2009.

335 " 'When you get ready to spend' ": Jim Montgomery, interview with author.

336 "plain fact": Barack Obama, remarks on My Brother's Keeper, February 27, 2014.

336 "I may not be a Marine": White House transcript, March 12, 2014.

337 Representatives approved: Food Resource and Action Center, October 2011, http://frac.org/about.

337 "When we send our kids": Michelle Obama, remarks in Alexandria, Va., January 25, 2012.

337 "I know that kids": Michelle Obama, remarks in Washington, D.C., September 12, 2013.

338 "You don't have to be": Michelle Obama, "The Campaign for Junk Food," *New York Times*, May 28, 2014.

338 "working hard to serve": Ibid.

339 "We simply can't afford": Michelle Obama, remarks at the White House, June 12, 2014.

339 "a stain on the soul": Kathleen Curthoys, "Helping Homeless Vets," *Army Times,* August 11, 2014.

339 "just wrong": Michelle Obama, remarks at Women's Veterans Care Development Forum, Arlington, Va., November 10, 2014.

339 "hard to know what to say": Michelle Obama, remarks in Chicago, April 10, 2013.

340 "And that, in the end": Ibid.

340 The need was clear: Martha J. Bailey and Susan M. Dynarsk, cited in White House fact sheet, "Increasing College Access for Low-Income Students," January 2014.

340 By 2014, the country: "Education at a Glance 2013," Organization for Economic Cooperation and Development.

340 where the 2014–2015 tuition: Sidwell Friends School, website.

340 "tilts the playing field": Barack Obama, remarks on higher education, White House, January 16, 2014.

341 "Because there are millions": Michelle Obama, remarks, White House, January 15, 2014.

341 "to seek them out and give them": Ibid.

342 "Are you listening": Michelle Obama, remarks, Atlanta, September 8, 2014.

EPILOGUE

343 "just wastes time": Michelle Obama, remarks, Atlanta, September 8, 2014.

343 only 36 percent: Editorial, "The Worst Voter Turnout in 72 Years," *New York Times,* November 11, 2014.

344 yawning gaps: Pew Research Center, "King's Dream Remains an Elusive Goal," August 22, 2013.

344 Michelle herself said: Michelle Obama, remarks in Topeka, Kan., May 17, 2014.

344 "incredible amounts of change": Marcia Chatelain, interview with author.

345 "playing a long game": Michelle Obama, speech, Democratic National Convention, September 5, 2012.

345 "I want to know": Jackie Calmes, "When a Boy Found a Familiar Feel in a Pat of the Head of State," *New York Times,* May 24, 2012.

345 "I want you to think": Michelle Obama, remarks to African Methodist Episcopal Church General Conference, Nashville, Tenn., June 28, 2012.

345 "something changed when": Michelle Obama, remarks at the White House, February 25, 2011.

345 "why, as first lady, I do this": Michelle Obama, remarks at Georgetown University, November 8, 2011.

346 "We have a black family": BET Honors, January 14, 2012.

346 "celebrated black women's": Michelle Obama, remarks in Winston-Salem, N.C., June 7, 2014.

Bibliography

Algren, Nelson. *Chicago: City on the Make*. Chicago: University of Chicago Press, 2011.

Axelrod, David. *The Believer: My Forty Years in Politics*. New York: Penguin Press, 2015.

Balz, Dan, and Haynes Johnson. *The Battle for America 2008: The Story of an Extraordinary Election*. New York: Viking, 2009.

Bell, Geneva. *My Rose: An African American Mother's Story of AIDS*. Cleveland: United Church Press, 1997.

Betts, Kate. *Everyday Icon: Michelle Obama and the Power of Style*. New York: Clarkson Potter, 2011.

Black, Timuel D., Jr. *Bridges of Memory: Chicago's First Wave of Black Migration*. Evanston, Ill: Northwestern University Press, 2005.

Bowen, William G., and Derek Bok. *The Shape of the River: Long-Term Consequences of Considering Race in College and University Admissions*. Princeton, N.J.: Princeton University Press, 1998.

Boyer, John W. *A Hell of a Job Getting It Squared Around: Three Presidents in Times of Change; Ernest D. Burton, Lawrence A. Kimpton, and Edward H. Levi*. Chicago: University of Chicago Press, 2013.

Branch, Taylor. *At Canaan's Edge: America in the King Years, 1965–68*. New York: Simon & Schuster, 2006.

Burroughs, Margaret Taylor. *Life with Margaret: The Official Autobiography*. Chicago: In Time Pub and Media Group, 2003.

Bush, Laura. *Spoken from the Heart*. New York: Scribner, 2010.

Cheney, Anne. *Lorraine Hansberry*. Boston: Twayne, 1984.

Cohen, Adam, and Elizabeth Taylor. *American Pharaoh: Mayor Richard J. Daley—His Battle for Chicago and the Nation*. Boston: Little, Brown, 2000.

Despres, Leon M., with Kenan Heise. *Challenging the Daley Machine: A Chicago Alderman's Memoir*. Evanston, Ill.: Northwestern University Press, 2005.

de Vise, Pierre. *Chicago's Widening Color Gap*. Chicago: Community and Family Study Center, University of Chicago, 1967.

Drake, St. Clair, and Horace R. Cayton. *Black Metropolis: A Study of Negro Life in a Northern City.* Chicago: University of Chicago Press, 1993.

Du Bois, W. E. B. *The Souls of Black Folk.* New York: Oxford University Press, 2007.

Givhan, Robin. *Michelle Obama: Her First Year as First Lady.* Chicago: Triumph Books, 2010.

Green, Adam. *Selling the Race: Culture, Community, and Black Chicago, 1940–1955.* Chicago: University of Chicago Press, 2007.

Grimshaw, William L. *Bitter Fruit: Black Politics and the Chicago Machine, 1931–1991.* Chicago: University of Chicago Press, 1992.

Grossman, James R. *Land of Hope: Chicago, Black Southerners, and the Great Migration.* Chicago: University of Chicago Press, 1989.

Grossman, James R., Ann Durkin Keating, and Janice L. Reiff, eds. *The Encyclopedia of Chicago.* Chicago: University of Chicago Press, 2004.

Halperin, Mark, and John Heilemann. *Double Down: Game Change 2012.* New York: Penguin, 2013.

Hansberry, Lorraine. *A Raisin in the Sun.* New York: Vintage Books, 1994.

———. *To Be Young, Gifted and Black,* New York, Signet Classics, 2011.

Henriques, Peter R. *Realistic Visionary: A Portrait of George Washington.* Charlottesville: University of Virginia Press, 2006.

Hirsch, Arnold R. *Making the Second Ghetto: Race & Housing in Chicago, 1940–1960.* Chicago: University of Chicago Press, 1998.

Hofstadter, Richard. *The American Political Tradition and the Men Who Made It.* New York: Alfred A. Knopf, 1973.

Jamison, Judith, with Howard Kaplan. *Dancing Spirit: An Autobiography.* New York: Doubleday, 1993.

Kantor, Jodi. *The Obamas.* New York: Little, Brown, 2012.

Kennedy, Randall. *The Persistence of the Color Line: Racial Politics and the Obama Presidency.* New York: Pantheon, 2011.

Kretzmann, John P., and John L. McKnight. *Building Communities from the Inside Out: A Path Toward Finding and Mobilizing a Community's Assets.* Skokie, Ill.: ACTA Publications, 1993.

Leeson, Richard M. *Lorraine Hansberry: A Research and Production Sourcebook.* Westport, Conn.: Greenwood Press, 1997.

Lemann, Nicholas. *The Promised Land: The Great Black Migration and How It Changed America.* New York: Vintage Books, 1992.

Maraniss, David. *Barack Obama: The Story.* New York: Simon & Schuster, 2012.

Marton, Kati. *Hidden Power: Presidential Marriages That Shaped Our Recent History.* New York: Pantheon Books, 2001.

McClain, Leanita. *A Foot in Each World: Essays and Articles by Leanita McClain.* Evanston, Ill., Northwestern University Press, 1986.

Mendell, David. *Obama: From Promise to Power.* New York: Amistad, 2007.

Mundy, Liza. *Michelle: A Biography.* New York: Simon & Schuster, 2009.

Obama, Barack. *The Audacity of Hope: Thoughts on Reclaiming the American Dream.* New York: Crown Publishers, 2006.

———. *Dreams from My Father: A Story of Race and Inheritance.* New York: Three Rivers Press, 2004.

———. *Of Thee I Sing: A Letter to My Daughters.* New York: Alfred A. Knopf, 2010.

Obama, Michelle. *American Grown: The Story of the White House Kitchen Garden and Gardens Across America*. New York: Crown Publishers, 2012.

Patrick, Deval. *A Reason to Believe: Lessons from an Improbable Life*. New York: Broadway, 2011.

Plouffe, David. *The Audacity to Win: The Inside Story and Lessons of Barack Obama's Historic Victory*. New York: Viking, 2009.

Powell, Colin L., with Joseph E. Persico. *My American Journey*. New York: Random House, 1995.

Remnick, David. *The Bridge: The Life and Rise of Barack Obama*. New York: Alfred A. Knopf, 2010.

———. *King of the World: Muhammad Ali and the Rise of an American Hero*. New York: Random House, 1998.

Robinson, Craig. *A Game of Character: A Family Journey from Chicago's Southside to the Ivy League and Beyond*. New York: Gotham Books, 2010.

Royko, Mike. *Boss: Richard J. Daley of Chicago*. New York: Plume, 1971.

Satter, Beryl. *Family Properties: Race, Real Estate, and the Exploitation of Black Urban America*. New York: Metropolitan Books, 2009.

Schmitz, Paul. *Everyone Leads: Building Leadership from the Community Up*. San Francisco: Jossey-Bass, 2012.

Scott, Janny. *A Singular Woman: The Untold Story of Barack Obama's Mother*. New York: Riverhead Books, 2011.

Sugrue, Thomas J. *Not Even Past: Barack Obama and the Burden of Race*. Princeton, N.J.: Princeton University Press, 2010.

Swarns, Rachel L. *American Tapestry: The Story of the Black, White, and Multiracial Ancestors of Michelle Obama*. New York: Amistad, 2012.

Tomer, Mary. *Mrs. O: The Face of Fashion Democracy*. New York: Center Street, 2009.

Travis, Dempsey J. *An Autobiography of Black Chicago*. Chicago: Urban Research Institute, 1981.

———. *An Autobiography of Black Jazz*. Chicago: Urban Research Institute, 1983.

———. *An Autobiography of Black Politics*. Chicago: Urban Research Press, 1987.

Tufankjian, Scout. *Yes We Can: Barack Obama's History-Making Presidential Campaign*. New York: powerHouse Books, 2008.

Turow, Scott. *One L: The Turbulent True Story of a First Year at Harvard Law School*. New York: Penguin, 2010.

Williams, Marjorie. *The Woman at the Washington Zoo: Writings on Politics, Family, and Fate*. New York: Public Affairs, 2005.

Willis, Deborah, and Kevin Merida. *Obama: The Historic Campaign in Photographs*. New York: Amistad, 2008.

Wilson, August. *Joe Turner's Come and Gone*. New York: Theater Communications Group, 2007.

Wilson, William Julius. *The Declining Significance of Race: Blacks and Changing American Institutions*. Chicago: University of Chicago Press, 1980.

Wright, Bruce. *Black Robes, White Justice*. Secaucus, N.J.: Lyle Stuart, 1987.

Wright, Richard. *Black Boy*. New York: Harper Perennial, 1993.

Index

ILLUSTRATION CREDITS

Marian Robinson: Obama campaign photo

Fraser Robinson: DuSable High School yearbook

Michelle and Craig: Obama campaign photo

Kindergarten photo: Theodore Ford

Michelle as a first-grader: Obama campaign photo

In high-school modern dance: Whitney Young High School

Michelle as a college freshman: Princeton University

Princeton University yearbook photo: Princeton University

With Stanley Stocker-Edwards: Kimberly M. Talley

With Susan Page: Kimberly M. Talley

With Barack in Hawaii: Obama campaign photo

Wedding: Courtesy of Obama campaign

In Kenya: OFA

At home in Chicago: *Chicago Tribune*, Zbigniew Bzdak

Public Allies: Courtesy of Public Allies

Election Day, 2000: AP Photo/*Chicago Sun-Times*, Scott Stewart

Iowa, 2007: AP Photo/Charlie Neibergall

Inaugural parade: Scout Tufankjian/ Polaris

After inaugural ball: White House photo

Official photo: White House photo

Fashion bangle: White House photo

Jacob Philadelphia: White House photo

Hula hoop: White House photo

Secret Service headquarters: AP Photo / Pablo Martinez Monsivais

Ferebee Hope Elementary: White House photo

Reach Higher: White House photo

Minnesota, 2012: AP Photo/Elizabeth Schulze

#BringBackOurGirls: White House photo

Basketball game: AP Photo/Alex Brandon

Gardening: *The Washington Post*

Tug-of-war: White House photo

Elmo: AP Photo/Pablo Martinez Monsivais

LeBron James and Dwayne Wade: White House photo

State of the Union: AP Photo/Jacquelyn Martin

Marian Robinson with Michelle: Scout Tufankjian/Polaris

Ad shoot: Scout Tufankjian/Polaris

A NOTE ON THE TYPE

This book was set in Minion, a typeface produced by the Adobe Corporation specifically for the Macintosh personal computer and released in 1990. Designed by Robert Slimbach, Minion combines the classic characteristics of old-style faces with the full complement of weights required for modern typesetting.

Composed by North Market Street Graphics,
Lancaster, Pennsylvania

Printed and bound by Berryville Graphics,
Berryville, Virginia

Designed by Cassandra J. Pappas